Everybody's History

A volume in the series
Public History in Historical Perspective
Edited by Marla R. Miller

Everybody's History

Indiana's Lincoln Inquiry and the
Quest to Reclaim a President's Past

Keith A. Erekson

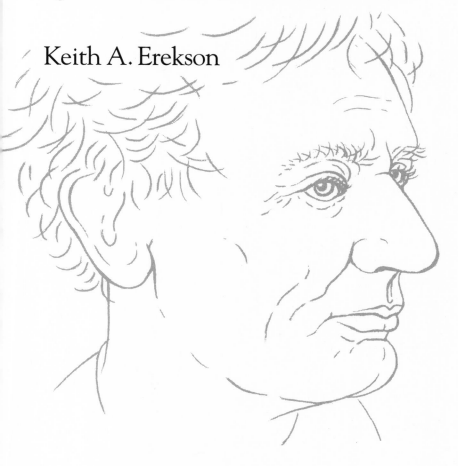

University of Massachusetts Press • AMHERST AND BOSTON

Copyright © 2012 by University of Massachusetts Press
All rights reserved
Printed in the United States of America

LC 2011045246
ISBN 978-1-55849-915-7 (paper); 914-0 (library cloth)

Designed by Dennis Anderson
Set in Sabon and Goudy Oldstyle by Westchester Book
Printed and bound by Thomson-Shore, Inc.

Library of Congress Cataloging-in-Publication Data

Erekson, Keith A.
    Everybody's history : Indiana's Lincoln Inquiry and the quest to reclaim a
president's past / Keith A. Erekson.
        p. cm. — (Public history in historical perspective)
    Includes bibliographical references and index.
    ISBN 978-1-55849-915-7 (pbk. : alk. paper) — ISBN 978-1-55849-914-0
(library cloth : alk. paper)
    1. Lincoln, Abraham, 1809–1865—Homes and haunts—Indiana—Spencer County.
    2. Lincoln, Abraham, 1809–1865—Childhood and youth.
    3. Southwestern Indiana Historical Society (Evansville, Ind.)—History.
    4. Spencer County (Ind.)—Historiography—History—20th century.   I. Title.
    E457.32.E74 2012
    977.2'31—dc23
                                2011045246

British Library Cataloguing in Publication data are available.

To Carolyn

Contents

Illustrations

Preface

I KNEW I had found something important when the attendant in the reading room took the aging letter from me, lifted it in the air, and shined a flashlight through it. Ordinarily, procedures at Indiana University's Lilly Library were far more austere: books must rest in cradles, fingers must not touch pages, loose sheets of paper must remain flat on tables, voices must not speak above a whisper. Compliance was strictly enforced by the human attendant and monitored by closed circuit cameras. But this was clearly no ordinary letter. A lawyer from Evansville, Indiana, wrote of a "coming death, which was undoubtedly anticipated," then mentioned a "leak," followed by reference to a "person of whom I have spoken but whose name I have not placed in this letter." My eyes widened. This unnamed person had "continually betrayed" the lawyer and the pair had "had a battle of rivalry" until. . . . The next paragraph had been almost completely blacked out by vigorous strokes of a thick, black pencil. "~~This breach of confidence would be serious if it got out of my letter but~~ . . ." the quirky, old typewritten font had been swallowed up by lead.

With my curiosity definitely piqued I motioned to a friend to come over, but she could not pick out any more of the words than I could. When the reading room attendant moved toward us I feared we would be reprimanded for being too noisy, but instead she smiled, pulled out the flashlight, and personally held the letter as we tried to read in reverse through the back of the page. With this breach of protocol, the entire reading room burst into commotion. Fellow researchers, strangers really, who had sat together for hours and days without speaking to one another now huddled around the letter, talking, pointing, guessing, laughing.

Finding this letter pulled me into the clamorous and competitive world of Lincoln Studies during the 1920s where deaths, rivalries, secret plots, and betrayals went hand in hand with witnesses, archival collections, and publications. The quest to understand Abraham Lincoln—and to reclaim him for Indiana—drew hundreds of Americans from all walks of life, lawyers and scholars, school teachers and sculptors, politicians and preachers. My quest to reconstruct this unfamiliar world drew me into contact with dozens of friends and colleagues who pointed me to sources, encouraged my efforts, and permitted just one more imposition on their time. One of the arguments made in the following pages is that history work is practiced within a wide social network of friends and colleagues. I am truly humbled as I reflect on the vital assistance I have received from so many people and institutions.

The sources on which my work rests have been preserved and shared by helpful archivists. Many of these sources would have remained unconnected were it not for the keen eyes of Patricia Sides, who noticed similarities in font and style among a variety of disparate collections at the Willard Library in Evansville, Indiana. That Pat had been working for years to reconstitute the collection, and that she welcomed me into the process of discovery, made the project enjoyable and rewarding. Similar patterns of collegiality and excitement marked the attention I received from Tom Schwartz, Bryon Andreasen, James Cornelius, Gary Stockton, Mary Ann Pohl, Jenny Ericson, and Cheryl Schnirring of the Abraham Lincoln Presidential Library (Springfield, IL); John Hoffman of the Illinois History and Lincoln Collections at the University of Illinois at Urbana-Champaign; Jane Westenfeld of the Pelletier Library at Allegheny College (Meadville, PA); Cindy Van Horn of the Lincoln Museum (now Allen County Public Library, Ft. Wayne, IN); Mike Capps of the Lincoln Boyhood National Memorial (Lincoln City, IN); Glenn Crothers, Jim Holmberg, Jacob Lee, and Mike Veach of the Filson Historical Society (Louisville, KY); Becky Middleton and Kris Manley of the Spencer County Public Library (Rockport, IN); Raymond and Patricia Dawson of the Lincoln Pioneer Village (Rockport, IN); Jill Larson of the Lewis Historical Library at Vincennes University (Vincennes, IN); Lou Malcomb of the Indiana University Library (Bloomington, IN); county historians John Fierst (Dubois), Dennis Latta (Knox), Tony Collignon (Perry), Sandra McBeth (Pike), David Ranger (Spencer), and Darrel Bigham (Vanderburg); and Mr. and Mrs. W. Robb Kell and Vivian Taylor of the recently reconstituted Southwestern Indiana Historical Society.

I thank also the staffs of the Library of Congress (Washington, DC), the Huntington Library (San Marino, CA), the Indiana Historical Society (Indianapolis), the Indiana State Library (Indianapolis), the Lilly Library

(Bloomington, IN), and a host of repositories throughout southern Indiana: the Alexandrian Public Library in Mount Vernon, the Boonville-Warrick Public Library, the Cannelton Public Library, the Chandler Public Library, the Evansville Museum, the Evansville-Vanderburgh Public Library Central Branch, the Grandview Library, the Lincoln Heritage Library in Dale, the Newburgh Public Library, the Perry County Old Courthouse Museum, the Pike County Public Library in Petersburg, the Princeton Public Library, the Tell City Historical Society Museum, the Tell City–Perry County Public Library, and the Warrick County Museum in Boonville.

As I attempted to assess my findings and articulate my thoughts, I benefited from willing readers, thoughtful responses, and critical conversations—held in archival stacks, conference sessions, hallways, restaurants, or during car rides—with David Thelen, Eric Sandweiss, James H. Madison, and Ed Linenthal; Sam Wineburg, John Bodnar, Jeff Wasserstrom, Wendy Gamber, Bill Bartelt, Tracy K'Meyer, Geoff Timmins, Alan Booth, David Pace, and Sean Brawley; Katja Hering, Bonnie Laughlin-Schultz, Karen Dunak, Jennifer Stinson, Dawn Bakken, Cynthia Gwynne Yaudes, Dan Gregory, Carolyn Erekson, and the participants in the public history reading and discussion group at Indiana University; Allen Safianow, M. Todd Bradley, Chris Miller, Amy Hay, Paul Edison, Sandy McGee-Deutsch, Sam Brunk, Ron Weber, Chuck Ambler, and Charles Martin; Richard Miller, Claude Clegg, Ken Pimple, and Glenda Murray; Adam Arenson, Dana J. Lightfoot, Lee Ann Westman, Josh Fan, and Matthew Desing; and Marla Miller, Clark Dougan, Carol Betsch, Kay Scheuer, and three anonymous reviewers at the University of Massachusetts Press. Many of the ideas were refined during my interaction with students at Indiana University, Indiana University–Kokomo, and the University of Texas at El Paso; school teachers in Howard, Brown, and El Paso counties; and genealogists and the "general public" in Bloomington, El Paso, and beyond.

This project would have been simply impossible without generous financial assistance from Ruth Lilly and the Ruth Lilly Philanthropic Foundation, the Illinois Historic Preservation Agency, the Indiana University Graduate School, the Society of Indiana Pioneers, the Filson Historical Society, and the History Department of Indiana University. A semester leave from the University of Texas at El Paso permitted me to pull everything together for publication.

I am grateful to the Oral History Association and Oxford University Press for permission to revise "Method and Memory in the Midwestern

'Lincoln Inquiry': Oral Testimony and Abraham Lincoln Studies, 1865–1938," *Oral History Review* 34, no. 2 (Summer/Fall 2007): 49–72; and to the Organization of American Historians and Oxford University Press for permission to use portions of "Putting History Teaching 'In Its Place,'" *Journal of American History* 97, no. 4 (March 2011): 1070–72.

The Indiana University Art Museum has graciously allowed reproduction of a panel from Thomas Hart Benton's famed Indiana Murals on the cover (a larger segment is reproduced on page 157). The murals are, in fact, part of the story that follows, but since they will not appear until Chapter Six I should explain here that Benton placed young Abraham Lincoln squarely in the midst of key symbols and figures of Indiana frontier life—a printing press; a one-room school house; the Rappites who followed the voice of the Angel Gabriel and Father George Rapp from Württemberg, Germany, to settle in New Harmony; Scottish industrialist Robert Owen, who purchased New Harmony in 1825 to found a utopian community based on scientific experiments and education; reformers, hucksters, and land speculators; debates about temperance, politics, and slavery; religious revivals, political gatherings, and corn huskings. The Hoosiers who worked to reclaim Lincoln also wanted to reconstruct this vibrant and forgotten world so vividly captured by Benton's brush.

Finally, it may be impossible to adequately thank five people—Carolyn, Emily, Alyse, Haley, and Lyndie—who joined me on this journey. Sometimes they visited yet another museum, often they prompted questions I had not thought to ask, always they looked at my photographs and listened to my stories about "the Lincoln studiers." Our shared experience in the presence of the past may perhaps best be illustrated by the occasion when, upon leaving the Lincoln display area of the Indiana Historical Society, our two-year-old looked over her shoulder and called out, "Bye, Lincoln!" to the friend she knew she would see again.

❧ Everybody's History

Introduction

"Lincoln Is Everybody's Subject"

THIS BOOK tackles the modern historical paradox in which Americans regularly report hating history in classrooms while they increasingly pursue the past in everyday life. Test after standardized test seems to suggest that younger people don't know the basic facts of history while a recent nationwide survey found that older people most commonly recall their history classes as "boring" and "irrelevant." Yet Americans purchase historical books and movie tickets, visit historic sites and museums, commemorate anniversaries and historic places, save old buildings and family heirlooms, and research genealogy and local history. History likewise permeates public life as presidents draw comparisons to their predecessors, war planners and pundits contrast current wars to previous conflicts, sports commentators cite statistics for every possible feat, community members debate the place of history in the school curriculum, and historically themed businesses and amusement parks draw some acclaim and abundant ire.[1]

With such widespread interest in the past, this book proposes that, rather than testing children for historical illiteracy or conducting an exit survey or visiting a series of historic sites, the best way to understand America's historical paradox is to go with Americans as they pursue pasts that are important to them. Two hundred years after his birth in 1809, Abraham Lincoln remains the most recognized and researched American. During the 2009 commemoration of the bicentennial of his birth, surveys of historians and the general public ranked him as the greatest American president of all time. That same year, an important document with Lincoln's signature set an auction record by selling for nearly three-and-a-half million dollars and the discovery of his fingerprint on a document in Ohio made national headlines. The two-millionth visitor passed through the technologically enhanced Abraham Lincoln Presidential Museum in

I

Illinois, and dozens of new books about him joined the more than twenty thousand other works already in print. Lincoln's two hundredth birthday was commemorated by blacks and whites, northerners and southerners, school children and scholars, movie stars and politicians. An uncounted number of speakers, curators, educators, and private club members hosted dozens of lectures, exhibits, teacher institutes, and commemorative dinners.[2] Even as funding sources wither, museum attendance declines, and university-based historians fret about the future of the humanities, fascination with Lincoln endures.

Over the past century, there has been a tendency to distinguish this popular appeal of Abraham Lincoln from the scholarly study of his life. As early as December 1934, Lincoln scholar James G. Randall complained that "Lincoln is everybody's subject." Reviewing the then 2,000-plus publications on Lincoln, Randall found such trivialities as "Lincoln and the Doctors" (written by a physician) and "Dogs were ever a Joy to Lincoln" (written by a dog-lover). Inscribed upon the large "granite temple" at Lincoln's birthplace were unreliable dates and incorrect parents! "The hand of the amateur," Randall concluded, "has rested heavily on Lincoln studies." Randall called for a new generation of "professional" historians— trained and employed at universities—to save Lincoln from the errors and problems perpetuated by amateurs. In time, academic historians also began to distinguish their work from that done by professionals in archives, museums, and historic sites. Descriptions of public historical practice soon differentiated truth from myth, realism from romance, scholar from audience, and producer from consumer.[3]

Efforts to distinguish professional from amateur, education from entertainment, or history from heritage continue to circulate in American society, but the differences prove far less enlightening than the convergences. Reflecting on his experience at the Illinois state historic site in New Salem where Lincoln lived as a young man, director Richard S. Taylor observed that "nowhere does academic history intersect with the public imagination in more complex and revealing ways than at historic sites, especially sites devoted to Abraham Lincoln's memory." The simple fact that so many people have been interested in Lincoln for so long offers an especially rich opportunity to reassess assumptions about the public, about the practice of history, and about the interactions among all who read, evaluate, challenge, and appreciate history.[4]

Why are Americans drawn to Lincoln? Historians have analyzed the political, sociological, and cultural uses of his memory, but as recently as 2008 Barry Schwartz stated, "No one knows what ordinary Americans think about Abraham Lincoln." Perhaps the focus on Lincoln's appeal has turned the most important question inside out. Rather than assuming that Americans are interested in history because they like Lincoln, what if we looked at their fascination with Lincoln as one expression of wider interest in history? Can understanding popular interest in the sixteenth president illuminate the way that historical insight operates more generally? What can Lincoln's popularity tell us about the value of history in public life?[5]

These questions prove more difficult to answer than to ask. After conducting their survey of American interest in the past, historians Roy Rosenzweig and David Thelen concluded that "the real issue was not, as pundits were declaring, what Americans did not know about the past but what they *did* know and think." In more pragmatic terms, oral historian Michael Frisch has suggested that "the issue for museums and historians who care about them would seem to be less a matter of generating interest than of learning more about what drives an existing interest." Museum curator Terry Fife hypothesized that an individual's connection to the past is "such a personal and subjective experience and the interaction is still virtually unknown and largely undefined."[6]

This book examines the largely undefined popular appeal of the past by seeking to observe Americans in the everyday acts of doing and making history. Would not our understanding increase dramatically if we could watch people define their topics, question witnesses, and seek out answers? How do everyday historians read sources? What motivates them to devote such extensive amounts of time to the pursuit of the past? How do they explain the importance of their work? How do they enlist others in the cause? How do they define and recognize authority? How do they react when others criticize their work? How do their activities change over time? How do they remain the same? In short, what happens when people do history?

FOURTEEN YEARS before James G. Randall complained about amateurs in the Lincoln field, a lawyer in Evansville, Indiana, founded the Southwestern Indiana Historical Society. From its small beginning in February 1920, the organization eventually drew over five hundred members from all walks of life and from across the nation. Three times a year for nearly two decades they came to southern Indiana from Maine, California, and Texas to hear historical papers read by each other—lawyers and politicians, university-trained historians and collectors, genealogists and high school drama teachers, college presidents and newspaper editors. They were primarily interested in the fact that Lincoln's biographers had neglected his years in Indiana. Young Abraham had moved to the Hoosier state in

1816 when he was seven years old and stayed there until age twenty-one. For one-fourth of his life, Lincoln felled Indiana trees, worked for Indiana farmers, learned from Indiana neighbors, and told Indiana jokes. He also buried his mother and sister in Indiana graves.

Two specific trends in Lincoln biography demanded society members' attention. First, in the aftermath of the Civil War, biographers saw Lincoln as a symbol of reconciliation and emphasized the fact that the Illinois lawyer had been born in Kentucky. In the Great Emancipator, the Savior of the Union, the charitable chief, biographers found a human link between North and South, some silently omitting his time in southwestern Indiana. Second, and even more damaging to Indiana pride, other biographers employed the rhetorical device of contrast to emphasize Lincoln's presidential greatness in spite of his humble origins. As Lincoln rose in public estimation over the years, the scene of his youth sank from the "extreme humility of border life" in an 1866 biography to the "stagnant, putrid pool" of William Herndon's 1889 characterization. One writer distinguished Lincoln from his Hoosier neighbors with an unsavory metaphor designed to touch both the eyes and nose: Lincoln was a "diamond glowing on the [Indiana] dunghill."[7] Most society members descended from those neighbors and so, reacting both out of familial respect and out of a sense of historical justice, they reasoned that Lincoln's boyhood must be understood in the context of his neighbors, that the evidence for those neighbors resided in the family stories of then-living grandchildren, and that the information would be lost forever with their deaths. Therefore, in order to be true to Lincoln and to their collective ancestry, it was incumbent upon the descendants of southern Indiana pioneers to carefully record and analyze their ancestral and community stories through a "Lincoln Inquiry."

The quest for Lincoln, family, and accuracy proved electrifying. Over the course of nearly two decades, some 250 individuals researched and presented papers treating the Lincolns in Indiana, pioneers and their families, and the histories of towns, schools, and local institutions. In their meetings, an elderly woman relating family pioneer lore shared the podium with a Johns Hopkins–trained historian explaining "scientific methods in historical research," followed by a local historian theorizing about "the preservation of the knowledge of old people." Outside of the meetings, participants interviewed elderly residents, indexed old newspapers, taught high school students how to research in the court house, wrote papers and newspaper articles, built monuments and a reconstructed pioneer village, memorialized the grave of Nancy Hanks Lincoln, and produced historical pageants. The breadth and depth of their activities simply defy stereotypical categorization.

A "local" society, the Inquiry drew attention and participation from across the country. Motivated by "familial pride"—that producer of specious pedigrees and family hagiography—participants critically evaluated published histories and local lore. Collectors of "antiquarian" documents and pioneer biographies, they used cutting-edge technology to engage a variety of audiences. Without academic training generally, they applied current trends in academic historiography, heard lectures on method, read the *New York Times Book Review,* and influenced the establishment of monuments and museums now operated by the National Park Service and private investors. Within two years from its founding in 1920, the Lincoln Inquiry constituted the largest and most active historical society in the state of Indiana. By the end of the decade, the director of the state's historical bureau credited the Lincoln Inquiry with "reviv[ing] interest in the fourteen years which Lincoln spent in this state" and "contribut[ing] powerfully to the revision of our interpretation of Lincoln's personality and its development."[8] The Lincoln Inquiry both encouraged participation in a public historical quest to understand Lincoln and contributed to that larger understanding.

The Lincoln Inquiry also fought tenaciously for a place in the crowded public history field of Lincoln studies during its "Golden Age" in the 1920s. As Americans returned to "normalcy" after World War I, major biographies of Lincoln were written by two preachers, a former senator, a poet, and a muckraking journalist. The Lincoln family published a genealogy, Randall wrote of constitutional problems during Lincoln's presidency, states and corporations founded societies and research libraries to collect Lincolniana. Statues sprouted up on town squares, the Lincoln Memorial was dedicated in Washington, DC, and automobiles carried increasing numbers of tourists to historic sites connected with Lincoln in Kentucky, Indiana, and Illinois. Witnesses to Lincoln's life and veterans of the Civil War began to pass away, Lincoln's son donated the father's papers to the Library of Congress, and neo-Confederates launched a revival that would spawn bestselling literature, monuments, and a nationwide political movement. In short, the 1920s witnessed significant transformations in the field of Lincoln studies, the discipline of history, and the nation as a whole.

In this context, the work of the Lincoln Inquiry is recoverable because of the vast array of sources it left scattered across the Midwest. The minutes of its meetings fill nearly 1,200 pages and are amplified by hundreds of pages of speeches and correspondence between society members and historians, journalists, and fellow workers. Regional, state, and national newspapers ran commentary on the society's work. Dozens of scrapbooks document members' achievements *and* their hopes, reflections, and motivations. This rich body of evidence permits us to approach these people as journalists or ethnographers would. We can sit with individuals in their living rooms as they open old dusty trunks filled with the artifacts and personal papers of an ancestor, we can walk with them through forests where Lincoln might have walked and pause with them at the gravesite of his mother, we can listen as they articulate the memories that rush over them while speaking to the assembled society, we can observe individuals alone in their studies as they draft and redraft narratives and arguments about the past. Like historians of lived religion who care less about the rhetorical structure of sermons and more about the expression of religiosity in everyday life, we can use these sources to open a window on the everyday processes of historical thought and action.[9]

Everybody's History uses the case of the Lincoln Inquiry to argue for a richer, more comprehensive view of public historical practice as a vast social network in which authority and methods are contested, evidence is debated, interpretations are challenged, and wide-ranging findings require selection, support, and synthesis. In reading, researching, writing, and sharing their findings, participants in the Lincoln Inquiry were just as much historians as their counterparts in the still-emerging academic historical profession. By creating a social network that accommodated academics and genealogists, lawyers and locals, collectors and novices, they inhabited a rich and vivid confluence of memory, history, consciousness, and practice.

Precisely because Lincoln is everybody's subject we are compelled to adopt a new model of historical practice that incorporates people from *all* walks of life who actively engage the past, who critically evaluate historical sources and evidence, and who substantively contribute to collective knowledge. Historian Ian Tyrrell has recently shown that since their origins in the late nineteenth century, academic historians have regularly reached out to the American public via schools, radio, film, and state and local history. The story of the Lincoln Inquiry demonstrates that the "public" also reached back. Though some of the characters in this story will articulate a critique of academic specialization, this book argues for the need to recognize a multiplicity of contributions from various domains of authority. Those who participated, from whatever their starting point and whatever their agenda, are considered public historians in the pages that follow.[10]

The public historians engaged in the Lincoln Inquiry understood history to be close, real, and personal. Because Lincoln's past and the nation's past unfolded within the local and family context of the Indiana frontier, society members remained attuned to the ways that the past, though gone, remained present. The Dutch philosopher of history Eelco Runia describes this approach to the past as "presence" or "'being in touch'—either literally or figuratively—with people, things, events, and feelings." He contrasts presence with the aspirations of preservationists, for example, who seek to "stop time, and preserve, respect, and honor what you happen to possess." In contrast, presence represents "a desire to share in the awesome reality" of human existence. Participants in the Lincoln Inquiry did not conceive the past as a foreign place but rather as something they could experience and engage nearby, in archives and conference presentations to be sure, but also when reading alone in an armchair, poring over courthouse records, opening trunks in attics, reflecting on the deceased at gravesites, contemplating human experience on a riverbank, or building replicas of pioneer log homes.[11]

The story of the Lincoln Inquiry unfolds over the first four decades of the twentieth century. Chapter One traces the formation of the Lincoln Inquiry in the lives of individual participants and the context of public history of the era. The society's formal structure accommodated fraternity and rivalry within as well as critique of past historians and correspondence with contemporaries. In Chapters Two and Three, the Lincoln Inquiry moves into the crowded field of public history in Indiana and the competitive field of Lincoln studies. As the society competed with other historical institutions in the Hoosier state for access to scarce resources, it levied the support of nationally renowned biographers. Yet its success also stirred up jealousies among other writers who criticized the Inquiry's methodology, calling forth a vigorous defense of oral testimony and an articulation of the authority of locals to interpret the experience of Lincoln on Indiana's frontier. Chapter Four closely outlines the Lincoln Inquiry's contribution to the field of Lincoln studies, both the discrete findings that were scooped up right away by competing biographers and the broader insights about the social context of Lincoln's Indiana boyhood that are still coming to be appreciated by historians. Chapter Five examines the way that the Lincoln Inquiry defended its interpretation of Lincoln's frontier experience against Indiana's civic leaders who wanted to erect a monument to Lincoln's mother in an effort to clean up the state's image after the Ku Klux Klan overran state government. Finally, after a decade of justifying and defending its approach and interpretations, the Lincoln Inquiry made several attempts to synthesize its findings for a variety of public audiences. Chapter Six explores a photo exhibit, a historical pageant, and a pioneer village to assess how participants understood their audiences and how they attempted—and ultimately failed—to produce a lasting public synthesis of their work. The Lincoln Inquiry carved out a space to practice history between state and local workers and within a competitive network of historical practitioners marked by research and rivalry, politics and prestige, witnesses and stories, secret combinations and public confrontations.

When Lincoln is everybody's subject, even he is not immune to critique. Individuals in these pages will celebrate his intellect, criticize his morals, and venerate his mother. His name will be invoked for professional ends, personal profit, and civic restitution. The Lincoln Inquiry itself maintained an ambivalent relationship with its subject, sometimes pushing the Lincoln theme while at others seeing it as a distraction. In studies of Lincoln's memory, Merrill Peterson and Barry Schwartz concluded that Lincoln endures because he is adaptable. Eric Foner, David Blight, and James McPherson point to issues that Lincoln dealt with—civil liberties, race, national identity—that remain part of American culture. For the Lincoln Inquiry, the sixteenth president became a useful way to combine local history and national influence, family memories and American identity, nearby history and larger significance. By undertaking a collective quest for meaning through local history and the lives of Indiana pioneers, the Lincoln Inquiry demonstrates that Lincoln's legacy endures because it provides the gateway for "everybody" to connect their historical interests.[12]

To all who have any interest in the past, whether authors or archivists, curators or commentators, professors or preservationists—by profession or avocation—*Everybody's History* serves as an invitation to explore the Lincoln Inquiry's work and worldview and to reflect on your own. Though this book is decidedly *not* a handbook of practice, it brims with learnable lessons and testable tactics. While library shelves bulge with prescriptive discussions of why history *should* matter to students or to tourists, *Everybody's History* tells a story about why history *did* matter so much that hundreds of Americans devoted their time and means to studying, preserving, and perpetuating it. In illuminating the reasons why previous Americans have found meaning in the past and pleasure in its pursuit, this story may bring specificity to public discussions that all too frequently speak only vaguely about history's role in creating good citizens or preserving democracy. All history is public history because, beyond filling course requirements, beyond teaching critical thinking, beyond preparing people for civic engagement, history possesses the power to whisper life, feeling, and meaning into the present human experience. To the Lincoln Inquiry, the quest to reclaim the sixteenth president combined national history, western history, state history, local history, family history, public history, human history, in short, everybody's history.

∂§ 1

The Lincoln Inquiry

JOHN IGLEHART typically spent his evenings reading history. By day he worked as the general counsel for a large railroad corporation—the Evansville & Terre Haute beginning in the 1870s and then its parent company, Chicago & Eastern Illinois, after 1912. He spent his off-work hours raising a family, tending a garden, and riding in his automobile, but by nightfall he preferred reading. After dinner he would, as he once described it, settle down in a "comfortable corner" and, by the light of "two good electric bulbs," immerse himself in old diaries and newspapers, collections of letters, narratives of travelers on the Midwestern frontier, and the annual agricultural reports for the state of Indiana. These sources from the past opened up to him the world of his ancestors who had emigrated from England in 1817 to settle in the Hoosier State only a few months after Abraham Lincoln's family had arrived. Iglehart liked to say the he had been born "in the wilderness" of Warrick County, Indiana, in 1848, but he knew that, unlike the pioneer generations before him, he had lived with modern luxury. He graduated from Asbury (later DePauw) University and was admitted to the Indiana bar in 1869, two years after the Methodist-owned college admitted its first class of women and the same year that the transcontinental railroad linked the nation's coasts and revolutionized American business and culture.

Living as he did in a day of electricity and modern inventions, Iglehart used reading to "shut out the lights" that surround modern people. He believed that anyone could "live in that time and in that period . . . if they will undertake it" through reading. And so he read—autobiographies and biographies of Midwestern pioneers, county histories, state histories, state history magazines, and histories of local institutions. Lincoln's biographers Ward Lamon, John Nicolay and John Hay, and William Herndon

9

wrote about the Indiana frontier, but they came from a generation of writers who had all known Lincoln personally without knowing Indiana and therefore emphasized Lincoln's later presidential greatness by contrasting it with his early life. In large measure, their depiction of the frontier mirrored Edward Eggleston's fictional portrayal in *The Hoosier Schoolmaster* (1871), one of the earliest in a stream of Hoosier writings that would to capture the dialect and customs of southern Indiana for an eastern audience. As a counter to this caricature of backwoods frontier life, Iglehart preferred the writings of nationally known historians such as Francis Parkman, Theodore Roosevelt, Albert Bushnell Hart, Woodrow Wilson, and Frederick Jackson Turner. Having read widely enough in the sources from the frontier period, Iglehart did not simply "consume" these written histories, he put them on the witness stand, so to speak, and critically evaluated their interpretations, lines of development, and use of sources.

Iglehart's personal preferences might have remained his own had he not been drawn into a more public role in history work in 1916. In that year Indiana celebrated its centennial with public pageants, parades, and publications. Evansville's mayor appointed Iglehart chair of a citywide centennial historical commission in order to lengthen the state's celebration into an observance of the city's anniversary the following year. In addition to his experience in reading history, Iglehart brought several other assets to his new public role—he was thorough and accurate in the courtroom to the point of being "exceedingly tedious" at times, agile and active despite his nearly seventy years of age, and well connected in the community as the brother and father of successful local businessmen. A fellow lawyer recalled him as "a rugged character, very determined and firm and always on the right side of civic questions." Such conviction was not always balanced by patience with those who did not share his views, and he once confessed, "I am volcanic sometimes in my methods of delivery." And, to top it all off, Iglehart was easily recognizable in public by his thick snow-white hair and beard—a blend of Santa Claus and Clarence Darrow.[1]

Iglehart plunged into the task of preparing for the city's centennial. He organized a two-pronged campaign to collect reminiscences from living persons and to scour local homes and libraries for old documents and artifacts. He wrote articles about Evansville's history and collaborated with the editor of the state's history magazine to produce a new history of Vanderburgh County.[2] Yet, by the time 1917 arrived, the previous year's wave of commemorative exuberance had crashed on the rocks of the World War. Believing the hype that the American "Doughboys" would end the conflict quickly, the city patriotically postponed its celebration. However, as 1917 passed into 1918 and as the enemy transformed from German soldiers into Spanish influenza, Evansville called off all plans to celebrate.

Though Iglehart never contracted influenza, he did become infected with another condition that would profoundly shape his future. To his

In 1920, Evansville lawyer John E. Iglehart founded the Southwestern Indiana Historical Society, which would draw hundreds of Americans into a quest to reclaim Abraham Lincoln's Indiana past as part of the "Lincoln Inquiry." Courtesy Willard Library, Evansville, IN.

extensive interest in reading and research, Iglehart had added the experience of organizing and promoting history in public, and he would continue to purse history as a public organizer, reader, and researcher for the rest of his life. On the basis of his past experience and interests, he founded a "Lincoln Inquiry" that would ultimately mobilize a large social network of historical practitioners, challenge the published writings on Lincoln and the Indiana frontier, and seek to share its findings with the widest possible audience.

Doing History Together

After the dissolution of Evansville's centennial committee, John Iglehart could have returned to his reading chair and envisioned himself as a solitary history writer. Two of his favorite writers—Roosevelt and Parkman—had inherited fortunes that allowed them to travel widely and write at leisure. During the 1880s, specialists in a number of scholarly disciplines began to form professional associations and develop more rigorous approaches to training and credentials. American historians began to seek doctoral training in universities and to define "professional historians" as individual authors of monographs and holders of endowed chairs at universities—Turner and Hart were stationed at Harvard, and before entering politics Wilson had held positions at several universities, most notably Princeton.

Local historians in the United States also tended to work individually as they collected and preserved artifacts and documents and compiled and wrote local histories. Looking around the nation in the early twentieth century, Iglehart could have decided to pattern his work after other local historians, such as the Kansas newspaper editor Lilla Day Monroe, who collected reminiscences of approximately 800 elderly pioneer women, or Oregon farmer Ezra Meeker, who retraced his 1852 emigration in an ox-drawn replica in 1906 and 1910 in an effort to preserve and commemorate the Oregon Trail, or even fellow Hoosier Marguerite Miller, who collected and published two volumes of old settler stories. In his history of local historians and antiquarians, David J. Russo tacitly underscored their individualistic approach by characterizing their work as "a many faceted enterprise" and a "vast, sprawling folk movement." But Iglehart chose not to remain in his comfortable corner. By 1919 he began casting around for assistance in forming a historical society. In so doing, he opted to do history collectively with others and stepped permanently into the wider world of public historical practice.[3]

In seeking to do history in public, Iglehart united a longer tradition of forming historical societies with the unique conditions of postwar America. Beginning in Massachusetts in 1791, historical societies sprang up in eastern states soon after the Revolutionary War and all over the Midwest before the Civil War, with Indiana founding its statewide society in 1830, only fourteen years after achieving statehood. Furthermore, historical study, collecting, and writing also found a home in the work of fraternal societies and women's clubs, on the programs of local lyceums and regional Chautauqua circuits, and in displays at world's fairs. During the last decade of the nineteenth century, a spate of lineage-based societies were organized—the Sons of the American Revolution (1889), the Daughters of the American Revolution (1896), Colonial Dames of America (1891), the United Daughters of the Confederacy (1894), and the Sons of Confederate Veterans (1896).

By the 1920s, Iglehart would also find support in Americans' democratic impulse for "joining" public associations and their Progressive Era culture of civic participation. Fraternal societies and women's clubs had drawn increasing numbers since the late nineteenth century. Contemporary civic-minded midwesterners founded the Kiwanis Club (1915) in Michigan, and Rotary International (1905) and the Lion's Club (1917) in Illinois. The Ku Klux Klan revived as a socio-political organization in Georgia (1915) and grew to approximately six million members in the 1920s. County historical societies and old settlers' societies sprang up throughout the Midwest. Local communities of the Progressive Era featured numerous civic associations dedicated to purposes ranging from paving streets, to installing electric lights, to mounting water fountains on public squares. In Indianapolis, for example, one 1929 edition of a local newspaper announced over 400 meetings of 171 organizations. Local historians also worked through hundreds of local associations, decorating graves, placing Civil War monuments on town squares, or campaigning to save Thomas Jefferson's Monticello.[4]

In Lincoln circles, the centennial of his birth had prompted the founding of a nationwide Lincoln Farm Association (1906) that purchased his birthplace in Kentucky, a Lincoln Centennial Association (1908) in Springfield, Illinois, and an Abraham Lincoln Association (1909) and Lincoln Circuit Marking Association (1915) that were active throughout Illinois.

Within this general context of public participation, Iglehart established a multi-layered social network for practicing history by creating an institutional home, recruiting participants, encouraging pleasant interaction, and soothing interpersonal frictions. He began by seeking advice and support for incorporating a public society according to the rules and procedures of the state of Indiana. Harlow Lindley of the State Historical Commission sent instructions for forming a society, and James A. Woodburn of the Indiana State Historical Society shared examples of organizational plans and objectives. As founding members, Iglehart invited his brother and a cousin, one former U.S. senator, two fellow lawyers, and four female acquaintances from Evansville's Walnut Street Presbyterian Church. In short order, the group signed articles of incorporation for a nonprofit, tax-free, non-stockholding, voluntary association. They proposed a quarterly meeting plan, set membership dues, agreed to follow Robert's Rules of Order, elected Iglehart president, and adopted three loose objectives to study, preserve, and publish history. Only the name of the society prompted debate. Iglehart proposed "Lincoln Club" to state officials, who rejected it for being too vague. He then decided on "Southern Indiana Historical Society," but the name had already been taken by a group in New Albany, so at last he settled for "Southwestern Indiana Historical Society," a name that would be shortened among members to simply "the Southwestern."[5] Though the change did not seem to bother Iglehart, it did foreshadow the society's ambivalent relationship with Lincoln. The nickname "Lincoln Inquiry" would come later.

The idea of organizing historical societies, of course, was not new, but a few features of the Southwestern distinguished it from other contemporary historical associations. Unlike lineage societies, for instance, the Southwestern did not restrict membership to descendants of Indiana's frontier. And, in a further departure from contemporary practice, the Southwestern invited membership of both men and women. The Southwestern would not be a male-only, black-tie dinner affair like the numerous Lincoln Day Dinners held around the country, nor would it develop separate men's and women's auxiliaries like fraternal or lineage societies. By opening membership beyond descendants and to both men and women, the Southwestern targeted all persons residing or interested in the history of the eight counties of Southern Indiana's "Pocket" region—Posey, Vanderburgh, Warrick, Spencer, Perry, Gibson, Pike, and Dubois—the southwestern corner of the state bounded on the south by the Ohio River, the west by the Wabash River, and the north by the east fork of the White River.[6]

While working to create an institution open to all, Iglehart also recruited specific individuals who would actively perform research and participate in the society. Iglehart aimed initially for "about half a dozen

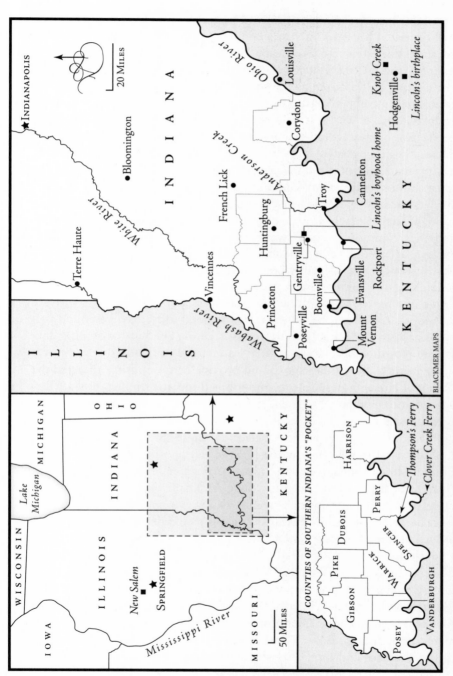

The Lincoln Inquiry drew much of its membership from the eight counties of southwestern Indiana's "Pocket"—the same region of the country in which Abraham Lincoln lived and worked from age seven to twenty-one. Map by Kate Blackmer.

people, not more than that, who will be active at the beginning, but they will be able, I hope, to interest a couple of dozen of our best people and get them started in an organization." These individuals were referred to in minutes and correspondence as "able workers," with one reference denominating half a dozen as the society's "kitchen cabinet." The effort to recruit new members followed a pattern in which, as one of the able workers explained, it was best "not to call a 'mass meeting'—which seldom is effective on any score—but assemble the interested people and make a definite beginning in each township." The result would be "a little band, a very small percentage of the population," or "a small group of us [who] must stand shoulder to shoulder in bearing the burdens."[7]

The strategy succeeded in drawing a cadre of "able workers" who brought to the society a range of experience with the variety of historical activities common in early twentieth-century America. Indianapolis insurance agent George Wilson had worked in Indiana's coal mines, served as surveyor of Dubois County, and taught and superintended in the county's schools. Known for his *History of Dubois County* (1910) and *Early Indiana Trails and Surveys* (1919), he also spent 30 years assembling a private scrapbook collection that ultimately contained forty massive bound volumes of historical data. Iglehart's cousin Albion Fellows Bacon of Evansville bore four children, wrote poetry and novels, organized local reform movements to fight tuberculosis and provide better housing, directed the National Housing Association, and lobbied Indiana's reluctant state legislature into passing a tenement law in 1913 and a housing law in 1917. Attorney Lucius C. Embree of Princeton was active in state and local politics and the grandson of frontier judge and U.S. representative Elisha Embree, a Whig who had joined Lincoln in opposing the Mexican War. Eldora Minor Raleigh was the niece of frontier lawyer John Brackenridge, who had loaned books to young Abraham Lincoln. Thomas de la Hunt of Perry County was the son of a Civil War major who inherited a large home and substantial means so that he could devote most of his time to local history. He contributed a weekly history column to the *Evansville Courier* and in 1916 authored a history of Perry County and wrote and directed the county's centennial pageant. Logan Esarey earned a Ph.D. in history, taught at Indiana University, and had served as editor of the *Indiana Magazine of History* since 1913. Sculptor George Honig and his wife, Alda McCoy Honig, a classically trained pianist, lived in Evansville. Rockport high school drama teacher Bess Ehrmann wrote pageants, plays, and historical sketches and urged her students to study local history. Boonville lawyer and judge Roscoe Kiper served two terms in the Indiana state house of representatives and was also a member of the Sons of the American Revolution, the Masons, and the Kiwanis Club. William L. Barker presided over Boonville's Peoples Trust & Savings Bank and maintained an intense interest in locating every place Lincoln had been. United by a desire to illuminate the history of frontier Indiana, members of the Southwestern brought experience in researching nearby sources, writing local history books and newspaper articles, teaching and lecturing on history, presenting the past in public pageantry and art, and applying history toward civic and political ends.

What differentiated these "able workers" from other Hoosiers? In the correspondence and minutes of the society, the distinction generally came under the vague terms of "interest," "historical instinct," or "historical sense" and most frequently in the negative: "Persons who have historical instincts in Indiana are very few"; "Historical instinct is not dead in Evansville, it has practically never existed"; "There has been up to this time practically no spirit of inquiry or historical instinct among our people."[8] Yet, in a few instances able workers identified affirmative attributes as being preparation, expert knowledge, and persistence. Banker William Barker explained that "some one with historical sense . . . could read an entry in the court records and get great historical value out of it, while another would see it as a law entry." Attorney Lucius Embree, whom Iglehart described as possessing "a strong historical instinct," explained, "There are a great many people . . . who are interested in the past history of their fathers and grandfathers, but they do not seem to have the knack of getting things together." Iglehart also emphasized the connected skills of discerning public interest and exercising discrimination, "the ability to select from a mass of material that which is of public interest—historical interest, from that which is mere uninteresting detail." It required hard work to produce what Logan Esarey termed "sound history"; such work, insurance agent George Wilson explained, was something that "lazy people do not covet."[9]

The society's archivist, Ethel McCullough, contrasted the Southwestern's able workers with Wisconsin historian Lyman Draper, a common target of criticism from historians at the time. Draper joined the staff of the Wisconsin Historical Society in 1854, and by the time of his death in 1891 his extensive collecting had made it one of the largest libraries in the Midwest. He nurtured dreams of using his materials to write bestsellers and important historical books that he never finished (and sometimes never started). McCullough explained that Draper "had the historical sense. He knew what he wanted and how to get it; but he did not know just how to use it after he got it. He lost his balance, his sense of proportion, and he left his great task unfinished." Someone with a fully developed "historic sense," she explained, would possess "a sense of discrimination; what is important or significant, what is unimportant and trivial" as well as "accuracy" and "faithfulness to the end." Thus, in the minds and practice of the members of the Southwestern, effective history workers distinguished themselves not by academic training or by professional affiliation, but by the possession and cultivation of the qualities of selection, discrimination, proportion, significance, and perseverance that produced "historical people" who were "kindred spirits in works historical."[10]

Not only did the society's able workers describe "historical instinct" with words such as "faithfulness" and "spirit," they also employed religious language in the discussion of potential members. Historical interest, they believed, was innate, but if "latent" it could be aroused through a process much like Christian rebirth. Referring to "the historical instinct that I believe we all have," high school drama teacher and eventual society president Bess Ehrmann noted "the awakening of the citizens to the possibilities of recording our pioneer history." Confessing the lack of work done in Posey County, Deidré Duff Johnson expressed "a contriteness of spirit and an awakened conscience." In language remarkably similar to describing an experience of conversion, Andrew Jackson Bigney, the president of Evansville College and a biologist by training with a self-described "sideline" of history, reported that he had not always been interested, but after visiting a historic site he "felt that spirit stirred within." Many of the society's meetings were held in churches and at one meeting, a call to society membership imitated the appeal of a revival meeting: "We invite everybody, for we take it that anybody who is not interested would not attend and therefore we take it for granted you are interested and with a view of expediting matters and taking the names of those who desire to join, I ask those who desire to join to stand up and we will take names and put you in the membership immediately, without any further delay." After a four-year separation from the society, former Indiana Historical Commission director John Oliver wrote that "every time I 'tune in' with your point of view, I find myself waxing enthusiastic over this whole subject matter. . . . How I wish I could come in more frequent contact with you and catch more of your burning enthusiasm!"[11] Studies of collective memory and the "myths" of heritage often describe public interest in history as a "civic religion" that replaced actual religion in America's secularizing society.[12] In the case of the Southwestern, however, the opposite appears to be true—instead of history functioning as religion, religious

experience and language served to construct and narrate the social practice of history.

Motivated by religious zeal, the society's able workers reached out to
their communities through social networking and the local press. Some
new members came through individual acquaintance with members of
the Sons of the American Revolution, the Daughters of the American
Revolution, the Grand Army of the Republic, or the Society of Indiana
Pioneers. At least a dozen of the society's active male workers shared connections in local Masonic lodges, which over the past five decades had
focused less on secret ritual and more on civic service. In Rockport, Bess
Ehrmann first lobbied the women's club to study local history as part of
their annual study schedule. Then, after a woman had presented a paper
to her peers, Ehrmann invited her to repeat the performance for the
Southwestern. In 1927 society members joined with the American Legion
and local veterans to host a commemorative service at Nancy Hanks
Lincoln's gravesite, and the society extended formal meeting invitations
to members of the Indiana Nature Study Club, the Lincoln Memorial
Commission, the Evansville Chamber of Commerce, the Tri Kappa Sorority
of Huntingburg, and the Newburgh Civic Improvement Society.[13]

At least eight members of the society owned and/or edited newspapers
in the area. The papers in several communities published announcements,
invitations, and programs before each of the society's meetings, and representatives from the papers regularly attended and reported on the proceedings. In Spencer County, Ehrmann pushed "to have every [research]
paper published in one of our county papers." Tom de la Hunt wrote a
weekly column on local history and addressed the society on the topic of
"Publicity in the Newspapers." He encouraged members to submit items
on Mondays—the down days—for they would be far more appreciated
than "the 'boiler-plate filler' that is in every other newspaper." In his own
writing, de la Hunt liked to vary topics widely and to drop in local names
because readers "like to see the names of their families and ancestors in
print as well as their own."[14]

Over the course of two decades, the society grew and its membership
rolls and meeting minutes eventually named over 500 participants. Approximately 80 percent came from the eight "Pocket" counties of southwestern Indiana with another 40 persons from around the state; two
dozen from Kentucky, California, Kansas, Michigan, and Washington; and
one each from ten other states. Men and women split the membership at
approximately 40–60 percent, and no record was made of members' race.
All of the 533 individuals are not recoverable from local census data or

county histories, but the available information proves revealing. Of the approximately one hundred for whom birth or death dates are available, four were born in the 1840s, seventeen in the 1850s, twenty-one in the 1860s, twenty-six in the 1870s, nineteen in the 1880s, five in the 1890s, and one in 1904; at least three lived until the 1980s, placing the majority of society membership in the ages between 45 and 75. Noting this, one member commented that "the quest for ancestors" was a "middle-aged occupation" and "not a disease which attacks the young who are quite too busy with the bustling present to catch the gentle murmur of the past." When not at meetings, members worked as farmers and school teachers, ministers and librarians, university professors and college presidents, newspaper editors and correspondents, lawyers and judges, and an artist, auditor, druggist, funeral director, grocer, jeweler, notary public, physician, and veterinarian. As its use of religious language foreshadowed, the society also drew Baptists, Lutherans, Methodists, Presbyterians, and Catholics—the last group would become increasingly significant over the course of the decade as the Ku Klux Klan fanned anti-Catholic sentiment.[15]

Thus, this primarily midwestern, middle-class membership does not seem to fit traditional characterizations of local historians, collectors, or genealogists. They did not come from an old elite who sought to bury themselves in the past as an escape from the industrial and social transformations of the early twentieth century. Nor can they be characterized as a rising generation of nativist reformers who labored to remake the memory and experience of arriving immigrants. Their interest in the past arose not out of a critique of modernity or a concern for cultural preservation so much as from a desire to promote their local community. Yet in advocating for their frontier Indiana communities they were not single-minded "brass band" boosters with eyes only for material gains, nor were they unaware that the region's past could influence its present. Like the midwesterners of Lewis Atherton's *Main Street on the Middle Border,* members of the Southwestern mingled idealism, optimism, and a faith in progress, but unlike Atherton's people they also criticized materialism and preserved the past by redefining its value in terms broader than "the immediately useful and practical."[16]

They bore traits characteristic of Indiana in general and of southern Hoosiers in particular. Historian James H. Madison observed that early twentieth-century Indianans held a particular "belief that Hoosiers were generally alike, that they avoided extremes, that they held on to past traditions, that they represented what was typical and perhaps even best about America." Residents of southern Indiana, in contrast with fellow Hoosiers in the north part of the state, "remained in the twentieth century more rural, more isolated, and more attached to the traditions and ways of life of the mid-nineteenth century." Like the members of the contemporary Society for the Preservation of New England Antiquities (founded ten years earlier, in 1910), they were educated, conservative, property-holding residents of small towns with family roots in the region.[17] Members of the Southwestern came from all walks of life to study and learn about the history of their families and their communities.

Common regional and ancestral ties played into the society's initiative to foster amiable interaction among members, an effort that found its most ardent advocate in newspaper columnist Thomas James de la Hunt. From his father, he had inherited enough money to do whatever he pleased in life; from his mother, he had inherited a two-story mansion brimming with relics. When he came of age, "Tommy" found enough evidence in old records to stretch the family name Delahunt into three more aristocratic-sounding words. Widely respected for his historical writing, de la Hunt cultivated high society connections in the state and nation through his active membership in the Society of Indiana Pioneers and the Sons of the American Revolution. And though local gossips suspected the lifelong bachelor was gay, no one faulted him for his social grace or hospitality. Noting that the Daughters of the American Revolution possessed five times more members than the Sons, he urged Iglehart to "take something from the 'Daughters' in lending our reunions a flavour of sociability, added to the purely historic side of coming together." The formula was simple, "in order to increase in numbers we must first interest eligible people by entertaining them."[18]

In public commentary on historical work, the charge of "entertainment" or "amusement" is often levied in criticism of topics and practices that are interesting to the general public. For example, the experienced twentieth-century cataloguer of local historical societies Walter Muir Whitehill once distinguished authentic historic preservation efforts from "historically veneered amusements, waxworks, and other dubious 'attractions' sprinkled among the nut stands, snake farms, and souvenir shops that prey on the traveling public." However, in de la Hunt's usage, "entertainment" referred not to amusement park rides, or to souvenir shops, or even to the dancing parties that had been abandoned by the American Historical Association after 1897, but instead to hospitality and sociability.[19]

The Southwestern regularly hosted receptions and pilgrimages to local historic sites marked by pioneer relics, guides in period costume, music, and food. Though formally prescribed by the bylaws, Robert's Rules of Order often yielded the floor to more enlivened rituals, as when the presiding authority invited a standing roll call of attendees from each of the eight counties that was invariably accompanied with applause. At a meeting in New Harmony, the president announced that the "ladies of New Harmony are appointed the official cake makers" of the society. More than once reference was made to the type of gathering that *might* have occurred had they organized themselves before the Volstead Act made alcohol sales illegal. Just as often, this lament was followed by the good-humored observation that many students believe "it did not take prohibition to make history dry."[20] Members of the Southwestern could enjoy both serious historical presentations and light-hearted socializing.

The society's minutes and addresses brim with references to the "pleasant associations" and the "beautiful friendships . . . formed . . . not from boisterous raillery of convivial social gatherings, nor the slap on the back of some one who wants to use you in his ambition, but the deep feeling which some people have for you, who really love and admire you for what you are, and who hang on to you for the good they can do to you." Harriet Powell called on this sociality in the preface to her presentation about her own family history: "It is very interesting to me and is next to my heart. It may not be interesting to every one of you, but there are some here who are interested because they like me." One member described the meeting times as a "day of getting together" that provided "the opportunity of coming into contact with a great many individuals whom I deem worth while." Another observed that the meetings "have brought together kindred minds from each of the counties, forming thereby, acquaintances and establishing lasting friendships in the work of preserving local history that could be done through no other medium." In at least one instance reported on record, societal ties became familial as the son of president Robert A. Woods married the niece of Albion Fellows Bacon.[21]

Finally, the interaction that permitted pleasant socializing also allowed for interpersonal rivalries. After working on a biography of one of Indiana's pioneer legislators, former Democratic U.S. representative Arthur Taylor heard George Wilson deliver a talk that thoroughly covered the subject from all angles. During his assigned time, Taylor humorously described his biography-in-process as a tale that included a trip to South America, the development of "probably one or two affinities," and a climax in which one lover jumped into the sea and drowned. His wife, he joked, would find it "heavenly," his lawyer would find it "bunk," and alas, Wilson had already written it! The audience enjoyed the fun, with one recalling Taylor's remarks as "a very delightful talk filled with great merriment and good humor."[22]

Other conflicts required formal resolution. Within a year of the society's founding, members from Gibson County began to call for a separate organization, citing "conflict of interest" and "friction" with the larger society. In a nutshell, they wanted their own officers who would control the disposition of their dues, instead of sending dues money to Evansville or having to pay both county and regional membership dues. Leaders of the Southwestern recognized that "the effect of it would be to throw cold water on the main scheme which is working out successfully." Iglehart responded by explaining that the past did not happen in tidy little compartments that paralleled modern counties. The pioneers had moved over the Appalachians to Kentucky, Indiana, and beyond, providing "one sufficient reason for the existence of the society, independent of mere local county organizations which have been found so far inadequate to work the field."[23]

Working in committees, in private, and in full session, group members evolved a solution whereby all members belonged to both the Southwestern and their county society and the dues were split evenly. Presidents of county societies became ex-officio vice presidents of the Southwestern, and county societies submitted names of their members to sit on the Southwestern's standing committees of finance and dues (each county treasurer), publicity and newspapers (each county secretary), archives (each county curator), membership, and historical research. The move pushed the society's leadership structure to over 50 positions at a time when membership hovered around 200 people. Iglehart explained, "It seems that unless somebody feels that he is ordered to do something, or got some title, or some office, that he can't do anything, can't get any work out of them." The tension persisted, for example when officers tried to correlate schedules so as to allow monthly county meetings that did not interfere with one another, but the structure diffused complaints for a while, and served to neutralize county rivalries by dousing them with bureaucracy.[24]

The Southwestern Indiana Historical Society provided the framework for hundreds of Hoosiers to do history together. By creating an institution, inviting active participation, encouraging socializing, and mediating rivalries, the community of history practitioners bridged differences of opinion and emphasis to establish a wide social network of historical practice. This social dimension of public history work remains underappreciated at best. Analyses of the act of historical writing rarely identify any relationships beyond faculty mentor and student while studies of state and local historical societies typically devote far more attention to institutional structure, physical facilities, or program development. After extended observation of Civil War reenactors, Tony Horwitz noticed a social dynamic at play that he characterized as "part frat party, part fashion show, part Weight Watchers' meeting."[25] The case of the Southwestern confirms that fraternity, public recognition, mutual encouragement, and interpersonal rivalries create a social atmosphere that engulfs the historical work of researching and sharing findings. The members set out to produce history collectively in a social process built on formal and informal ties. Interacting with fellow historians also made it easier to engage with other historians who had worked or were working on the subject of Lincoln's Indiana frontier. The quest to portray Lincoln's frontier neighbors accurately would transform the social network into a focused research initiative.

From Society to "Lincoln Inquiry"

In 1908, *Indiana Magazine of History* editor Christopher Coleman outlined the numerous possibilities for history work in the state but observed that "the trouble seems to be not so much in the inability to do anything or in the lack of means, but in the lack of an interesting and important purpose or of intelligent direction." Throughout the twentieth century, historical societies have defined their purpose and direction in reference to two models identified by Walter Muir Whitehill in his 1962 nationwide survey *Independent Historical Societies*. On one end of the spectrum, the privately owned Massachusetts Historical Society (est. 1791) pursues preservation and publication; on the other, the publicly funded Wisconsin Historical Society (est. 1846) emphasizes education and outreach. Institutional decision-making is often therefore viewed as a choice between preservation or outreach. Over the course of the twentieth century, for example, the Historical Society of Pennsylvania (est. 1824) opted for the former and the Chicago Historical Society (est. 1856) for the latter.[26] Preservation, publication, education, and outreach each found a place in the work of the Southwestern, but members of this social network found their energizing purpose less in the "product" of their efforts than in their relationship to previous scholarship. They saw both preservation and education as means for correcting the errors perpetuated by past writers, particularly those who had written about Lincoln.

The society came to this focus on Lincoln only reluctantly. In his inaugural presidential address at the society's first meeting in 1920, Iglehart noted that Lincoln had lived in southern Indiana but emphasized that he was "only one of a number of subjects." Iglehart warned that undue focus on Lincoln might overshadow the rest, for "there are many names that should be remembered and many deeds that ought not to be forgotten." Two years later, however, he changed his mind. "I have come to the conclusion," Iglehart explained, "that the missing chapter in Lincoln's life in Indiana results in a substantial degree from the fact that there is a missing chapter—which fact we all recognize—in southern Indiana life." Lincoln's boyhood could not be separated from the history of his neighbors on Indiana's southern frontier. Research into southern Indiana's history would yield insight into Lincoln's experience and the history of a nation as a whole. Instead of sponsoring a dinner or founding a museum, the Southwestern would host a "Lincoln Inquiry" to carefully record and analyze family and community history in order to write the "missing chapter" in Lincoln's life and in the region's history. The endeavor would also correct the errors prevalent in past historical writing.[27]

Chief on the list of southern Indiana's historical critics were biographers of Abraham Lincoln. Boston resident and Lincoln biographer Josiah Holland had written of "the extreme humility of border life . . . and the paucity of its stimulants to mental growth and social development." Lincoln's law partner William Herndon had called frontier Indiana "a stagnant, putrid pool," and Chauncey Black, the ghostwriter for a biography published under the name of Lincoln's bodyguard Ward Lamon, had distinguished Lincoln from his Hoosier neighbors as being a "diamond glowing on the dunghill."[28] In lawyerly fashion, Iglehart identified two problems with the biographies. First, he condemned the biographers as outsiders "who spent only a short time in Indiana." Next, he impeached the prosecution's most important witness, Dennis Hanks. A cousin of Lincoln's mother, Hanks had lived with the Lincoln family in Indiana but parted ways with Abraham after moving to Illinois. In addition to being cited by Herndon as an essential witness, Hanks began to dress in a top hat, peddle artifacts connected with his assassinated relative, and give contradictory testimony to other biographers. In Iglehart's estimate, Hanks was an "illiterate and ignorant braggart" who was "entirely unreliable."[29] But Iglehart did not single out Lincoln studies for blatant inconsistencies because he recognized that the perception of Indiana's backwardness resonated in wider literature.

Beyond Lincoln studies, society workers contended with more widely read novels—in particular Baynard Rush Hall's *The New Purchase* (1843) and Edward Eggleston's *The Hoosier Schoolmaster*. Hall had come to Indiana from Philadelphia to teach at the seminary in Bloomington (later Indiana University). When the school passed him over for the position of president, he responded first by feuding with school officials and then by returning to the East, where he wrote a thinly veiled memoir that castigated his former neighbors. Iglehart branded the book "cowardly libel" because it "breathes a contempt for western character" and because the author "makes no effort to disguise his bitterness as a bad loser."[30] In contrast to the out-of-place easterner, Edward Eggleston was born in southeastern Indiana but left the Midwest to pursue a literary career in New York City. His novel humorously portrays southern Hoosiers as poor, uneducated, ignorant, and villainously corrupt, though the story's hero does manage to reunite an orphaned boy with his mother. Iglehart thought Eggleston possessed a "charming personality" and considered him the "greatest prose writer of his time," but *The Hoosier Schoolmaster* had been "hurriedly written" and its characters represented "the scum of the earth." "Eggleston's story is a dialect story, and in it dialect is true to life," Iglehart explained, "but the story is located among the most disgusting class of humanity of the lowest instincts, and these books have created an impression of early pioneers in Indiana, which I feel does not do justice to a class of Native Westerners and pioneers who were more intelligent and less illiterate."[31] Though Eggleston eventually transitioned into more strictly historical writing and later served as president of the American Historical Association, the novel remains his most significant work.

Even historians seemed to get the picture wrong. Iglehart and his colleagues identified a host of published errors—Reuben Gold Thwaites and Theodore Roosevelt had both confused the father and son founders of Evansville, and commercially published county histories related incorrect details and errant stories about places and events. More troublesome, perhaps, was the general neglect of southern Indiana, in national histories certainly but also in histories of the state produced by writers in Indianapolis and other northern parts of the state settled primarily by New Englanders. Such "mistakes" were "natural for the reason that" most published histories "are almost silent" in regard to southern Indiana, so writers had no place in which to find the correct information.[32]

As a first step, members of the Lincoln Inquiry responded to past interpretations by citing present authorities. At home in Indiana, they found Logan Esarey, a native of southern Indiana and professor of history at

Indiana University and editor of the *Indiana Magazine of History*. Esarey had written an article in 1918 titled "The Pioneer Aristocracy" in which he identified three "classes" of people in pioneer society: an educated and cultured "aristocracy," a large middling class, and a small lower class of illiterate rowdies common to all societies. Iglehart hailed the piece as "a normal and sane-minded description of a society which deserves the fairest and best treatment" and characterized Eggleston and Hall as having "taken the bottom layer to represent the whole people." Pleased to find a sympathetic audience, Esarey participated regularly in society meetings because he, too, had "never taken kindly to such caricatures of our people."[33]

In 1921, Iglehart reached out to the national academic community by writing to Frederick Jackson Turner, the Harvard University professor renowned for a body of work that began in 1893 with a famous essay titled "The Significance of the Frontier in American History." Turner argued that America's unique society—characterized by democracy, independence, inventiveness, and optimism—originated in the experience of Americans on the frontier. The widespread appeal of his ideas propelled him from Wisconsin to Harvard, where he began to train a new generation of historians who applied his thesis to various regions and time periods—and spawned a generation of critics who challenged its claims. Even in the twenty-first century, the Turner thesis remains a central component of academic debates about the American West as a generation of "New Western Historians" tries to define itself in opposition to it. The theme has grown increasingly potent in popular culture, as the clash of civilization and savagery became the stock narrative of Hollywood Westerns, the westward moving line of civilization leapt off the earth during the Cold War's space race for the "final frontier," and the concept of homegrown American exceptionalism continues to inspire conservative political movements.[34]

Turner received a steady stream of correspondence from historians seeking his advice. Academics, local writers, and graduate students often wrote for his guidance—including a young James Randall who spoke of teaching history at Kokomo High School in northern Indiana. Despite such correspondence, the use that members of the Lincoln Inquiry proposed to make of his work was new to him.[35] Introducing himself to Turner via letter, Iglehart complimented the professor's work, described his legal career, and mentioned the he had already published two articles in the state history journal that cited the "Frontier Thesis." He then asked Turner for advice on applying the thesis to Lincoln's individual neighbors on the Indiana frontier. Turner responded graciously, thanking Iglehart for the compliment and expressing his own interest in the lawyer's work. On the application of his national typological thesis to specific pioneers, Turner wrote: "As you know, I have worked more upon mass movements than upon individual factors; but no one appreciates more than I do that the mass can't be understood unless one generalizes from the study of individuals as well as groups. So your investigation into the [individual pioneers] is very useful research."[36]

From his location in local, public history work in Indiana, Iglehart sensed that Turner's Frontier Thesis provided, in the later words of historian Ian Tyrrell, "an important example of the incorporation of grassroots history" into an "explanation of the West that enlarged the scope and significance of national history."[37] By situating Lincoln's frontier within the very process that made Americans American, the Lincoln Inquiry would not simply investigate local or family history. It would contribute to the understanding of America. Turner would watch the society's work approvingly over the coming decade.

Correspondence with Turner connected the Lincoln Inquiry to a network of academic historians. Members of the Inquiry read Turner's books and cited him in their papers. Pursuing the leads in Turner's footnotes and in his letters, Iglehart and his colleagues were introduced to Harvard historian and Pulitzer Prize winner Edward Channing, Yale historian Max Farrand, and *Mississippi Valley Historical Society Quarterly* editor Milo Quaife. They discussed the work of academic historians Charles and Mary Beard, Vernon Parrington, and Arthur Schlesinger; popular historical writers James Truslow Adams, Ray Stanard Baker, and Gerald Johnson; literary critic Lucy Lockwood Hazard, and essayist Simeon Strunsky. Turner also introduced them to the work of his promising students, Cornell historian Carl Becker and future University of Wisconsin historian Merle Curti, who would pioneer approaches to social, intellectual, and quantitative history. Correspondence with Turner also prompted Lincoln Inquiry members to subscribe to the scholarly journals published by the Mississippi Valley Historical Association (later the Organization of American Historians) and the American Historical Association as well as to the *Atlantic Monthly, Historical Outlook,* and the *New York Times Book Review.* Several members joined the Mississippi Valley Historical Association, attended the annual Indiana History Conferences, and spoke on panels at the American Historical Association.

Grounded as it was in the work of fellow historians of the past and present, the Lincoln Inquiry cast a wide methodological net. A circular

letter sent to vice presidents in April 1920 called on members to take in-
ventories of local resources, write biographies of pioneers, create scrapbooks, establish museums, preserve documents and relics, mark historic
sites, and index county histories and newspapers. Workers soon identified sixty-two families contemporary with the Lincolns and systematically set out to preserve their family stories. Over the course of two decades the society met 46 times to hear the reading of 369 presentations.
Of the 217 papers located in a variety of local and family collections, 116
were biographies, 99 local histories, 65 on Lincoln, and 65 on the methods
of historical work. It should also be noted that 139 of these were published
in state history journals or newspapers, or by private printers.[38]

Drawing upon his own experience leading the legal office for a major
railroad corporation and upon Turner's example as a mentor to doctoral
students, Iglehart lined up workers with their topics. He later explained
to Lincoln biographer Carl Sandburg, "I exercised in a very full manner
the authority of selecting the workers and assigned to each the particular work which they seem to me to be fitted to do." Every member who
joined the society promised to prepare at least one paper to present at a
meeting, and many of the papers presented over the next decade and a
half make references to having been assigned. On one occasion the
speaker joked, "I am not very happy to stand here before you and tell
you about [my own ancestors in] the Barker family. Judge Iglehart has
been ding-donging me to prepare this paper for quite a while . . . and in a
moment of weakness I yielded to the Judge, and have regretted it since."[39]
Because a stenographer recorded all proceedings, the society also welcomed those visitors who could add any information to addresses. "It is
not only the long papers that we want to get hold of but the little items,"
Albion Fellows Bacon urged. "There isn't one of you but what has something about your ancestors, or some of your neighbor's ancestors, that
are just some of the best things in the world." Tommy de la Hunt added,
"Don't wait for the committee to come to you and ask you for it, but
send it to them." In 1924, the society passed a resolution charging vice
presidents to collect "brief historic items of interest" and submit them to
the executive committee "for publication in any way found suitable."[40]

By simultaneously engaging the historical literature and encouraging
every contribution larger or small, the Lincoln Inquiry articulated a unique
significance for its work. One common criticism of local historians is that
they focus on only those things with a direct link to a person or event in
a narrow geographical locality. By invoking Turner's frontier thesis and
situating the Indiana frontier experience amidst the national process of

settling throughout the West, Iglehart explained that the Inquiry could not "confine [its] writing to local matters" but had to treat regional history "as part of a greater whole." Because Lincoln and his neighbors lived in many counties and because documentary records survive in disparate locations, the Inquiry simply could not "be split into county units or by county lines or boundaries." Citing the more poetic words of Woodrow Wilson, Iglehart urged the Lincoln Inquiry to do history "with uplifted eye," seeking to connect the facts on the ground in Indiana with the larger developments in "the making of the West" and "the birth and growth of American democracy."[41] The story of the Indiana frontier was the story of Lincoln, the story of the West, and the story of America.

The Urgency of Oblivion

The establishment of the Southwestern Indiana Historical Society and its quest to restore the missing history of Lincoln's frontier Indiana community acquired a sense of urgency from the convergence of popular opinion and the inexorable passage of time. The imperative to correct public understanding was heightened by the perception that the truth about Indiana's pioneer past was rapidly passing out of existence. "One by one," Wilson wrote, "the old pioneers faded out of our lives, the clinging hands let go, the feet that marched in step with us dropped out so gradually that we scarcely knew it until, at last, there came a day when we suddenly realized that we had hardly one old pioneer with us." Embree noted that "the ashes of oblivion" were rapidly "obscuring" the memory of Indiana's pioneers. And so participants in the Lincoln Inquiry labored "to rescue from oblivion." "This historical material must be preserved by this generation," Ehrmann urged, "or much will be lost that can never be supplied by a later generation." Thus, participants in the Lincoln Inquiry saw themselves as existing at a unique moment of time that provided them access to a near but rapidly receding past. They felt a duty "to rescue from oblivion" the findings that only they themselves could provide.[42]

This duty also found expression in the religious language of a calling. Iglehart ended his first address to the society by referencing "the call from the dead," saying that they should "not permit the record and memory of the deeds and character of those worthy pioneers to perish." He concluded, "To that solemn call in behalf of this Society I summon the worthy descendants, wherever they may be, of those worthy pioneers and ask their aid in our work."[43] Just as Lincoln himself had invoked the recent deaths at Gettysburg in a call to reunite and reinvigorate a nation divided by war, so too did Iglehart use the passing of the frontier to motivate the Lincoln Inquiry to bring new life to the study of Lincoln's boyhood.

The Lincoln Inquiry thereby constructed a proximate relationship between past and present. In this view, even though the past is gone, traces of it remain in the present. These traces demand a response from people in the present, who may choose to commemorate, understand, demand retribution, or seek reconciliation. In his analysis of memory and historical distance, Mark Salber Phillips reminds us that "distance is not simply given, but is also constructed, and the range of distance-constructions is really quite broad." Members of the Lincoln Inquiry recognized that "the past is gone, the present is as thin as a knife blade," and they saw their historical activities as occurring in the place "where yesterday touches today." A college president transposed the temporal concept into a spatial one, picturing history as an iceberg lying chiefly in the past while projecting into the present a tip bearing messages of appreciation and guidance.[44]

Accordingly, the past could "give its meaning to the present" because "it enables us to accumulate past experiences, and by their aid look into the future with some acquired knowledge." Wilson emphasized that "the reading of history should give us such wisdom as will enable us to divine the range of our affinities," but he also warned that "the lessons of the past must be read with wisdom or they will betray the reader. There is danger in an appeal to history unless it is an intelligent appeal and one made for a purpose that is right. Hate should have no place in such an appeal." The best historian "tries to interpret the present and knows it is not final. The effort is better than none at all."[45] By viewing the past as present in the lives and records of southern Indiana, the Lincoln Inquiry laid the foundation for arguments about the significance of its contribution and its authority to make the study.

Members believed that the Lincoln Inquiry could easily provide correct information to those who would seek it, but the task of reversing false popular impressions about Indiana pioneer life appeared far more daunting. George Wilson compared the popular view of southern Indianans as poor white trash to a Supreme Court decision that had already "soaked" popular opinion, admitting "it is hard to reverse such a decision." One member reported overhearing a conversation on a train one day in which a man said, "Those Southern Indiana folks are hill-billies, ignoramuses, cheap-skates, they are damn skunks." In commentary that drew laughter from the crowd, the listener joked, "I grabbed the sides of my seat and held on for dear life to keep from killing him and the only reason I spared him was I knew a big liar like him was in no condition to die." In a more sanguine vein, Logan Esarey hoped simply that the Inquiry would "ultimately convince a few people." He did not seek to replace poor white trash with rich Indiana nobility, but simply wanted the public to regard Hoosiers as "at best mediocre."[46]

The Lincoln Inquiry argued for the value of its work on a variety of grounds. The element of state and local pride was certainly evident. George Wilson urged "history as a source of local state advancement" and there clearly was much to be gained by connecting southern Hoosiers to Lincoln instead of the backwoods characters of popular novels. In his *Lincoln in American Memory*, Merrill Peterson characterized the society's workers simply as "Hoosier patriots," but there was far more at issue. "There is the personal phase of this subject," said Iglehart, "upon which I do not trust myself to speak without restraint, and I cannot speak of it with patience." The stereotypes were not abstractions to southern Indianans; they represented their parents and grandparents. And there was a further generational sense that children and grandchildren would someday be grateful as well. "We study the past not to glorify our own ancestors and our neighbors at the expense of others," said Christopher Coleman, "but we do it in order to understand all the factors that enter into this complex thing, human life." They asserted that the "history of Indiana has never been written" because the history of southern Indiana had not yet been understood, thereby making the society's workers into "pioneers in history-making for Indiana." By enlisting hundreds of Americans, the Inquiry held that "the aggregate of our work, however interesting to individuals in its details, is of wide importance." The collective endeavor would be valuable precisely because it bore the impress of so many individuals, neighbors in southern Indiana, contemporaries in the historical work, and predecessors in historical writing and interpretation.[47]

In the early years, the Lincoln Inquiry did not devote a lot of time to defining its audience and certainly never discussed hosting an audience survey or focus group. They assumed widespread general interest in Abraham Lincoln, and they were correct. The 1920s would become known as "the Golden Age of Lincoln Studies" because so many individuals and groups would claim the right to collect, preserve, research, and write about the sixteenth president. Lincoln's public image would remain popular throughout World War II and would decline only in the second half of the century as civil rights leaders questioned his views on race and presidential scandals eroded American confidence in politicians in general. Statements in the society's minutes refer to making the Inquiry's work available "to the world" for "general interest." The editor of *Time* magazine during the 1920s, Henry R. Luce, identified his readers as an "outward-looking middle-class audience in search of summary"—Americans who wanted more than the daily news reports but did not want to wade through the dense text of the *New York Times*.[48] In search of this same audience, Lincoln Inquiry workers also assumed that once they had placed their findings "out there" future historians would use them to correct past errors of fact and interpretation. A decade of participation in the tempestuous field of Lincoln studies would refine their views on both the public and historians.

Addressing themselves to the general public, their fellow historians, and the rising generation, participants in the Lincoln Inquiry felt both duty-bound and authorized to bear witness. "We can hardly blame the world for believing Eggleston," wrote Logan Esarey, "so long as we do not furnish any better evidence." Speaking to the society in May 1920, he urged, "it is not too late now to begin gathering the documents we can find and give them to the people and to future generations to interpret, together with all the interpretations we ourselves can give them. We owe this duty to the neglected history of the Hoosier state." The problems in Lincoln studies and in southern Indiana history turned out to be the same—"you cannot separate the history," declared Iglehart, "It is all one."[49]

IN CRITIQUING the inadequate work of historians, Lincoln biographers, and popular writers, the Lincoln Inquiry mobilized a vast, socially interconnected network of local history workers and academic historians into a focused quest to do history in public. Iglehart's solitary reading and writing expanded into a broad social network of practitioners who embraced a range of methodologies and constructed their relationship to the past in proximate terms. Perhaps the energy and nuance are best captured in accounts of the society's 1921 meeting in Cannelton. As trains brought passengers from Evansville, Indianapolis, Louisville, dozens of southern Indiana towns, and other places as far away as Colorado, a welcoming committee presented each arriving guest with a commemorative badge bearing the words "La Fayette We Are Here." Four years earlier, the phrase had celebrated the arrival of John J. Pershing at the Parisian tomb

The Lincoln Inquiry met three times a year for nearly two decades to present new research findings, to debate their conclusions among themselves and with rival historians and Lincoln biographers, and to socialize, as in this 1921 visit to Lafayette Springs in Cannelton, Indiana. Courtesy Willard Library, Evansville, IN.

of the Marquis de Lafayette in particular and of the American Expeditionary Force in France in general.[50] On this day, May 24, 1921, the words formed the theme for the society's spring meeting and pilgrimage. In the morning, society members visited the site where Lafayette's steamboat had sunk while he toured the nation in 1825. They drank from a nearby freshwater spring that had reportedly served Lafayette while he awaited rescue and took a photograph of the group framed between the spring on one side and an American flag on the other. After a lunch prepared by the Womans Travel Club of Cannelton, the afternoon meeting at the local Catholic parochial school opened with orchestral music and welcomes from community and society leaders. Then high school students presented the episode from Cannelton's Indiana state centennial pageant that pictured Lafayette's visit with "pioneers who came to greet and touch his hand." Dr. John Oliver of the Indiana Historical Commission "emphasized the importance of educating the children along historical lines," an elderly resident gave his "early impressions" of Perry County, the wife of a local sculptor rendered Liszt's "La Campanella" on the piano, a local woman read a sketch she had written about her ancestor, and the crowd sang the "Star-Spangled Banner." After a brief business meeting, the festivities then moved to Tommy de la Hunt's "Virginia Place" mansion where, the minutes note, "tea was served on the lawn by a bevy of attractive young women." In the evening, those whose trains went westward stopped at the grave of Nancy Hanks Lincoln where they agreed that "every Indiana school boy and girl should be taken on a pilgrimage to this park."[51]

With its blend of socializing and scholarship, pilgrimage and presence, research and recollections, the Cannelton meeting put the one-year-old Southwestern Indiana Historical Society on the map. The society's call of "We Are Here" sounded not only to Lafayette's ghost but also to the community of historical practitioners in Indiana and the Midwest. A local newspaper observed that the society was "recognized as perhaps the leading society for historical research in Indiana." Logan Esarey told readers of his *Indiana Magazine of History* that the meeting was "the most successful that has been held" since the society's founding. John Oliver wrote to Iglehart that he hoped to pattern the meeting of Indiana's state historical societies after that of the Southwestern. At the group's next meeting five months later in Rockport, city officials called a municipal holiday to host the more than three hundred people who turned out.[52]

Though at first ambivalent about its relationship with Lincoln, the society gradually came to see its role as writing the history of Lincoln and southern Indiana. Able workers were being mobilized, the past was still within their grasp, and the future needed them now more than ever. And yet, by staking a claim to the right to interpret the early life of Lincoln, the Lincoln Inquiry set itself on a collision course with a host of other contenders in Indiana and beyond.

᪥ 2
A Crowded Field

O N LINCOLN's birthday in February 1924, half a dozen of the Lincoln Inquiry's able workers met for a "smoker" in Evansville. For two hours the assembled lawyers, insurance agent, former state senator, artist, and journalist examined their "historical and society work and the outlook in southwestern Indiana." The outlook was not good. An eight-page memo documenting the evening's exchange reveals that the men agreed unanimously that the Indiana State Historical Commission had "deliberately snubbed" the society's workers and introduced a new "policy of restrictions" in an effort to censor the society's work and control its agenda. Redirecting Eggleston's imagery onto state bureaucratic officers, the memo lambasted "the provincialism of Indiana schoolmasters, from the eastern, central and northern part of the state" who failed to recognize that the Lincoln Inquiry's work came out far in "advance of anything which is being furnished at Indianapolis."

Another tension went unspoken in the meeting. Just as state officials had grown jealous of the society's agenda, only four years into their enterprise its leaders had grown jealous of one another. In particular, the society's founding president, the grizzled corporate lawyer John Iglehart, and his elected successor, the wealthy socialite Tommy de la Hunt, had ceased speaking to each other. Only the state's treacherous attack could temporarily suspend the "antagonisms" felt between them.[1] The Evansville smoker of 1924 did not feature a pilgrimage, or pioneer relics, or even physical facilities planning. Leaders of the Lincoln Inquiry had discovered that the public practice of history necessarily involves politics and power.

Though twenty-first century commentators often frame debates over museum exhibits or school curricula as the outgrowth of modern "culture wars," the public interpretation of history has always been contested. John

Adams and Thomas Jefferson offered different interpretations of the Revolutionary War during the contentious election of 1800, and Republicans
claimed both Lincoln and the moral high ground by "waving the bloody
shirt" in the decades after the Civil War. In the field of Lincoln studies,
James Randall's effort to rhetorically claim the field for academics came
after dozens of others claims had already been made by Lincoln's acquaintances, by his biographers, by state and local historical associations,
and by the Lincoln Inquiry.

By recruiting members, setting agendas, conducting research, and publishing their findings, participants in the Lincoln Inquiry made a bid for
the rhetorical historical territory that had already been claimed by previous historians and historical institutions. Numerous state agencies and
institutions were already trying to preserve and tell the history of Indiana. In the field of Lincoln studies, the 1920s witnessed a surge of work
by genealogists, collectors, monument builders, and biographers. The ex-
ternal pressures and enticements coming from the state history community and the Lincoln community threatened the internal cohesion of the
Lincoln Inquiry. Once a paper was read at a meeting, could anyone scoop
its findings for their own book or newspaper column? Who had the right
to edit a paper, or to decide whether it was good enough to be published?
Why should someone present research findings at a meeting in southern
Indiana when a famous author might pay for the work in cash or compliment? These and other questions forced themselves upon the Lincoln
Inquiry as it became yet one more competitor in an already crowded field
of contenders seeking scarce funding resources, access to publishing outlets, and the power of defining the goals and outcomes of public historical work.

A General Mania for Lincoln

The Lincoln Inquiry began its work at a time of growing public interest
in Abraham Lincoln. The twentieth century opened with a widely popular
two-volume biography of Lincoln authored by journalist Ida M. Tarbell
that moved with quick prose over the solid foundation of documents,
portraits, and relics. Collectors of Lincoln memorabilia became increasingly active in searching out new sources and cataloging their holdings. The
centennial of Lincoln's birth in 1909 witnessed the creation of the Lincoln
penny, a new postage stamp, and dozens of books and poems; it also
fostered a handful of associations that remained active in promoting
Lincoln. The Lincoln Farm Association had raised money to purchase his

Kentucky birthplace and by 1911 had dedicated a reconstructed log cabin within a massive Greek temple on the site. Progressive Era reformers used Lincoln as a symbol of inclusion for immigrants, as an example of state power for their reform interests, and as a guide for both capitalists and socialists who saw in Lincoln both a confidence in open markets and a compassion for the working class. In 1916, as the United States moved toward participation in World War I, British author and philanthropist Godfrey Rathbone Benson (Lord Charnwood) authored the first biographical examination of Lincoln from an international viewpoint. Three years later, British playwright John Drinkwater's play *Abraham Lincoln* opened on Broadway to phenomenal success and played in nearly every major theater in the country over the next half a decade. Though many of Lincoln's contemporaries had died in the late nineteenth century, a significant number of people who had known Lincoln in life continued to tell their stories, the single most important remaining witness being Lincoln's son Robert, who closely guarded the family name and his father's personal papers.[2]

By the early 1920s, as the Lincoln Inquiry established its agenda and held its first public meetings, interest had grown into a torrent. Congregational clergyman William E. Barton opened the decade with books on Lincoln's religion and his parents. After exposing corruption at Standard Oil and successfully working as a muckraking journalist, Tarbell revisited her early subject to write a *Boy Scouts' Life of Lincoln* (1921). Jesse Weik, once William Herndon's young research assistant, returned to the subject after a successful career in law and business to author *The Real Lincoln* (1922). That same year the federal government finally unveiled its own monument to Lincoln on the national mall, a massive granite temple that would become the most visited historical site in America and the setting for numerous rallies and public events. The Lincoln family genealogist produced a massive tome chronicling Lincoln genealogy back to 1630s Massachusetts, and a second generation of collectors began to assemble what would become the largest private Lincoln collections in history.[3] It was with marked understatement that Iglehart observed that "the mania for writing a history of Lincoln has become very general."[4]

The first Lincoln biographer to sniff out the work of the Lincoln Inquiry was William E. Barton. Known as a "bloodhound after facts," the former Congregational preacher was rapidly amassing a large personal collection of Lincolniana, and he greatly desired to parlay his earlier books on Lincoln's religion and ancestry into a full-length biography. In May 1922 he wrote to Iglehart asking about the effect of Indiana on

Lincoln's career, though the questions revealed his partiality to the stereotypical portrayal of southern Indiana life: "What effect did Indiana
have upon the career of Abraham Lincoln? Was his life in any material
respect influenced by reason of his 14 years in Indiana? Would it have
been as well for him if he had continued to live in Kentucky and gone
from that state in 1830 to Illinois; or if in 1816 he had gone direct to Illinois from Kentucky?"[5]

Iglehart responded with a warning and a lecture. "I think there is too
much opinion evidence in historical work and too much of an effort to
make the facts which are furnished prove the pre-conceived views of the
author," he began. As for the questions, the lawyer explained, "I would
not undertake to answer them at random nor in too condensed form. The
Gladstonian method involves sometimes comprehensive discussion of a
wider field centering upon the exact question in issue, and is therefore
somewhat more elaborate than any attempt to furnish categorical answers
to direct questions. I shall be glad at my leisure to answer them if you
care for them in the line of this suggestion." In other words, Iglehart proposed to work deductively from the widest possible base of contextualized
evidence before stating any conclusions. He offered to forward copies of
publications, and Barton willingly accepted. The lengthy, contextualized
answers seem to have been neither solicited nor written.[6]

In November 1922, Iglehart received a letter from the leading Lincoln
biographer of the day, Ida M. Tarbell. Now in her sixties, Tarbell had
graduated from Allegheny College and worked as a teacher for two years
before finding her career as a writer. After four years as managing editor
of *The Chatauquan,* she went to Paris to pursue post-graduate study and
prepare a biography of Madame Roland. Samuel McClure hired her to
write a series of essays on Napoleon Bonaparte for *McClure's Magazine,*
and then she moved on to Lincoln. Reluctant at first, she soon wrote over
twenty essays that doubled the magazine's subscriptions to a quarter of a
million. The articles were first compiled into a heavily illustrated volume
before Tarbell reworked them into her two-volume *Life of Abraham
Lincoln: Drawn from Original Sources and Containing many Speeches,
Letters and Telegraphs Hitherto Unpublished* (1900). She went on to write
a trenchant exposé of John D. Rockefeller's Standard Oil Company. Although known as a muckraker and a pioneering investigative journalist,
Tarbell never abandoned Lincoln, returning to him every so often to write
short stories or small pamphlets.[7]

Like the members of the Lincoln Inquiry, Tarbell had challenged the
dour portrait created by Lincoln biographers of the nineteenth century.

Assembling a host of previously unused sources and reminiscences, Tarbell wrote of a Lincoln who succeeded *because* he had been a backwoods frontiersman, and her two-volume biography was welcomed by readers who had been repulsed by Herndon's negative portrayal and bored by the ten-volume biography written by Lincoln's secretaries John Nicolay and John Hay. She also understood the competitive nature of the field of Lincoln studies. When she first began her work on Lincoln, she had visited Nicolay, who coolly told her that everything worthwhile had already been done. When she persisted, he warned, "You are invading my field. You write a popular Life of Lincoln and you do just so much to decrease the value of my property." As a result, she welcomed newcomers and encouraged other writers, though, in her ardor for discovery, she sometimes tried too hard to pump information out of people. She admitted that she could be a "dreadful sponge" but her enthusiasm, knowledge, and national stature made her the dominant figure in the field, or, as one historian who noted that her middle name was Minerva quipped, the "goddess of Lincolniana."[8]

Tarbell asked Iglehart for everything he could tell her about Lincoln in Indiana. Omitting the warning he had given to Barton and still trying to decide whether to emphasize Lincoln or southern Indiana, Iglehart explained that he had no Lincoln documents and that he had "never had special felicities for dealing in detailed relation to Lincoln's life or residence in Indiana." At the present moment he was more concerned about the people of southern Indiana, for until their history was written Lincoln would have to wait—there was "no shortcut on getting into the Lincoln Inquiry." He sent Tarbell copies of his addresses and some relevant papers from society meetings. She wrote back thanking him for the gift and confessed that she had not "sufficiently studied the intellectual and moral and social environment" of southern Indiana. "I feel," she wrote, "that in my previous Lincoln work I have been too much interested in picking out the facts and incidents which could be directly connected with Lincoln." In December, while in New York City for the holidays, Iglehart visited Tarbell to explain the rationale of the Lincoln Inquiry in person.[9]

While Iglehart was in the east, an editorial in the *Indianapolis Star* caught the eye of Indiana's former U.S. senator, Albert J. Beveridge. Born in Ohio and raised in Illinois, Beveridge graduated from Asbury University almost 20 years after Iglehart had. He, too, practiced law and was elected to the U.S. Senate in 1899 in a campaign in which he drew parallels between himself and Lincoln. Though some who knew him personally found him arrogant and self-centered, he was popular with Indiana voters and soon became an outspoken advocate of American imperialism, child labor reform, and food regulation (he sponsored the Meat Inspection Act of 1906). After losing his seat in 1910 he followed Theodore Roosevelt into the Progressive Party but never again held office. Unable to shape current politics, he shifted his attention to the past. In 1916, as Iglehart chaired Evansville's anniversary committee, Beveridge published the first part of an eventual four-volume biography of Supreme Court Justice John Marshall. In 1920, as Iglehart launched the Lincoln Inquiry, Beveridge received the Pulitzer Prize for Biography. The Marshall biography placed its subject within what Beveridge saw as the nation's grand imperial expansion. After another failed campaign in 1922 he again turned his attention to writing the story of American nationalism, picking it up where he had left it in the life of Marshall and following it through the life of Lincoln.[10]

In January 1923, Beveridge wrote to Iglehart that the work of the Lincoln Inquiry was "of vital interest to me at present." Iglehart responded by first inviting Beveridge to attend the society's next meeting in Evansville. When Beveridge agreed, Iglehart coaxed him into giving an extemporaneous talk at lunch before a combined meeting of the society and the Evansville Chamber of Commerce. However, three days before the event Beveridge came down with the flu and his doctor forbade him to travel.[11]

Iglehart filled in for Beveridge by reporting on the correspondence he had received from Barton, Tarbell, and Beveridge. Of Tarbell he said he had "always regarded her work as the fairest to the people of the State of Indiana." Explaining Beveridge's absence, he hoped that "we will have the chance to see Senator Beveridge yet. For my part I hail his entrance into the historical field. It has been lonesome down here not to have some man of vision who was able to sit with us and aid us in this work." He quoted the Indianapolis editorial that had caught the former senator's attention in predicting that the Lincoln Inquiry would become "one of the chief assets of the state." In this moment of reverie, Iglehart recalled that "when this society was organized, I said to my associates that if we carried out our plan as proposed, the American historians would have to come to us for the facts which we would develop. They have come sooner than I expected."[12] He also failed to estimate how short this historical honeymoon would be. In time, the Lincoln Inquiry would politely challenge Tarbell and defend against attacks from Beveridge and Barton.

Between Scylla and Charybdis

As the Lincoln Inquiry drew the notice of nationally respected writers, it also caught the attention of history workers throughout Indiana in general and at the state capital in particular. As with the field of Lincoln studies, individuals and institutions devoted to Indiana history had also flourished over the past several decades. The Indiana Historical Society, founded in 1830 but defunct for nearly half a century, was revived in 1886 and began a modest but steady program of publishing papers on state history. When an Indianapolis journalist founded the *Indiana Magazine of History* in 1905 he noted that only thirteen active local historical societies existed in the state's ninety-two counties, but the state's 1916 centennial prompted the organization of more county societies and the formation of a state historical commission. Indiana University's history department soon acquired the state history magazine, and descendants of Indiana's pioneers formed a lineage society that began hosting an annual conference of historical societies in 1919. After World War I the governor charged the historical commission with documenting the state's wartime contributions and the commission soon published a bulletin, promoted county history work, and entered the field of historic preservation. By 1925, sixty-five Indiana counties would host societies.[13]

The director of the state historical commission had earned a Ph.D. from the University of Wisconsin, and when he arrived in Indiana he was "especially appalled by the multiplicity of historical agencies." John Oliver devised a scheme by which he could centralize all the Hoosier historical activities into an arrangement in which the state library, archive, museum, and publisher were all coordinated under his unified direction. The model had worked in Wisconsin, but Indiana proved more complicated. In the first place, the state historical society was privately managed and could not be taken over by the state. Second, the library predated the historical commission and was already managed as an independent state department. Finally, there was the Lincoln Inquiry. Oliver's plan imagined county societies as responsive appendages of the state's centralized body. He had not planned on encountering a regional society determined to direct the work of its own county societies.[14]

In March 1921, Oliver appointed Iglehart to a new state committee charged with overseeing the execution of archeological surveys for every Indiana county. The letter's tone and content suggest that Oliver expected Iglehart to be honored by the appointment, but Iglehart refused to be distracted from the Lincoln Inquiry. Oliver attended the society's' February

1922 meeting in an attempt to repair the relationship, and his conciliatory speech tried to emphasize statewide unity in light of neighboring states—such as Wisconsin—known for "sending their special agents into Indiana and robbing us of the historical material that rightly belongs here." After Oliver left, Iglehart explained that the state wanted them to perform work but "refuses to aid us directly." Therefore, he "resisted" their effort "to impose upon us" and "refused as an officer of the Southwestern Indiana Society to permit the machinery of this society to be sidetracked, so to speak, and be diverted to the line of inquiry which was altogether different from the conception that we had of the work that we were doing."[15] The Lincoln Inquiry had no intention of carrying out Oliver's projects.

Beyond resisting statewide centralization, the Southwestern soon bothered state officials by speaking out on issues of state historical activity. In 1921, the society called on the state to build a highway near the historic Lincoln sites. The following year, Iglehart complained publicly: "We have a State Historical Commission—I don't quite understand its purposes—we have a State Historical Society that ought to do the work we are doing here, but they do not do it." The society's archivist added that "the State Library is not especially interested in developing our history down here." Later the society called on the state to purchase and preserve the Lafayette Spring to which members had made a pilgrimage during their meeting in Cannelton. Whatever the state institutions were doing, their inaction to care for southern Indiana history was a "shame and disgrace."[16]

Oliver responded with an offer to meet one of the society's most pressing needs. Society members had desired a publishing outlet for their work, but had yet to find a suitable option. *Indiana Magazine of History* editor Logan Esarey invited contributions, but at least one influential society member "thought if [their work] were published in one of the Evansville papers it could be read more widely." Indianapolis insurance agent George Wilson opted simply to bind his papers into a private collection of large scrapbooks.[17] In August 1922, Oliver proposed to publish the society's proceedings at the expense of the state, and Iglehart quickly accepted. Three months later, the report of the society's February 1922 meeting rolled off the press in Indianapolis. In the prefatory announcement, Oliver praised the Southwestern as "the largest and most active sectional society in Indiana," lauded its members as "some of our ablest and most enthusiastic students and writers of Indiana history," and endorsed their papers and their "lines of historical investigation" as comprising "one of the primary sources of our state's history."[18] By offering access to publication and public praise of the society's size, membership, and agenda, Oliver laid the groundwork for a peaceful political alliance—but it would not last for long.

Trouble came from competing egos within. Long a member of elite social circles in Indianapolis, Tommy de la Hunt craved a position on the state historical commission. He asked Iglehart for an endorsement from the society and for an introduction to former U.S. senator James A. Hemenway, and Iglehart complied. Iglehart had known de la Hunt only by reputation when he invited him to be a guest speaker at the society's first meeting. He introduced de la Hunt as "the greatest historical authority in the River Counties in Southern Indiana," and the published version of the talk included a statement from the president of the state historical society endorsing his "excellent" history of Perry County as "one of the best county histories produced in Indiana." De la Hunt responded initially by promoting the society's work in his weekly newspaper column, "The Pocket Periscope."[19]

In February 1923, de la Hunt succeeded Iglehart as president of the society, and the latter was designated lifetime honorary president. This move introduced structural tension because it granted Iglehart power to choose which duties he would keep and which he would pass on, leaving de la Hunt feeling slighted. When Iglehart assigned him to do research about a Perry County pioneer, de la Hunt refused because the pioneer had lived in Tell City and not de la Hunt's own Cannelton. De la Hunt also worried about the relative prestige of other society members. As president, he refused to invite fellow Perry County native Logan Esarey to the society's meetings and he tried to exclude one of George Wilson's articles from publication as part of the society's proceedings. On August 25, 1923, Deidré Johnson, another of the society's "able workers," opened the Evansville *Courier* to the "shock" of finding the paper she had presented at a recent society meeting published in de la Hunt's weekly column. Though de la Hunt expressed appreciation to Johnson, she and Iglehart privately fumed at the "gleaner" who performed no original research but earned his livelihood from the work of others. After the squabbling and interpersonal politics, this literary theft served as the final straw, leading Iglehart to quash an initiative to publish a collection of de la Hunt's "Periscope" articles. The two men stopped speaking with each other.[20]

In the midst of the crisis with de la Hunt, the relationship with the state also turned sour. John Oliver left the state historical commission to accept a faculty position at the University of Pittsburgh and was replaced by Harlow Lindley, a professor of history at Earlham College who also served as the part-time director of the State Library's Department of History and Archeology. Lindley set out immediately to complete Oliver's unfinished business of statewide centralization and had no use for a historical society that would not cooperate with statewide initiatives. In October 1923, while preparing the second issue of proceedings for publication, Lindley retained the references to the society's size and enthusiastic workers, but struck the praise of their ability and the endorsement of their work and approach to history. Two months later, Lindley cancelled the agreement to publish all of the society's proceedings and made himself the sole selector and editor of any society work that might be published.[21]

Thus, by the close of 1923, the Lincoln Inquiry faced a reopened conflict with state history authorities and an internal rivalry between its founder and its current president. Iglehart wrote to George Wilson that the society was "sailing between Scylla and Charybdis." Just as Odysseus could afford to sail neither too close to six-headed Scylla nor into the great whirlpools created by Charybdis's gaping mouth, so too the society's path lay between state history workers seeking to devour their work on one hand and a vortex of internal rivalry on the other. As public history imitated Greek mythology, members of the Lincoln Inquiry found themselves "fighting for the life of the society" and "having no end of trouble."[22]

From Smoker to Safety

The new threat from Lindley forced Iglehart and de la Hunt into the same room in a "smoker" with Wilson, Lucius Embree, sculptor and society treasurer George Honig, and former state senator Roscoe Kiper. At the gathering, all agreed that Lindley's downgrade of the estimate of the society's work constituted a "snub" and abhorred the proposed policy of Lindley's sole control over publishing. The group explored possibilities for publishing, including the *Indiana Magazine of History* and the state historical society's publications, but feared that Lindley's centralization mission would eventually overtake both venues as well. They would have to negotiate with Lindley. Meanwhile, oblique references in personal correspondence and executive committee minutes suggest that several women in the society pushed Iglehart and de la Hunt toward an "entente cordiale." As the emissary of the Lincoln Inquiry, Wilson returned to Indianapolis with a message intended to prod Lindley on the basis of his own objective: If the state would not negotiate, the Lincoln Inquiry would publish its findings independently—surely the state could not afford competing publications.[23]

In May 1924, Iglehart and de la Hunt met with Lindley on neutral ground at the annual meeting of the Mississippi Valley Historical Association in Louisville. There, they reached a new agreement: Iglehart would head an internal publication committee charged with selecting and editing papers to be published by the state and, if they were kept within pre-arranged space limits, Lindley would perform only copy-editing. As a gesture of goodwill, Iglehart invited Lindley to speak at the society's next meeting in June, expressing his "hope that everything will pass off quietly—that we will not have any *fireworks* to disturb the serenity of the meeting."[24]

At the June meeting in Huntingburg, however, both the entente cordiale between Iglehart and de la Hunt and the new arrangement between the Lincoln Inquiry and the state broke down. As presiding officer, de la Hunt publicly took credit for brokering the deal with the state, angering Iglehart and Wilson. For his part, Lindley obliquely criticized the Inquiry by declaring county organization to be the "best unit" for accomplishing historical work and reissued the call to participate in the statewide archeological survey. He complimented the society's activity and inquiry, but further antagonized it for not keeping records "as completely as might be done." Later that month, the state published another set of society papers, lumped together, as Iglehart later observed, "with Lucy Elliott's gossip and picnic bulletins"—"a second class performance" that he felt was "deliberately imposed upon us without our knowledge or consent." Iglehart unburdened himself to Logan Esarey, who responded in sympathy: "I have had to deal with such men for the last fifteen years in everything I have done along this line and what is worse in most cases I have had to hold my temper. I am not even permitted to swear at them in public." In the summer of 1924, the state's Scyllan attack appeared insurmountable.[25]

Charybdis continued to whirl within. Facing the last six months of his presidency, de la Hunt began dropping hints that he would be honored to serve a third term while Iglehart began searching for a replacement. He approached Bess Ehrmann, the Spencer County drama teacher and club woman who had so actively led that county's historical activities, but she declined out of friendship for and fear of de la Hunt, or "Mr. X," as they referred to him in their correspondence. "The duel which Mr. X and I have fought out," Iglehart began, "was a tragic affair and must leave its traces in our Society. I have already seen evidences of the chilling of enthusiasm

and without enthusiasm I think disintegration will come." He expressed
no remorse for blocking de la Hunt's proposed volume of news articles,
saying only that "I thoroughly vanquished him and the wisdom of my
course has been so thoroughly vindicated." Iglehart no longer felt any
desire for reconciliation: "If he does not hate me, he ought to" and "while
I have no feelings toward him, I have no faith in his promises." Hoping to
entice Ehrmann, Iglehart added that "there are several women in the Society more capable of running it than the men who are eligible." Iglehart
even tossed out the possibility of his quitting the society and directed
Ehrmann to burn the letter.[26]

In fewer than five years, the Lincoln Inquiry had mobilized hundreds of
Hoosiers to research the history of southern Indiana. The call to write the
history of their community and the missing chapter in Abraham Lincoln's
life had energized participants and drawn the attention of national
writers. It had also drawn the society into direct competition with state
agencies and exacerbated interpersonal tensions. Working in county- and
committee-level positions, the women who had tried to navigate a peace
between Iglehart and de la Hunt did not occupy any formal position with
power to hold the society together. And the leading female member of the
society refused to step into such a position. The social dynamics at play
between competing male egos on one hand and silent female guidance on
the other were not uncommon in historical societies of the period. If left
to the options within its own control, the society might have disbanded
under the weight of interpersonal politics and the power exercised by
state officers. But the politics and power at play within this debate were
subject to influences from wider circles. Scylla might not be the largest mon-
ster in the world, and, in a larger sea, Charybdis might be no more than an
eddy.

Suddenly, in the summer of 1924, the sea of public history politics in
Indiana changed. Under increasing scrutiny from state legislators hoping
to cut expenditures, Lindley left the state historical commission and the
director of the state library stepped down. When the state appointed Christopher Coleman to direct the commission, the Indiana Historical Society
named him executive secretary of its operations and the state library
offered him office space to pursue both tasks. The consolidation of state
agencies that had once appeared impossible on paper now blossomed in
practice.

Coleman, who had received a degree from Columbia University (Ph.D.,
1914) and had edited *Indiana Magazine of History* before Logan Esarey, taught history at Butler College in Indianapolis. At the time of his

appointment, the chain-smoking Democrat known for his puns had spent seven years as the college's vice president. From his proximity in Indianapolis, George Wilson reported the news to Iglehart but did not know how to predict what would happen. "One gains an impression from Dr. Coleman something akin to the 'air of the East,'" he noted. "You will notice he says very little; he lets you talk, and absorbs history, tradition, and so on in that way. He was very gentlemanly, courteous and comes nearer being Dr. Oliver than Dr. Lindley was." Wilson also observed that Coleman's $4,000 salary more than doubled that of Oliver and that his wife appeared to be "a lady of means."[27]

What would Coleman do about the issue of publishing? Instead of waiting, Iglehart sprang into action. He invited Coleman to the society's October meeting scheduled to be held in Lincoln City. There, at the boyhood home of Abraham Lincoln and the grave of his mother, the society would show off the level of its expertise and range of its accomplishments. And the Lincoln Inquiry had in the meantime secured a new national endorsement from the field of Lincoln studies that would not fail to impress. Iglehart and de la Hunt agreed to overwhelm the state with a display of proficiency and prestige.

On a crisp October morning, Coleman joined over two hundred of the society's members who had come from throughout the Midwest to attend the third meeting of the calendar year. Scattered through the crowd were businessmen, lawyers, and civic leaders; as well as school teachers, university history professors, farmers, and a college president. Near the front sat a leading advocate of women's rights and municipal hygiene; next to her a high school drama teacher. Down the aisle sat a noted collector of Lincolniana; twenty-two people had caravanned from nearby Dubois County. Excitement filled the air as people greeted one another and enthusiastically reported their activities since the last gathering.

Tommy de la Hunt stepped onto the speaker's podium carrying a heavy wooden gavel, carved from the tree under which the earliest settlers of Indiana had drafted their state's first constitution in nearby Corydon. As he cracked the gavel down to calm the bustling crowd he likely thought of his grandfather who had been at the "Constitutional Elm" on that fateful day, but when he opened his address he spoke of his mother who had taken him to Nancy Hanks Lincoln's grave site to tell the sad tale. The Lincoln family had come to Indiana in December 1816, less than six months after the meeting under the Corydon elm tree. Two years later, nine-year-old Abraham's mother fell victim to "milk sickness," chemical poisoning transmitted in the milk of cows grazing on the white snakeroot plant that flowered in the underbrush of the Indiana frontier. After that first visit with his mother, de la Hunt had come alone, with friends, as the tour guide to governors and dignitaries, and in each of the different seasons of the year, but "at no time have I been so deeply thrilled as here."[28]

De la Hunt conducted society business and then state senators Roscoe Kiper and Charles J. Buchanan addressed the audience, followed by two members of the commission appointed to formally mark Nancy Lincoln's grave. An auto caravan took visitors to the nearby Santa Claus campground where an "old-fashioned chicken dinner" awaited. In the afternoon, Rev. Louis Warren of Morganfield, Kentucky, argued that "The Mystery of Lincoln's Melancholy" lay not in his family history but in the experience of life on the Indiana frontier and the loss of his mother and sister. In an early call for psychohistory (and an uncanny foreshadowing of late twentieth-century cognitive science), Warren urged, "If we are students of William James instead of William Herndon we shall not prowl around in the dusty attics of traditions nor shake the genealogical tree of either the Lincoln or Hanks families in hopes that some spoiled fruit will fall to explain the mystery of Lincoln's melancholy, but we shall conclude from the evidence in hand that the grooves of sorrow made in the plastic mind of the boy Abraham, were made deeper and deeper by each successive tragedy, until each thought wave passed through a valley of sadness."[29]

De la Hunt then read a poem by Albion Fellows Bacon, a nationally renowned public housing reformer from Evansville. The three-part poem argued first for Lincoln's local significance, noting that while "the world claims his manhood," Indiana bore exclusive right to his boyhood. After an allusion to Joseph of Egypt, Bacon's poem concluded by calling Lincoln a "mystic seer." George Honig, a young artist and sculptor, asked the assembly, "What does the face of Lincoln reveal?" and then enumerated his answers: courage, fortitude, sacrifice, sympathy and love, a knowledge of nature, and the touch of a mother's hand. "There is something intensely human about old photographs," he continued. "In them still lives one who is absent. The expression on the face, the light in the eye, the kindness and forgiveness of the mouth; one can almost feel the heart beat beneath it; the man comes back." Such a visual connection was important. "You may read the hundreds of books on the story of Lincoln, but not until you look upon his portraits will you understand the real character of man. Upon his face is written the history of a nation and the hopes of a people—the face of Democracy."[30]

Then Coleman was invited to the podium. "We are now in the beginning, I think, of a great historical revival," he observed. Noting the recent rises in book publishing and readership, in the membership of historical societies ranging from the American Historical Association to the revived Indiana Historical Society, in monument construction and relic collection, Coleman asked: "Who can estimate the value of this historical renaissance in our American life today, when the material things seem to absorb most of our attention? It may very well be said that this reaching back in affectionate reverence to the past will be the saving breath of life to our intellectual development. We study the past, not to exalt the past over the present, but to make the past give its meaning to the present. We study the past not to glorify our own ancestors and our own neighbors at the expense of others, but we do it in order to understand all the factors that enter into this complex thing, human life. We do not want to live in the past, but we want to make the past live in the present and enrich the present with these treasure-troves of greatness of character and of achievement and of utterance."[31] Perhaps Coleman's vision of rebirth would keep the society from dying.

Bess Ehrmann next outlined thirty-four projects completed by the Lincoln Inquiry during its first four years of existence. The society had obtained a letter written by Lincoln in 1860 to a friend from his Indiana boyhood and photographs of some of his Indiana neighbors. Elderly residents had recorded stories of Lincoln borrowing books and saving his family's farm. Society members had written biographies of members of the Boone, Brackenridge, Casselberry, Gentry, Grass, Grigsby, Hall, Johnson, Lockhart, Morgan, Pitcher, and Prince families. In a gesture of equanimity, she complimented both Iglehart and de la Hunt for their respective histories of Vanderburgh and Perry counties. She emphasized that "the people who live near the scenes of Lincoln's early life . . . are best able to interpret its environment," that the history "could never be written by outsiders," that "this historical material must be preserved by this generation or much will be lost."[32]

Then, at the very end, Kiper again took the stand to report that in a recently published book, the nationally renowned Lincoln heavyweight Ida Tarbell had praised the Lincoln Inquiry. "There has been in the last few years," she wrote, "a considerable amount of solid work done on the character of the men and women who settled this corner of the state," which "gives us a better basis for judging the caliber of the men under whose indirect influence at least Lincoln certainly came at this time, than we have ever had before." It was a stellar endorsement from the most popular Lincoln biographer of the era. Kiper compared this new volume with her earlier biography and concluded, "there is quite a change of view point of Miss Tarbell with reference to the early surroundings and influences on the life of Lincoln, and she attributes a great deal of that and the influence of that to the Southwestern Historical Society."[33]

THREE DAYS after the meeting Iglehart wrote Coleman and asked to start over in such a way as to be "treated as [we] have been by Dr. Oliver and Dr. Esarey." Coleman responded with grace and gratitude, complimenting Iglehart on "the great service you have rendered the State and the whole country by organizing the historical society." They met in person twice over as many months to work out their concerns through "plain talk." Iglehart asked specifically that the state continue publishing the Lincoln Inquiry findings without asserting "any claim of full power" over selection and editing. Coleman expressed the desire to publish the society's work but informed Iglehart that the state would consider only unpublished materials, that he wanted to see "every statement buttressed by reference to the source," and that he would not make changes without consulting the society's president.[34]

As the conversations unfolded, Iglehart slowly realized that the balance of power in Indianapolis had shifted so that Coleman now needed the society's help. Though Coleman did not show his cards all at once, Iglehart pieced together the fact that Coleman was under pressure from the state assembly. In 1923 it had failed to pass a bill to merge the historical commission into the library. Republican Ed Jackson won the nomination for governor in 1924 and called for a review of all state boards and commissions; word leaked that he intended to dissolve Coleman's historical commission. To keep the commission alive—and his job—Coleman wanted an endorsement from the largest and most active historical society in the state of Indiana. Iglehart agreed to endorse the commission, but if Coleman ever displayed the same "contemptuous condescension" as Lindley or "sought to impose" a permanent "stranglehold" on their work the he would personally testify against the commission before the legislature. The deal was sealed.[35]

On January 23, 1925, three days after the governor's committee officially recommended abolishing the Indiana Historical Commission and terminating all publishing except the governor's annual messages, the Lincoln Inquiry passed a resolution on behalf of its over 500 members expressing approval of the commission's "new method of procedure" and "entirely competent" new director; it also warned of the "serious interference and injury" that would result from dissolving the commission. Within weeks the resolution landed on the desks of the governor and the representatives of all of the counties in "the pocket." The next month society members elected former state senator Roscoe Kiper their new president.[36] The Lincoln Inquiry was ready to play politics.

Coleman kept his job, though the once-autonomous commission was transformed into a subset of the library and renamed the Indiana Historical Bureau. He credited the Lincoln Inquiry's "prompt and decisive action" with helping defeat the proposed abolition. The dream of a unified state history program in Indiana effectively died with this compromise. Unlike the unified programs in Wisconsin, Minnesota, Ohio, and Illinois or the multiple autonomous agencies in Maryland, Pennsylvania, and New York, in the state of Indiana separate entities run by the same people out of the same building would thenceforth conduct history work.[37]

The Lincoln Inquiry's entrance onto the crowded field of public history in Indiana illustrates the connections between local, state, and national history work. Though it began as a social network among descendants of southern Indiana pioneers, the Lincoln Inquiry's practice of historical study drew it into larger networks, both of historiographical analysis of past writers and of correspondence and professional association with contemporary historians and writers throughout the nation. Local historians, public history professionals, academics, and nationally known biographers corresponded and competed with each other and also found themselves operating within the larger context of the state's electoral politics. In an environment marked by the scarcity of access to publishing and funding, the public practice of history necessitated the pragmatic practice of politics.

Iglehart came away from the exchange believing Coleman to be "sincere," and Coleman now acknowledged Iglehart as "a very good friend." When he later overheard someone say that Iglehart fought like a panther, Coleman responded with a qualification: "A panther fights for its young, but Judge Iglehart fights for his children and his forefathers."[38] Through the successive tenures of John Oliver, Harlow Lindley, and Christopher Coleman, the Lincoln Inquiry had defined and defended its place among Indiana's state and county history workers. Its entrance had caught the attention of Lincoln biographers and earned the praise of the field's most popular writer. And yet, while the field of public history in Indiana had shifted beneath the feet of the Lincoln Inquiry, so too were transformations under way in the field of Lincoln studies. A new generation of writers, hoping to stake their own exclusive claims to Lincoln's legacy, prepared to topple Tarbell and anyone else with her. The battleground would shift from politics and power to methodology and meaning.

The Best Witnesses

As the Lincoln Inquiry secured its place on the landscape of public history in Indiana, competitors in the field of Lincoln studies stepped up their pressure on its work. Two different encounters serve to encapsulate the developing tensions, illustrating the weight Inquiry members would place on direct experience and face-to-face encounter at a time when historians in general and those in the field of Lincoln studies in particular would argue for the primacy of written sources preserved in archives. As some historians urged distance and "scientific" objectivity, the Lincoln Inquiry emphasized proximity and personal encounter.

On the same trip to Indianapolis on which John Iglehart hashed out a publishing arrangement with Christopher Coleman, the Lincoln Inquiry founder also met with former U.S. senator and Pulitzer Prize–winning biographer Albert J. Beveridge. Now at work on a proposed four-volume biography of Lincoln, Beveridge had shared with Iglehart a draft of the first three chapters in which he dismissed the work of Ida Tarbell and employed an apparent host of evidence to paint Lincoln's Indiana neighbors as immoral, illiterate backwoods yokels. As Iglehart would later tell the story, he called on Beveridge in his room in the Claypool Hotel in between sessions of a history conference in Indianapolis. Beveridge extended a cordial greeting, and though both his breath and his room bore evidence of the four cocktails he had consumed within the recent past, he listened patiently at first, as Iglehart recited the rationale of the Lincoln Inquiry and outlined the classes in frontier pioneer society. The prize-winning biographer grew more agitated, however, as Iglehart provided evidence for Lincoln's acquaintance with neighbors of character and good values. Finally, having laid the necessary groundwork, Iglehart climaxed with a direct attack in the paraphrased words of historian Frederick Jackson

Turner: "You, Mr. Beveridge, are smothering your hero in the 'scum of the earth'!"[1]

An earlier encounter of a different sort had been described more than four years previously at a meeting of the Lincoln Inquiry in the tiny town of Poseyville. Local resident A. R. Beach told the story of a relatively unknown battle of the American Revolutionary War which had occurred on Indiana soil in 1781 when Mohawk Indians, acting in conjunction with the British forces, ambushed a small group of Pennsylvania militiamen. Without a single casualty, the Mohawks killed thirty-seven Americans and took the remaining sixty-four or so captive back to Detroit. With probably a little flourish, Beach narrated the escape made by four brave prisoners who hid by day, marched by night, and lived on dog meat until they returned home, "pale and emaciated, weak, wan and bedraggled." Beach went on to explain that two ancient Indian mounds overlook the site of the ambush and that he himself had spent many an hour exploring the site and the mounds. He confessed that sometimes he would sit on one of the mounds and imagine what the ghosts of the Mound Builders must have thought about the battle. "They must have been greatly disturbed by the sound of the guns and have come forth from their dusty abodes to witness the conflict." Shakespeare, Beach noted, always found a ghost to help him out of tight places, but the ghosts of the Mound Builders proved "very shy." Only occasionally, "when the signs were right and the shadows began to fall," did he imagine that he heard their voices saying, "It was a brave fight, but the odds were too great."[2]

The real encounter between Iglehart and Beveridge and the imagined one between Beach and the Mound Builders share the individualized intimacy of direct historical dialogue. In the former, two contemporary historians debated with each other the strengths of their evidence and the merits of their conclusions. In the latter, a story teller in the present longed for confirmation from an authorized narrator of the past. It is significant to note that Beach did not want to speak with the participants—the Mohawks or militiamen who fought on that soil—but rather with observers who could not only describe *what* had happened but also provide the summarizing commentary that explained *why*. He did not want to relive the experience of the soldier but to learn its significance from an authorized analyst. In the practice of history, proximity to the past, access to sources, and authority to narrate are bound up as tightly as two historians locked in a face-to-face confrontation. Beveridge, Iglehart, and Beach all approached the past with different claims to authority: systematic research or comprehensive experience, a personal visit to a site in the present or a privileged narration by a witness from the past.

During the 1920s, the field of Lincoln studies split over the issue of oral testimony. Beginning in 1865, Lincoln biographers had sought, often haphazardly, for witnesses to the events in the life of the sixteenth president. In his thorough 1994 study *Lincoln in American Memory,* Merrill Peterson observed that "the tide of reminiscence rose slowly after Lincoln's death, became a flood in the 1880s, and crested at the centennial of his birth in 1909."[3] But reminiscences did not simply rise and fall like the tide, they were solicited and suppressed, collected and condemned, relished and rejected for a variety of reasons in a variety of settings. This ongoing debate about witnesses was also bound up with struggles over the definition of sources, access to them, and the authority to interpret them. Lincoln's secretaries Hay and Nicolay became suspicious of reminiscences while working in the 1880s, Beveridge openly attacked both reminiscers and those who believed them in the 1920s, and James Randall and his students would attempt to nail the coffin shut after the 1940s.

The debate over oral testimony necessarily involved numerous important questions that proved as difficult to answer then as now. Were witnesses a part of the past that survived unchanged into the present, or did they simply create memories of the past to suit present needs? Could witnesses get closer to the past than other kinds of sources? Was proximity or distance more valued in considering the past? Who had the authority to answer these questions? Whose work would be endorsed or endangered by those answers? In their quest to certify or condemn the content of witness testimony, students of Lincoln have overlooked the way that discussions about witnesses restructured the balance of power among the numerous claimants who aspired to understand and explain Lincoln's past. Within the long context of seeking for witnesses and within an immediate crisis in which the claims of witnesses were contested, the Lincoln Inquiry articulated a rationale for identifying the "best witnesses" available. Their interests and efforts resonate with later oral history practices and theories about memory, method, presence, and authority. Seeing their work as existing on the edge of oblivion, Lincoln Inquiry workers reached back to the past and pulled witnesses into an innovative, interpersonal encounter in the present.

Varieties of Historical Witnesses

Almost from the moment of Lincoln's death in 1865, Americans interested in learning and writing about his life called on witnesses, albeit through various means and to sometimes opposing ends. Lincoln's death on Good Friday prompted a host of memorial sermons that emphasized the compelling symbolic story of the poor son of a frontier carpenter who was raised to the heights of national power only to sacrifice his life to emancipate a race. In Springfield, Massachusetts, Josiah Holland stepped down from the speaker's stand and vowed to turn eulogy into biography. A newspaper editor, popular copy-book writer, and ardent Republican, this "dapper, walrus-mustachioed New Englander" made a two-day trip to Illinois within the month after Lincoln's death. In 1866, his "instant history" rolled off the press, eventually to sell over 100,000 copies. Holland presented a Lincoln who was virtuous, valiant, and Victorian, concluding that "the almost immeasurably great results which [Lincoln] had the privilege of achieving, were due to the fact that he was a Christian President." That conclusion launched a debate about Lincoln's religiosity and spirituality that continues to this day, and it also marked the beginning of the debate over the use of witnesses to study the life of Lincoln.[4]

To Holland goes credit for writing the first comprehensive biography of Lincoln and for seeking oral testimony to do so. He sought out people who had known Lincoln, listened to their tales of frontier life, and then, in a day before audio recording devices, he requested a letter stating all that had just been related. Armed with his pre-packaged, symbolic, Christological narrative, Holland looked for testimony to fit. When he asked Lincoln's law partner William Herndon about Lincoln's religion, the latter replied, "The less said the better." With a wink, Holland reportedly declared, "O never mind, I'll fix that." He did not interview Mary Todd Lincoln, her sons, or any of Lincoln's cabinet members. In Holland's hand, witness testimony served primarily as a decorative façade hung upon the framework of his pre-existing narrative. The storyline belonged to Holland and, at times, so too did the sentiments of the informants themselves. Facing the witness did not so much reveal Lincoln's life as prove that Holland had been—ever so briefly—to the Illinois frontier.[5]

Disagreeing flatly with Holland's interpretation of Lincoln, William Herndon also took a decidedly different approach to collecting oral testimony. Having known his law partner professionally and politically for over two decades, Herndon felt himself supremely qualified to present Lincoln "in his passions . . . *just* as he lived, breathed—ate & laughed."

Examining court records, back copies of the local newspaper, and campaign biographies, Herndon encountered irreconcilable statements that prompted the lawyer to rely on his professional expertise in cross-examining living witnesses. In so doing, Herndon chose to employ witnesses as windows into a past that they themselves may not have fully understood. Relying, as he put it, on his "mud instinct" and "dog sagacity" he wanted "to see the men's & women's faces when they talk," to "read their motives," and thereby see "to the gizzard." Dusty documents from the past concealed too much, he thought, so Herndon adopted face-to-face encounter as a research methodology that moved his study past mere chronicle toward the analysis of true motivation.[6]

Herndon's approach can be illustrated by his interview with Lincoln's stepmother, Sarah Bush Johnston Lincoln. Sarah joined the Lincoln family in 1819, the year after Abraham's mother died, and lived with him for twelve years. He visited her occasionally throughout his life, the last time being in 1861 before leaving for Washington, DC. Herndon's notes indicate the he originally found her to be "old and feeble" and that he "did not Expect to get much out of her." However, after some questioning, "she awoke—as it were a new being—her Eyes were clear & calm," and then Herndon believed he had found a trustworthy witness. He therefore recorded her recollections about young Abraham's education, work, interests, and home life. In the following transcription of part of his notes, we see that Herndon the questioner is absent in the notes, but his presence in the exchange can be felt in the tug and pull between her desire to tell a story about her family's life and his desire to identify books that Abraham had read:

Mr Thos Lincoln & Myself were married in 1819—left Ky—went to Indiana— moved there in a team—think Krume movd us. Here is our old bible dated 1819: it has Abes name in it. Here is Barclay's dictionary dated 1799—: it has Abe's name in it, though in a better hand writing—both are boyish scrawls—When we landed in Indiana Mr Lincoln had erected a good log cabin—tolerably Comfortable. This is the bureau I took to Indiana in 1819—cost $45 in Ky Abe was then young so was his Sister. I dressed Abe & his sister up—looked more human. Abe slept up stairs went up on pins stuck in the logs—like a ladder—Our bed steds were original creations—none such now—made of poles & Clapboards—Abe was about 9 ys of age when I landed in Indiana—The country was wild—and desolate. Abe was a good boy: he didn't like physical labor—was diligent for Knowledge—wished to Know & if pains & Labor would get it he was sure to get it. He was the best boy I ever saw. He read all the books he could lay his hands on—I can't remember

dates nor names—am about 75 ys of age—Abe read the bible some, though
not as much as said: he sought more congenial books—suitable for his age. I
think newspapers were had in Indiana as Early as 1824 & up to 1830 when
we moved to Ills—Abe was a Constant reader of them—I am sure of this for
the years of 1827–28–29–30[7]

Beginning around 1980, some Lincoln scholars began to promote
Herndon as "a kind of proto-professional oral historian," but that characterization is not fully accurate.[8] Herndon did spend nearly two years
traveling to speak with those who had known Lincoln, and when finished, he ordered all of his materials copied and bound as a protection
against loss of the originals. However, most of his collected materials were
letters or prepared statements signed by the informant. He approached
potential informants haphazardly, often without recording anything:
"Some I conversed with on the roads and other places and had no chance.
Things which I did not deem of importance I paid not much attention to,
but now I regret it, as I have often wanted the very things I rejected."
Herndon approached witnesses largely as a lawyer seeking a deposition.
He would arrange a formal interview, identify the opportunities the witness had for possessing firsthand knowledge of Lincoln, ask a series of
questions, and often read the statement back to the subject and ask for
amendments and approval. He also confessed, "I did not take down in writing 100th part of what I heard men and women say, they talked too fast for
me, not being a stenographer."[9]

From Lincoln's close friends, Herndon learned that Lincoln held un-
orthodox religious views; from neighbors in Illinois he learned that
Abraham was engaged to Ann Rutledge and descended into depression
after her death; from relatives in Kentucky he reported that Lincoln's
mother was illegitimate and hinted the future president might have been,
too. The resultant work—a series of lectures delivered in 1866 and a biography published in 1889—has proven both controversial and essential.
Herndon's own biographer observed that Herndon's biography of Lincoln prompted "appeals to Anthony Comstock for suppression, shocked
cries of indignation, a measure of discriminating praise, and not a little
extravagant eulogy." By the 1920s, therefore, the Lincoln Inquiry was
only one in a long line of protestors of Herndon's portrayal.[10]

Herndon used oral testimony to craft a portrait of Lincoln that func-
tioned as what twentieth-century oral historians would come to call an
"anti-history" to Holland's "Victorian pseudobiography"—a counter-
narrative that reverses the dominant, culturally accepted narrative by, in this
case, revealing things too intimate for late nineteenth-century sensibilities.

Looking at and through the faces of the witnesses, Herndon also claimed for himself the authority to open a door to truth that only he could open.[11]

Unimpressed by either Holland's decorative or Herndon's door-opening uses of oral testimony, Lincoln's former clerks John Nicolay and John Hay distanced themselves from witnesses and their reminiscences. With the sixteenth president still in the White House, the pair decided they would compile a history of his wartime administration. During the 1870s and 1880s, Nicolay interviewed several of Lincoln's contemporaries in both Illinois and Washington, and in the process grew skeptical of human memory. Hay explained to a friend that when they began work on the biography "we thought we should have great advantage in personal conversation with Lincoln's contemporaries in regard to the important events of his time, but we ascertained after a very short experience that no confidence whatever could be placed in the memories of even the most intelligent and most honorable men when it came to narrating their relations with Lincoln." Nicolay considered most reminiscences to be "worthless to history." Instead of relying on witnesses, the pair negotiated with Lincoln's surviving son Robert to use his father's personal papers. Robert granted them access on condition that he be allowed to review their manuscript. The son who removed a reference to young Abe's having sewed the eyes of hogs shut in order to load them onto a flatboat would never have countenanced the findings of Nicolay's interviews about Abraham's depression in the months preceding his marriage to Mary. The resultant ten-volume *Abraham Lincoln: A History* (1890) contained little information from firsthand interviews; it also sold poorly and has been criticized as a "court history" written by Lincoln's loyal aides under the close supervision of his son.[12]

It is ironic that Nicolay and Hay moved away from oral testimony at precisely the same moment that public interest pulled in the opposite direction. Three large volumes of recollections about Lincoln rolled off the press in the 1880s, followed by another volume almost every decade until the end of World War II.[13] Ulysses S. Grant's bestselling *Memoirs* (1885) spawned dozens of magazine serials recording the recollections of other Civil War–era figures. In the wake of Reconstruction, the theme of political and national reunion gained increasing poignancy, especially when told from the intimate perspective of brothers who fought against each other or veterans who now exchanged handshakes instead of gunshots. A veritable cottage industry grew up publishing made-to-order county histories and "mugbooks" featuring the pictures, biographies, and memories of aging pioneers and aspiring town fathers. A host of new periodicals sprouted to provide new outlets for aspiring writers and new competition for established newspapers. This fervor for reminiscing produced documentation of soldier experience in the Civil War, pioneer experience on the American frontier, and the experience of life under slavery, perhaps the most famous example of which came at this time from the lips of the son of Thomas Jefferson and Sally Hemings.[14] Even though early drafts of the work of Nicolay and Hay ran in the *Century Magazine*'s popular "War Series," they ultimately chose not to invoke their authority as the pre-eminent witnesses to life inside Lincoln's White House, probably to the detriment of both their final product and its bottom line.

This ambivalence toward oral testimony manifested itself in the early work of Ida Tarbell. Long before she would expose Standard Oil or compliment the Lincoln Inquiry, she had had to decide what to do with the recollections of witnesses. She began her Lincoln work by reading, visiting Kentucky, and hiring interviewers in Indiana and Illinois. However, finding the same contradictions that had stymied Herndon, she opted not to face the witnesses but instead to take her stand on material artifacts and written documentation. After combing the country for yet-unpublished photos, speeches, letters, and other documents, Tarbell produced a biography that contained a nearly two-hundred-page appendix of written documents.

But while her biography touted its documentary sources, Tarbell nevertheless also realized the powerful appeal that witnesses could have for her twentieth-century audience. In a series of stories that would be repackaged in numerous formats over the years and become known simply as "Billy Brown stories," Tarbell removed every other voice from the narrative except that of the witness Billy Brown. The earliest encounter opens, "Did I know Lincoln? Well, I should say. See that chair there? Take it, set down. That's right. Comfortable, ain't it? Well, sir, Abraham Lincoln has set in that chair hours." The reader sits at the feet of a garrulous old man who appears to be responding to the reader's questions: "Tell stories? Nobody ever could beat him at that . . . ," "Was there much talk about his bein' killed? Well there's an awful lot of fools . . . ," "Ever see him again? Yes, onct down in Washington. . . ." The format occludes Tarbell and immerses the reader in the face-to-face discovery experience as the lively witness regales his audience with firsthand accounts of life with Lincoln. Contrary to the practice of naming witnesses employed in varying degrees by Holland, Herndon, and later writers, Tarbell specifically declines to connect her "Uncle Billy" to an individual, stating that she had met one particularly charming "Billy Brown" in Springfield but that there were also "Billy Browns" in numerous Illinois towns throughout the 1890s. By presenting her stories without her own explicit authorial mediation, Tarbell brought the reader into close enough proximity to "hear" the witness. Precisely because the encounter with Billy Brown happened nowhere, it could happen anywhere, wherever the reader sat.[15]

Though Nicolay and Hay had avoided oral testimony, the practice had gained wide popular appeal among both readers and practitioners. A Wisconsin educator sought out statements from Lincoln's family, friends, bodyguards, telegraph operators, and biographers. An Iowa preacher journeyed to Kentucky, Indiana, and Illinois to speak with "persons who personally knew Mr. Lincoln" and to visit the places "where the feet of Abraham Lincoln pressed the earth." One researcher tracked descendants of Lincoln's mother's family to Arkansas to interview them. In Indiana, a teenager collected stories from former Lincoln neighbors, a school teacher interviewed locals and commissioned photographs of people and places, a Methodist preacher from New Albany collected stories from those on his southern Indiana circuit, the newspaper editor in Boonville gathered and published over two dozen affidavits of the Lincoln family's passage through the village, and scores of individuals and families told stories about ancestral connections to the Lincolns.[16] The Lincoln Inquiry was by no means unique in seeking oral testimony, but its workers would put oral testimony to uses that would both follow past practitioners and draw them into conflict with others who claimed authority to interpret the life of Lincoln.

"We Reach Back Eager Hands"

The founding rationale of the Lincoln Inquiry articulated a tight relationship between southern Indiana, interpretive authority, and the society's able workers. Precisely because Lincoln had lived in Indiana, and because the evidence of Indiana frontier life had been passed down through Hoosier families in the form of stories and material culture, the Lincoln Inquiry saw itself in the single best position to soak in all of the necessary details about the history of southern Indiana. Lincoln's past remained very close to present-day southern Indiana. Holland had visited Illinois for two days, Herndon had spent five days in southern Indiana, and Tarbell had reportedly stopped only one night. By contrast, members of the Lincoln Inquiry had lived their entire lives among the places, people, and relics that had survived from that earlier day. Iglehart's cousin, the social reformer Albion Fellows Bacon, described their interpretive authority in verse:

> Great Lincoln, neighbor of an earlier time,
> The world your manhood claims; to us alone
> Belongs your youth. We reach back eager hands
> To clasp your own.[17]

By speaking with witnesses who had lived on Lincoln's Indiana frontier and who remained accessible only in southern Indiana, twentieth-century Hoosiers could reach back and clasp the hand of Lincoln, their neighbor. Collectively, by sharing their interviews and comparing their findings, the Lincoln Inquiry sought both the immediacy of face-to-face encounter and the reliability of aggregate patterns.

Because audio recording technology was still generally unavailable, Lincoln Inquiry interviewers kept handwritten notes and shared their findings as reported conversations. For example, in 1881 eighteen-year-old Will Fortune traveled from Boonville to neighboring Spencer County, Indiana, to "talk with the survivors." In "a much faded little notebook" he recorded "notes, mere fragments of information" at times, but at other times he wrote "word for word." "They were intended at the time to be mere reminders," he explained, "except that a few of the interviews were rather fully noted in the language of the persons who were interviewed." When presenting his findings to the public, Fortune used both word-for-word and words-to-the-effect material from the interviewee, thereby permitting him to frame those words with descriptions of setting, sounds, and body language. Sometimes Fortune recorded only sentences: "The testimony of the survivors was without exception, as I recall their words, that 'he was a great reader', 'he wasn't like other boys,' 'he didn't take much part in the social pleasures of the time, but he could nearly always be seen reading a book.'" On another occasion, Fortune introduces an interviewee "out of the blur of impressions that come with the lapse of time": "Mrs. Crawford was a very bright woman and quite vivacious. Her memory seemed quite clear and definite. She talked rapidly. She was a woman of more than usual refinement of speech and manner, and yet, in her conversation, there was a good deal of the dialect that belonged to the early days of Indiana." The reference to dialect set up her telling of the young Abraham's being the "awfullest plagued boy she'd ever seen" after he had borrowed a book from her husband and the rain damaged its pages.[18]

Such framing not only presented the audience with a mental image of the interviewee; it also foregrounded the fact that interviewer and interviewee shared in creating the encounter. In the early 1890s, Alice Hanby visited the home of the aged Judge John Pitcher. Pitcher had practiced law in Indiana when Lincoln was a teenager and owned two volumes of *Blackstone's Commentary* in which the boy had signed his name. Hanby's framing of the encounter sets up a tense moment in which she challenged Pitcher's past judgment:

> An instant later and Judge Pitcher had risen to greet me. For the moment he stood, a somewhat majestic figure in the dim light, yet he was not tall, scarcely taller than the average. As I shook hands with him, I said with perhaps a touch of reproach, "And you advised Lincoln not to study law! Why?" He answered quite promptly, "Yes. He was nothing but a long, lean, gawky country jake. In fact, I didn't think he had it in him." This last was spoken hurriedly, yet with such emphasis as to leave a keen sense of Pitcher's opinion of Lincoln—in those days. Also, that last sentence sounded to me almost a defense of such opinion. However, before I could venture a reply, Pitcher changed to personal matters, and no more was said on the subject of Lincoln.[19]

Without audio recording devices, without transcription methods designed to indicate tone or velocity, Hanby illustrated the position recently taken by oral historian Allesandro Portelli to characterize oral history: "the narrator is now pulled into the narrative and becomes part of the story. This is not just a grammatical shift from the third to the first person, but a whole new narrative attitude. The narrator is now one of the characters, and the *telling* of the story is part of the story being told."[20] Compared to Herndon's attempt simply to look through the witness to the story he wanted to tell, or to Tarbell's effort to remove herself entirely, this approach allowed Lincoln Inquiry narrators to interact with witnesses to Lincoln's life. Their subsequent interaction with twentieth-century audiences created a new pattern that interwove past and present experience through a narrative of witness and encounters.

Being "present" to "see" the witnesses brought other advantages. For Herndon, the clarity and calmness of the subject's eyes indicated that he or she could be trusted. Watching the witness—especially the face—provided clues for questioning a witness's reliability. In 1895, Ida Tarbell employed school teacher Anna O'Flynn to research Lincoln in southern Indiana. O'Flynn met and photographed half a dozen women who claimed to have been Abe's boyhood "sweetheart." But, with the passage of seven decades, how could one know? On another occasion, one interviewer resolved the issue this way:

[First interview:] A Mrs. Oskins who enjoyed smoking a cob pipe, frequently came to the home . . . and often spoke of having known Abe Lincoln. On one occasion, Mrs. Oskins said, 'Well, Abe used to go with me . . . But law! He was so onery and shiffless, I wouldn't keep company with him.'"

[Second interview:] An old lady named Lukins, who also loved a cob pipe, was sitting in a chair tipped against the wall. During the course of the conversation, Mrs. Lukins removed her pipe from her mouth and said, "I could a' been Abe Lincoln's wife, if I'd wanted to, yes siree, I could a' been the first lady of the land." [Interviewer] "Now, Sarah, what are you talking about, you know you couldn't." "I could, too," said Mrs. Lukins. [After being pressed further she said,] "Well, Abe tuk me home from church oncet."[21]

Here one small facial detail—the cob pipe—repeated in both incidents, proved the key to assessing validity. Logan Esarey applied Turner's frontier thesis to Lincoln's midwestern frontier to argue for three classes of pioneer society—an educated aristocracy, a large middle class, and a lower class of ruffians and scoundrels, or, in Turner's phrase, "the scum of the earth." Those ruffians and scoundrels had been popularized by Edward Eggleston's novel *The Hoosier Schoolmaster,* in which the nasty, old, conniving, lying character Mrs. Means was never without her cob pipe.[22] By seeing the witness—and in this case her pipe—students of Lincoln's life discerned who could be trusted to tell the truth about Lincoln. In an era before criminal psychology or electronic lie detectors, the assessment of a witness's reliability rested on interpersonal interaction, human experience, and probably a little applied phrenology. In this particular case, the judgment reflected both a critique of the reliability of the lowest class of pioneer Hoosiers and the conclusion that Lincoln had not been a permanent part of that class.

Among the society's records is one occasion of oral history performance. John Shanklin Ramsay had joined the Union Army in Evansville at age 17. Before he reached the field, a cannon ran over his foot, and he was reassigned to provost guard duty in Washington, DC. There, on April 14, 1865, he slipped away from his assigned duties to attend Ford's Theater, in the process becoming a witness to Lincoln's assassination. Discovering that Ramsay, the "only known survivor" of the local unit, still lived in the region, society members invited him to speak at one of their meetings, but age and ill health prevented his acceptance. On April 18, 1930, John E. Morlock interviewed the octogenarian. The next day he presented a report of the conversation publicly as Ramsay listened approvingly. The following year, the performance was repeated for the entire society at a

"GIT A PLENTY WHILE YOUR'E A GITTIN'," SAYS I.

During the 1890s, elderly women who had grown up with Lincoln on the Indiana frontier confessed to having been his boyhood "sweetheart." Nancy Beard (top left) attended apple peelings and corn huskings with young Abraham while Ruth Crawford Huff (top right) claimed to be a close friend. Participants in the Lincoln Inquiry rejected some claimants on the basis of context clues, such as a corn cob pipe that identified the narrator as belonging to a lower, less trustworthy class of pioneer more inclined to exaggeration. This cultural view was illustrated by Mrs. Means (bottom), a character in Edward Eggleston's *Hoosier Schoolmaster* who was openly nasty and conniving, and always carried her cob pipe. Courtesy Lewis Historical Library, Vincennes University.

meeting held on Lincoln's birthday. Woven through the performance of Ramsay's memories are strands of contingency, unfulfilled desire for vengeance, and the present tangibility of death:

> Booth jumped to the rail of the box and sprang for the stage. As he sprang his spur caught in the big American flag and he fell, injuring his leg. I was in a position where, if I had had a gun, I could have shot him two or three times, but I had nothing. I was in the theatre without permission from my commanding officers and so I began a hasty retreat, knowing that an immediate call would be sent out from my company. As I went through the narrow lobby of the theatre, Lincoln's body was being carried out. His head brushed my sleeve and when I reached the barracks, I found my coat sleeve was covered with the president's blood.[23]

Interviewees were not just lifeless authorities, but living beings with audible dialects. By re-performing their original encounters with witnesses, the interviewers reopened what a twenty-first-century oral historian has characterized as "an especially charged, contingent, reflexive space of encountering the complex web of our respective histories." Audiences could listen as Hanby pressed Pitcher for details, as Fortune recalled his encounters out of a "blur of impressions," as Morlock perpetuated the brush with Lincoln's lifeblood. By reporting their actual experience with interviewees, the interviewers became witnesses to the past and tokens of its "presence" at the meetings of the Lincoln Inquiry.[24]

By drawing together many people interested in interviewing witnesses to the life and death of Abraham Lincoln, the Lincoln Inquiry created a community of practice that had been unavailable to isolated biographers such as Holland, Herndon, or Nicolay and Hay. The concentration of interviewers therefore allowed for theorization about reliability, memory, and human experience. In his massive scrapbook collection, insurance agent George Wilson worked out a rough typology of memories from those that were "commercially true, that is ninety percent the truth; ten percent embellishment" to those that were simply "courthouse yarns" composed of ninety percent embellishment. He also noted that "kaleidoscopic memories" shifted with each telling and should be verified by "official records and legal documents." In a talk titled "Preservation of the Knowledge of Old People," local judge Lucius C. Embree shared a story about a pioneer mother and children who heard "a wild and piercing outcry" one night just before dusk. Fearing an Indian attack, the mother armed herself with an ax and her eleven-year-old son with a rifle, and the pair stood guard all night, "believing all the time that the next moment would bring to their ears the savage yells of the enemy." Nothing happened.

The next morning the mother sent her boy to reconnoiter, and he found the neighbor's cabin intact; nothing seemed to have been disturbed. After questioning, the family recalled that their cow had stepped on the bare foot of their eldest daughter whose screams were imitated by her brothers until the cow finally moved. Embree observed: "The effect upon the defenseless family a mile away was somewhat different. This was an Indian massacre in which no lives were lost, but it made an impression upon one family which remained vivid to one of its survivors for more than eighty years. Does it not throw light upon the life of early Indiana?" Like oral historians of the future, the Lincoln Inquiry dealt with likelihood, memory, and silence.[25]

The work of the Lincoln Inquiry was not, of course, as sophisticated as that of the oral history movement of the late twentieth century, but in contrast to previous efforts to dismiss oral testimony or to use it as a decorative description, a doorway to the soul, or a direct channel to the past, the Lincoln Inquiry contributed useful innovations.[26] Collectively, the members' interpersonal encounter with witnesses permitted listening, questioning, theorizing, and performance. The process provoked new commentary from John Pitcher, revealed fraudulent witnesses, and produced awareness of the evolving relationship between memory and experience. Part reminiscence, part legal deposition, and part emerging vision of shared authorship, the oral history work of the Lincoln Inquiry soon became the basis for an attack on the methods and, by extension, the authority of southern Hoosiers to claim to understand Lincoln's experience on the midwestern frontier.

The Attack on Witnesses

From the perspective of the able workers in the Lincoln Inquiry, the assault on their work with oral testimony originated with a trio of aspiring Lincoln biographers. Coming from divergent geographical and professional backgrounds, Albert Beveridge, William Barton, and Louis Warren drew on the emerging academic model of "scientific" history to argue for the exclusive use of written, documentary sources. They rejected Tarbell's willingness to engage evidence whatever its source and, in theory, reversed Herndon's original conclusion that contradictory written sources could best be resolved by cross-examining the witness. In practice, their argument necessitated some rhetorical gymnastics as the definition of "source" became bound up with struggles over who had the clearest "authority" to rightly interpret the evidence. This particular struggle within the narrow field of Lincoln biography mirrored broader trends within the American historical profession, both to elevate written sources and to claim greater historical authority for those with the training and access to read them.

After the case of the grippe kept Albert Beveridge from the Lincoln Inquiry's February 1923 meeting, he worked only intermittently on his proposed life of Lincoln. He passed the summer in Switzerland trying to regain his health, and the following winter he spent much of his time trying to shape the national Republican agenda by writing *Saturday Evening Post* articles on foreign affairs, the judiciary, railroads, and the presidency. By the late spring of 1924, after shaking off a recurrence of the grippe mixed with a bad case of sinusitis, Beveridge was ready to recommit full time to his work on Lincoln. On Sunday, June 15, he spent an hour with Iglehart in Newburgh. "His talk to me was general," Iglehart recorded. Beveridge outlined his plan of research and his intention to focus on Lincoln's education and political experience during the Indiana years. Iglehart recorded two compliments from the former senator: that Iglehart "was the only man he had talked with who did not seek by his views to fortify some preconceived ideas, but whose mind was entirely open to deal impartially with the evidence," and that Iglehart's work on the life of local lawyer Ratliff Boone was "important, tremendously important."[27] The themes of evidence, open-mindedness, and significance would permeate the debates over the coming year.

The further Beveridge plunged into the literature on Lincoln's life, the more he became convinced that no one had yet done justice to the sixteenth president. Though he had never received academic training in history, his work on Marshall had drawn him into contact with university-based historians who, for the past forty years, had been establishing their profession on the basis of a German model that emphasized archival research in written, documentary sources. Beveridge joined the American Historical Association (AHA) and served in both elected and appointed positions. In April, he complained to J. Franklin Jameson—the first person to earn a Ph.D. in history from an American university, the first Ph.D.-holding historian to preside over the AHA, and the editor of the association's influential *American Historical Review*—that the literature on Lincoln was a "morass." To the iconoclastic and influential historian Charles Beard he wrote that working through the "tangle" was proving "infinitely harder" than his work on Marshall.[28] In Beveridge's estimate, Nicolay and Hay had not conducted enough research, lacked impartiality, and were poor writers. Charnwood's biography was "spotted with errors of fact so plain that they are glaring" and compilations of reminiscences were "utterly untrustworthy." To Beard he wrote that "the dear old girl" Tarbell offered nothing more than a "pathetic" attempt to "fumigate" Lincoln.[29] Casting around for a response to the "slush and rot" in the literature, Beveridge sought for archival sources and found his way, inadvertently, back to the work of William Herndon.

University-based historians such as Jameson, Beard, and Frederick Jackson Turner advocated a new "scientific" approach to history that emphasized dispassionate and exhaustive archival research into contemporary written sources. The degree to which an open-minded historian can be "objective" has been debated extensively, but this generation of historians held objectivity out as an ideal that could lead to the writing of a truly "definitive" work of history.[30] From his associations with academic historians, Beveridge imbibed this ethos and desired more than anything to write the definitive, last word on Lincoln. To do so, he would have to locate and integrate all possible archival sources. The problem, however, lay in the fact that Lincoln documents were either rushed into print or hoarded in private collections. After writing their ten-volume history of Lincoln's presidency, Nicolay and Hay put out another fourteen volumes of Lincoln's letters, speeches, and writings—the first of a flood of collected works.[31] Finding and using archival sources in the 1920s required personal connections. Friends at the Library of Congress, the New Hampshire Historical Society, and the Illinois State Historical Society allowed the nationally renowned author to take copies from their collections, and Lincoln collector Oliver Barrett opened his private collection. Beveridge was furious, however, that Robert Todd Lincoln would not permit access to the papers used by Nicolay and Hay—on the same day that Robert refused Beveridge he signed a deed of gift to the Library of Congress that closed the collection until twenty-one years after his own death. Beveridge was so "desolated" that he considered abandoning the biography. "I wish to make this book definitive," he wrote to a friend, "and do not care to waste several years of my life writing something that will be merely a stopgap."[32] His spirits would revive with access to the private collection of a fellow Hoosier.

For nearly three years Beveridge had been soliciting Jesse W. Weik for access to the research notes of William Herndon. As a young lawyer with an interest in famous people, Weik had helped Herndon write the controversial biography in 1889, and he had inherited the notes after Herndon's death two years later. When Beveridge learned Weik was working on a book titled *The Real Lincoln,* he interceded with Houghton Mifflin to publish it and offered to give it a favorable review. In an attempt to bargain for access, he variously flattered Weik that his review would increase the sales of Weik's book, talked his contact at the press into pressuring Weik, delayed writing the review, and promised that his own biography would bring Weik attention and added profits.[33] When Weik finally relented, Beveridge was overjoyed as he now had the archival source base from which to operate as a "scientific" historian. Though Herndon had begun to collect correspondence and notes after Lincoln's death in 1865, the passage of time allowed Beveridge to recast them as archival sources. By citing them as the "Weik Manuscripts," Beveridge demonstrated both his debt to Weik and his endowment of Herndon's interview notes with the enhanced status of written sources. Casting his lot with Herndon, Beveridge reframed him as a "truthful, honest and thorough man" who possessed "to an uncommon degree, the scholar's mind and habit of thought." Beveridge assured Jameson that he had "no doubt at all about [Herndon's] veracity." Beveridge knew that Herndon had sought "to make deductions and examine the 'souls' of men and women," but he also trusted in his own ability to discern Herndon's soul analysis from the "statements of fact." As Beveridge assured Weik, Herndon had received a "rotten deal" from "the historical propagandists and the preachers and the women of the Mid-Victorian period of the eighties and nineties."[34] As a skilled scientific historian, Beveridge would rescue both Herndon and Lincoln from the field of Lincoln studies.

After his visit to southern Indiana, Beveridge spent the summer of 1924 writing the first three chapters of his manuscript, one each on Lincoln's early life in Kentucky, Indiana, and Illinois. He pored over the Weik collection and would later explain, in good scientific historical fashion, "My idea of biography and history is that the writer has no business making deductions, inferences, and stating his conclusion. On the contrary, his business is to assemble all of the facts and place them in just proportion—these facts, thus arranged, tell the story and make the conclusion." Even in the 1920s, long before the challenge of postmodernism, philosophers and practitioners of history were debating this position. Beveridge, opponents would claim, selected the information that he endowed as "fact" and the very act of arranging the facts renders a "conclusion," whether the author admits it or not. Though he did not admit it to himself, Beveridge left evidence that he, in fact, brought a conclusion to his research and writing. As a senator, Beveridge had been thoroughly dedicated to the cause of American imperialism, arguing for the expansion of American power across the Pacific and throughout the world. He had told this story through the life of John Marshall and intended to continue the narrative by "weaving it around the life and career of Abraham Lincoln." His strategy would be "to mass a large number of small facts so that the meaning behind them will be apparent without preaching." The other fact that Beveridge would not admit to himself was that he was growing tired of slogging through the Lincoln field. Secretly he hoped in vain that Calvin Coolidge would tap him as his vice presidential running mate in the election of 1924.[35]

By August 1924 Beveridge had finished the first chapter and sent it to Weik to show him, as he explained, "the manner in which I am handling your collection and giving you credit in the foot-notes." By October, he was sending all three chapters to academic historians and local historians throughout the country. He explained that the drafts remained "crude in the extreme," would still require "months of artistry" in the revision process, and were "over-annotated." The latter characteristic was intentional, however, because "this is the controverted period which the remnants of the Mid-Victorians have tried and are still trying to Tarbellize" and because he hoped "to inspire in the readers a feeling of confidence right at the start" so that they would "believe what I say in the more important parts that follow." Having thus laid the groundwork to challenge Tarbell, he turned his attention to the campaign, still not wanting to close the door on another chance at the senate in 1926.[36]

Responses to the draft varied by individual but showed an interesting pattern in relation to the background of the reviewer. The academic historians—Jameson, Beard, James A. Woodburn at Indiana University—all disclaimed any specific knowledge of the details of Lincoln's early life and therefore focused on Beveridge's writing style, with the general consensus that the extensive notes made the first chapter unwieldy but that the prose got better as the story moved forward. Lincoln's psycho-biographer Nathaniel Stephenson of Yale liked the documentation and thought the chapters achieved "exactly the right spirit, with neither fear nor favor, and with a powerful grasp on essentials." The secretary of the Kansas State Historical Society, who would later protest Beveridge's treatment of the Kansas-Nebraska Act, declared the chapter on Lincoln's Indiana years to be "the best description of the wilderness into which the pioneers of the Ohio Valley plunged, which I have ever seen."[37]

The able workers of the Lincoln Inquiry reacted differently. Bess Ehrmann rejoiced, "*At last* there has been a history of Lincoln that tells something of his boyhood and young manhood in Indiana." Will Adams thanked Beveridge for an interesting read. Roscoe Kiper wondered if

Beveridge might not want to at least acknowledge that alternate traditions existed. J. Edward Murr, who had traveled extensively in southern
Indiana in the late nineteenth century, responded with a seventeen-page
review and recommended that Beveridge pay more attention to the work
of John Iglehart.[38] Iglehart, still negotiating a publishing agreement with
the Indiana Historical Commission's new director Christopher Coleman,
explained that he had not read the chapters thoroughly but had read
enough to see that he would have to respond with detailed "criticism
backed by candid reasons" and promised a response by the year's end. But
Beveridge could not wait. "I am wondering if it would be too much
trouble to write me just a line telling me what 'vital' point it is that you
find wrong." He also dropped hints that several "distinguished scholars"
had already approved of the manuscript and that the "meticulous research by the scientific methods of modern scholarship has wiped out
many things" that had previously been reported about Lincoln's youth.[39]
In this brief exchange, Beveridge foreshadowed a longer struggle that
would pit "scientific methods" of archival research against the work of
the Lincoln Inquiry.

Iglehart agreed to meet Beveridge in Indianapolis in December at the
state's conference of historical societies. The annual gathering had begun
in 1919 and had grown to feature papers on state history topics, words
from invited speakers, and reports of state and local history activities.
The secretary of the Southwestern, Susan Garvin, reported on the society's founding and rationale at the second meeting, Iowa state history
superintendent Benjamin Shambaugh attended one year and explained
the organization of work in his state, Lincoln scholar James Randall
would speak on historical revisionism in 1937. After Beveridge asked the
president of the Indiana Historical Society, James A. Woodburn of Indiana University, to read the draft of his first three chapters, Woodburn
invited Beveridge to preside over the conference in December, and the
former senator accepted.[40]

In Indianapolis, Beveridge reunited with two other men—both
preachers—who were engaged in researching and writing about Lincoln.
William Barton had started writing about Lincoln while Beveridge was
still working on Marshall. Favorable reviews of the Congregational clergyman's first book on Lincoln's religion only whetted his appetite for
fame and for eviscerating popular Lincoln myths . The book's successful
sales also facilitated his private collection of Lincolniana, which he maintained at his summer home in Foxboro, Massachusetts, in its own separate building affectionately nicknamed the "Wigwam." By 1924 he was

in the final stages of writing a full biography. He had already written to Iglehart for information about Lincoln's Indiana youth and in private correspondence, at least, he had already begun to contend with Ida Tarbell over her use of witnesses and the birth of Lincoln's mother—Tarbell had sided with genealogists who claimed Nancy Hanks was legitimate, while Barton sided with Herndon in calling her illegitimate.[41] The second preacher, Louis Warren, became interested in Lincoln soon after he began a pastoral assignment for the Disciples of Christ in Elizabethtown, Kentucky. When not preaching, he walked from town to town, sifting through dusty court records in search of all references to a Lincoln or a Hanks. His discoveries persuaded him that Lincoln's father had not been lazy or shiftless and that both sides of the family had been maligned by Lincoln biographers. Far less certain of his historical skills, he had corresponded with Barton until the latter slipped some of Warren's findings to the media in an effort to force him to sell his research notes.[42]

For his part, Beveridge had been trying to pull any information he could out of both Barton and Warren, offering to help their future books find a suitable publisher. Barton yielded quickly and Beveridge enlisted his help in persuading "young Warren." But Warren remained reticent and soon Beveridge began chiding him for being "unduly apprehensive." As Beveridge and Barton dropped hints that perhaps no publisher would pick up Warren's book, Warren responded that he believed his "scientific approach" to "duly authorized public records" would overturn Herndon's collection of "the traditions of old men and women who never thought of the Lincolns for forty years after they left Kentucky." On the same summer trip in which he had met with Iglehart, Beveridge went to Kentucky, but he had failed to locate Warren's sources, and by fall he was growing impatient. When he learned he would preside at the Indianapolis meeting, Beveridge took the opportunity both to warn Warren "to go slow on the theory that Thomas Lincoln was a man of any importance or prosperity" and to invite him to stay in the Beveridge home.[43] Warren had a spot on the conference program, and he hoped to use it both to convince Beveridge that the Kentucky court records surpassed Herndon's notes and to demonstrate to Barton and Beveridge that his findings on the family's economic status were correct. Along the way to challenging both of them indirectly, he devised a critique of witnesses. Iglehart understood the paper and the setting as a coordinated attack on the work of the Lincoln Inquiry.

In his introductory remarks before a packed house at the Claypool Hotel, Beveridge mentioned generically that "local pride has a great influence in distorting history." He and Barton then looked on as Warren laid out a general taxonomy of historical method with specific reference to work on Lincoln. Warren categorized inferior Lincoln work as being performed by two classes: "interviewers" and "interpreters" who relied, respectively, on personal and bibliographical sources. While the latter never left his library (or, one might say, his "Wigwam"), the former (like Herndon) "was a social being and, above all, a conversationalist. He was adept at learning every detail of a dramatic story. In pumping his auditor dry he often caught in his bucket of information much matter that was spurious. This foreign substance found its way into his text. While we shall always be under a great debt of gratitude to the Interviewers for preserving the early traditions and folklore of a race, we wish that they might have been more discriminate in the use of much untenable traditional matter which they released." Warren then heralded the day when true and objective Lincoln studies would be carried out by "investigators" who relied only on documentary evidence, such as that which might be found in Kentucky courthouses. He closed the talk with a nonchalant "word about 'The Lincoln Inquiry,' an expression coined by John E. Iglehart": "Most of the material gathered under the inspiration of this slogan, and much of it very valuable, has been contributed by Interviewers, or Interpreters."[44] Though nearly deaf, Iglehart clearly understood the charge.

Early the next morning, Iglehart met Beveridge face-to-face in his hotel room and defended the work of the Lincoln Inquiry. No record of the encounter has survived from Beveridge's perspective, but two months later he wrote to Bess Ehrmann to thank her for sending a "delightful paper" that summarized the work of the Lincoln Inquiry. Then he summarily dismissed the entire initiative in a single stroke: "I am writing exclusively from sources. As you know, modern scholarship sternly rejects secondary material and has nothing to do with inference, deduction and supposition." The following month, he repeated his categorical rejection of their work in a book review published in the *Indianapolis Star*.[45] Though intended for Beveridge and Barton, Warren's blow landed squarely in the face of southern Indiana witnesses, challenging the rhetorical and methodological grounding of the entire Lincoln Inquiry.

The conference session at the Claypool Hotel illuminates the way that conversations about Lincoln, historical sources, and the authority to interpret them were complicated by overlapping rivalries in the field of Lincoln studies in the mid-1920s. Beveridge and Barton attacked Tarbell, the biggest name in the field, by criticizing her popular Uncle Billy stories and her upbeat portrayal of Lincoln as a backwoodsman. From his base on the Kentucky court records, Warren criticized Barton for his armchair research methods, Beveridge for his reliance on the notes Herndon had bequeathed to Weik, and the Lincoln Inquiry for using witnesses. The Lincoln Inquiry criticized Eggleston and Herndon for their negative interpretation of frontier life and Herndon and Tarbell for not spending sufficient time with the people of southern Indiana.

In addition to criticizing their competitors, all four challengers argued for their authority in historical interpretation based on their nearly exclusive access to certain sources. Warren saw Kentucky court documents that Beveridge could not find, Barton admired the vastness of his own collection, Beveridge trumpeted his use of notes unseen by anyone but Herndon and Weik, and the Lincoln Inquiry emphasized its proximity to and participation in southern Indiana culture. Furthermore, each promised findings that would be noteworthy, unique, even definitive, because no one else in the world could even access their sources. The Lincoln Inquiry argued that no outsider could truly understand their community, Warren that no one else could devote the same amount of time to dusty volumes, and Barton that no one else knew his collection as he did. Beveridge remained the most vulnerable, arguing publicly that Herndon had "carefully, thoroughly and impartially" collected "facts" and hoping privately that Weik would not share the notes with anyone else.[46]

The exchange also formally introduced the metaphor of scientific investigation into the struggle to reclaim Lincoln's past. Scientific historians elevated written sources because their content was fixed and therefore presumably replicable by any given researcher on any given day. Living witnesses posed a problem to the scientific model precisely *because* they were alive and therefore able to answer new questions, forget past answers, or give a new scoop to the solicitation of a competing writer. They also, eventually, died, making further cross-examination impossible. The language of science also brought rhetorical advantages. Beveridge used the metaphor to cover his weakness by reinventing Herndon's interview notes as the static, archival documents found in the "Weik Manuscripts." Warren invoked science both to play up his strength in courthouse record research and to circumvent the need to engage either Herndon's notes or Barton's collection. The move served as the historical equivalent of a lawyer arguing against the admission of evidence to a courtroom. The former lawyer Beveridge did not miss a beat in making the same application in his letter to Ehrmann and would later use this same justification to mock and ignore the 1926 biography of Lincoln written by poet

·l Sandburg.[47] Lawyer Iglehart also fully understood the potential of scientific history rhetoric to undermine the entire Lincoln Inquiry, but instead of abandoning their witnesses, the society's able workers expanded the role of witnesses to permit the analysis of aggregate patterns. These new witnesses united the best of first-person observation and investigative analysis.

Engaging the "Best Witnesses"

In private, the criticism brought out the fighter in Iglehart. Warren "called me by name with a flat reference and threw a little dust and a lot of arbitrary definitions of this work, but sought to preempt the field," he explained in a letter to George Wilson. Iglehart reasoned that Warren served as the mouthpiece for an unholy trinity with Beveridge, a known partisan of Herndon's degrading view who presided at the session, and Barton, a man already on record for wanting to dismiss the Indiana years entirely. The Kentucky and Illinois historians were angered by the society's "maxim and corollary" that one could not understand Lincoln without understanding his Indiana years and that one could not understand the Indiana years without spending some time in southern Indiana. "They cannot accept it; they dare not controvert it," he explained, so they are trying to ignore it. But Iglehart, the "panther," fresh off the victory of a renewed publishing agreement with the state historical commission and freed of his rivalry with de la Hunt by the election of the politically astute Kiper, relished this new challenge. "I want a little bit of spur to keep the thing active, and I am enjoying it hugely."[48]

The Lincoln Inquiry officially responded by calling its members to the witness stand at their public meeting in Princeton, Indiana, in November 1925 to address two related questions: the "best evidence" and the "best witnesses." Iglehart conceded that "the witnesses who knew Lincoln and whose memory was of historical value are all dead," but—his lawyerly training at play—"there remains what from the standpoint of the rules of evidence is called the best evidence which can be produced at the time of the investigation. We are now entering a new field of inquiry." This field encompassed "all persons living available who have . . . in the past interviewed men and women who knew Lincoln." The interviewees may have died, but the interviewers remain available "to give us a description of these people with a view to show that they were a respectable class of people."[49] In other words, Iglehart proposed to turn the interviewers into interviewees to publicly answer for their qualifications, methods, and findings. Authorship and authority blended, as experience with aging pioneers provided interviewers with authority to stand as the "best witnesses" to the "best evidence" of pioneer life. Here, in a public crafting with stenographer at hand, interviewers became interviewees, "narrators and historians, preservers and creators of memory."[50]

Among the interviewers called to testify at the meeting were Bess Ehrmann, who had grown up in Spencer County; Will Fortune who, as a young man, had interviewed Spencer County residents in 1881; Anna O'Flynn, a school teacher from Vincennes who had conducted the interviews that Ida Tarbell decided not to use; and J. Edward Murr, a Methodist minister who had grown up with Lincoln relatives (cousins) in Harrison County and whose circuit in 1898–1902 had included Spencer County, where he frequently interviewed his aging parishioners. Iglehart invited Jesse Weik to attend, but he declined. Each witness emphasized the fact that she or he had descended from pioneers who lived in southwestern Indiana. Their current reputation also came in for scrutiny; Murr, for example, was found to be "very well known through entire southern Indiana, especially in southwestern Indiana, having been the pastor of a prominent church." Murr also spoke for all witnesses when he contrasted his qualifications with those of Herndon, who had "spent five days in and about Lincoln's old home," and Tarbell, who had "spent one and only one night in Spencer County and interviewed but one associate of Lincoln." After describing their work, the witnesses faced questions from each other and from the audience. O'Flynn answered Fortune's questions about precisely when she had done her interviewing, Ehrmann's question about the "personal appearance" of the people interviewed, and a variety of inquiries regarding how long she had worked with witnesses, whom specifically she had interviewed, and how Tarbell had "edited" her work. The interviews were recorded by stenographer, archived with the society's proceedings, and later published in edited form.[51]

Through the public cross-examination of the "best witnesses," the Lincoln Inquiry transformed interviewers into interviewees and proposed a unique combination of qualifications stemming from life experience and historical skill. O'Flynn and Murr had spent an extensive amount of time in southern Indiana, and Ehrmann and Fortune also descended from Indiana's pioneers. Yet they did not commit the fallacy of assuming that self-knowledge was historical knowledge by thinking that they know about people in the past simply because they shared the same social or demographic characteristics. Over the course of long exposure, the best witnesses talked with, associated with, and became personally acquainted with many of the original pioneers and their families. One worker noted that "when one has lived in a town more than sixty years one has not only imbibed its history, but knows its people pretty thoroughly." Ehrmann summarized it best, noting that "it is the people who live near the scenes of Lincoln's early life who are best able to interpret its environment. They are intimately acquainted with the descendants of his boyhood friends, have heard the stories of his life as related by their elders and therefore ought to be in a position to write more understandingly of those early days and those pioneer people." The work "could never be written by outsiders who would perhaps spend a few days or a few hours in investigation."[52] Ancestry, firsthand experience, and understanding made residents of southern Indiana the ideal candidates.

In light of the critique from scientific history, the qualification most noticeably absent from the best witness list of qualifications is formal training. Over the years, and especially in response to Warren and Beveridge, the society developed both a defense of the right of amateurs and a critique of the limitations of professionals. Anyone could—and members of the society did—read as much of published historical literature as they desired. Iglehart further insisted on "the right of an amateur, a man who is not a historian or a history teacher, and who is not a specialist, to have views of his own in research." Iglehart did not want "any claims which the facts may not warrant" but he did claim the right to hold "whatever views I am able to establish." Such views were not opinions or dreams or fancies, but must be conclusions drawn from one's own research. Too exclusive a focus on research, however, brought its own problems. Specialists, Iglehart argued, develop "a certain impairment of an accurate sense of proportions in importance" between things in their field and things in the outside world. From the time of its organization, the society had never paid anyone to participate in its activities.[53]

This defense of the amateur and critique of the specialist found expression in the words of the British psychologist and social reformer Havelock Ellis, shared among society members: "The world's greatest thinkers have often been amateurs, for high thinking is the outcome of fine and independent living, and for that a professional chair offers no special opportunities." The Lincoln Inquiry's specific critique of professional appeals in the Lincoln field formed part of a broader critique of the regimentation and specialization promoted throughout the Progressive Era in general. Borrowing a phrase popularized by an arctic explorer of the day, Lincoln Inquiry members held that specialization brought the "standardization of error." Centralized schools forced curious children into uncomfortable desks, so the society advocated taking students to the archives; centralized state history workers forced their agenda on local workers, so the society resisted Oliver and Lindley. The Lincoln Inquiry would not permit a trio of Lincoln scholars to corner the entire field, especially when the language in the mouths of a former senator and two preachers amounted to little more than authoritative posturing. The history of Lincoln and southern Indiana was far too important to be left to experts. But instead of rejecting experts outright, members of the Lincoln Inquiry pushed to expand the definition of expertise beyond academic training.[54]

By turning interviewers into witnesses of their interviewees, the Lincoln Inquiry invested its "best witnesses" with an informed, summarizing, interpretive role. They would not be the passive recipients of Herndon's soul-searching gaze nor the invisible listeners to Uncle Billy's tale but rather a combination of observer and narrator, much like the ghosts imagined by A. R. Beach who could report both *what* happened at a Revolutionary War battle and *why*. Traditional witnesses say, "I know because I saw," whereas the best witnesses could say, "I know because I spoke with many people who saw." The best witnesses could report first-hand testimony, identify patterns in the aggregate, and speak to the concerns and questions of the audience. Their appearance at the meeting in Princeton would be something akin to inviting Studs Terkel and Stetson Kennedy to speak about American history in the 1930s and 1940s. The best witnesses fit the definition offered years later by Peter Novick, who, in his critique of the American historical profession's quest for objectivity, concluded that the "historian is less like the author of a logical demonstration" and "more like a witness to what has been found on a voyage of discovery." Having completed a successful voyage, the best witnesses operated in two realms at once, equally close to the vanished past and to the interested present. They possessed, in Iglehart's words, "that indefinable thing" that united "their knowledge of pioneer life" with the ability "to describe these conditions as they have never been described before." Being both observer and analyst, a remnant of the past and alive in the present, the best witnesses offered the benefit of both interpersonal relation and distanced analysis.[55]

The creation of "best witnesses" as observers and analysts adds an important dimension to the discussion of historical authority. The scientific model locates authority within the archival researches of an academic or the informed interpretation of the curator. Because the "conscience of society" needs only to teach, not to be taught, the duty of professionals is to share their expertise with the masses, often stamping out popularly held myths in the process. Oral historian Michael Frisch has noted that interviewing, by its very nature of being the product of a conversation between two individuals, produces a unique historical source that is co-authored by two persons who together assume and share the authority. In theory, such "shared authority" democratizes history and requires mutual trust, collaboration, and shared stewardship. In practice, however, the sharing of authority has proven harder to accomplish. Those who possess authority are typically reluctant to share it, viewing the exchange as a linear condescension at best or at worst a zero sum game in which their exclusive authority is lost when shared. If any compromise is reached, it is over the far narrower terrain of "negotiating interpretation." In the Lincoln field of the 1920s, Beveridge had no time to waste in reading Sandburg, Nicolay feared that Tarbell's success would come at his expense, and no one as yet appeared willing to negotiate.[56]

In contrast to models of authority-sharing as linear relinquishment or co-authorship, the best witnesses served as a combination of witness and informed guide to the past. They reported their observations of the first-hand comments and characteristics of older residents, made informed commentary on the basis of their collective observations, and responded to audience questions originating in the hearers' interest in the topic and understanding of historical literature. Authority therefore emanates from numerous domains—the life experience of the original witnesses, the combined experience and analysis of the interviewer turned best witness, and the questions posed by the audience that provoke additional reflection from the best witnesses. Original experience, local knowledge, perceptive analysis, and the reading of scholarship thus represent different domains of authority that converged in the shared experience of hearing and interrogating the best witnesses. By demonstrating the value in collectively presenting local and family knowledge, the Lincoln Inquiry articulated a cogent model for sharing authorities across multiple domains of authority or expertise. Because Lincoln's boyhood must be understood in the context of his neighbors, and because the evidence for those neighbors resided in the family stories of then-living grandchildren, and because the information would be lost forever with their deaths, the best witnesses were uniquely positioned to meet the historiographical need with the best available evidence.

MEMBERS OF the Lincoln Inquiry felt confident about their defense. Iglehart predicted that the records of the meeting "will be the crowning step in this work" and that "the time will come when this method of proof will probably settle the doubts with men like Beveridge." In memorable imagery that played both on Warren's ministerial training and on the political climate of the era of Prohibition, Iglehart proclaimed that "this testimony of Philip Sober as compared with Philip Drunk will cry out, trumpet tongued, against the deep damnation of Warren's taking off when he was put forward at the head of this little firing squad." Indiana University history professor Logan Esarey confessed, possibly with some rhetorical exaggeration, that he "would place much greater dependence on these witnesses of Murr's than on Lincoln himself."[57]

Speaking at the meeting in Princeton, Christopher Coleman credited the Lincoln Inquiry with "contribut[ing] powerfully to the revision of our interpretation of Lincoln's personality and its development." Over the next three months, Coleman reported to Iglehart that Tarbell, Weik, and Barton had all expressed their approval. Barton, in particular, "spoke very warmly of you and of the work of the Southwestern Indiana Historical Society. I am persuaded that you will have to class him now with Miss Tarbell as having become really interested in the work which you are doing." Others in the state history establishment in Indianapolis "seemed interested in it and very complimentary about the fire with which you delivered it." In 1927, Warren requested membership in the Southwestern Indiana Historical Society and then slipped quietly into southern Indiana to conduct his own research. When the local paper announced his presence, Iglehart exulted: "Of course it is like searching in last year's bird's nest. The nearest we can now get to that field is filling out and putting in proper form the work of interpreters [the best witnesses] who were nearer to the living witnesses."[58]

The approval of Weik and Tarbell and the reversal of Barton and Warren prompted a medley of metaphors from Iglehart: "certain small historians" or "buzzards and hyenas" who were little more than "workers in a fog" had "trained their guns" and "shelled the woods" in an effort "to take possession of the subject." Now those "buzzards and hyenas" were "fighting for their lives" as they watched the Lincoln Inquiry soar with "the eagle's flight." Iglehart and the best witnesses would not "be made the football of the little historians who are seeking to build a wire fence around this field." The Lincoln Inquiry had "survived a secret campaign of rivalry and destruction" and the work had become "altogether more effective on account of . . . the rivalry of Barton and Beveridge and Warren."[59]

Beveridge, however, remained unconvinced. After the Princeton meeting he continued to complain privately about both the "reminiscers" who "were considerably muddled in their recollections" and the "Babbitts and sob-stuff people generally" who believed them. For Beveridge, reminiscers remained connected to "local pride" that "induced people to conjure traditions." He had previously warned Kiper that traditions lead to "all kinds of swamps," but as he worked through Lincoln's early political life he grew discouraged by the "magnitude and complexity" of the task and talked about "throwing up the sponge." Lincoln, it turned out, had not been the nationalist statesman of Beveridge's heart but rather a calculating politician, a partisan Whig, and a critic of the Polk administration's expansion into Mexico. The same month that the best witnesses met in Princeton, Indiana's senator Ralston died and friends began lobbying for Beveridge to fill the vacancy.[60] Perhaps a new career politics would give him the face-saving option of stepping away from Lincoln.

The Lincoln Inquiry, on the other hand, had seen the merits of stepping up to face the witnesses and to face-off against rivals. The concept of an informed witness—articulated in the imagination of A. R. Beach at the Indian mound and enacted in the "Best Witnesses" meeting—proved useful to the Lincoln Inquiry and persuasive to many in the community of history practitioners. Placing the witnesses on the witness stand allowed for the integration of several domains of historical authority, from life experience, to firsthand testimony, to critical cross-analysis. The Lincoln Inquiry located authority in numerous experiences and activities and conceptualized authority not as a commodity to be hoarded through scarcity but as a resource to be magnified through aggregation. Over time, the Inquiry mounted enough evidence to understand Lincoln's life on the Indiana frontier in a way that was both different from contemporary rivals and, as we shall see, underappreciated by subsequent historians.

ॐ 4

Lincoln's Indiana Environment

THE "BEST WITNESSES" meeting at Princeton marked the first attempt by the Lincoln Inquiry to synthesize its information into a single presentation. For half a decade, Inquiry workers had not only been interviewing witnesses but also scouring courthouse records, searching out documents and artifacts, plumbing old newspapers, reading written histories, and thinking critically about what had been uncovered and about where missing information might still be found. By encouraging and assigning hundreds of people to pursue questions about local and family history, the Lincoln Inquiry sought to produce—eventually and collectively—a rich history of southern Indiana that would provide the proper context and perspective for understanding Lincoln's Indiana youth.

Knowledge about Lincoln would come from hundreds of direct and indirect attempts in a collective effort that would ultimately occupy thousands of hours and produce hundreds of papers. A representative participant was Deidré Johnson. A resident of Mt. Vernon, the forty-two-year-old had been invited to attend the society's first meeting and, over the next nineteen years, she attended regularly, served as vice president from Posey County, read two formal papers at society meetings, and became regular fixture on the "kitchen cabinet" that ran society business behind the scenes. In her writings and speeches she articulated the aspirations and emotions she shared with her peers in the work of discovering new sources, reading engaging literature, and connecting fact with emotion.

Members of the Lincoln Inquiry enjoyed uncovering hidden sources and sharing them at society meetings. Numerous papers quoted a previously unpublished letter, identified a book that Lincoln read, or revealed the contents of a diary. Here is Johnson's description of the experience of opening a newly discovered trunk with a friend: "At the first opportune time a large wooden chest was taken out of storage and brought to my home in the early autumn of this year. Mrs. Von Behren and I had it carried to a sunny room and opened. Here we have spent hour after hour in this historic gold mine, finding a wealth of private, state and national history undreamed of, books of personal memoirs, private letters written by [former Indiana governor] Alvin P. Hovey, letters from men whose names blazon across the pages of time, newspaper articles of worth, unpublished poems, speeches, comments upon war, politics, philosophy, in fact everything of any importance between the period 1821 and 1891 is mirrored either large or small within its confines."[1] Sunshine, gold mine, wealth, and importance all demonstrate the value the Inquiry placed on finding all manner of documentary sources.

But sources alone did not create a complete history. While preparing a formal paper on the life of a Methodist preacher ancestor who traveled the circuit on the southern Indiana frontier, Johnson read an estimated ten thousand pages of archival and published materials in order, as she put it, to "steep myself in the atmosphere of the period, then place this pioneer in his proper background." The resultant paper narrated the development of the earliest religious institutions in Indiana and interpreted them in light of contemporary historical scholarship. The Lincoln Inquiry valued this ability to connect an individual to the wider context, both in its members' own work and in the work of others. On another occasion, when she faced fall housecleaning, garden harvest time, volunteer duties with the Red Cross, a local outbreak of influenza, and a stack of unanswered letters, Johnson picked up Gerald Johnson's *Andrew Jackson: An Epic in Homespun* (1927) and Charles and Mary Beard's *The Rise of American Civilization* (1927) because "I wanted once more to be thrown back into the Jackson Era." Sources and narrative combined to create a world, or as the Inquiry preferred to call it, an "environment" populated by people, nature, and culture.[2]

Finally, the reconstruction of a past environment through exhaustive immersion in all available sources was not complete without stirring an emotive connection. Johnson described her experience of such a connection before the unveiling of a new monument: "As I sat looking and listening to the lineal descendants of those kinsmen they had gathered there to honor, I was conscious of an amazing number of emotions, as varied as the lights and shadows sifting through those forest trees; wonder—at the fortitude of the men who first heeded the call of expansion, then braved the hardships along and beyond the Wilderness Trail;—pride—in the success and magnitude of their individual, if not their collective endeavors;—kinship—for had not my own forefathers waved farewell to the luxuries of tidewater Maryland and of the Old Dominion, then trecked into Kentucky over pretty much that self-same road? Then gratitude; reverence for their indomitable spirits; a veritable gamut of emotions, swinging back again and again to a recognition of that warp and woof of character, woven from the Loom of Life." Good history could— even should—provoke feelings of awe, pride, connection, gratitude, and respect.[3]

If we multiply Johnson's experience with original documents, written narratives, and emotional connections by the five hundred members of the Lincoln Inquiry we begin to sense the variety of experiences and expectations that filtered into the Inquiry like light through the shadows of the leafy forest canopy. By searching for sources, placing individuals within a broader context, and attempting to document and write about all aspects of southern Indiana's frontier, the Lincoln Inquiry aimed for much more than simply identifying where Lincoln walked or what he read. Those narrower questions were examined, but they were kept within the wider angle of the entire frontier experience. The Lincoln Inquiry sought, in Ida Tarbell's words of advice, to "trace and authentically establish the intellectual, social and religious conditions of Southwestern Indiana" in order to create "an authentic picture of the atmosphere in which Lincoln lived."[4] The spatial metaphors of "atmosphere" and "environment" would be invoked to describe the members' comprehensive study of everything related to the frontier. In practice, the society adopted an operational agenda to examine artifacts and relics, identify historic places, and write biographies of individual and family experience. The Lincoln Inquiry approached Lincoln through an ethos forged through competition with contemporary Lincoln scholars and grounded in a view of the frontier as a symbolic representation of all of American history. Most of the Inquiry's discrete biographical findings were scooped up by Lincoln biographers then and later, but their broader effort to contextualize Lincoln on the frontier has yet to yield all of the insights that they knew could be found there. In the ongoing historical quest to locate Lincoln on the frontier of Indiana's past, the Lincoln Inquiry's contribution provided both direct answers for the field in the 1920s and enduring questions for the future, clearly illustrating the value of involving everybody in the historical process.

The Lincoln Inquiry's Approach to the Past

By the time the Lincoln Inquiry was organized in 1920, there were already two interpretations of the sixteenth president's early life in Indiana. Lincoln scholar Mark E. Neely Jr. captured the contrasting views in the original language of some of their most colorful proponents. The "dung hill" thesis, as Neely calls it, emphasized the crudities and barbarism of the frontier to depict Lincoln as the poor, illegitimate son of a shiftless, lazy father and an illegitimate, illiterate mother. Indiana brought only hardships and obstacles that had to be overcome by the boy who fortuitously escaped them. On the other hand, the "chin fly" thesis emphasized the benefits and delights of frontier life to depict Lincoln as a child of nature who gained priceless wisdom and experience. Indiana made Lincoln into a man of the people and a storytelling sage. The dung hill thesis originated in the perceptions of eastern writers and the oral testimony and research agenda of William Herndon, who shared his notes with Ward Lamon and Lamon's ghostwriter Chauncey Black, who positioned Lincoln as "the diamond glowing on the dunghill." The chin fly thesis found its articulation in the work of Ida Tarbell, both her early biography and the subsequent genealogical volume that praised the Lincoln Inquiry and elevated the "horse, the dog, the ox, the chin fly, the plow, the hog" into the "companions" of Lincoln's youth that "became interpreters of his meaning, solvers of his problems in his great necessity, of making men understand and follow him."[5] During the 1920s, the Lincoln Inquiry would criticize both positions by looking beyond them to the work of western historian Frederick Jackson Turner. Their application of Turner's "Frontier Thesis" has gone unrecognized in the field of Lincoln studies.

During the renaissance of Lincoln work in the 1920s, biographers and interpreters sorted themselves into one of these two pre-existing camps. Relying heavily on Herndon's notes, Albert Beveridge emphasized the harshness and incivility of the Indiana frontier. He joined William Barton in challenging popular myths and attacking the romanticism of Tarbell with hard-scrabble realism. Tarbell stuck to her position throughout the decade and was joined by Louis Warren's courthouse researches in Kentucky and by Carl Sandburg's poetic biography that, together with the film it inspired, became probably the single most influential depiction of Lincoln's early life in American historical consciousness. The two sides typically disagreed on everything. The hastily constructed half-faced cabin that Thomas Lincoln built in Indiana was criticized by Beveridge as evidence of Thomas's laziness, whereas Warren would rhapsodize about the salutary effects of "the aroma of newly cut timber." Barton argued that Lincoln's mother was illegitimate on the basis of an original court record that he refused to let anyone see while Warren expanded the work of past genealogists to locate Nancy Hanks's parents in another Kentucky family.[6]

From its formation, the Lincoln Inquiry openly criticized Herndon's interpretation, along with similar readings from novels and other popular stereotypes. And as the "Best Witnesses" meeting demonstrates, they also began to line up against contemporary historians who appeared to take the same view. However, the Lincoln Inquiry also criticized Ida Tarbell's interpretation. In her latest book, *In the Footsteps of the Lincolns,* Tarbell had followed six Lincoln generations from Massachusetts to Indiana. She concluded that they manifested the "pioneer spirit" or the "migratory spirit" that "pushed" them "into unbroken territory, allured by the hope of larger wealth, of greater freedom of action and thought, of more congenial companionship, and always by the mystery of the unknown, the certainty of an adventure." Abraham's father had been "the child of an advancing pioneer army." Writing to Tarbell, Iglehart reasoned, "Of course Lincoln as a Frontiersman, and as a backwoodsman has been discussed and the fact has been emphasized by many writers," but the Lincoln Inquiry proposed to contribute something more by contextualizing the family of backwoodsmen within the experience on the Indiana frontier. Therefore, for example, to the debate about the relative comfort of the half-faced cabin, Christopher Coleman looked not to laziness or luxury, but instead cited the diary of an Ohio riverboat captain who recorded sub-zero temperatures in the region for that winter.[7]

This approach distinguished the Lincoln Inquiry from its contemporaries and from subsequent historians. Though they sought to defend their ancestors and the history of their communities, the Lincoln Inquiry researchers were not members of the "chin fly" camp; they challenged both sides of the debate. Half a century later, when Neely articulated the contrast between the "dung hill" and "chin fly" theses, he proposed to move beyond the binary options by looking to Lincoln for a resolution of the two interpretations. Reviewing Lincoln's first political platform and his autobiographical statements, Neely rightly observed that Lincoln found little to admire in frontier life and that he had worked his entire life to escape from the frontier.[8] The Lincoln Inquiry, on the other hand, did not view the question of interpretation of the Indiana frontier as a biographical problem to be resolved by consulting Lincoln's opinion. Instead, the

Lincoln Inquiry cast the problem as historical and decided to settle the question by turning to the history of the frontier.

The Lincoln Inquiry interpreted the Indiana frontier of the 1820s as symbolic of the entire American experience on the frontier, and to make their case members relied on the scholarship of Turner. Shortly after the "Best Witnesses" meeting, the irregular and formal correspondence between Iglehart and Turner transformed into a regular, informal, and personal relationship. They met at professional meetings, and Turner hosted Iglehart at his summer home in Wisconsin. Iglehart became Turner's warm friend, devoted disciple, and enthusiastic supporter while Turner became an authoritative endorser of the Lincoln Inquiry's work and its mentor in the refinement of historical method.[9]

Turner's "Frontier Thesis" operated on an abstract, symbolic level. Responding to a generation of academic historians who were emphasizing the ties between Europe and the Unites States, Turner argued for the uniqueness of American society and attributed it to two great social processes that came to a head on the frontier. On one hand, the American West that stretched from the Alleghenies to the Pacific Coast had provided an unlimited supply of "free land." Second, this space became the site of a perpetual encounter between civilized European Americans and the "savage" Native Americans. Watching "the procession of [American] civilization" parade through the Cumberland Gap one sees not genealogically identifiable individuals but "the fur-trader and hunter, the cattle-raiser, the pioneer farmer" wending their way in succession over the American continent. When individuals are named—such as Andrew Jackson, or Abraham Lincoln—they are elevated to heroic typological status, serving as thumbnails for the entire mass of white, westward-moving immigrants of their respective eras.

In the work of the Lincoln Inquiry, three Turnerian passages were quoted most frequently. First, members cited Turner's assertion that American democracy "came stark and strong and full of life from the American forest." Second, they followed Turner in locating the "transitional zone" of the "New West" in southern Indiana and the Midwest in the 1820s. Third, they adopted Turner's use of Lincoln as "the very embodiment of the pioneer period of the old northwest" and saw Lincoln in contrast to the lower class of frontier life characterized by Turner as "the scum that the waves of advancing civilization bore before them." Instead of categorizing all settlers as either civilized or scum, Turner and the Lincoln Inquiry recognized distinctions of class and culture.[10] American democracy originated on the frontier, in the 1820s this crucial process churned through southern Indiana, and the life of Lincoln symbolized the experience of an entire generation.

By locating Lincoln on southern Indiana's Turnerian frontier, the Lincoln Inquiry responded to past interpretations of Lincoln's early life. Yes, southern Hoosiers had been poor, "but it was the independent poverty of the western wilderness and it made men of those who fought their way out of it." The unsavory aspects of frontier life emphasized in the "dung hill" thesis could be explained away as being the trash and driftwood that floats on top of powerful societal waves. Like skimming across the surface of water, a quick research trip to southern Indiana might yield contact with the scum, but only those who experienced the depth of the wave would truly understand its force and power. As for the "chin fly" thesis, the Lincoln Inquiry elevated Lincoln from a happy-go-lucky backwoods frontiersman into a typological symbol for all of frontier life. Lincoln was not just a "Backwoodsman of the Alleghenies" or a "Man of the Western Waters" in Teddy Roosevelt's phrases, but rather the representative of agricultural democracy, indeed the first great American.[11]

In applying Lincoln as typological figure to the pioneers of the southern Indiana frontier, the Lincoln Inquiry pulled Turner's abstract national thesis down to a concrete, local level. Whereas Turner worked up from the mass of westward moving migrants to identify Lincoln as a symbolic summary, the Lincoln Inquiry reversed the logic to pull Lincoln's estimable qualities back down onto their pioneer ancestors individually and collectively. At its most earthy level, this model paralleled common farming knowledge that prizewinning horses inherit traits from similarly gifted sires and dams; Lincoln was simply a very good representative of southern Indiana stock. At a more symbolic worldview level, by reapplying the frontier thesis and Lincoln to specific pioneers, the Lincoln Inquiry found means for projecting historically significant content onto lost and sometimes anonymous ancestors. If an ancestor had been merely "ordinary," his or her life gained meaning by participation in the frontier experience. Lincoln became the prism through which one might "see what qualities the pioneers of the Middle West possessed." This symbolic extrapolation also compensated for one of Turner's weaknesses. Whereas Turner had summarized the history of the west as a parade of male figures—trader, hunter, farmer—the Lincoln Inquiry added women to the types and united the experiences. In one visual example, George Wilson sketched an image in his notebook in which five frontier figures hold hands: a female pioneer and female weaver with a male trader, merchant, and trapper. The Lincoln Inquiry widened Turner's linear historical process into a collective portrait of southern Indiana's pioneer community. By sharing this new understanding of the past with each other, the rest of the state, and future generations, the members of the Lincoln Inquiry defined their social relationships with their predecessors, contemporaries, and successors.[12]

The Lincoln Inquiry also used their social application of Turner's frontier thesis to navigate the crowded field of Lincoln studies in the 1920s. Iglehart openly confessed that "complications in our Lincoln work practically drove me to frontier work." Placing Lincoln on the Indiana frontier sidestepped psychobiography and the debate over ancestry by shifting the focus from nature to nurture. The frontier provided a place on which to ground undocumented reminiscences through biographical and local historical sources. The frontier thesis supported the Inquiry's founding rationale that the local history of southern Indiana was relevant to the biggest questions about American history and national character. And, if competitors were going to criticize the Lincoln Inquiry on "scientific" or methodological grounds, Iglehart and his colleagues rested their findings on contemporary scholarship that described the American frontier and discussed the soundest methods for research and writing about history. Not only did Inquiry participants read Turner, they, like Deidré Johnson, also read widely and cited the work of his students and supporters: James Truslow Adams's application of the thesis in *Revolutionary New England* (1923), Frederic L. Paxson's prize-winning *History of the American Frontier* (1925), William Mason West's argument on the advantage western settlers had over eastern settlements. This cadre of contemporary academic historians served as a counterweight to Beveridge's professional ties and Warren's categorical dismissal. In Iglehart's words, reading modern academic histories put the Inquiry "into strict historical lines of work."[13]

The Lincoln Inquiry's application of the frontier thesis also reinforced its collective approach to historical research and writing. The Inquiry invited any substantive contribution from anyone able to offer it. In addition to formal papers, the society's meetings also offered times to share brief notices and thoughts. Often a formal presentation would prompt a memory or reminiscence that was recorded by the society's stenographer. They looked for "scraps of information here and there," which could be "pieced together by careful study into a connected though necessarily meager story" or taken in the aggregate. "The value of the evidence of this kind may be greater or less," Iglehart explained to Tarbell. "Some of it is of supreme value. All of it has probative value and a good deal has circumstantial evidence." Albion Fellows Bacon captured the excitement generated by this collaborative ethos when she wrote of "untold sources of historical wealth that have not been reached." When the city attorney of Tell City provided the local welcome at the society's October 1923 meeting he noted the recent discovery of the tomb of Egypt's King Tutankhamen and wondered if a similar treasure "may be discovered right here in Perry County." "Why shouldn't you unearth something wonderful in Perry County?" Bacon replied, "That is the spirit of Americanism." If Johnson found a treasure in an attic, how many other treasures still remained hidden? Democracy may have been created on Turner's frontier, but the descendants of those pioneers also claimed it as the basis for their right to contribute to historical knowledge about Lincoln and southern Indiana history.[14]

In encouraging a range of contributions, the Lincoln Inquiry also developed the analytical and rhetorical means by which to bring disparate information together. Like Johnson, they read deeply in published literature in a practice they called "steeping." In contemplating a new writing project, Tommy de la Hunt wrote that "I must concentrate, must steep myself again in its memories before putting pencil to paper afresh." They also read critically and encouraged one another to corroborate sources and draw informed inferences. They understood "facts" as "real events" in need of context: "One never really knows facts," Wilson recorded, "until he knows their inner meaning. Unless one knows all the setting, relation and purpose back of the facts he does not know the facts." Inquiry workers distinguished facts from opinions, myth, tradition, eulogies, "biography, family genealogy, or literary production," but recognized the limits of dogmatic categorization.[15] At one society meeting, Esarey observed that "it is generally assumed that when a tradition is confronted with contemporary written evidence the latter should prevail. Such a rule would greatly simplify matters but in the application it frequently leaves grave doubts. The famous diary of John Quincy Adams, if taken literally, leaves no doubt as to his premiership among the statesmen of his time, but the dead weight of tradition, that he had little influence at Washington, leads one to doubt." On the other hand, Wilson noted, "A careful analysis of tradition often leads up to the discovery that the so-called tradition was an absolute fact." The best course, he concluded, was that pursued by Herodotus: "He called facts, facts, if he saw them; he called impressions, impressions; observations, observations; fiction, fiction;— and tradition, tradition;—a lesson all of us may well afford to read and follow."[16] And yet there were also times to simply draw a line to end absurd speculations. "If Thomas Lincoln had made all of the cabinets attributed to him while living in Spencer County, he would have had superhuman ability."[17]

In describing their work, the members of the Lincoln Inquiry invoked a mishmash of metaphors that emphasized the different aspects of their practice. The unlimited possibilities of their work and the potential value of their findings often found expression in mineral terms: "There is an unworked mine," "our field is like the Comstock lode, the ore of which is pure gold," "we have untold sources of historical wealth that have not been reached." Like gold, the truth about Indiana's frontier lay hidden and mixed with tradition, but it could be discovered and sorted out through diligent work. When they spoke of their interpretive work, pioneer imagery guided their efforts to "hog-tie facts" and "blaze afresh every trail" through the forest of growth surrounding the dung hill and chin fly theses. The act of speaking at a meeting or publishing one's findings drew on imagery of light and darkness: they were "throwing" the "searchlight of investigation and publicity" and "plucking" historical things "out of the mists of more than a century ago." And, they worked collectively with each other and with past and future historians to create "another link in the chain of evidence" or yet more "bricks in the kiln ready to be laid in the mortar." The Lincoln Inquiry engaged the length and breadth of the historical process, from archival research to interpretation to publication, in a collective endeavor. As one member summarized the entire process, "Part of the charm of local history lies in the fact that one can not read it all, in a book, at one sitting, but must construct the story one's self by the aid of old books, old letters, and pictures, a bit of narrative from that person or this. Sometimes, a year or two elapses before one finds the missing bits of the puzzle which, when put together, complete the story."[18] The Lincoln Inquiry found the pieces of the puzzle of Lincoln's early years within reach in southern Indiana. Working collectively with each other and in dialogue with past and contemporary interpreters of Lincoln's Indiana years, members endeavored to place Lincoln firmly within the context of southern Indiana's frontier environment.

Lincoln's Frontier Indiana Environment

First and foremost, the Lincoln Inquiry set out to understand Lincoln's "environment." The word was not uncommon in history writing at the time and was often used as a substitute for "local history." In the usage of the Lincoln Inquiry, the term referred to the nexus of geography, culture, and human action, and envisioned the Lincoln homestead as the "hub" around which his environment existed. Participants in the Inquiry used the metaphor of modern film to explain the need to pay attention to the "background" as well as the principal actors, thereby justifying their study of plants, animals, waterways, rock formations, and weather. But the environment also included what later would be called culture, or in George Wilson's words, "an accumulated mass of beliefs, thoughts and experiences." In the environmental metaphor, culture was the "atmosphere" in which Lincoln and his contemporaries lived. And yet, mountains, rivers, and forests became significant to the extent that humans interacted with them by scaling a peak, traveling a river, or settling within a forest. The resultant environment made up the nurture component that interacted with hereditary traits passed on through nature and ultimately became something larger than the individuals that interacted with it. In fact, while witnesses may recall specific events, the total picture of a person's environment was "too complex" and "beyond the vision" of participants, making the reconstruction of Lincoln's environment a task suited to the historian who would combine witness testimony with additional sources and analysis.[19]

In practice, the Lincoln Inquiry pursued Lincoln's environment through the study of artifacts, places, and biographies. In presidential addresses, circular letters, and personal correspondence Inquiry workers repeated the call to preserve any relic, identify any place, and preserve the story of the life of any person connected to Lincoln's southern Indiana frontier environment. Part of the urgency stemmed from the fact that much had not been written, writings had been lost, and the courthouse closest to the Lincoln homestead in Spencer County had burned in 1834.[20] To compensate, participants searched for evidence in letters, diaries, court records, probate records, family albums, newspapers, store ledgers, church records, military records, maps, music, deeds, wills, old books, family Bibles, contracts, photographs, clothing, heirlooms, furniture, and quilts.[21] Speakers illustrated their talks with artifacts and often described their excitement upon finding sources—tingling nerves, "breathless eagerness," Deidré Johnson's opening of the family trunk—and their faith in the unknown possibilities still hiding in attics.[22] The society held its meetings in historic communities, hosted pilgrimages to specific places, and erected plaques in dozens of locations.[23] Most significantly, society members prepared over three hundred biographies of individuals and families as well as papers on local history, culture, and institutions. Some of the biographies contained little more than a listing of genealogical data, but most made some attempt to connect the subject to his or her time and place. Many became collective biographies of family members living during the 1820s, and some expanded to include the generations before and after. Society members read and commented to each other on William R. Thayer's recent *Art of Biography* (1920), which encouraged biographers "to learn how [the] environment in time and in places affects" the subject (and it did not hurt that he, too, criticized Nicolay and Hay's biography of Lincoln, the "greatest American of the century").[24] The goal in all of this work was to create a "chain of sketches which will link the people of all these counties together in a degree never properly recognized in any literature."[25]

At the center of this frontier environment stood young Abraham Lincoln. He provided the main outline of his life in Indiana in two statements he prepared for the 1860 presidential campaign: his family arrived in 1816, his mother died two years later, he spent most of his time at work and little of it in school. After working several years as a hired hand on other farms and on flatboat work on the river, the Lincolns left the state for Illinois when Abraham was twenty-one years old.[26] The additional findings proposed by the Lincoln Inquiry would prompt debate among contemporary Lincoln biographers.

By the time of the Lincoln Inquiry's work in the 1920s, it seemed that objects connected to Lincoln turned up everywhere. The records of the Inquiry note cabinets allegedly made by Lincoln and his father, rails split by the teen, brick molds used by the hired laborer, the grindstone used to sharpen his ax, a knife with his initials carved in the handle, a kettle. Pieces of the cabins occupied by the Lincolns had ended up as paperweights, gavels, and souvenirs.[27] Though Thomas Lincoln could not have made all of the cabinets without "superhuman ability," two of those whose provenance was verified were placed by the Lincoln Inquiry in the courthouse in Rockport and a museum in Evansville.[28] After a copy of a letter from Lincoln to David Turnham was shared at a society meeting, members helped secure the original.[29] These relics and many others—pioneer furniture, china, household implements, guns, swords, textiles, and Indian relics—were often shown at society meetings and then preserved in city and county museums throughout the eight counties of southern Indiana's "Pocket."[30]

Interviews with elderly residents produced numerous stories about young Abraham's love life. William Herndon identified three girls who may have stirred the boy's heart while he lived in Indiana, Ida Tarbell added a fourth, and Jesse Weik rounded the number out to five.[31] The interviews reported by the Lincoln Inquiry identify at least seven more who offered small insights: Abraham had carried Elizabeth Tully's shoes, Nancy Beard had gone to apple-peeling and corn-husking parties with him, and Polly Richardson recalled that Abraham had saved her and her mother from a pack of wolves with his ax, though by the 1920s it proved impossible to confirm whether the eight-year-old boy had actually done so. "Best Witness" Anna O'Flynn photographed two of the claimants, Elizabeth Wood and Ruth Crawford, in 1896.[32] From the "chin fly" perspective, Warren almost categorically denied any romantic interest for the virtuous young Lincoln in Indiana, attributing most of the stories to Herndon's malice or subsequent mythmaking, though he did allow that Lincoln watched a sunset with Anna Roby after she was married and in the presence of her husband Allen Gentry. For his part, Beveridge passed over the issue almost entirely, concluding that "there was nothing attractive in Abraham's appearance." Yet, here he willfully ignored Herndon's evidence, simultaneously acknowledging that Lincoln spent a lot of time with Anna Roby while citing her as the authority that he "did not go much with the girls."[33]

Another point of debate involved Lincoln's relationship with two lawyers living in the region. Herndon had communicated with John Pitcher, who reported loaning books to Lincoln and encouraging him to write. In January 1922, Alice Hanby reported visiting Pitcher in the 1890s, seeing Lincoln's signature in Pitcher's copy of William Blackstone's *Commentaries,* and hearing him confirm that he had dissuaded Lincoln from studying law. In his own correspondence Lincoln only mentioned reading Blackstone in Illinois, and the book later burned in a fire, leaving the debate unsettled.[34] Herndon had also reported that Lincoln watched John A. Brackenridge defend a case, but at the same January 1922 meeting Inquiry worker Eldora Raleigh, Brackenridge's niece, cited family tradition that Lincoln walked from his home to Boonville to hear her uncle many times, that he occasionally visited the home, and that Brackenridge loaned him law books as well. Raleigh's statement, in particular, drew attention and criticism. When challenged to support her claim that Lincoln knew Brackenridge, Raleigh agreed that she could not "prove" her family's tradition, but she could also not "prove" her own birth even though she was present. She did, however, offer a signed deposition that "Abraham Lincoln knew my Uncle John A. Brackenridge, walked miles to hear him plead law and borrowed books from him."[35]

As in the response to Lincoln's young romance, contemporary comment on these findings likewise fell out along pre-established lines. The year after Hanby spoke of Pitcher's dissuasion, Jesse Weik announced that when he had interviewed Pitcher, the lawyer reported encouraging Lincoln to study law. Tarbell had named only Pitcher as an influence on young Abraham in 1900 but, on the basis of Raleigh's work, she added Brackenridge to her 1924 volume.[36] With Tarbell on board, Beveridge had to oppose. He followed Herndon in citing Lincoln's acquaintance with John Pitcher, but he explicitly denied any "evidence to support the speculations" that Lincoln knew Brackenridge, ignoring Raleigh's paper and attributing the very idea to "Tarbell's well-meaning imaginings." Warren ultimately came down in support of both acquaintances, though he debated the location of the Brackenridge home and took the opportunity to criticize Beveridge for sloppy source work on Brackenridge.[37]

Some of the Lincoln Inquiry's findings forced contemporary writers to leave their default positions. When "Best Witness" Will Fortune identified *Quinn's Jests* as a book of humor that Lincoln read in Indiana, he let Tarbell know right away, but she did not mention it in her new book. Beveridge, on the other hand, snapped up the finding as soon as he could, but he chose not to share any of the jokes, noting that the "humor is heavy, the so-called jests often indecent and sometimes so filthy that they cannot now be introduced." In this case even Beveridge sided with Tarbell's effort to "fumigate" Lincoln's ribald humor. Warren, his ministerial sensibilities still acute, dismissed the entire book, reasoning that something so vulgar would not have "be[en] of interest to pioneer youths."[38] When Iglehart demonstrated that a poem Herndon had attributed to Lincoln was actually an English folk ballad, Tarbell and Beveridge left it alone, Barton failed to find any other origin, and Warren actually credited Iglehart with exposing the error.[39]

One of the Inquiry's most significant findings received very little attention then and has been largely overlooked since. In 1865, David Turnham told Herndon that he had loaned Lincoln the first law book that the future lawyer ever saw, a copy of *The Revised Statues of Indiana* (1824). Nearly every biographer since has mentioned this volume, but few have known what to do with it. Herndon's conclusion, that study of the book "no doubt . . . led Abe to think of the law as his calling in maturer years," has been repeated by many. Tarbell got her hands on a copy and saw that it contained the Declaration of Independence, the constitutions of the United States and of Indiana, and the Northwest Ordinance of 1787, followed by nearly four hundred pages of statues. So what would a teenage boy make of that? In 1900, Tarbell first assumed he read it all and reasoned that through the book "he understood the principles on which the nation was founded" and how the state of Indiana was governed. Later

she suspected he only read the founding documents in the book's opening pages. Beveridge judged that "through this volume Lincoln acquired
a fair understanding of the elements of law and government" and Warren
mused that the boy "must have read" the Declaration and Constitution
"over and over again." Frederick Trevor Hill, on the other hand, in his
monograph on Lincoln as a lawyer, ridiculed the "absurdity" of young
Lincoln reading something so "dull."[40] The book sat on Iglehart's shelf for
over fifty years while he was a practicing lawyer. In his early writings, he
repeated the conclusions of others and agreed that Lincoln must have
read the front matter. In time, however, he realized that the volume had a
more profound influence. Iglehart's notes about his reading and speeches
reveal that he discovered a connection between the Indiana statues and
Lincoln's first political platform in which the Hoosier, only two years after
leaving Indiana, spoke to residents of Sangamo County, Illinois, about
transportation and education in language reminiscent of the debated
statute book.[41] Thus, the Indiana law book's most demonstrable impact
came not in Lincoln's later legal career but in his early political life.

The Lincoln Inquiry's method of collectively compiling findings sought
accuracy in the long run but could not prevent foul play in the short term.
At the society's June 1928 meeting in Gentryville, Tommy de la Hunt announced that in the past forty-eight hours Perry County residents had
discovered an affidavit from 1866 in which a Jacob Weatherholt Jr. testified that his father had carried the Lincoln family across the Ohio River
from Kentucky to Indiana in 1816 on his ferry at Clover Creek. This assertion directly challenged the previous consensus held from Herndon
through Tarbell that the family had crossed on Thompson's Ferry, a site
near Troy on the boundary between Spencer and Perry counties that had
already been commemorated jointly by the two counties. The Clover
Creek claim meant that Lincoln's first step on Indiana soil would have
been solely in present-day Perry County near Tobinsport. The announcement provoked remonstrations from Spencer County residents, but de la
Hunt replied coolly that a local judge had certified the authenticity of the
affidavit. In a show of submission intended to support the claim and provoke the society, de la Hunt confessed that he had cited the traditional
site in his centennial pageant, but now he was forced to accept the certified proof to the contrary. For unrecorded reasons, the Lincoln Inquiry
endorsed the findings, but questions soon arose. First, Weatherholt named
William Booth as Lincoln's assassin, though John Wilkes Booth's name
should have been well enough known the year after the assassination.
Second, the affidavit claimed that the Lincoln family spent the night at the

same place where the Marquis de Lafayette stayed when his ship capsized in 1825, a coincidence that proved too timely for a county whose officials were appealing to the growing numbers of automobile tourists who visited Spencer County Lincoln sites. Though no direct charge of forgery was ever made, growing suspicion and the weight of previous testimony led writers to abandon the affidavit within the decade.[42]

Over the next three decades, Lincoln biographers and writers picked up other findings of the Lincoln Inquiry. In 1937, Gerald McMurtry used its local history sources to document "The Lincoln Migration from Kentucky to Indiana." Four years later John F. Cady cited Roscoe Kiper's work in an article titled "The Religious Environment of Lincoln's Youth." In 1942, future Lincoln biographer Reinhard H. Luthin named books by Ehrmann and Beveridge and McMurtry's article as the key sources for Lincoln's early years. Travel guides of the 1950s and 1960s routed tourists to sites marked by the Inquiry. In his study of Lincoln in Indiana published in 1959, Warren ultimately accepted the work of "Best Witnesses" Murr and Fortune as well as other informant testimony reported in Ehrmann's book and the newspaper columns of society members Thomas de la Hunt and Charles Baker.[43] In the field of Lincoln biography, the Lincoln's Inquiry's discrete findings found their way into the broader stream of Lincoln scholarship.

But while various Lincoln biographers have plucked individual Lincoln Inquiry findings, none have fully pursued the larger argument the members made about Lincoln's frontier Indiana environment. The Lincoln Inquiry seized on a recollection from one of Lincoln's adult contemporaries that averred that Lincoln had read everything within a fifty-mile radius of his Indiana home. While some of the members looked for books in probate records or wondered why Lincoln never checked a book out of the public library in nearby Rockport, the Inquiry also leveraged the statement into an argument to view Lincoln within a much wider world on the frontier. Biographers before and since the Lincoln Inquiry have focused on what has come to be called the Pigeon Creek Neighborhood, a cluster of homes occupied by approximately 120 people in 14 farming families. The fifty-mile radius, however, draws in Boonville and Princeton, the larger towns of Evansville and Vincennes, a settlement of British immigrants, and the Ohio River towns of Cannelton, Rockport, and Newburgh. In Lucius Embree's words, Lincoln did not live in one "small, compact community," but in a network of communities connected through "preachings, camp meetings, public gatherings, house raisings, log rollings and political assemblages." Residents of these communities moved in and out quite regularly, with many of the newcomers arriving from Kentucky. The flow of people and trade moved south-to-north as well as eastward and westward. Borrowing a word of recent coinage from the bull economic markets of the 1920s, Iglehart described the communities as being "fluid, not frozen."[44] Thus, far from Herndon's "stagnant, putrid pool," the Indiana frontier, with its access to the Midwest's main waterway, was constantly being renewed by the circulation of people and ideas.

Many events in Lincoln's young life make more sense within this fluid model of the Indiana frontier. Lincoln carried his family's harvest to mills on the Noah Gordon farm (2 miles away), on Anderson Creek (16 miles), and in Troy (17 miles), and on at least one occasion took wool to Princeton to be carded (40–45 miles). In his hiring out, he found his way to the Ohio River, cutting cord wood for passing steamers, ferrying travelers across Anderson Creek, rowing passengers out to meet steamships in the middle of the Ohio River—and eventually riding a flatboat to New Orleans. Biographers beginning with Herndon have cited these experiences without sensing their implication for the fluidity of life on the Indiana frontier.

Recent historians freed from focusing on Lincoln's biography, however, have been making the fluidity argument about an even broader midwestern region termed the "Trans-Appalachian frontier." In the hands of Malcolm Rohrbaugh, Nicole Etcheson, Andrew Cayton, and Richard Nation, southern Indiana has come to be seen as part of the broader Ohio River valley in which incoming settlers converged from the upland south via the Ohio River system and from New England via the Great Lakes region. In southern Indiana, upland southerners predominated, bringing with them a hatred of planter aristocracy and a wariness of New England wealth, identification with democracy and independence, and distaste for Yankee cultural imperialism. The region also became home to settlements of Catholics, Baptists, British immigrants, and utopian planners. Social institutions from law to politics to taxation evolved on the frontier and debates over internal improvements, land policy, public education, immigration, and temperance grew into political divisions between Whigs and Democrats and eventually divided loyalties between North and South in the Civil War.[45] This early nineteenth-century frontier environment provides the obvious context for Lincoln's early speaking and writing about temperance, his awareness of debates over slavery, his early acquaintance with Andrew Jackson's Democrats and his choice in Indiana to side with Henry Clay and the Whigs, his encountering of

British folk ballads and jokes, and his deep familiarity with the compromises and contradictions between northern and southern culture. The context also foreshadowed the twentieth-century tensions that the Southwestern Indiana Historical Society would face with state history workers and officials in Indianapolis.

The Lincoln Inquiry proposed to understand this fluid Indiana frontier by researching the lives of the people who passed through it. From its earliest meetings, the Inquiry began to compile a list of families who had lived in southern Indiana in the 1810s and 1820s. Some of the sixty-two family names are familiar to Lincoln biographers—Gentry, Crawford, Grigsby, Turnham, Jones, and Lamar.[46] Others, such as Britton, Ashworth, DeBruler, Boone, or Morgan, are not. Over the course of nearly two decades, Inquiry workers produced nearly three hundred biographies of individuals and families. The purpose was not to somehow prove or allege that all these people knew or even met Lincoln, or to seek to create a day-by-day listing of every book or person he encountered on every day of his life in Indiana. Rather, the aim was to amass enough material from which to view "a composite photograph of the Indiana pioneers."[47]

These biographies were never submitted to formal prosopographical analysis, but several patterns emerged that prompted commentary on various occasions. Noting that so many of the families had come from or through Kentucky, Inquiry workers endorsed a growing tendency among biographers to describe Lincoln's nearest neighbors as a "transplanted" Kentucky community, though they probably would not have gone as far as one recent Kentucky writer who claimed that "the Kentucky Influence was so pervasive in southern Indiana that one could almost suggest that the youthful Lincoln had never left the farm at Knob Creek."[48] They noted that many of the residents joined Thomas Lincoln in squatting on their land—some for several years—before purchasing it from the federal government.[49] They noted the presence of preachers and lawyers on religious and legal circuits and found evidence of contemporary discussion over slavery.[50] They saw the marks of a culture of literacy in the subscriptions to newspapers, public library holdings, family and probate records of book ownership, traditions of book sharing, and even an advertisement from an individual in an 1819 issue of the *Indiana Gazette* calling on delinquent book borrowers to return loaned books.[51] They sought out pioneer superstitions of the period, not to cite and re-cite them as evidence of ignorance, but rather to produce a fuller understanding of the beliefs and culture of those who lived on Lincoln's Indiana frontier.[52]

In placing Lincoln in the context of southern Indiana's frontier, Lincoln Inquiry participants frequently described him and his family as "typical," but they never called him "average." Their usage of the word "typical" followed Frederick Jackson Turner's application of Lincoln as a "type" or symbolic category through which to view the development of American history. Roscoe Kiper imitated Turner best in noting Lincoln's "sterling characteristics which made him the great and good and noble American citizen." He was a "typical American citizen because his life materialized the ideals of America."[53]

This conclusion, reached by the Lincoln Inquiry in the 1920s, was not revisited until 2001 when Kenneth J. Winkle applied social history methods to understand the social "winds" that lifted "the young eagle" from the frontier to the Oval Office. Winkle placed Lincoln's experience within the social-historical context of his ancestors and contemporaries and repeatedly found the Lincolns "typical," "traditional," "unexceptional," and "commonplace." He notes the transplanted Kentucky community and the prevailing southern influence in Indiana. The family "practiced classic subsistence agriculture" and "observed the traditional sexual division of labor" with Abraham and his father farming, cabinet-making, and hunting while his mother and sister cooked, washed, sewed, and cared for the children. Even in the death of his mother did Lincoln remain within the norm: one in four frontier children lost at least one parent before reaching age 15, and among nineteenth-century U.S. presidents one-half lost a parent before reaching adulthood. When Thomas Lincoln remarried, he acted like most pioneer men—and the same as all three of his Lincoln ancestors who had lost their wives. The hiring out of young Abraham revealed the growing prosperity of his family, and the flatboat trip to New Orleans moved his labor from a subsistence to a market economy. Reviewing Winkle's book in the *American Historical Review*, Allen C. Guelzo lauded the approach: "The question that the vast bulk of Lincoln studies want to ask is *what made Abraham Lincoln so extraordinary?* It takes an extraordinarily different way of looking at Lincoln to ask entirely the opposite question: in what ways was Lincoln actually quite typical of his times? Asking that question seems only to have occurred to Kenneth J. Winkle, and the job he has done of answering it gives us for the first time what we might call a social history of the sixteenth president." Reviewing the scholarship on Lincoln through 2009, Matthew Pinsker praises Winkle and adds that the most pressing need for understanding Lincoln's private life is "to expand knowledge of the social and cultural context of Lincoln's childhood." However, Winkle's "extraordinary"

question and the need for "expanded" context had actually already occurred to hundreds of practitioners of history in Indiana's Lincoln Inquiry during the 1920s and 1930s. And though they sought for answers
differently, historians in the Lincoln Inquiry came to the same conclusion
that debates over "dung hill" and "chin fly" interpretations of Lincoln's
Indiana experience are best replaced by an exploration of conditions and
processes typical of the time and region.[54]

It does not appear that the Lincoln Inquiry ever questioned what
Lincoln might have thought about the fluid frontier on which he lived.
Most likely they simply assumed that he liked it and never closely examined this idea, preferring instead to devote their time to identifying all of
the features of his frontier environment. It would be left to later historians to argue, as Neely did, that Lincoln spent his life trying to escape from
the frontier. In fact, it was the fluidity of the frontier that permitted such
an escape. More recently, William C. Harris has added nuance to Neely's
conclusion, agreeing that Lincoln was self-conscious of his pioneer heritage but also proud of it, especially of his grandfather and namesake,
who had been one of the earliest settlers in Kentucky.[55]

THE EFFORTS of the Lincoln Inquiry to place Lincoln within the context
of Indiana's frontier environment—illustrated in the experience of Deidré
Johnson and multiplied across hundreds of society members—challenged
the field of Lincoln studies in the 1920s in various ways. The concepts of
"environment" and "frontier" combined traditional Lincoln biography
with the work of contemporary academic historians through Frederick
Jackson Turner's frontier thesis. The emphasis on preserving relics, places,
and biographies added to the interviews, reminiscences, and documents
collected by Inquiry members and previous interviewers. By rooting Lincoln in a specific community, they sought not to distinguish him from his
neighbors like a diamond from a dunghill, but rather to identify the way
that he and their ancestors navigated the same constraints and survived
in the same "atmosphere." Lincoln was not a lone eagle who miraculously
took flight on his own. He was, in the poetic words of Albion Fellows
Bacon, part of a family of eagles: "Here grew a new Democracy/ Here was
the eaglet's nest,/ Where his wings grew strong for his after flight—/ Here,
in our Middle West."[56]

By the second half of the 1920s, the Lincoln Inquiry had begun to turn
the heads of Lincoln biographers and historians. In 1925 Ida Tarbell wrote
that she was becoming "more and more interested" in the Lincoln Inquiry.
"The longer I roll over the idea in my mind," she wrote, "the more con-

vinced I am not only that it is the right approach to any study of Lincoln in southwestern Indiana, but that it is probably a much wider and richer field than any of our biographers have yet appreciated." Christopher Coleman declared that the Inquiry's work "contributed powerfully to the revision of our interpretation of Lincoln's personality and its development." From his new position in Pennsylvania, John Oliver wrote that he had been following the Inquiry and believed its members had "hit a new note in the extent to which [they] emphasized the environment and human association in which Lincoln grew up to young manhood. [They] have truly interpreted in a correct manner the frontier view of history in southern Indiana during the first quarter of the nineteenth century." Even the editor of the *Mississippi Valley Historical Review* judged that "ideas and accumulated data will inevitably prove to be a valuable contribution to existing knowledge of the Great Emancipator."[57]

Having organized a broad network of local history practitioners, established its right to participate in public history work in Indiana, defended its use of oral testimony, and labored to forge a new interpretation of Lincoln's frontier experience, the Lincoln Inquiry still sought ways to persuade the general public to abandon its stereotype of southern Indiana. When Bess Ehrmann attempted to publish a summary pitched for a general audience, the paper was rejected by the editor of the *Atlantic Monthly* and two other national magazines where it was judged too narrow and more appropriate for a local history publication.[58] Little could she or her colleagues predict that the Lincoln Inquiry would soon be drawn into one more struggle in which they would again face off against Beveridge, Warren, and the state agencies in Indianapolis. Only this time, the public would be watching as the memory of Nancy Hanks Lincoln and the presence of the Ku Klux Klan turned Indiana's past into a battleground for its future.

♔ 5

The Klan and a Conspiracy

O N THE rounded crest of a small, tree-covered hill in southern Indiana's Spencer County lie the buried remains of Nancy Hanks Lincoln,
the mother of the sixteenth president. After succumbing to milk-sickness,
a chemical toxin transmitted to humans who drink the milk of cows that
have grazed on the white snakeroot plant, Nancy was buried in a wooden
box built by her husband with the likely assistance of her nine-year-old
son. Her grave rests with others of her generation who were likewise buried in the rough, pioneer-era cemetery. A succession of markers has
identified the site, but the trees and terrain have remained largely the
same. And yet, somewhat surprisingly, visits to the site have prompted a
range of reactions. The variations and the constancies in the reports of
three visits illuminate the powerfully personal impact of the intertwining
of place, memories, and stories.

On September 14, 1865, exactly five months after Abraham Lincoln
had been shot, his former law partner William Herndon visited Nancy's
grave. The trees and undergrowth had become dense, "wild and grand,"
he wrote. He found no fence or headstone, only a sunken spot in the
ground. He thought, and later wrote in his notes, about Nancy, her son,
and himself. "If I could breath life into her again I would do it. Could I
only whisper in her Ear—'Your Son was Presdt—of the U.S. from 1861
to 1865,' I would be satisfied. I have heard much of this blessed, good
woman. I stood bare headed in reverence at her grave. I can't Say why—
yet I felt in the presence of the living woman transported to another
world. 'God bless her,' said her Son to me once and I repeat that which
Echoes audibly in my Soul—'God bless her.' . . . After looking at the
grave and Contemplating in Silence the mutation of things—death—

immortality—God, I left, I hope, the grave, a better man—at least if but for one moment."[1]

In October 1924, the same month of the year in which Nancy had died one hundred and six years previously, Tommy de la Hunt addressed a meeting of the Lincoln Inquiry held near the site of Nancy's grave. A native of neighboring Perry County, de la Hunt had visited the grave often; he had come in every season of the year; he had given tours to Indiana's governors, to state officials, and to national figures, including Ida Tarbell. "Many memories come thick and fast about me as I stand here this morning," he declared, "of people passed on, with whom I have walked under these trees and stood beside yonder mound. The dearest of all these recollections is that the first time I came here was in boyhood, hand in hand with my own wonderful little mother. She told me the pathetic story of Nancy Hanks Lincoln, and made an impression that all the later biographies of Lincoln that I have ever read failed to do."[2]

In February 1927, one hundred and eighteen years after the birth of Abraham Lincoln, the governor of Indiana issued a proclamation to formally preserve the grave and sent Anne Studebaker Carlisle to visit the site. Her father was one of the five brothers who founded the successful Indiana-based car company that shared their name, and, forty years earlier, he had been so ashamed of the state's neglect of the site that he erected a stone monument there at personal expense. In a letter addressed to the governor and published in newspapers throughout Indiana, Carlisle reported that while she was standing atop the small hill crest her attention had been drawn away from the grave. "As we looked up into the branches of the friendly trees nearby the thought came to me, 'You friendly trees, did you know Abraham Lincoln?' And then it seemed to me that one particular knarled [sic] oak whispered back, 'Yes, indeed, I knew Abe Lincoln. We all knew him well and loved him much.' And finding an appreciative audience, the friendly oak told again the wonderful story." Before his mother's death, young Abraham had played in the grove and afterwards he returned often to meditate and to cry. Noting the governor's recent proposal to preserve the grave, she enjoined, "It is a great honor to be identified with this splendid undertaking and I invite every woman in the state of Indiana to share in it."[3]

For Herndon, de la Hunt, and Carlisle the site of Nancy Lincoln's grave prompted reflection, a feeling of proximity, and a sense of participating in a larger conversation. All three approached the grave on an anniversary, telegraphing their desire to synchronize both time and place in a symbolic encounter. The experience pricked sensorial imaginations, with Herndon feeling Nancy's presence and hearing Abraham's voice while Carlisle listened to the trees who had been observer-witnesses. All three were moved to think of a mother—Herndon of the particular mother buried on the site, de la Hunt of his own mother, and Carlisle of universal motherhood. These mothers were also embedded within a communicatory process that found its focus at the time of visitation. Herndon became the bearer of a message from Abraham to Nancy after both had died, de la Hunt transmitted the emotion felt in the presence of his mother to the assembled audience, and Carlisle passed a story from the friendly witness trees to civic-minded mothers throughout the state of Indiana. All three people visited the same spot of earth, surrounded by the same cluster of trees, concealing the remains of the same woman. None had ever met her, and yet they imagined her in different roles and within three different storylines. Herndon thought of the biographical story of a mother and son, de la Hunt recounted an ancestral story that connected his present to Indiana's pioneer past, Carlisle told a universal story that united nature itself with eternal motherhood.

Because neither facts nor historical documents speak for themselves, we must pay attention to the way that specific details—in this case, the grave of a mother—are placed within a larger storyline. Or, to borrow terminology from the philosophy of history, we must observe how details are emplotted within a larger narrative framework that is sometimes called a meta-history or a schematic narrative template. These schematic narratives exert tremendous influence and yet are frequently unacknowledged in the study and teaching of history. For example, in history classrooms, students easily forget the facts hung on the stupefying storylines cobbled together by textbook committees while they can vividly recount the facts presented in a film whose Hollywood production team spent hours sequencing the storyboard before ever powering on the camera to film the first scene. Media accounts of public debates over museum exhibits or school curricula so often emphasize the facts in question—the number of people killed by a bomb, the percentage of Americans who celebrate Christmas, or the contributions of Thomas Jefferson—that they largely omit analysis of the broader schematic narratives at play. Symbols and slogans make reference to truth or citizenship without revealing the underlying values, ideologies, and implications wrapped around the storyline. In discussions of public history "battles" and "wars," competing narratives remain the least examined aspect of American historical consciousness.[4]

Insurance agent and Lincoln Inquiry worker George Wilson spoke of the schematic narrative when he observed: "One never really knows facts until he knows their inner meaning. Unless one knows all the setting, relation and purpose back of the facts he does not know the facts."[5] For Wilson, de la Hunt, and the rest of the Lincoln Inquiry the "purpose back of the facts" was a narrative of Americanism forged on the frontier of Indiana in the 1820s. This frontier story connected Lincoln and his greatness with the experiences shared by all who had lived in southern Indiana in the decade and a half after the state entered the union, the parents and grandparents of the Lincoln Inquiry workers of the 1920s. Herndon's visit to the grave revealed his work underneath a schematic biographical narrative that led him to interview living witnesses and long to speak with those that were dead. Albert Beveridge applied Herndon's notes to his own narrative of American imperialism, and Anne Carlisle was part of a conscientious effort on the part of Indiana politicians to refashion the state's image—they saw Nancy's bones not as the link to a particular woman or to a generation of women who lived one hundred years before but instead as a call to mobilize women and mothers in the present.

Neither the Lincoln Inquiry, nor popular biographers of the 1920s, nor the state of Indiana challenged the interpretation of Lincoln as the Great Emancipator. However, the Lincoln Inquiry differed from contemporaries by locating the sources of Lincoln's greatness in his Indiana environment rather than his unique personality or his singular mother. The Lincoln Inquiry employed a different schematic narrative and pushed against other narratives. From the outset, the Inquiry resisted the narrow biographical focus on Lincoln employed by Herndon, Beveridge, and other writers.

While that struggle continued, another erupted in the second half of the 1920s as desperate politicians in Indianapolis crafted a new schematic narrative intended to apply Lincoln's memory toward civic ends. They cared little for the exact biographical details of Herndon or Beveridge and less for the Lincoln Inquiry's reconstruction of the experience of Hoosier ancestors on the frontier. This new civic story—told by friendly trees to faithful mothers everywhere—would feature a Lincoln uniquely suited to erase the embarrassments of a modern Hoosier state overrun by the machinations of the Ku Klux Klan. Relying on its experience in establishing a place on the crowded landscape of public history in Indiana, the Lincoln Inquiry resisted this civic appropriation of Lincoln. The resultant struggle over three stories—biographical, frontier, and civic—involved a tangle of tensions from racial undertones to gendered assumptions, civic devotion to religious expression, regional rivalry to political posturing. As state politicians attempted to paper over Indiana's racialized present with an idealized version of past womanhood, the Lincoln Inquiry dug in for a fight that soon circled around to include Beveridge and an apparent conspiracy of Lincoln biographers. The resultant clashes and contestations illuminate the often unseen ways that narratives shape both our understandings of the past and our uses of it in the present.

A Pioneer Mother Versus the Klan

"Scalp Lieber!" Lincoln Inquiry member J. C. Jolly wanted no misunderstanding of his opinion of the recent decision by the head of Indiana's Department of Conservation, Richard Lieber, to close Nancy Hanks Lincoln Park to the public. In this August 1925 letter to the editor of the *Rockport Journal* that was reprinted widely throughout the state, Jolly openly criticized the "big man" in Indianapolis who ruled by fiat from afar without even visiting the gravesite. "We have been complimented by numerous visitors," explained Jolly, who appreciated the park's pleasant condition. If Lieber cares so much about Nancy's grave, Jolly challenged, "where has he been all these years?"[6]

For decades, the state of Indiana had mounted only a mixed record on the issue of caring for the grave of Nancy Hanks Lincoln. The humble pioneer cemetery had been largely forgotten throughout the nineteenth century, until 1879 when Peter Studebaker, second vice president of the Studebaker Company of South Bend, paid for a tombstone and Rockport residents contributed toward the cost of a protective fence and organized an oversight commission. In the 1890s, Indiana's governor rejected an appeal from southern Hoosiers to assume care of the site, so they organized a private association that secured a $1,000 donation from Abraham's son Robert Todd Lincoln to erect an elaborate monument carved from the discarded stone of the monument at his father's tomb in Springfield, Illinois. In 1907, Indiana's general assembly assumed responsibility for the site and appropriated funds to erect an iron fence around the property, to build a macadamized road from the highway, and, for reasons left unexplained, to install life-sized sculptures of lions at the entrance. But the state did nothing else—even after the location of the Lincoln cabin was identified in 1917—so by the 1920s, a chorus of voices joined Rockport residents in calling for help. Lincoln biographer William Barton

and Fort Wayne Journalist Claude Bowers wrote editorial pleas in 1921
and 1922. Citizens from across the state began to raise money to purchase additional property in 1923. A school teacher in Vincennes lobbied
unsuccessfully to build a trade school near the site, and in 1924 the
Boonville Press Club began hosting an annual picnic that eventually
drew over 16,000 participants. In its early years, the Lincoln Inquiry
provided advice and political endorsements wherever useful.[7] In March
1923, the general assembly created a Lincoln Memorial Commission
charged with raising money to purchase additional property and build
structures, while immediate care of the site passed to Lieber's Department of Conservation.[8]

Richard Lieber had immigrated to Indiana from Germany. Born into
wealth, he learned to play several musical instruments, had a personal
allowance since childhood, and was "inclined to be extravagant." Those
who knew him well reported that he was physically lazy, that his temper
was easily aroused, and that he was bored by small talk though he liked
to hear himself speak. As a young man in Terre Haute he went into business, but he much preferred traveling and reading history. He served on a
variety of community boards and when, in 1916, he was appointed to
lead Indiana's conservation efforts, he began an intensive effort to create
a statewide system of parks. Just as the state had attempted to centralize
and systematize its historical institutions, so also had it created a Department of Conservation under Lieber in 1919 and assigned it to oversee
maintenance of Nancy's grave in 1923.[9]

The state's efforts to raise money to purchase the site yielded few contributions, and neighbors held out on selling in hopes that the new demand would raise the value of their property. After two years of inaction
and upon hearing reports of the grave's "deplorable condition" and ru-
mors that picnic parties were "desecrating" the grave site, Lieber closed
the park to all automobile traffic and prohibited all meetings except those
of explicitly religious or moral function. He was not prepared for the reaction of southern Hoosiers.

Jolly's letter to the editor called for physical violence. A calmer editorial
explained that Spencer County had donated the land to the state and argued that its tax-paying citizens expected access to the property they had
gifted. Lieber quickly traveled to Lincoln City, where he met with local
residents but "remained firm" on his decision, promising vaguely: "If they
will possess their souls in patience they will find that there are much big-
ger things on the horizon than finding a parking place for automobiles."
Unafraid to engage in state politics, local residents threatened to take the

issue to the governor, but when G. W. Patmore suddenly sold to the state his 47 acres adjacent to the site the debate quieted. After the state sorted out an error in the property's deed, the issue remained dormant for over a year.[10]

Driven by his objective of creating a statewide park system under his control, and motivated by the prize property containing Nancy Lincoln's grave that had fallen into his lap, Lieber itched for action. By the summer of 1926, the funds allocated by the state had all been spent, leaving no money even to enforce the park's closure. How could he persuade the state to allocate or raise more money? Could he pull the machinery of state politics to move in his favor? What kind of effort would unite voters and politicians in a crusade to achieve his desired ends? Over half a century of appealing to Americanism, honor, duty, and state pride had only coaxed Spencer County to donate land and state lawmakers to install stone lions. To bring about so dramatic a change of public opinion and policy would require a tactful appeal to shame and embarrassment, and by 1926 the conditions were perfect in Indiana.

Two years earlier, during the election of 1924, the Ku Klux Klan had overrun Hoosier politics. Whereas the original Klan had operated as a diffuse vigilante network in southern states after the Civil War, this second Klan had come into being in 1915 at a meeting of neo-Confederate sympathizers at Stone Mountain, Georgia. The Klan of the twentieth century spread throughout the nation, from Oregon to Maine, and eventually drew an estimated four to six million members, with a particularly strong membership in Indiana. From its beachhead in Evansville in 1920, just a few months after the organization of the Lincoln Inquiry, the Hoosier Klan grew to include one-fourth to one-third of Indiana males, making its membership larger than that of the state's Methodist churches. With a message that blended Lost Cause mythology, medieval English chivalry, religious primitivism, and one-hundred-percent patriotism, the Indiana Klan targeted primarily Catholics and foreign-born residents, though its rhetoric also mentioned blacks, adulterers, gamblers, prohibitions violators, and thrill-seeking teenagers. The national organization made its headquarters in Indianapolis from whence its leader, Grand Dragon D. C. Stephenson, coordinated national activities through the publication of a national newspaper that singled out enemies, identified Klan-friendly businesses, and endorsed political candidates. The Klan was particularly successful in Indiana's 1924 election, sweeping into power its gubernatorial candidate, Ed Jackson, and every state representative on the ballot.[11]

With the support of the Klan to pay back, incoming legislators promised to use the session of 1925 to root out corruption everywhere, especially in parochial schools and wherever they could identify Catholic influence. They threatened to consolidate the historical commission and reduce funding to the state library, thereby forestalling any hope Lieber had of seeking additional funding while simultaneously providing the context that pushed Christopher Coleman and John Iglehart into the truce that exchanged publication in state periodicals for a unified endorsement. Internal feuding among Klan-backed office holders and the traditional Hoosier resistance to state interference in education muted the Klan's attack on schools, and the historical commission survived. As the legislative session drew to a close in March, Grand Dragon Stephenson assaulted and raped an Indianapolis woman who then took poison and died in April. By November, Stephenson had been convicted of second-degree murder and sentenced to life in prison.[12] The Klan's formal organization withered quickly, Governor Jackson survived tenuously, and Lieber saw his opening in the resultant legacy of local racism and statewide shame. If Indiana's reputation had been blackened by the public sin of racism, could it not make restitution by erecting a tribute to the Hoosier boy who became the Great Emancipator?

In July 1926, Lieber invited two men to in his Indianapolis office for a private consultation about Indiana's reputation. Will Hays had grown up in the tiny town of Sullivan in southwestern Indiana and practiced law before entering politics. He chaired the Indiana Republican Party in 1916, led the Republican National Committee in 1918–1921, managed Warren G. Harding's 1920 presidential campaign, and was appointed Postmaster General in Harding's cabinet. In 1922, however, Hays resigned from the cabinet to accept a $100,000 salary (eight times his cabinet salary and more than Harding's) to lead the newly established Motion Picture Producers and Distributors of America, a pioneering public relations initiative designed to blunt media attacks on the debauchery of Hollywood. He therefore brought to Lieber's plan a combination of love for his home state, familiarity with Indiana politics, and experience in cleaning up after public relations disasters. Marcus Sonntag hailed from Evansville, headed the state's World War I memorial commission, and had campaigned throughout the state to marshal historical societies—including the Southwestern—into documenting and celebrating the state's participation in the Great War. He brought ties to the state's historical establishment and connections with donors who had supported monuments in the past. After a brief meeting that produced a ready consensus, the trio immediately took their idea to Governor Jackson, who excitedly endorsed the concept.[13] The plan would require a show of leadership, the mobilization of public support, and a manifestation of virtue directed at a nationwide audience. Along the way, it would strengthen Lieber's control over a statewide system of parks.

Five months later, on December 22, 1926, Governor Jackson published a proclamation (written by Lieber) declaring Indiana's desire to "pay off a debt of long standing which the people of our state owe to the memory of the greatest American whose life in the formative stages of his youth was spent in Indiana—Abraham Lincoln." The proclamation named officers, an executive committee, and one hundred twenty-five "ladies and gentlemen" who supported the formation of an Indiana Lincoln Union (ILU). The list read like a "Who's Who" in Indiana leadership circles at the time, including Republicans and Democrats, businessmen and authors, educators and the wives of former governors. Writers Booth Tarkington, Meredith Nicholson, and George Ade claimed places on the list, as did ten members of the Lincoln Inquiry, including Iglehart, Coleman, and Kiper. Albert Beveridge was also named, but a combination of ill health and strenuous exertion on his biography of Lincoln would contribute to his death by heart attack before the end of April. Anne Studebaker Carlisle presided over the ILU, Republican Hays and the widow of former Democratic senator John W. Kern (William Jennings Bryan's 1908 running mate) served as vice presidents, and Democratic political boss and French Lick resort owner Thomas Taggart kept the treasury. Lieber chaired the executive committee. Over the coming months, the rollout would include a graveside wreath laying, speeches, and a swank banquet in Indianapolis at which famous storyteller George Ade regaled potential donors.[14]

The push for public support began quickly as well. Governor Jackson's open letter was followed by a resolution of support from the state assembly in January 1927 and a public call for donations in February. "To Indiana belongs the privilege of caring for the grave of Nancy Hanks Lincoln," Jackson declared. "It is fitting that on the birthday of her son we should dedicate ourselves to the duty of erecting on the grounds where she lived and died a monument of our appreciation." Jackson's letter was published in the press, read in schools and churches, and endorsed by various local civic organizations. Throughout 1927, the campaign sponsored a series of newspaper advertisements and pamphlet publications, hosted a speech contest in schools, and organized fundraising districts throughout the state to manage mailing and door-to-door subscription requests. By setting the audacious goal of raising $1.25 million in a single year, organizers argued that Hoosiers would best show their appreciation for Lincoln by donating money toward the construction of his mother's memorial.[15]

The campaign appealed to Indianans in two primary ways. First, it drew on a long tradition of comparing Indiana to its neighbor states. From the earliest unofficial calls for a memorial to Lincoln, commentators had noted the elaborate tomb in Illinois (completed in 1874) and the magnificent Greek temples erected at Lincoln's Kentucky birthplace (1911) and in Washington, DC (1922). Editorials frequently reported that Kentucky or Illinois had "done its part" and complained that Indiana had "all but forgotten" or "done practically nothing." In September 1927, the Indiana Lincoln Union published a pamphlet with photographs and descriptions of existing Lincoln Memorials around the country. All of the Lincoln Union's newspaper advertisements ended with the challenge: "Fourteen states;—30 Cities in the United States—have Lincoln Memorials—Indiana has none. . . . What Will Indiana Do?"[16]

A second appeal invited the participation of Hoosier women on the basis of their womanhood and motherhood. During the 1920s, "new women" were casting their vote, striding into the workplace, and raising their hemlines. The Klan had already capitalized on growing concerns about the stability of traditional society by calling for a defense of virtuous womanhood. Governor Jackson's Lincoln proclamation picked up where his Klan-supported rhetoric left off, describing the campaign as an "opportunity to commemorate Abraham Lincoln's mother . . . the brave and gentle mother who gave him good faith and led him with a kindly hand for a little while along the path to greatness." Just after Lincoln's birthday in 1927, ILU president Anne Studebaker Carlisle made that visit to Nancy Lincoln's gravesite in which she imagined that the trees told her "the wonderful story" of Lincoln's carefree boyhood, his mother's death and burial, the tears they saw him shed, and his confession that his mother loved violets. Carlisle returned home and wrote up the experience in a letter to the governor that was published throughout the state. She closed the letter by inviting "every woman in the state of Indiana" to join in "paying their tribute to the wonderful pioneer woman and mother" buried in Spencer County. Three months later, in May 1927, Carlisle presided over a public ceremony at the grave in which she laid a wreath "in the name of Indiana mothers." She spoke to Nancy and mothers everywhere: "from this humble environment your influence, through your immortal son, has radiated around the world—a challenge to motherhood."[17] As

promotional materials for the site would later announce, "We are erecting here a shrine to Motherhood and the family hearthstone."[18]

Jackson and Lieber did not invent the image of a pioneer mother, but
in selecting it as the rallying cry of their campaign they wisely chose a
symbol of stability that also happened to have proven quite flexible in
adapting to a variety of causes. The massive societal translocations of the
industrial revolution had already provoked Progressive Era reformers to
protect women in the workplace and commemorate Mother's Day. During the first three decades of the twentieth century, sculptures, log cabins,
and forests dedicated to mothers sprang up in Kansas, Missouri, California, and Oregon. Midwestern writer Hamlin Garland won the Pulitzer
Prize for his biography of the daughters of the Middle West and followed
the book with a tribute titled *A Pioneer Mother.* The Daughters of the
American Revolution added a religious dimension when they commissioned twelve statues to pioneer mothers and children that dotted the
nation from Maryland in the east to California in the west along what
would later become U.S. Highways 40 and 66. These "Madonna of the
Trail" monuments celebrated the "vanishing womanhood" that had con-
quered the wilderness by establishing homes. The savage reality of the
recent world war and the growing industrialization of the nation prompted
calls for making homes the "saviors of civilization" that was threatened
by materialism, warfare, and bureaucracy.[19]

The image of a pioneer mother proved adaptable in many ways. In
Portland, Oregon, white women seeking to push their suffrage agenda
into the 1905 centennial of the Lewis and Clark expedition erected a
statue to Sacagawea as a "pioneer mother," thereby allowing a Native
American woman to symbolize their message of empowerment. In Santa
Fe, Native American rights activists protested the DAR's monument depicting an Anglo woman defending small children with a rifle.[20] The image also surfaced in Lincoln studies. In her first biography of Lincoln
published in 1900, Ida Tarbell devoted only half a sentence to Nancy's
death, and that merely to serve as a transition between moving from
Kentucky to the arrival of the new stepmother who brought books for
Abraham to read. Two-and-a-half decades later, however, Tarbell spoke
of the "irreparable tragedy" caused by Nancy's "sudden death" and
praised "this simple pioneer woman" for being "the mother of our greatest American." The question of motherhood likewise underlay the debate
raging between William Barton and Louis Warren about the births of
Abraham and Nancy. They had agreed that the son had been born within

the wedded bonds between Thomas and Nancy but fiercely challenged each other in Nancy's case.[21]

The pioneer mother, the public support, and the statewide leadership coalition all contributed to the campaign's major purpose of convincing the rest of the country—and particularly opinion shapers in the east— that Indiana had not lost its soul to the Klan. To that end, there seems to have been little debate among the executive committee of the ILU that the person most capable of designing a fitting memorial was Frederick Law Olmsted, Jr. Not only had Olmsted inherited his father's name and architectural firm; he had established his own reputation for promoting wildlife conservation and developing national parks.

After visiting the site in March 1927, Olmsted drew up a plan that would combine ecological and commemorative elements. He wanted to remove the lion statues and cast-iron gate near the entrance, to reroute a nearby railroad crossing and highway, and to replace exotic vegetation with frontier flora and fauna of the 1820s. He also proposed that this restored forest give way to an open commemorative walkway that connected the gravesite with a broad plaza featuring a colossal American flagpole. Characterizing the present site as a "town picnic grove" or "conventional 'landscape cemetery,'" Olmsted proposed creating a "Sanctuary" and explained to Lieber that "the controlling factor in the situation is the intimate association of this piece of land with certain events in the early life of Lincoln" and his "first great sorrow, which speaks directly from the grave where he buried his mother and from the vacant site of his early home." Olmsted felt it his "prime duty to let these simple familiar associations speak for themselves" for they were "capable . . . of arousing in any thoughtful and informed person ideas concerning Lincoln as deeply moving as any that can come to him."[22]

The entire project rode on the explicit rhetoric of religious redemption for the unspoken sins of the Klan. Governor Jackson's open letter called for a "spiritual awakening" in Indiana that would bring about the creation of what Lieber most frequently called a "shrine." Dating back to his closing of the park to auto traffic, Lieber had argued that the site's best purpose would be not as a "playground" or "a picnic ground, but rather as a shrine." It was Indiana's duty and opportunity "to hallow the ground where [Lincoln] spent his childhood and where his mother died." Olmsted's proposal offered only "sanctuary" for mediation, so the ILU added to his original design a massive cathedral-like building—a 200-square-foot structure containing a 150-foot tower, a large pipe organ,

After the Ku Klux Klan overran Indiana state politics in the mid-1920s, civic leaders hoped to clean up the state's image by erecting a shrine with this massive, cathedral-like memorial to Lincoln's mother. Participants in the Lincoln Inquiry protested the effort for its replacement of the totality of Indiana frontier experience with the veneration of a solitary, mythologized mother. Indiana Lincoln Union, *The Indiana Lincoln Memorial* (1938), 34.

and cloisters decorated with frescoes. Within Olmsted's frontier forest, the ILU would further add a trail of twelve stones retrieved from places significant to Lincoln's life, such as his birthplace, his store in New Salem, and the Illinois state capitol. Winding through the Hoosier hardwood trees, this trail provided an explicit connection to the Passion of Jesus Christ as commemorated in the twelve Stations of the Cross in Catholic liturgy.[23] With its cathedral and Christian symbolism, this shrine would not be a historic site cloaked in the language of "civil religion" but in fact a religious site devoted to the civic end of absolving Indiana's recent sins.

In the fall of 1927, the redemptive mission took on an even greater urgency. Throughout the early months of the initiative's rollout, Lieber had spoken openly about the fact that the site, as part of his statewide system of parks, would attract its share of an estimated 40 million annual American auto tourists.[24] The emphasis in Lieber's speeches shifted dramatically, however, after the general stain of the Klan attached itself to Governor Jackson personally. After the Klan's grand dragon Stephenson had received his final sentence, he expected to be pardoned by the man whom he had placed in office. When Jackson refused, Stephenson retaliated by revealing all of the Klan's ties to the state's public office holders. Lieber's typically perfunctory diary contains an entry for September 9, 1927, that reflects his concern over the revelation: *"Governor Jackson indicted by Marion Co. grand jury!"*[25] Though Jackson was acquitted on a technicality, his reputation, and the projects he had endorsed, suffered. Afterwards, Lieber's speeches suddenly emphasized the religious dimension: "Each tree that is planted, each stone that is laid, will have a spiritual value as significant as its utilitarian purpose in the completed Lincoln Memorial expression." The site would "perpetuate not only Lincoln's spirit as it existed in him, but also its influence upon our own lives. This shrine, therefore, can not be otherwise than a testimonial to our own intelligence, because it shall express our recognition and appreciation of those principles of honesty and tolerance that Lincoln exemplified."[26] From history to honesty, site to spirituality, trees to tolerance, Lieber made the leap of faith that Lincoln and his mother could atone for the Klan.

In December 1927, Lieber traveled to Washington, DC, to explain Indiana's mission to President Calvin Coolidge, hoping to secure an endorsement. As Lieber discussed world history, American settlement, midwestern pioneers, and the Lincoln Union's fundraising plans, he noted that Coolidge simply "sat and listened." Lieber later recalled, "The more he listened the more nervous I became. He has a habit of listening and looking at you and you never know just what is on his mind. Finally I blurted out that *certain things* that have happened in Indiana have shown that we need Lincoln more than ever and that we were very busy claiming him as a Hoosier." After two years in which Stephenson, the Klan, and eventually Governor Jackson made national headlines for continual revelations of repulsive and corrupt activities, both Coolidge and Lieber understood what "certain things" made Indiana "need Lincoln more than ever." That need drew out the state's civic leaders, prompted a campaign for public support, invoked interstate rivalry, and emphasized pioneer mothers and religious redemption as an antidote for contemporary Hoosier racism and Klan-led corruption. Coolidge simply smiled and endorsed the project.[27] If Indiana had earned the shameful reputation of being the place where modern mothers raised Klansmen, then certainly the time had come for it also to be known as the place where one mother raised the Great Emancipator.

Indiana's political climate pushed this battle for Indiana's past out of private and into public life. Backroom deals work best when kept secret while appeals to civics and state pride require a public hearing. The emphasis on motherhood and the appeal to Indiana women also placed women in leading public roles that had typically been occupied by men. Aside from the exceptional participation of Ida Tarbell, squabbling over Lincoln had been primarily a man's affair, best conducted in private smokers or in hotel rooms over cocktails. But the "new" women who entered the broader workplace of the 1920s created a demand for other women to step forward to defend tradition. Anne Carlisle was tapped to direct the ILU because of both her family wealth and her gender. The resultant campaign also transformed the place of gender in the public discussion of Lincoln's early life. It was one thing to debate Lincoln's paternity or the women he loved, but the discussion now transformed into a question of womanhood, both on the pioneer frontier and in the civic world of Indiana in the 1920s. Instead of exploring Nancy Lincoln's life on the frontier, this new schematic civic narrative brought assumptions about the necessarily blessed influence of inherently self-sacrificing mothers. This elevation of universal motherhood over a contextualized view of the Indiana frontier of the 1820s soon provoked the ire of the Lincoln Inquiry.

The Lincoln Inquiry versus . . . a Conspiracy?

Women had played a central role in the Lincoln Inquiry from its very inception. Though the idea originated with Iglehart, the development of bylaws and a constitution had occurred in conversation with half a dozen women who would become the society's founding members. Bess Ehrmann, Albion Fellows Bacon, and Deidré Johnson had proven some of the most able of workers and after the fallout between Iglehart and de la Hunt they had been summoned into an informal "kitchen cabinet" that directed much of the society's internal affairs. Women comprised 60 percent of the society's membership and, as the years passed, they contributed an increasing number of papers at society meetings, from one of every nine in 1920 to one of every three in 1926. Women had also come to occupy a majority of the society's elected offices, from one-quarter in 1920 to two-thirds in 1926. In the fall of 1926, while Lieber and Jackson worked out their plans for the Indiana Lincoln Union, members of the Lincoln Inquiry finally persuaded Bess Ehrmann to accept the society's presidency.

Women had long been active in public efforts to preserve and commemorate American history. In the nineteenth century, individual women worked in local communities, and organized women's groups had hosted successful campaigns to preserve George Washington's Mount Vernon estate, Andrew Jackson's Hermitage in Tennessee, and the Alamo in Texas. Though such monuments appear traditional by modern standards, they represented important avenues for women of the time to engage in contemporary political issues. At Mount Vernon, for example, women from the north and south tried to unite the nation around Washington's memory on the eve of the Civil War. In southern states, the monuments erected by the United Daughters of the Confederacy moved beyond mere commemoration into the creation of a new Confederate tradition bent on vindication. Yet, though they had been active in public history for decades, women began to feel themselves being squeezed out by the 1920s as a new generation of male "professionals" moved into the field.[28] The Indiana Lincoln Union's use of Anne Carlisle illustrates this development. The selection of Ehrmann recognized her credentials and responded to politics within the Lincoln Inquiry.

Ehrmann's name had been proposed in 1922 to become the society's second president after Iglehart, but she declined on account of her school teaching, family responsibilities, and active club work. She continued to decline the invitation, even after Iglehart's rift with de la Hunt. The society's third president, Roscoe Kiper, brought necessary political experience, but he also aspired to write the definitive history of Lincoln in Indiana, so during his tenure he prohibited the publication of society papers and demanded that all stenographic reports—including those of the "best witnesses"—remain in his possession. By 1926, Iglehart suspected de la Hunt and Kiper of planning to "make a combination" to remove Spencer, Perry, and Warrick counties from the society. When approached again in September 1926, Ehrmann begged, "*Please* name some one beside me," but after two months of persuading she accepted. A high school drama teacher, a close friend of Ida Tarbell and Tommy de la Hunt, one of the "best witnesses," and the author of a thorough defense of the Lincoln Inquiry's rationale and accomplishments, Bess Ehrmann assumed the presidency of the society in February 1927 at the same time that Anne Carlisle's letter about the friendly trees hit Indiana newspapers. As president, Ehrmann rewrote the society's bylaws to match its practice and began to systematically collect and archive the papers presented at meetings. She also coordinated the response to the Indiana Lincoln Union.[29]

The inclusion of ten members of the Southwestern Indiana Historical Society among the one hundred twenty-five organizers of the Indiana Lincoln Union was originally taken as a compliment to the society's prominence, but the warm feelings quickly cooled. At the public unveiling of Olmsted's design, it became apparent that decision-making for the project would occur within tight political circles in Indianapolis. As a result, the ILU asked the Southwestern simply to provide a list of the flora and fauna that would have greeted the Lincolns upon their arrival in 1816.[30] Iglehart expressed his concern to Coleman, who shared and stoked it. Coleman had already "urged" Lieber and the ILU executive secretary Paul Brown to "recognize all organizations and workers already in the field." But, as a fellow operative in Indianapolis politics, Coleman had already observed that Lieber's "method of work in all matters is to proceed with his own plans without making much effort to co-ordinate other organizations." And though Lieber was "very competent and effective," he was also "rather inconsiderate." Iglehart or Ehrmann were not excluded from any meetings because none were held. But Coleman also encouraged patience: "I believe the whole development shows that there has been no intentional slighting of anybody and no tendency whatever to belittle the Southwestern Indiana Society." Both Coleman and former senator (and Southwestern member) D. Frank Culbertson of Vincennes began to lobby to place Ehrmann on the executive committee. Because Lieber was raising good money and doing good work, Coleman recommended supporting him, however tactless his methods.[31]

If Coleman's letter placated Iglehart, the fundraising banquet in Indianapolis pushed him over the edge. There, in the midst of the state's movers and shakers, the ILU praised and fêted Louis Warren as its Lincoln expert. For the purposes of the state's redemptive mission, Warren made a good fit. He was both a pastor and a historian, and his meticulous documentary study *Lincoln's Parentage & Childhood* (1926) depicted Thomas Lincoln as a hard-working pioneer father and defended both his marriage and that of his wife's parents against the charges of illegitimate childbirth. At a meeting of the Southwestern in 1924 he had, in fact, eulogized Nancy Hanks as one of many pioneer mothers who "suffered most in the birth of western civilization." His acceptance of a new pastorate in an Indianapolis suburb made him readily available to give public lectures on behalf of the Lincoln Union. But Iglehart had not forgotten Warren's December 1924 critique of the Lincoln Inquiry that prompted the meeting of the "best witnesses." More threateningly, from his new home in Indianapolis Warren now contemplated a second volume on Lincoln's Indiana years.[32]

Seeing the ascent of Warren into the inner circle of the ILU exacerbated longstanding tensions between Hoosiers in the southern and northern parts of the state, tensions that had already been exposed in the efforts of state history workers to engulf the Lincoln Inquiry under a centralized agenda. Part of the differences stemmed from the state's settlement history—its northern residents had come from New England while the southern residents migrated from the Carolinas and Virginia through Kentucky and across the Ohio River. Southern Indiana developed into a distinctive sub-region of the state, dominated in the nineteenth century by intense localism in government, economics, and moral behavior that left southern Hoosiers democratic in a republican state, agricultural in an emerging market economy, Calvinistic amidst an ethos of postmillennial perfectionism. By the 1920s, science had come to the aid of Hoosiers in the north as enterprising eugenicists in Indianapolis had begun to systematically document the differences of the "Kentucky Hill-Folk" in the southern counties and to lobby for government programs to sterilize or institutionalize them. For their part, southerners resented northern intervention. Iglehart personally writhed under the "New England spirit of condescension and the central and northern Indiana spirit of flunkeyism, which looks to the man higher up and seeks for a man lower down to be kicked."[33]

In Iglehart's view, the sudden elevation of Warren and the actions of Indianapolis politicians pointed to a deeper threat that he traced to the late Albert Beveridge. When Beveridge ran for public office in Indiana he had skillfully tied up resources and blocked out competitors. Was not the same thing happening in the politics of Lincoln's Indiana history? Beveridge had secured from Jesse Weik sole access to William Herndon's notes and had drafted a chapter that thoroughly reinforced the erroneous stereotype of southern Indiana. Though Beveridge had not lived to finish his biography, William Barton had published a two-volume biography of Lincoln that contained an obscure reference to the value of building a monument to Nancy Hanks Lincoln in Indiana. Barton was a known partisan of the impact of Kentucky and Illinois on Lincoln and he had been present during the December 1924 attack by Warren and Beveridge. Kiper and de la Hunt had expressed their approval of state history activities, and now Warren, the erstwhile attacker, stood as the single historical adviser to a statewide campaign aimed at raising over one million dollars to commemorate an artificial pioneer mother on the very landscape of southern Indiana. The more he looked over the field, the more Iglehart saw the connections between Beveridge, Barton, Warren, and the Indiana Lincoln Union—the Lincoln Inquiry now faced a unified conspiracy. Iglehart never spelled out the entire conspiracy in writing, though at times he came close, despite the passages that he blacked out of his letters. Warren's new role in Indianapolis surely suggested that he was picking up where the late Beveridge had left off.[34]

Iglehart's colleagues dismissed his conspiracy theory. Deidré Johnson did not think the state had snubbed southern Indiana, Ehrmann reasoned that "*at least* we are causing the up state people to know we live down here," and Coleman continued to urge restraint. As they lobbied the governor to place Iglehart and Ehrmann on the ILU executive committee, society member Frank Culbertson of Vincennes reasoned that the Inquiry simply suffered from "thick-headedness on the part of those starting the movement."[35]

With the jury out on the existence of a conspiracy, the Lincoln Inquiry nonetheless returned a unanimous verdict on the inadequacy of the state's proposed pioneer mother monument. They saw no use for a redemptive mother to atone for the sins of the entire state and preferred instead a monument to a frontier boy who could typify the experiences and attributes of all of their ancestors. The Lincoln Inquiry did not challenge the interpretation of Lincoln as the Great Emancipator, but its workers differed from civic leaders in locating the sources of Lincoln's greatness in the collective environment on the frontier rather than his singular mother. This nuance between the frontier story and the civic story is significant in light of the fact that studies of Lincoln's memory and image in American culture treat the Great Emancipator as an image that had appeal after the

Civil War but declined in the twentieth century. In his prize-winning study *Race and Reunion: The Civil War in American Memory,* David Blight argued that the national impulse for sectional unity squeezed out concerns for African Americans and their rights and that by 1915 reconciliation overwhelmed emancipation. Sociologist Barry Schwartz attributed the decline of Lincoln's emancipator image to the new nationalism "forged" in the first decades of the twentieth century.[36] And yet, in the midst of the 1920s the image remained central to the civic mission of Indianapolis politicians. In Indiana, the division was the byproduct not simply of nationalism or worldwide wars but also of regional rivalries and local legacies. In the Hoosier state, the contest did not divide along national or racial lines so much as it did along lines of place and practice, region and interpretation. This struggle reveals that the most meaningful contests to interpret and commemorate the past occur not on the Mall in Washington but in spaces closer to home.

At the June 1927 meeting of the Southwestern, Iglehart introduced a resolution calling on the Lincoln Union to expand its memorial proposal to include "a somewhat broader phase so as to cover the subject of Pioneerhood and Frontier life of Abraham Lincoln in Indiana," and, conditioned upon such an interpretive move, he offered the society's "unqualified support in its undertaking and the use of said material and data." Privately, Iglehart fired off letters to Ida Tarbell, Frederick Jackson Turner, and Carl Sandburg, reporting recent developments and asking for an endorsement of the society's resistance. Tarbell responded that Olmsted's plan was "an uplifting suggestion, and so fitting"; she hoped it succeeded. Turner praised Olmsted's desire to remove modern obstructions, liked the monumental flag pole, and thought the only thing missing would be a monument "to the 'pioneer mother,'" just as the DAR was erecting, provided that "funds and the *right* sculptor could be found."[37] Had the conspiracy reached even Tarbell and Turner?

Iglehart politely explained to Turner that an overemphasis on Lincoln's mother would obscure the significance of Lincoln's experience on the Indiana frontier. "We recognize that proper recognition should and no doubt it will be given to Nancy Hanks Lincoln," he wrote, "We also appreciate that Abraham Lincoln, the Emancipator, is recognized as such throughout the world." However, "this Society recognizes you as the first true interpreter of the frontier in American history," and "we ask your judgment upon the question of whether or not there should be, and if so what, recognition of Abraham Lincoln as a pioneer." Turner caught the implications and responded to Iglehart with a rigorous endorsement of the Lincoln Inquiry's work, an application of his frontier thesis to the Indiana memorial, and permission to use the letter when necessary. "Your society, (the work of which I have followed with interest and profit)," Turner wrote, "does well, in my opinion, to study the life and conditions of the pioneer folk of the region which gave birth to Lincoln and to that Indiana society which influenced him in his formative years. To write of him, or to perpetuate his memory by an Indiana memorial without emphasis on the frontier phase of his life, without adequate recognition of this pioneer society and its ideals, would be 'like the play of Hamlet with the Hamlet left out.' " The memorial "must take full account of the place of the frontier" because "Lincoln represented what was best in frontier qualities." The letter rises to a poetic climax: "It is, as you say, well to recognize Lincoln's frontier mother. It is well also to celebrate Lincoln, the 'Emancipator', and Lincoln the 'Savior of the Union.' But, fundamentally, all these things are causally related to the Lincoln whose ancestors pioneered from New England through the Middle States and the South to the new West; to the native of Kentucky; to the Lincoln of the woods of Indiana and the prairies of Illinois; to the Lincoln of the frontier." From a monumental standpoint, this meant that "the axe and the log cabin (symbol of the neighborly house-raising) and the rails that fenced the clearing of the pioneer should be part of the work of the sculptor or architect who would commemorate Abraham Lincoln."[38] From a story-telling standpoint, Turner and Iglehart cast Lincoln as a character on Indiana's past frontier instead of its contemporary civics. Armed with Turner's authoritative endorsement, the Lincoln Inquiry was ready to challenge the Indiana Lincoln Union.

In August, ILU executive secretary Paul Brown contacted Iglehart to secure the cooperation of the Lincoln Inquiry with the ILU in general and with Warren in particular. Iglehart simply forwarded Turner's endorsement of the Lincoln Inquiry and refused to work with Warren. In a flurry of letters, phone calls, and a closed-door meeting at the French Lick Resort at which no minutes were taken, Iglehart issued a warning and an ultimatum. "I warn you against permitting Warren to steer you," Iglehart wrote to Brown. Though the ILU probably did not know it, Warren was an "evil genius" at the head of a "historical cult." All of the pieces fit together: Beveridge began a biography that ignored the Indiana frontier, Barton predicted a park that celebrated only the pioneer mother instead of the entire community, Warren was appointed spokesman to attack the Lincoln Inquiry in public while Beveridge and Barton looked on, and the Lincoln Union had been manipulated into focusing on Nancy at the expense of the southern Indiana frontier. The "Beveridge spike is over your organization from the bottom and foresides to the roof." Characterizing the ILU as "a self-constituted committee, self-created, self-perpetuating, responsible to nobody but their executive committee," Iglehart explained that the Lincoln Inquiry had not yet published a systematic summary of its work and would not share its findings unless the ILU made amends "in good faith" for "the most offensive snub of the Governor."[39]

No doubt the person most surprised by this accusation was Warren. He, like all of the persons named by Iglehart, had cooperated with Beveridge, but in the end each felt abused by Beveridge and jealous of the others. Weik was angered by Barton's attack on Herndon (and implicitly on himself), but when he asked Beveridge to refute Barton in a book review the former senator declined because he had convinced the reluctant Bobbs-Merrill publishing house to take Barton's biography in the first place.[40] But though Beveridge had helped Barton publish, he had also hamstrung Barton's work by persuading Weik not to share the Herndon notes with Barton.[41] Beveridge had also offered his influence with publishers to Warren, but when Warren ultimately decided not to share his notes Beveridge blocked publication while professing his sincerest (two-faced) regrets.[42] Even Beveridge ended up skeptical of all the others and afraid that any public comment about his research would lead to theft of archival materials.[43] Warren and Barton feuded both in public and in private, and in correspondence with all but Warren, Barton alternated between calling Warren his "pupil" and criticizing his work.[44] Bewildered by Beveridge and Barton, Warren moved toward Tarbell, criticized Herndon, and further alienated his competitors.[45] In reality, Warren's December 1924 talk criticized everyone in the field, but Iglehart had seen only the attack on the Lincoln Inquiry.

Still not convinced of the existence of a conspiracy and not wanting to burn all bridges with the ILU, Iglehart's colleagues began to work around him. Ehrmann corresponded with Warren and reported that he "spoke in glowing terms" about the work of the Lincoln Inquiry. Warren explained that Iglehart had not been placed on the executive committee because the appointments had gone to people who donated the most money. Coleman made inquiries of all his contacts in Indianapolis and removed all doubt about the ILU being manipulated by Warren and the ghost of Beveridge. "You were dead wrong about Warren being at the bottom of this whole thing," Coleman wrote to Iglehart. Brown had simply found Warren's book in the state library and, upon learning that he lived in Indianapolis, invited Warren to give lectures. "The whole plan," Coleman explained, "is the creation of the Department of Conservation, which I think really means that the inception and control lies in Richard Lieber." And, unfortunately, Coleman did not have the authority to interfere with another state department. Rising above the contention, Coleman reminded Iglehart that the question of historical flora and fauna remained most important and should not be lost in the struggle.[46]

With Iglehart somewhat mollified—and with Governor Jackson's Klan indictment making headlines across the country—Lieber and Brown offered a compromise. They proposed the formation of a historical research committee, chaired by Coleman, to oversee cooperation between Warren and the Lincoln Inquiry. Coleman declined and recommended Ehrmann, to which Lieber agreed only if Warren could retain the role of special adviser. Iglehart accepted the structure, but only in conjunction with a signed statement on the arrangements from Lieber, an explicit endorsement from the ILU of the work of the Lincoln Inquiry, and a written statement from Warren explaining his December 1924 address.[47] After nearly two months of negotiation, Brown complied. He sent notices to state newspapers about the committee and the Lincoln Inquiry and compelled Warren to respond in writing as a condition of maintaining his appointment as a lecturer and receiving an appointment as special adviser. Warren, who aspired to a full-time Lincoln research career and who barely made ends meet as a pastor, saw no option but to comply.[48]

Warren began cautiously, "I will gladly comply with your request for a written statement as to my interpretation of my address," and followed with an itemized response: he had never "entertained in [his] mind a single thought of hostility" toward the society, did not know until recently that the paper had caused a controversy, was unaware of the charges made against him at the Princeton "best witnesses" meeting, had long cherished the idea of researching Lincoln and therefore did not undertake "a deliberate invasion of the Indiana field" or "any attempt to assault or attack the organization or any of its members." As for the paper itself, Warren explained that he had chosen the subject of his own will and "certainly intended to cast no reflections on the good start that had been made" by the Lincoln Inquiry. By means of a hypothetical situation, Warren tried to argue the contrary: "having in mind the author in New York [i.e., Tarbell] who might be trying to write a history on Lincoln in Indiana, without the necessary atmosphere and without any means of testing the reliability of his source material in the form of bibliography," Warren argued that such a "production would or might be 'readable but not reliable.' " On the other hand, the Lincoln Inquiry comprised "historians who were on the ground to test the reliability of the source material that came to hand." Warren closed with a declaration of innocence blended with an apology: "If I felt that I had been guilty of any intentional wrong towards the society I should be very glad to apologise for it, and if my presentation of my subject matter was so faulty as to convey a meaning which I did not intend, I regret it very much." Iglehart accepted the apology, and the working arrangement with the ILU.[49]

Yet in Warren's statement, Iglehart also found evidence for the Beveridge conspiracy. Because Warren had provided "no excuse," he therefore, "in substance and by necessary inference, although in an evasive manner," had also produced "an absolute confession."[50] This evidence steeled Iglehart to keep up the fight. Beveridge's widow announced that her husband's incomplete manuscript would be prepared for publication by Worthington C. Ford, the editor of numerous presidential papers and a former president of the American Historical Association. Using "Best Witness" Will Fortune to gain an introduction to Ford through Mrs. Beveridge, Iglehart welcomed this "last chance to mitigate the infamous chapter 2 of Beveridge in his estimate of the people of early Indiana." On the same day that he demanded of Brown a written explanation from Warren, Iglehart wrote what he termed "a polite but somewhat ominous letter" to Ford. Two days later, Iglehart went to New York City, only to find that Ford had deliberately missed their meeting. Ford did accept Iglehart's offer to send him material by mail, and over the next four months, the former lawyer filled Ford's mailbox, sometimes daily, with lengthy letters and research materials—articles, notes, dictations, and lists of prominent southern Indiana pioneers. When it became clear that Ford only wanted to know if Lincoln's neighbors had southern ancestry and that he would not tell Iglehart what, if any changes, he was making to the chapter on Indiana, the correspondence broke down.[51]

Meanwhile, the ILU historical research committee foundered. At the October 1927 meeting of the Southwestern Indiana Historical Society, the members passed a resolution "heartily and unreservedly" endorsing the Lincoln Union and pledging "support and assistance" in the project. During the lunchtime intermission, Ehrmann convened the committee, but attendees—including Warren—spent most of the hour trying to discern the committee's role. Logan Esarey expressed his "amuse[ment] at the situation in which Rev. Warren was placed" but observed that the Lincoln Union had called its own meeting on the same day in Indianapolis "so that no one with even presumptive authority would be present in Petersburg." He believed the Union meant to leave the committee in the dark so that the "sentiment of the state which is very kindly toward Lincoln is to be liquidated." Coleman confided to Iglehart that Lieber was so devoted to raising money that "he did not make any definite promise of turning over any particular authority to this committee."[52]

Still hoping to make a difference, Ehrmann wrote Brown asking for a clarification of the committee's role and duties. Lieber gave the committee a triple mandate to identify Indiana's influence on Lincoln, provide a report of flora and fauna to the building committee, and "disseminate such information." He also asked them to "eliminate . . . the vast amount of controversy over alleged incidents in Lincoln's life in Indiana."[53] Though Iglehart had hoped for some interpretive authority and for some control over the project's spending, Lieber offered neither. The mandate was both vague and unhelpful. The only specific task had been assigned months earlier when Olmsted asked for a list of flora and fauna. At the February 1928 meeting of the Southwestern, Ehrmann appointed three sub-committees to study frontier flora and fauna and to identify events suitable for inscriptions or depictions in murals, but none of the committees seems to have produced any reports that were forwarded to the Lincoln Union.

The work of identifying frontier flora and fauna was seized by George Wilson. Drawing on his surveyor experience and vast private collection of local history data, Wilson set out on his own to identify the ecological elements of the Lincolns' Indiana frontier. By the first part of January 1928, he produced a comprehensive and illustrated report titled "The Lincoln Forest, Field, Flora, and Family, 1816–1830." Continuing the Lincoln Inquiry's emphasis on neighbors, the report opened with a list of residents and a map of their property acquisitions. Using period surveyor reports from the early nineteenth century, Wilson documented water resources and the location of a brook, commented on the impact of the region's elevation, and identified forty-two types of trees and twenty-three vines and bushes, noting the relative composition of the forest. Iglehart called the report "a gem" and Ehrmann pronounced it "the most perfect report in every way." A copy of it arrived on Lieber's desk by the end of the month.[54] As a result of the struggle with the Lincoln Inquiry, Lieber's stock speech that he gave throughout the state contained a new paragraph describing the ILU proposal not simply as a tribute to Lincoln's mother but as "a memorial to Indiana's pioneer environment."[55]

BY THE time Wilson's report on flora and fauna reached Lieber, the conservator had put the fundraising campaign in full stride. Some Hoosiers responded to the twin appeals to motherhood and interstate rivalry, but the ILU did not reach its goal of $1.25 million before the stock market crash of 1929. That year additional property passed into the possession of the state; one year later, 9,000 trees were donated and planted.[56] Iglehart's relationship with Warren, Brown, and Lieber remained tense—"there may be dynamite still there," he wrote—but uneventful. Iglehart reported to Coleman that he had grown "tired of too much friction" and concluded that he and the other society members had "won our fight for life."[57]

After his clash with the Lincoln Inquiry Warren feared that his career in the Lincoln field was drawing to a close, as the demands of supporting his family required more attention to his pastoral position. But, in February 1928, while giving a speech in Ft. Wayne, Warren impressed Arthur Hall of the Lincoln National Life Insurance Company. Founded in 1905, the company had grown successful, and its managers now sought a way to repay their debt to Lincoln's memory. They hired Warren to build a research library and manage an outreach program that would include lectures and a monthly bulletin. Accepting a salary that nearly doubled that of his Indianapolis position, Warren became a full-time Lincoln professional and moved out of direct competition with the Lincoln Inquiry.

As the Indiana Lincoln Union rolled forward and Warren moved to Ft. Wayne, Albert Beveridge's biography of Lincoln was published. Though he had envisioned four volumes, Beveridge had drafted only two of them before his death. Ford's editing amounted to little more than touching up grammatical errors and rounding out source citations—the text of the Indiana chapter remained almost identical to the draft seen in 1924 by the Lincoln Inquiry. Beveridge cited "Best Witnesses" Murr on the poverty and superstitions of southern Hoosiers and Fortune on the book of dirty jokes Lincoln read while in Indiana. The text denied that Lincoln borrowed books from Brackenridge, though a footnote acknowledged that Kiper believed Lincoln did so. In Beveridge's hand, the pioneers of southern Indiana were ignorant, superstitious, dirty, immodest, and drunken.[58]

Early reviews of Beveridge's *Life of Lincoln* were mixed. Some offered praise for a diligent public servant and recently deceased researcher. The *Chicago Tribune* called it a "stupendous piece of work," and Beveridge's friend and future biographer Claude Bowers complimented the "Lincoln of reality" found within its pages. Paul Angle of the Lincoln Centennial Association guessed that Beveridge "probably utilized more source material than any other" biographer, but Beveridge's friend and fellow Lincoln biographer Nathaniel Stephenson thought the work's thick background got away from its subject. William Barton called the work "a noble fragment," praising its depiction of Lincoln as a politician but criticizing its heavy reliance on the recollections of Herndon's informants (which Beveridge had blocked from Barton). Fresh from publishing a two-volume biography of Lincoln's early years and still stinging from the criticism levied by academics, Carl Sandburg judged that Beveridge only "rattles the dry bones of Lincoln." In the *Indiana Magazine of History,* Richard Arnold Tilden echoed Barton's criticism of the extensive use of Herndon material as a "lack of adequate sources" that "caused misstatements of facts." Tilden suggested that, as a "result of his legal and political training," Beveridge accepted "unproved statements" and "unverified and misleading sources" simply on the basis of their contemporaneousness and not on the basis of verifiability. Iglehart called Barton's review a "sledge-hammer attack" and felt that Beveridge's critique of the Lincoln Inquiry could now be put to rest.[59]

Though it secured official recognition and a formal assignment from the Indiana Lincoln Union, the Lincoln Inquiry failed to alter the ILU's overarching schematic narrative. Both the Lincoln Inquiry's efforts to situate the Lincolns in Indiana's frontier and its competitors' attempts to isolate Lincoln biographically from his Indiana neighbors lost out to the state's quest for civic redemption. The image of Nancy Lincoln as a pioneer mother and the development of a site commemorating her alone grew out of the desire of Hoosier politicians to rescue the state's reputation in the wake of the Ku Klux Klan scandals that reached all the way to the governor's office. The frontier and biographical narratives were replaced with a civic narrative that occupied the Lincoln family homestead.

The exchange also illustrates the power of schematic narratives to shape modern historical practice. Iglehart's conspiracy theory provided a storyline that helped him make sense of his interactions with competitors in the present. The power of schematic narratives is reflected in the reluctance of both the ILU and Iglehart to relinquish their storylines in light of contrary evidence. These overarching narratives frame not only the understanding of the past, but also the understanding of ongoing historical work.

For nearly a decade, the Lincoln Inquiry had defended its right to practice history, to employ oral testimony, to interpret the history of Indiana's frontier, and to participate in statewide commemoration activities. At each juncture the demands of the present contest overwhelmed the Inquiry's ability to make a positive statement of its findings. Always on the defensive, the Lincoln Inquiry had yet to offer its own comprehensive picture of Lincoln's frontier environment. The failure to change the commemorated message at Nancy Hanks Lincoln Park and the failure to persuade Beveridge or his editor forced the Lincoln Inquiry to rethink its relationship with the general public and to experiment with new ways of publishing its findings. In order to synthesize its sprawling work for the public, the Lincoln Inquiry would have to shift from defense to offense.

6

In the Lincoln Atmosphere

THROUGHOUT THE decade of the 1920s, the Lincoln Inquiry took its message to the American public in a variety of ways. When the society was organized, its members expressed the vague belief that if they researched southern Indiana's frontier environment then their correct findings would be cited by future writers. However, through their clashes with Indiana's public history establishment, the state's civic promoters, and Albert Beveridge and other Lincoln biographers, they slowly learned that it was not enough just to research about the past and publish in obscure journals—they needed to put their findings into a format that was both accessible and engaging to the widest range of persons possibly interested. In time, participants in the Lincoln Inquiry synthesized their findings for the public by designing a photograph exhibit, hosting pageants, experimenting with film, building a historical village, taking students into local archives, and writing for scholarly and public readerships.

Each of the Lincoln Inquiry's individual efforts to synthesize its findings for the public shared a common assumption about engaging public interest. Just as their research sought to put Lincoln in the context of life on the Indiana frontier of the 1820s, participants in the Lincoln Inquiry wanted to immerse the modern public in the environment and atmosphere of the past. A cartoon that ran in the *Evansville Courier* in 1922 perhaps best illustrates the application of this immersive objective. In the foreground, a beautiful young maiden identified as the Society escorts a stubby fellow, labeled "Public," through an open gateway in a thick brick wall that protects what appears to be a paradisiacal "Land of Romance-Sentiment-Knowledge." Walking arm-in-arm with the woman, the "Public" says, "Indeed we owe you much for maintaining such as this," to which the Society replies "Our pleasure!"[1] Here the past is conceived not as something lifeless in need of memorization but rather as something real to be encountered and entered. Knowledge about the past was united with romance or excitement and sentiment or feeling. In this journey of collective discovery, the Lincoln Inquiry's role became one of escorting,

The Lincoln Inquiry approached the public as a partner willing to be immersed in the environment and atmosphere of the past. Members conceived of the past not as something lifeless in need of memorization, but rather as something real to be encountered in the present. In this journey of collective discovery, the Lincoln Inquiry's role became one of escorting, guiding, and welcoming the public into a place it has never been but at which it is grateful to arrive. *Evansville Courier,* January 29, 1922.

guiding, and welcoming the public into a place it had never been but where it was grateful to arrive. Christopher Coleman explained, "We do not want to live in the past, but we want to make the past live in the present." For Deidré Johnson, this approach helped people to "feel that our lives are interlocking, dependent on other lives, some that have gone before." In this imagined immersion in a reconstructed past, the Lincoln Inquiry used old photographs, historic sites, and dramatic narrations to enable the public to, in the words of the *Courier*'s owner, a Lincoln Inquiry member, "drink in the historical atmosphere" and thereby "absorb so much of Lincoln and his life" as to feel "a part of the early settlers."[2]

Of course, the Lincoln Inquiry did not invent photographic curation, historical pageantry, or historic preservation. Neither did its productions engage contemporary practitioners in those fields in the way that its work had engaged the field of Lincoln studies. Nevertheless, the participants' efforts to disseminate their findings to public audiences reveal the tensions between research and presentation, discovery and synthesis, argumentation and experience. By aspiring to the idea of immersing the audience in an experience of the Indiana frontier, the Lincoln Inquiry displayed a range of practical applications and a willingness to experiment with new media. By bringing together many of the society's findings, the Lincoln Inquiry sought an elusive public synthesis that would be rhetorically, rationally, and experientially persuasive enough to immerse the audience in the Lincoln atmosphere.

Words, Pictures, and Character

In 1920, the Lincoln Inquiry began with incomplete assumptions about the process of sharing its findings with the public. Iglehart and the society's ablest workers fought mightily against the entrenched public history practitioners in Indiana and ultimately worked out a deal by which the state historical commission published the papers deemed most worthy of publication by the society's internal publications committee. Occasionally, additional papers appeared in the *Indiana Magazine of History* or as installments in the state historical society's publication series. The result, however, was far from successful. Coleman reported to Iglehart that reviewers typically "display no great enthusiasm" for the volumes of society papers, with the most common complaint noting a lack of source citations. He increasingly steered the society members' writing away from "excessive wordiness" and subtly pushed for "documentary evidence and strictly contemporary witnesses."[3]

   Though Lincoln biographers did scoop up individual findings, the
Lincoln Inquiry's new interpretation of the Indiana frontier garnered mixed
acceptance. A doctoral student at Indiana University named Charles G.
Vannest adopted the approach almost entirely for his self-published dissertation, *Lincoln the Hoosier* (1928), but reviewers likewise criticized
its lack of citations.[4] On the other hand, Albert Beveridge rejected the
interpretation in his lifetime, and his editor would not adapt the work after
his death. When it became clear that Worthington Ford would not adjust
Beveridge's interpretation of the southern Indiana frontier, the Lincoln
Inquiry once again set out to respond to Beveridge. This time, instead of
calling the "best witnesses" to the stand, members invited the audience to
look into the faces of Lincoln's long-departed neighbors.
   Before Beveridge's book was published, Iglehart circulated a copy of
the draft of chapter two among the Lincoln Inquiry's able workers. He
was correct in guessing that the final version changed very little and he
probably could have predicted the response of his colleagues. An unsigned
response, which appears to be by Albion Bacon, notes "a large amount of
disgusting material in this chapter" concerning living conditions and speech.
Deidré Johnson took a pragmatic stance. "It will do *no* good to rail with
sermons or threats hurled at such men as Beveridge or Ford—it will be
but a beating of wings against a wall," she reasoned. "I do not personally
take the extreme view of a few of the active workers in our Society, that
such a portrayal of pioneers is a disgrace to the memory of our Indiana
pioneers," but she did object to "his *generalizing* for *pages* in the most
graphic terms, from just this one low type" of pioneer to all others. Iglehart
objected to the "cat and dog idea of sex life."[5] When the published volume came out in September 1928, they listed six objectionable statements within a four-page span that cast Lincoln's neighbors (their ancestors) as men *and* women who were "ignorant, rough mannered, vividly
superstitious" consumers of "incredible quantities of whiskey" and to-
bacco, and inclined to "chewing, smoking, snuffing, and corn cob pipes
puffing." Their "sense of modesty was embryonic," they lived in cabins
that were "ill-kept, dirty in the extreme, infested with vermin," and their
"fighting and swearing were accompanied by low thinking, repellant living, filthy talk."[6] Once again, as in the work of Eggleston, the rude lower
class of pioneer society had been substituted for the whole of it.
   In public, society members expressed their anger. Speaking at the society's meeting in June 1928, Ehrmann cited the letters, linen samplers,
silver heirlooms, furniture, and documents "that showed that those early
people of Southern Indiana were worth while people." "I am sure it makes

your blood boil," she charged, "as it makes mine boil to read articles by
historians who say that the people of early times in Southwestern Indiana were the 'scum' of the earth." But the conversation also broadened
beyond rage. At the October meeting Lucius Embree pointed out that
"the people of Southwestern Indiana haven't kept many records," and
artist George Honig reported having collected much relevant data. Iglehart felt that "instead of being excited and abusive or denunciatory," society members "ought to state the facts and deal with the controversy in
a humorous quasi sarcastic vein, which the facts may justify, granting all
the time, all of the merits and good things that may be said in favor of
Senator Beveridge in his lifetime." And, this time around, the best "antidote to the Beveridge poison" would be to publish their findings.[7]

The first strike followed the established pattern of presenting at a
meeting a paper that would be published by the state, but this instance
also brought a new twist. At the October meeting, Ehrmann, Johnson,
and Bacon challenged Beveridge's work and stood up in defense of their
ancestors who could no longer speak for themselves. In much the same
way that the "best witnesses" had responded on behalf of Lincoln's
neighbors at the 1925 meeting in Princeton, Ehrmann introduced the
program: "The noted people that I have chosen to speak about were all
residents of Spencer County during the fourteen years that the Lincolns
lived there, and it was my privilege to see them, to talk to them, and to
note what type of people they were." Ehrmann denied that her grand-
mother had drunk whiskey or smoked a pipe, and Johnson refused to
allow her ancestors to be "thrown . . . en masse into the ranks of 'drunken
plowmen and women of uncertain morals'!" The trio of women also
articulated the basis for their authoritative presentation of evidence.
Ehrmann emphasized that they spoke "from our memories" and "it was
my privilege to see them, to talk to them, and to note what type of people
they were." She also philosophized about how to understand individuals,
past or present: "there is something about each person that we meet and
know that immediately, so to speak, catalogs them for us. There is a
something that is indefinable and indescribable about each person that
lets us know on short acquaintance whether he or she is worthwhile or
otherwise, whether intellectual or not, and the many things that go to
make up a personality." Eight years in the fight had taught Johnson that
"while prejudices cannot be blotted out, within a generation, it is worth
our effort" to speak on the record.[8]

In addition to speaking as witnesses of Indiana's past residents, the
women also articulated "word pictures" of their subjects. Ehrmann's

words are highly illustrative: "Then I will paint for you a word picture of his wife, Mrs. Richardson. Well do I recall her sweet face, her hair parted in the middle, combed smoothly back, neatly dressed. She was a large woman. She, too, was so hospitable, welcoming everyone to her home, and such hospitality was never found greater in any place than it was in the Richardson home." But listeners need not limit their fact-finding to her face alone, for, Ehrmann noted, "The descendants of that family are living in our county today. They have always been representative people. They have owned large farms, and have been people of force." Thus, "the people who lived here in the early days are gone. They cannot speak for themselves. Likewise, their children are gone, but the third and fourth generation live on, and are able to give testimony of those who have gone before."[9] Word pictures were created by description and by encounter with living descendants.

The idea of "Word Pictures" prompted Lincoln Inquiry worker Carrie Halbruge to take the argument one step further. Over the next few months she assembled more than two hundred daguerreotypes, oil paintings, silhouettes, and photographs of pioneers who had lived on Indiana's frontier in the 1820s. Most were created later in the century, and they had ended up in the possession of dozens of descendants. The collection was displayed publicly in February 1929 for audiences to walk through and look into the pioneer faces. The exhibit received local and regional press coverage, leading at least one commentator to the desired conclusion: "One realized in looking into these faces that they were a fine, sturdy class of people." Ehrmann saw the images as "another link in our chain of evidence as to the type of our ancestors," and she penned a brief summary of the collection that was published in state newspapers with a selection of the photographs.[10]

When viewed from the twenty-first century, the photographs appear an unremarkable assortment of old, dour, pioneers. But viewers in the 1920s did not bring to the exhibit the experience of daily encounter with headshots in news, entertainment, and social media; they did not bring a vocabulary that reduced faces to thumbnails or pixels. Viewing this collection in 1929 drew on a different set of cultural experiences that made encounter with a face in a portrait or photograph something much more intimate and significant. Lincoln Inquiry sculptor and society treasurer George Honig explained the feeling that accompanied seeing: "There is something intensely human about old photographs. In them still lives one who is absent. The expression on the face, the light in the eye, the kindness and forgiveness of the mouth; one can almost feel the heart beat

After biographer Albert Beveridge characterized Lincoln's Indiana neighbors as ignorant, drunken, and dirty, the Lincoln Inquiry responded by mounting an exhibit of over two hundred daguerreotypes, oil paintings, silhouettes, and photographs of pioneers who had lived on Indiana's frontier in the 1820s. The exhibit invited viewers to look into the eyes of Indiana's pioneers and understand their character. The public would not be taught *about* Lincoln's neighbors so much as it would be introduced *to* them. Undated newspaper clipping, photograph by the author.

beneath it; the man comes back." This re-experience of one who had died brought its own kind of knowledge. Again, Honig explained, "You may read the hundreds of books on the story of Lincoln but not until you look upon his portraits will you understand the real character of the man."[11]

Honig's comments highlight several dimensions of the Lincoln Inquiry's experience of looking and photographic encounter. First, unlike modern conceptions of photography that distinguish the represented person from his or her representation in a photograph, Honig suggests that the photograph instead contained what Susan Sontag would later describe as "a material vestige of its subject." Long after the subject had passed on, the vestige remained, making a photograph something like an archive of a portion of a person. Additionally, this preserved vestige could become reanimated with proper looking: the heart could beat again, the man could come back. And when the person did come back, the viewer encountered not just the visuality of the subject's clothing or movement, but also aspects of the subject's personality—kindness, forgiveness, character. Photographs reminded viewers that the subjects were absent while simultaneously keeping them present. Perhaps this understanding found expression in the reluctance of at least one of Lincoln's neighbors, Redmond Grigsby, to be photographed—he agreed only if he could hide his face.[12]

So in mounting a collection of pioneer photographs, the Lincoln Inquiry was not treating them the way that Peter Burke has characterized historians' use of photographs as "mere illustrations" that simply "illustrate the conclusions the author has already reached by other means." The Lincoln Inquiry had spent nearly a decade building an interpretation of southern Indiana's past, but the photographs led to the conclusion not as evidence in a rhetorical syllogism but as a gateway through which the public could experience the Inquiry's conclusions by encountering vestiges, reanimating them upon viewing, and sensing the character of Lincoln's neighbors. The public would not be persuaded *about* Lincoln's neighbors so much as it would be introduced *to* them.[13]

The Lincoln Inquiry's way of looking at photographs of faces was part of a broader cultural reaction to the relatively new experience of viewing photography made possible by the convergence of technology, genealogy, and popular science. Images of Lincoln played a central role in the process and chart its development nicely. During his presidency a host of print media offered Lincoln's appearance to the American public: lithographs and steel engravings hung in homes, his portrait dotted family albums, political cartoons circulated first in periodical pages and then also as individual prints. Lincoln submitted numerous times to early photographic technology, and twice he sat for the preparation of plaster life masks. A Democratic campaign song begged Lincoln's supporters not to "show his picture," and the story of the origin of his whiskers—a recommendation to make him more handsome among the ladies—remains well known.[14]

But for all the joking and the exaggeration, people who met him remembered his face. The year after Lincoln's death, in one of the earliest reminiscences of the martyred president, Francis Carpenter vividly remembered Lincoln's face: "I intently studied every line and shade of expression in that furrowed face. In repose, it was the saddest face I ever knew. There were days when I could scarcely look into it without crying." A painter, Carpenter had been hired to observe and recreate Lincoln's

face—most notably in his painting "The First Reading of the Emancipation Proclamation Before the Cabinet" (1864)—but others were also
similarly inclined to recall Lincoln's face. In published reminiscences,
again and again Lincoln's face is mentioned, frequently as a summary of
his life and character. Allen T. Rice, editor of one collection published in
1885, observed that "the face of Lincoln told the story of his life—a life
of sorrow and struggle, of deep-seated sadness, of ceaseless endeavor."[15]

It was a previously unpublished image of Lincoln that brought Tarbell
into Lincoln studies. After Nicolay tried to warn her out of the field, she
went to Robert Todd Lincoln who gave her the same answer about his
father's papers that he would later give to Beveridge and anyone else who
asked. As a show of kindness, perhaps, Robert offered the earliest daguerreotype of Lincoln, which had never been published. Tarbell later
recalled, "I realized that this was a Lincoln which shattered the widely
accepted tradition of his early shabbiness, rudeness, ungainliness. It was
another Lincoln, and one that took me by storm." Readers who encountered the image on the front cover of the November 1895 *McClure's
Magazine* felt the same exhilaration. Letters to the editor commented on
Lincoln's neatness, the exact knot of the cravat, and the "scrupulous care"
of his appearance—but they also encountered something more. Lincoln
biographer John T. Morse saw "the man in the making." Woodrow Wilson, still a young professor at Princeton, found the image "both striking
and similar," and contrasted this early view with Lincoln's presidential
visage: "The fine brows and forehead, and the pensive sweetness of the
clear eyes, give to the noble face a peculiar charm. There is in the expression the dreaminess of the familiar face without its later sadness." Charles
Cooley of Michigan noted "the same pleasant and kindly eyes, through
which you feel, as you look into them, that you are looking into a great
heart." Massachusetts Institute of Technology president Francis Walker
noted "that the present picture has distinctly helped me to understand
the relation between Mr. Lincoln's face and his mind and character, as
shown in his life's work. It is, far away, the most interesting presentation
of the man I have ever seen. To my eye it explains Mr. Lincoln far more
than the most elaborate line-engraving which has been produced."[16]

This last comment hints at an important technological transformation
that greatly facilitated posthumous visual encounters with Lincoln. Photographic technology had existed in America since the antebellum years,
but its cost prohibited reproduction for widespread publication. As a
result, those Americans who never met Lincoln in person knew his appearance only through woodcuts and engravings. In the mid-1890s, "the

new, cheap technique of photoengraving known as the halftone" revolutionized the field. With the going rate for woodcuts hovering around
$300 per page, a halftone could be made for less than $20. McClure
founded his magazine just as the cheaper photoengraving became available. The first issue, published in June 1893, included 100 illustrations in
just under 100 pages. Frank Luther Mott, a historian of American magazines, observed that "a considerable proportion of these pictures were
artistically mediocre or worse" and "were poorly engraved and printed."
By today's standards, the pictures "make a rather poor impression," but
"the passion of readers of the mid-nineties for portraits of the great and
near-great would be hard to over-state, and the pictures at once became
one of the most popular features of the new magazine." McClure also
launched a "Human Documents" feature that combined portraits and
biographies of "Eminent Men," such as Gladstone, Napoleon, Bis-
marck, Dwight Moody, James Whitcomb Riley, U. S. Grant, and Lincoln
(prepared by Tarbell). The advertising slogan for the series promised "the
story of their lives written upon their faces," and one reviewer wrote that
the first issue "throbs with actuality from beginning to end."[17] A generation of readers found themselves looking—for the first time, and then
regularly—into the face of the vanished past.

This explosion of photographic reproduction occurred within the lifetime of the participants in the Lincoln Inquiry, shaping both their knowledge about the past and their sense of how the past might best be encountered. At the same time that Tarbell published the daguerreotype
obtained from Robert Lincoln, a twelve-year-old James G. Randall, still
decades away from becoming the premier academic Lincoln historian of
his generation, found himself mesmerized by the craggy face of Lincoln
that soon filled his boyhood sketchbooks and watercolors. Circulation of
Lincoln's photographic image only increased during the Lincoln centennial celebration in late 1908 through February 1909.[18]

As with Lincoln, so with the witnesses to his life. Popular publications
on Lincoln in the 1890s and 1900s frequently contained photographs of
the witnesses from whose mouths flowed the dazzling new revelations.
Tarbell's report of the testimony of Christopher Columbus Graham featured a photograph of the old man looking almost prophet-like with his
white hair and grizzled beard. Who could doubt the testimony of Samuel
Crawford, leaning back in his rocking chair, legs crossed, eyes closed in
peaceful recollection? For the centennial of Lincoln's birth, Iowa minister
J. T. Hobson presented the sober portraits of nine old Hoosiers from whom
he deduced that Lincoln would certainly have supported prohibition.[19]

The caption of an undated print of a Matthew Brady photograph preserved in southern Indiana makes judgments about both the shape and origin of Lincoln's head: "One of the grandest heads ever modeled by the Creator." Technology brought the faces of the past into the experience of the public, but what about the faces of which no photograph survived?

In 1928, while constructing the memorial and tablets for its Nancy Hanks Park, the Indiana Lincoln Union lined up twelve models and held a public vote to decide which should be used as reference by the sculptor. George Wilson proposed doing the same thing on a much grander scale to "reconstruct" the most significant "missing face" in popular Lincoln interest—that of Nancy Hanks Lincoln. Iglehart excitedly reported that "recent science has developed what is called composite portraiture . . . eliminating all differences and emphasizing kindred traits. I have seen a picture of a hundred consumptives condensed into one and to this day in passing strangers on the street I will see the consumptive face."[20] If traits were passed down the generations, would it not also be logical to work back to the past from traits of living persons? And if the process might not work in specific cases, should it not work in the collective?

Popular science and genealogy here blended with academic and local history. Charles Darwin's evolutionary theory found application in social Darwinism and eugenics. Throughout the 1920s, Indiana reformers promoted "better breeding" and hosted "better baby" contests at the state fair. The practice resonated with Hoosiers who had experience in livestock raising. At one meeting, Iglehart spoke of one of Indiana's early governors by noting that a grandson was "a very good representative of that stock." This idea is only one step removed from Frederick Jackson Turner's argument that the experiences of Americans on the frontier had produced a new American character that was passed down to Americans at the turn of the twentieth century. Turner mapped the progression across the geography of the nation while popular eugenics mapped it across the generations. If favorable traits were passed down the generations, the laws of scientific reflexivity prescribed those same traits for the ancestors of eminent individuals such as Lincoln. History and science combined to dictate for the savior of the Union equally worthy forebears.[21]

This assumption also animated the debate raging in the field of Lincoln studies over the legitimacy of Nancy Hanks. Herndon had opened the can of worms with insinuations in his 1889 biography, and genealogists, journalists, and preachers eventually joined the fractious conversation. William Barton disproved theories of seven purported fathers of Abraham, including Chief Justice John Marshall and South Carolina senator John

C. Calhoun, but the records for Nancy were not so clear. Merrill Peterson treated this exchange as an amusing relic of the pre-professional era— "The woods were full of fanatics who continued to believe such stories well into the twentieth century"—and Kenneth Winkle passes it off as "romanticism," but there was much more at stake. After following five generations of Lincoln's ancestors from Massachusetts to Illinois, Tarbell concluded, "These Lincolns were behind him." Lincoln's ancestors were not just genealogical predecessors, but equals—participants in the inheritable essence that flowed through him. "When I finished my journey," she later recalled, "I felt that I had quite definitely and finally rescued the Lincolns from the ranks of the poor white trash where political enemies had so loved to place them." Her book included photographic comparisons of Lincoln and his relatives published side by side, leading Iglehart to report to Carl Sandburg that her photo display was "altogether more convincing and worth more to the world than all Barton has ever published."[22]

The Lincoln Inquiry's exhibit of pioneer photos became the starting point of a project to gather photographs of women—living or dead— born in the Lincoln states of Kentucky, Indiana, and Illinois, and who, at the time of the photograph, were approximately the same age as Nancy Hanks when she died in 1818. The collection of evidence does not survive, nor does it appear to have been submitted to scientific analysis, but it did inspire artist George Honig to produce Nancy Hanks in both sketch and doll form. In 1933, the doll won fifth place in a nationwide art contest hosted by the American Legion. A southern Indiana newspaper praised the doll and its purpose: "There is no picture of this sainted lady in existence and the artist has depended upon history and legends for the conception that he has so skillfully put into this masterpiece of his hand. The doll possesses a delicate and charming refinement in its expression," and Honig "has woven a semblance of Abe's expression that is very impressive."[23] Genealogy, science, faces, photographs, and facts had converged to produce a Nancy Hanks Lincoln that could now be seen and touched.

By engaging witnesses and photographs, members of the Lincoln Inquiry approached the past through its presence in their lives. For them, history existed in forms close enough to influence the present through "the touch of the past." Face-to-face encounters with Lincoln, his neighbors, and their descendants through both interviews and photographs brought life, proximity, and trust to the story of the sixteenth president. After retiring from the editorship of the Evansville *Courier,* William B.

Carleton told a meeting of the Southwestern about his birth within a mile of the Lincoln cabin and his frequent visits to Nancy Lincoln's grave. "We intimately knew men and women whose fathers and mothers were on close terms with the Lincolns. From their lips we have heard over and over again the stories." Such proximity and lived experience constituted a "Lincoln atmosphere," in which southern Indiana residents "live, breathe and have our being." As a result, the "more we live in the Lincoln atmosphere" the "more we feel like we are a part of the early settlers" and "a part of the Lincolns."[24]

Pageant, Village, and Atmosphere

The Lincoln Inquiry's photo exhibit was developed at the same time that participants were working on a historical pageant and a reconstructed historical village. But whereas the exhibit began with photographs and opened into an encounter with the past, the pageant and village began with a story and sought for effective ways of telling it. In the field of history, sequence matters. If one begins with an object and then tells a story about it, the object takes on the status of relic, a discrete and tangible link to the past. If, however, one begins with a story and then adds an object, the object takes on the status of evidence, providing legitimacy to the broader narrative. Beginning with the object limits the power of the story to the particular object or perhaps, at most, other objects of the same type. Beginning with the story allows for a wider range of claims that become valid and authentic because of the existence of objects. The pageant tied the story of Lincoln's youth to the spot on the Ohio River from which he set out on a flatboat journey to New Orleans in 1828. The village attempted to bring all of Lincoln's frontier experience into a single site in the community of Rockport. Both initiatives carried the participants and findings of the Lincoln Inquiry to the wider public.

As high school drama teacher Bess Ehrmann wrote her pageant "When Lincoln Went Flat Boating from Rockport," she would have been well aware of the popularity of pageantry in the United States at the turn of the century. The state of Indiana had called on each county to produce a pageant for the state's centennial in 1916, and a few scenes of the pageant Tommy de la Hunt had written for Perry County were performed at one of the society's early meetings. Dramatization had also reached the field of Lincoln studies. The Lincoln Inquiry pushed the city of Evansville to stage a performance of John Drinkwater's popular play about Abraham Lincoln, de la Hunt's pageant told the story of Lincoln's landing in Indiana, and in 1918 the community of New Salem had already hosted a pageant about Lincoln's Illinois years. In 1923, the Rockport Improvement Association opened a new park in the community by hosting athletics, vaudeville stunts, a moving picture, and a historical play by Ehrmann.[25]

The Lincoln pageant began small. After members of the Rockport Business Men's Association saw a Hollywood film that downplayed the role of Lincoln's Indiana years, they approached Ehrmann to write a pageant that would get the story straight. "When Lincoln Went Flatboating" was performed in the fall of 1926 with a cast of approximately one hundred. Two years later, with the Lincoln Union at work on the Nancy Hanks Lincoln Park and Beveridge's biography under preparation for publication, the situation called for something more. In 1928 the city of Rockport spent $700 to install circus seats, Ehrmann swelled the cast to over four hundred, and the performance date was moved from the fall to the fourth of July. The sponsors sent broadsides and leaflets to Hoosiers across the state, and Ehrmann persuaded her friend Ida Tarbell to plug the pageant in the *New York Herald Tribune*. "The 'Lincoln Inquiry' of Southwestern Indiana has thrown new light upon the boyhood of the Great Emancipator," Tarbell began, and "probably no more interesting monument will ever be raised to Abraham Lincoln" than the pageant that portrayed "the result of its findings." Ehrmann hoped the production would bring "almost world wide publicity."[26]

The pageant integrated the Lincoln Inquiry's findings with its approach to contextualizing Lincoln on the Indiana frontier. Ehrmann aspired "to give a true and honest picture of pioneer life in Indiana—in the dress, in the properties, in every detail." Many of the actors wore original pioneer costumes, and among the props were original fans, parasols, and muskets. One scene also included a wagon, five horses, and a dog. When one boy in modern clothing stepped onto the stage during one of the performances, Ehrmann "nearly had a fit." The pageant hit all of the key events in Lincoln's Indiana life—entering the state, his mother's death, schooling and book borrowing, acquaintance with John Pitcher—before focusing most of the action on the 1828 flatboat trip that sent Lincoln out of Indiana to New Orleans and back. The Lincoln Inquiry's conclusion permeated the piece: "Kentucky gave him his birth, Illinois gave him his political career, but Indiana molded the man." In keeping with custom of the era, the historical scenes were introduced by heralds symbolic of "The Spirit of History" while nature was represented through the choreographed dancing of water nymphs, wood nymphs, bees, and storm clouds.[27]

Building on the experience of encounter present in photographs of Lincoln's neighbors and their descendants, Ehrmann cast numerous descendants in the roles of their ancestors, making the production in her words *"real* history repeated" and in the press releases "a Living Memorial to America's Greatest Citizen." When ancestral ties were unavailable, as in the case of Lincoln, for example, Ehrmann cast an actor who was a descendant of someone who knew Lincoln. In a further cue to historical synchronization, the pageant stage sat on the bank of the Ohio River and the actors actually launched a boat into the river as part of the performance. The audience sat facing southward so that the river and the Kentucky hills formed the natural backdrop for the performance on stage. Rivers—and the Ohio River in particular—show up throughout the Lincoln Inquiry's work as a symbol of the way that time flows ever onward. "All else is changed," wrote Albion Bacon, "except the stream, that changes not, but sweeps, like history, on!" Like a river, the "stream of humanity" moved across the continent on Turner's frontier, and the Lincoln Inquiry passed its work on to future generations who would appreciate their effort. Ancestors and descendants, actors and audience, historians and future generations lived interlocking lives.[28]

In order to bring the event to the widest possible audience, Ehrmann's friends worked tirelessly to have the pageant filmed and distributed as a motion picture. As early as 1928, correspondence began with Will Hays, a native of southern Indiana, sponsor of the Lincoln Union, and for over half a decade the director of the Motion Picture Producers and Distributors of America. Hays equivocated, hinting that D. W. Griffith or John Ford might be working on a Lincoln film while also claiming the public would not be interested in a film about Lincoln. He ultimately said no one would be interested, so Iglehart talked his brother into paying a local cinematographer to make a silent film of the July 1930 performance. Later that year, however, D. W. Griffith released his own "talkie," *Abraham Lincoln,* with a screenplay by Stephen Vincent Benét and starring Walter Huston as Lincoln. By ignoring Lincoln's Indiana years, the film earned over five hundred critics in the Lincoln Inquiry, but it sent Iglehart back to Hays in another round of eager pleading met with disinterested deflection. Iglehart pushed for historical accuracy, but eventually conceded that enough evidence might be pulled together to add a romantic love interest to the story. In the end, Hays terminated the discussion, citing Griffith's recent success and the fact that the Lincoln Inquiry film was silent; he could not even pull strings with a distribution company, as that would be seen as favoritism. The silent film debuted at a meeting of the Southwestern Indiana

Historical Society in February 1931, ran in southern Indiana movie houses and schools, and for two years was distributed by the Iowa State School of Visual Instruction.[29]

The pageant at Rockport bore several limitations in terms of reaching an audience. First, access to it was limited by the fact that it was staged only every two years and there was only one copy of the film. Second, from the standpoint of the Lincoln Inquiry's mission to contextualize Lincoln on the frontier, the fact of its location at the point where Lincoln began his flatboat trip exerted a strong pull, emphasizing that single event out of the entirety of Lincoln's fourteen-year experience on the frontier. The pageant brought that site to life, but it could not do justice to all of the sites, experiences, and neighbors in Indiana of the 1820s. Was there a way to immerse the audience in something more?

George Honig called art the "silent language" that "everyone can understand." A sculptor, artist, and designer, Honig, born in Rockport, had trained at the National Academy in New York and worked on the statue of George Washington in that city's Washington Square Park. He married fellow Spencer County native Alda McCoy, a concert pianist trained at DePauw University and with private tutors in London and Vienna. After World War I the pair returned to Evansville for a sculpture contract and then stayed for the rest of their lives. Over the next several decades, George was commissioned to produce numerous sculptures in bronze, stone, and plastic throughout the Midwest. As a boy he had listened to old timers talk of Lincoln, and as a man he created numerous plaques, busts, and sculptures of the Great Emancipator. It was said of Honig that he spoke of Lincoln "in the present tense and in the manner of an eye-witness observer," both the human eye and "the eye of a vivid imagination." He participated with the Lincoln Inquiry from its earliest days, reported often on his interviewing and research, and testified as one of the "best witnesses" at the Princeton meeting. Honig's livelihood came from the contracts he received from others, but in his heart he longed to create something big enough to do justice to Lincoln and the Indiana frontier.[30]

By the early twentieth century, an international trend in historic preservation had already translated Scandinavian folk museums into an American outbreak of outdoor villages and period rooms in museums. In 1918, residents of New Salem, Illinois, erected four log buildings to commemorate Lincoln's presence; in 1926, John Rockefeller, Jr., launched a massive restoration project at Colonial Williamsburg in Virginia; and in 1929, Henry Ford dedicated his Greenfield Village, which brought together historic buildings and artifacts from across the nation. As the economic realities of the 1930s set in, Lincoln sites were seen for their economic value as well—the state of Illinois took over New Salem, and the Lincolns' Knob Creek homestead in Kentucky opened with a cabin reconstructed on the advice of Louis Warren and a tavern that benefited from the repeal of prohibition. Ida Tarbell had already expressed her preference for New Salem over marble temples, and the Lincoln Inquiry failed to persuade state officials away from creating a shrine to Nancy Hanks. Honig's work was well received, and he was encouraged by at least one historian who thought that "the person who can translate his ideas into a bronze tablet or a sculptured bust really does more to acquaint society with an individual than does the historian who is limited to the printed page."[31] The great depression gave Honig the opportunity to shift from contracted sculptor to project designer.

In 1933, Honig and his wife moved to Rockport, where he worked with the city council and the Spencer County Historical Society to secure funding through President Hoover's Federal Emergency Relief Administration (FERA). The city and local donors contributed $2,500 in materials, and FERA paid the $3,500 in labor costs necessary to employ dozens of men in hand-cutting trees to erect eleven log buildings that would recreate a pioneer village from Lincoln's era on a four-acre lot donated by the city. Next door, an industrial school would teach students technical skills as they produced souvenirs for sale at the park, including replicas of Honig's Nancy Hanks Lincoln doll. Honig estimated the whole venture would earn $10,000 annually in entry fees. Construction began in 1934, and 10,000 visitors celebrated the village's opening on July 4, 1935, with parades, speeches, and a pioneer dinner. Honig and the city leveraged this immediate success into a second proposal for $20,000 from the New Deal's newly created Works Progress Administration (WPA). Employing another hundred men for four more months, Honig added athletic fields with bleachers, a five-acre lake, an island, and a 400-foot sand beach. The dedication of the new facilities drew another 15,000 people in addition to the 25,000 visitors who had come in the intervening year.[32]

Unlike the state's shrine to Nancy Lincoln, the Lincoln Pioneer Village was designed as "a memorial not only to Lincoln but to his pioneer neighbors." The village contained recreations of the Lincoln family's last cabin and the home that Sarah Lincoln occupied after her marriage to Aaron Grigsby. Other recreated structures were tied to Lincoln's education—an old schoolhouse, the home of Josiah Crawford, who loaned Lincoln a book on Washington, the law office of John Pitcher, who loaned law books, and the store of William Jones where Abraham read newspapers and listened to the Whig owner talk about politics. Lincoln's work experience found expression in places where he hired out, such as Reuben Grigsby's cooper shop, the Pigeon Creek Baptist Church he helped to build, and the home of James Gentry, who hired the youth for farm work and flat boating—a reproduction of the flatboat carried visitors to the island in the lake. The remaining structures imitated other parts of the community, from the home where the county's first court session was held, to the first tavern, and a mill, inn, and market house. The homes were furnished with pioneer furniture, quilts, and implements, many of which were heirlooms donated by the descendants of Lincoln's neighbors. Scattered throughout the grounds were wells, a wagon and oxcart, hitching racks, grindstones, plows, and a pioneer garden.[33]

Government reports, newspaper coverage, and promotional materials all emphasized the village's attention to detail. Honig and others had dedicated "years of research" to produce structures that were "painstakingly" "exact to the last detail." The FERA employees who felled the trees shunned mechanized saws for old-fashioned axes. The wooden pegs that served as nails and hinges and the hand-split shingles drew attention, as did the heirlooms that could be traced to specific individuals. In contrast to the "shrine" the state was building to Nancy Lincoln seventeen miles away, the Lincoln Pioneer Village was "a faithful and eloquently accurate reproduction of a frontier village of Lincoln's time."[34]

The valuation of accuracy, reproduction, and attention to detail places the Lincoln Pioneer Village squarely within the tensions surrounding historic preservation in the 1930s. Rockefeller's investment at Colonial Williamsburg had set a new standard for preserving material evidence, even while doing so for patriotic ends. Ford's Greenfield Village likewise emphasized historical buildings, though his removal of the structures from their original locations in the name of education would later provoke criticism. An emerging professional ideal of authenticity would, by the 1940s and 1950s, define preservation as the unification of original buildings with an original site and original contents. The Lincoln Pioneer Village fell far short of this standard: it contained new buildings, arranged on a new site, and stocked with merely representative samples from the approximate time period. Furthermore, it introduced recreation into the mix, an effort that would later be stigmatized as "Disneyfication" after another investor who combined amusement and profit with reproductions of past scenes. Honig's village does not seem to have drawn out any criticism in the 1930s, though the continual promotional emphasis on accuracy suggests he was at least aware of the possibility.[35]

But to judge Honig's village by later standards of preservation misses the opportunity to understand the values of the Lincoln Inquiry and to explore how its members envisioned the interests and expectations of the touring public. Honig's reproduced village blended the Lincoln Inquiry's educational mission with Depression-era demands for economic stimulus and long-term development. The Lincoln Inquiry's work had already revealed an interest in synchronization over authenticity. It meant something to visit Nancy Lincoln's grave or to gather on Abraham's birthday, thereby synchronizing space and time. The "accurate reproductions" in the village likewise served to synchronize sentiment. Speaking at the 1935 dedication, Indiana's attorney general, Philip Lutz, explained: "Most of the things we cherish in life are sentimental things—the really worth while things in life are sentimental. Our home is a sentiment. It is built of brick, mortar, wood and stone; it has four walls and a roof; it is a place to eat and sleep—but a home is more. It is an abode of deep sentiment, memories of deep love, trials, tragedies, successes and joys." In emphasizing the wooden pegs and the heirloom shawls, Honig did not try to "stage authenticity" or to commodify history, but rather to open up the gateway for an emotional engagement with Indiana frontier life. As at New Salem, the "visual verisimilitude" of the tangible objects moved beyond the water nymphs of the allegorical pageant toward a higher kind of "spiritual authenticity." The effect was perhaps best articulated by Mark Twain's explanation of the difference between knowledge and realization. "The mere knowledge of a fact is pale; but when you come to realize your fact, it takes on color. It is all the difference between hearing of a man being stabbed in the heart, and seeing it done." By means of accurate reproductions and actual artifacts, visitors realized the spirit of Indiana's frontier and the character of its pioneer inhabitants. Honig and the Lincoln Inquiry hoped this portrayal would strike at the heart.[36]

In the Lincoln Inquiry's photographic exhibit, riverside pageant, and outdoor village museum, we can identify several elements of a collective aspiration to immerse the audience within a synchronized experience of the past. The photographs, descendant-actors, and accurate wooden hinges each served as a gateway to the vestige of an ancestor, to the genealogical heir of the past, and to the realization of sentimental reality. In each case, the journey pointed the public toward an understanding of the collective character of Indiana's pioneers and to the cultural climate and atmosphere of Lincoln's frontier. In serving as curator, director, or designer, members of the Lincoln Inquiry acted as guides who escorted the public through the gateway and into a world the guides had already experienced. Furthermore, the collective acts of sharing and learning seem to have benefited from attention to synchronization: seeing the same photographs, watching a pageant on the spot of Lincoln's flatboat departure, visiting or participating on the anniversary of a relevant date. This alignment employed a tangible trace of the past to align the present with the past, not by reversing the stream of time but by circling around to re-encounter, re-animate, re-live, and realize something previously unknown and inaccessible.

These Lincoln Inquiry projects continued to receive the praise of contemporary writers and historians. Christopher Coleman credited the Inquiry with contributing "powerfully to the revision of our interpretation of Lincoln's personality and its development." Indiana University historian James A. Woodburn endorsed the Inquiry's conclusion that to consider southern Indiana pioneers as "an inferior people, an outlandish folk, steeped in ignorance, illiteracy, boorishness, immorality, degradation and crime" could not be "farther from the truth." From the Lincoln field, William Barton wrote to Iglehart that his "conclusions and those of Mrs. Ehrmann seem to me correct" and Ida Tarbell judged that the Inquiry had made an "invaluable contribution to our knowledge of the conditions under which the boy Lincoln lived."[37] The Lincoln Inquiry reached out to the public with a message that continued to persuade Indiana historians and Lincoln biographers.

Students, Scholarship, and Synthesis

The Lincoln Inquiry's philosophy of immersion and synchronization found expression and frustration in other attempts at synthesizing the approach and findings for the public. As its influence grew, the society was approached by school districts requesting training for teachers and ready-made lesson outlines for class use. George Wilson, himself a former teacher and superintendent, believed that modern education methods generally undermined interest in history. Catechized questions bore "no human interest and quite often hardly any connection between a question and the one before or after it." School materials were "usually compiled in such as way as to be of little or no interest to a child." He humorously observed that when he "was a boy at school history was the driest subject on the program. . . . The class, as a unit, was sure that the island Noah's dove found should be called History, because it was the only dry spot during the flood. Nothing could have been drier. All regretted that the flood did not cover it." Beyond personal experience, members of the

Lincoln Inquiry also based their critique of public schooling on the rationale that Lincoln had become the greatest American with less than two years of formal schooling. Had they lived half a century later, these society members could have been advocates for critical thinking—they complained that students were taught to repeat answers "but not to think or initiate," the "jar of memory was crowded but his 'thinkbox' was empty," "The trouble with History is that too much is taught and not enough learned. The child is stuffed with data and not fed."[38]

Instead of responding to school district requests, the Lincoln Inquiry developed its own program of engaging students in the very activities of the society members—conducting archival research and reporting at society meetings. The goal would not be to help students perform well on an exam, but to take history "straight at the . . . boys and girls" and help them "take up the work forty years sooner than they would otherwise"—to nurture future participants in the Lincoln Inquiry. They bypassed the classroom and curriculum and pushed "school teachers to send their classes out to do some real first-hand research work." They urged teachers to take their students to Nancy Lincoln's gravesite or to Honig's pioneer village. "It is so much easier to get our children interested in the study of county history," drama teacher Bess Ehrmann observed, "if they can really see and examine these things."[39] Field trips and archival research immersed students in the traces of the past and would encourage them to write up their findings. A local college president offered the college newspaper as an outlet for publication, and Tommy de la Hunt happily reported that students "have taken this material to the papers and the papers have given it space." Ehrmann organized a club in which the students drafted a constitution, elected officers, invited local historians to speak to them, conducted research, published their own newspaper, and presented a collectively prepared paper at one of the Lincoln Inquiry meetings.[40]

The ideal of synchronized immersion proved harder to achieve in the Inquiry's attempts at written synthesis. The power struggle between the Lincoln Inquiry and its competitors both in the field of Lincoln studies and among civic-minded politicians in the state had effectively ended John Iglehart's writing. In 1925 he told Christopher Coleman that the Inquiry had focused so much on producing work that it had neglected organizing it. And as his conversations with Frederick Jackson Turner became more frequent, Iglehart began to read more and more and felt less and less secure in writing down his own thoughts, always stating the need to read just one more book before doing so. As a result, though he gave several speeches—including one at the American Historical Association—he went nine years without writing a paper, all the while reading and preparing for one final synthesis of the Lincoln Inquiry findings that William Barton encouragingly called the "Iglehart thesis." A decade of reading and discussing contemporary historical literature with Turner and at professional meetings of historians let Iglehart see himself as part of a broader historiographical conversation. How he saw his place in the discussion is identified by one of the early titles he proposed for his final synthesis: "The Significance of the Frontier in American History (1893) by Frederick Jackson Turner—Confirmed by the Voice of Science in the Analysis of Professor Merle E. Curti, Smith College (1931) and Other Authority: Relating to a History of a New Race Formed by Pioneering of Many Races in an Empty Continent with Free Land, and Manhood Suffrage, the First Record of Such an Event in History." The final paper, with the more modest title of "Standards and Subjects of Historical Society Work," opened with the proposition that the West had been treated insufficiently by eastern writers. After a quick caveat that he was not criticizing the pioneers who originated in New England, Iglehart devoted most of the paper to a sequential analysis of works about the American frontier published over the previous thirty years.[41] He produced a review of the literature but failed to locate the Lincoln Inquiry's contribution to the discussion.

The struggle for synthesis faced a variety of social factors. In the first place, the rivalries between counties continued to seethe beneath the apparent calm. Beginning in 1926, residents of Warrick, Perry, and Gibson counties began an extended debate about the route traveled by the Lincoln family that eventually generated forged documents and much bad blood. In 1930, several women of the society sparred with the new editor of the *Indiana Magazine of History,* William Lynch, after he criticized their work and their ancestors. These interpersonal difficulties were compounded by financial straits. Iglehart funded the society's activities for the first three years, dues kept it afloat during the second half of the 1920s, but after 1931 memberships and dues payers dropped dramatically. In 1932, the society's bank account balanced out at thirty-two cents. The crisis also hit state funding. In 1932, Coleman found his bulletin reduced to sixteen pages, and the following year the assembly called for an official study of expenditure reduction, effectively putting a moratorium on publishing. Iglehart's thesis would be the last of the Inquiry's papers ever published by the state.[42]

The Lincoln Inquiry might have survived the financial crisis had it not been for another category of loss that would prove irreparable. In 1922 the society began a tradition of offering a formal resolution expressing regret upon the deaths of its members, but by 1930 the trickle had become a torrent. At the February meeting, Eldora Raleigh reported that the deaths of *Boonville Republican* editor Thomas E. Downs and local judge Edward Gough had crippled the Warrick County organization. At the next meeting, in June, Raleigh herself was memorialized, along with another founding member, Judge W. D. Robinson. The minutes of the June meeting, held at the Boonville Methodist Church, register a profound sense of loss running through the entire proceedings. In addition to the loss of friends, Roscoe Kiper reported the loss of a nineteenth-century portrait and newspaper clippings from 1853. Deidré Johnson told of the theft of 10 boxes of historical "Lincoln Data" from a home in Mount Vernon. When roll was called, five counties were not represented. In 1932, Bess Ehrmann memorialized founding member Lucius Embree and George Clifford, the husband of her close friend Emily. At the March 1934 meeting in Evansville, resolutions of regret were passed for Tommy de la Hunt and Albion Fellows Bacon. The expressions were not heard by society president Arthur Fretageot, who was ill, and John Iglehart, who was in the hospital; both were memorialized at the next meeting.[43]

In 1933 the society dropped one of its three yearly meetings and ceased taking a stenographic record of the proceedings. Two years later, members moved to meet annually, and at the 1939 meeting they voted to cease meeting altogether. Kiper and Barker died in 1937, George Wilson followed in 1941. When Iglehart's sister died in 1928, he called himself "the last of my generation." Upon de la Hunt's death, Wilson typed into his fifteenth scrapbook that the "author of a history of Perry County was a personal friend of the writer for sixty-five years." Of the "active leaders" of the society's inner circle, only Ehrmann remained to lament, "we have lost by death so many of our best members and workers."[44] Friendship and writing, membership and work, collegiality and Lincoln, the ties of collective historical practice were severed by death. The collective weight of so many deaths dissolved the social network of historical practice.

After presenting the flatboating pageant in 1926, 1928, and 1930, Bess Ehrmann hosted a pageant about George Washington in 1932 for the bicentennial of his birth. By 1934, the city's interest had been diverted into George Honig's village, and the pageant never ran again. In 1938, Ehrmann published the Lincoln Inquiry's last work. *The Missing Chapter in the Life of Abraham Lincoln* provides a little bit of summary and synthesis in the form of a scrapbook. The first part of the book summarizes the history of Spencer County, Lincoln's life, and the Indiana environment. It described

The work of the Lincoln Inquiry circulated widely. In addition to hundreds of speeches and dozens of publications, the society fostered county historical societies, marked historic sites, and encouraged local museums. When Missouri painter Thomas Hart Benton was commissioned to paint murals depicting Indiana's history for the 1933 Chicago World's Fair, he read the Lincoln Inquiry's findings and portrayed young Abraham surrounded by southern Indiana's frontier life, with an ax in one hand and a book in the other. Photograph by Michael Cavanagh and Kevin Montague, courtesy Indiana University Art Museum, Bloomington, Indiana.

the origins of the Lincoln Inquiry and cataloged 141 projects completed under its auspices. The second part reproduced the testimonies of "Best Witnesses" Will Fortune, J. Edward Murr, and Anna O'Flynn and compiled a list of Lincoln neighbors together with photographs of two dozen of them. The final section of the book described Lincoln's 1844 return to Spencer County, reported on developments at the graves of his mother and sister, and published the script of Ehrmann's pageant and a description of Honig's village. It also announced the recent discovery by WPA local history workers of the will of Thomas Sparrow that contained Nancy Lincoln's "mark," a sign of her existence and illiteracy. The volume concluded with a description of cabinets made by Lincoln and a poem by Albion Fellows Bacon. "How does a life like Lincoln's help us?" wrote Ehrmann in her final words. "It gives us strength to bear our trials, to do the tasks before us without complaint, and to go our way with quiet dignity."[45]

Though the society disbanded, its work and legacy did not disappear but rather trickled into dozens of institutions across southern Indiana. Most of the county societies that had been affiliated with the Southwestern continued to function independently. Several of the Inquiry's papers were collected in the Indiana State Library and the Evansville Public Library, and others were published as part of a Federal Writers' Project–sponsored *History of Spencer County, Indiana* (1939). Many of the sites marked by Honig and commemorated by the Inquiry were integrated into automobile tours aimed at drawing tourists to "the Lincoln Country." A vast collection of minutes, correspondence, and stenographer's notes begun during Iglehart's presidency now formed the basis for a large local history collection in the Willard Library in Evansville. The cabinets and heirlooms collected wound up in museums in every county that participated in the Lincoln Inquiry. When Missouri painter Thomas Hart Benton was commissioned to paint murals depicting Indiana's history for the 1933 Chicago World's Fair, he read Vannest's summary of the Lincoln Inquiry findings and portrayed young Abraham Lincoln, surrounded by southern Indiana's frontier life, with an ax in one hand and a book in the other.[46]

IN ITS mission to take its findings to the public, the Lincoln Inquiry both succeeded and failed. It succeeded in mobilizing over five hundred Americans to participate in historical inquiry, in uncovering archival and oral sources, and in calling attention to the need to contextualize Lincoln's early life on the Indiana frontier. Hailed as Indiana's largest historical society in 1922, it remained by the end of the decade "the most active of the inter-county historical organizations in the state." Its work stands in stark contrast to standard criticisms of local history work as being "relentlessly local" or characterized by interest without knowledge. Though members wrote individually about a single family or community, the collective mission of providing context for Lincoln's life and the call for a crowd approach that welcomed contributions from any source gave meaning to even the smallest of findings—the name of a book read by Lincoln, the hinges on doors, or the face of a pioneer. The Lincoln Inquiry likewise inspired interest in hundreds of Hoosiers, many of whom went into the archives, faced the witnesses, and told their stories in public and print. The quality of this knowledge—like all useful knowledge—was challenged and debated by contemporary Lincoln biographers. Unlike local historians of the nineteenth century who lacked the capacity to find larger meaning for their work, the Lincoln Inquiry forced its way onto a crowded field, defended its approach to evidence, and lobbied biographers and civic leaders to adopt its interpretation.[47]

Yet throughout all the struggling, the Inquiry failed to produce a lasting synthesis for public consumption. A public synthesis is not unanimity, or consensus, or even a single story, but rather the single expression of all of the varieties of approaches, findings, and conclusions. The photo exhibit and pageant proved moving but also transitory, engaging but also ephemeral. The village provided employment, drew crowds, and remains part of the community landscape, but the enthusiasm that enlivened the tours diminished with time. Iglehart's written synthesis surveyed the literature on the American frontier and Ehrmann's chronicled the Inquiry's activities, but the two were never joined, and the Inquiry's accomplishments never became part of broader conversations about Lincoln or about the Indiana frontier. The individual findings that interested Lincoln biographers were scooped up as discovered and never collected into a single overarching statement about Lincoln in Indiana. The biographies of hundreds of pioneers and their families were never brought together into a social or community history of southern Indiana. No one stepped forward with a history of Lincoln and southern Indiana that could rival Paul Angle's 1935 history of Lincoln's Springfield.[48]

One reason for the failure to synthesize can be attributed to the complexity of the undertaking. From a topical perspective, the Lincoln Inquiry's agenda to recreate the entire biographical, social, cultural, intellectual, economic, and political environment of the southern Indiana frontier was extremely ambitious. And, as the information mounted up, it proved easer to call for the restoration of a "missing chapter" than to sort out the contradictions inherent in any emerging body of knowledge about the past, especially when such contradictions were exacerbated by the potential economic benefits to be gained from being the first to publish a finding or being selected as part of the route to be traveled by uncountable future tourists. The public history enterprise integrates myriad functions that are often unnamed and overlapping. The Lincoln Inquiry necessarily dealt with information about past events on Indiana's frontier, the voices of witnesses to those events who spoke out for years afterward, the ongoing conversation about the role and significance of the frontier in American history, its efforts to reconstruct the past, interview the witnesses, and engage the larger conversation, the effort of stenographers and archivists to preserve documents from past events and from the present labors, and the need to synthesize all of this so that it made sense to an outsider who picks up a book or visits a village. And the entire process occurred within the ongoing flow of time, leaving the Inquiry no good way even to know that a paper presented in 1934 had duplicated materials presented in 1921. Perhaps modern computer software, such as a wiki or a Second Life module or a humanities Geographic Information Systems platform, could have helped, but even in the twenty-first century these tools are not yet refined enough to capture facts and narrative elegance, social history and archival provenance, wooden hinges and the environment and atmosphere of Lincoln's Indiana frontier.[49] In life, the Lincoln Inquiry guides successfully invited the public to be immersed in their reconstructions of the past. In death, their knowledge, their commitment, and their public syntheses passed with them.

Conclusion

"A Thousand Minds"

EIGHT MONTHS after John Iglehart's death, James Randall called for the banishment of "amateurs" from the field of Lincoln studies. Born in Indianapolis, the young boy who liked to draw Lincoln's face grew into a constitutional historian trained at the University of Chicago. In the 1920s, he turned his attention to the field of Lincoln studies and was not impressed. The Greek temple at Lincoln's birthplace enshrined errors in granite carving, a host of publications trivialized Lincoln and his legacy, Carl Sandburg's poetic and popular biography of Lincoln was defective. As a solution to the host of historical errors that had arisen around the memory of Abraham Lincoln, Randall proposed simply to clear the field of all past and present work by reminiscers, biographers, journalists, preachers, politicians, poets, local historians, state history institutions, civic organizers, pageant directors, filmmakers, sculptors, and tourism promoters. In their absence, historians who had received scientific training, who held academic appointments at universities, and who researched primarily in written manuscripts would be able to provide accurate history for the general American public.[1]

Randall's message provided a clarion call for a new generation of "professional" historians who, like the Lincoln Inquiry in the decade before, wanted to enter the crowded and competitive field of Lincoln studies. Like members of the Lincoln Inquiry who organized a society, joined associations, attended state and national conferences, and corresponded with other writers, the professionals would forge their own networks through correspondence, formal memberships, scholarly journals, and personal interaction. But as the Lincoln Inquiry looked backward to craft a sense of urgency based on the deaths of knowing witnesses, the professionals looked forward to find hope in new sources that would become available. Like the Lincoln Inquiry, these newcomers would call on the field to pay attention to their preferred sources, replacing family memories and local records with archival manuscripts. Like the Lincoln Inquiry, the professionals would argue that their privileged access to their chosen sources granted them privileged authority to interpret the past. Unlike the public in the Lincoln Inquiry cartoon that walked arm-in-arm with the society into the land of historical knowledge, the scholars' public could not participate, only receive. And, like the rivals encountered by the Lincoln Inquiry, the new professionals also learned to draw boundaries. Randall's rhetorical division of the field into professionals and amateurs was reminiscent of Louis Warren's 1924 critique of his competitors that outlined a taxonomy of interviewers, interpreters, and investigators. And the professionals soon found data to support their claims. In 1929, after the *Atlantic Monthly* published love letters reputed to be between Lincoln and Ann Rutledge, Ida Tarbell endorsed them as authentic, William Barton remained suspiciously silent, but the bristling young professionalist Paul Angle called them a fraud. Further investigation revealed that the letters had been produced in a séance by a woman romantically entangled with Barton. The "affair" sank Barton's career, reflected badly on Tarbell, and cast a chill over publishers' interest in Lincoln that was felt by Bess Ehrmann as she tried to synthesize the Lincoln Inquiry's findings. Academic historians would later see this moment as a turning point in which, in the alliterative language of Lincoln biographer Benjamin Thomas, the realists "routed" the romanticists.[2]

Outside of the rhetorical boundary-drawing of the new professionals, however, life in the field of Lincoln studies carried on much as it had in the 1920s. Almost immediately after Angle had supposedly "banished" Tarbell and Sandburg from the field, he co-authored a book with the poet. Tarbell's readers continued to enjoy her new essays and to purchase reprinted editions of her past work. When Randall's student David Herbert Donald published his dissertation on William Herndon, Sandburg wrote the introduction. Sandburg added four more volumes to the two he had written previously, and the combined work—larger in word count than the ten volumes produced by Nicolay and Hay—became the best-selling, most widely read, and most influential Lincoln biography of all time. After reviewing Sandburg's initial installments critically, Randall mellowed in his view of the poet so much that he dedicated the fourth volume of his work on Lincoln's presidency to him, wrote a tribute to "Carl" in 1952, and welcomed Sandburg to his bedside three days before dying. Adapted for the stage and for television, the work of the poet—not the professional—led one recent analyst to judge that "probably more Americans have learned their Lincoln from Sandburg than from any other source."[3]

Though Americans of the twenty-first century look back on Abraham Lincoln as a historical figure, in his day he, too, looked to the past for lessons to guide his present. One year before he won the presidency, Lincoln spoke on the history of inventions and discoveries, observing that printing revolutionized human knowledge because "a thousand minds were brought into the field where there was but one before." Printing ended the "dark ages" by providing for everything from the explosion of scientific findings to the placement of spelling books in the hands of unlearned boys on the Indiana frontier. Thus "emancipated" from a reliance on the educated few, all Americans could contribute to the "advancement of civilization and the arts."[4] The story of the Lincoln Inquiry demonstrates that "a thousand minds" can collectively shape the practice of history as well, an observation borne out by the subsequent development of oral history, Nancy Lincoln's grave, and the field of Lincoln studies. The long-term impact of the Lincoln Inquiry suggests new ways of conceptualizing the public practice of history.

Though the Lincoln Inquiry had to defend its use of oral testimony in the field of Lincoln studies in the 1920s, other historians were embracing the practice. During the 1930s, the Federal Writers' Project (FWP) put dozens of unemployed historians to work by sending them out to interview former African American slaves and aging Native Americans. An FWP recruiter visited one of the Southwestern's meetings in 1936, society member Ross Lockridge briefly served as Indiana's state supervisor of FWP work, and several of the society members—including one of the "best witnesses"—are mentioned in the acknowledgments of the resultant *Indiana Guide*. In 1938, the same year that Ehrmann published the "best witness" testimony, journalist and historian Allan Nevins called for a reinvigoration of history by using oral testimony as, significantly, a "Gateway to History." Ten years later he organized an oral history project at Columbia University.[5]

In Lincoln circles, however, academic historians mounted a full-scale attack on the practice that centered on the work of William Herndon. In 1929, after debunking the fraudulent letters in the *Atlantic Monthly*, university-based historians quickly traced the problem to its root in Herndon's interviews. In his four-volume history of Lincoln's presidency, Randall included an appendix on Rutledge that dismissed the entire relationship on the basis of "the vagueness of reminiscences," "the doubtfulness of long-delayed memories," and "statements induced under suggestion, or psychological stimulus." Randall's student David Herbert Donald carried the critique further in his biography of Herndon, characterizing the informants as "the lunatic fringe," "those who had axes to grind," or "garrulous old men of long memory." Though not an academic, Louis Warren welcomed the company and chimed in to suggest that Herndon's collection of "recorded traditions, fragments of folklore, and personal reminiscences" made him "the master Lincoln mythmaker."[6]

Within another generation of scholarship, however, the tide turned back in the other direction for two reasons. First, a "professional" oral history movement began in 1966 with the formation of a professional association and a scholarly journal, and these new practitioners quickly deflected criticism of their craft regarding unrepresentative informants, inaccurate memories, intrusive subjectivity, and social bias.[7] Second, Lincoln scholars independently came around to the same conclusion that John Iglehart had reached decades before: though not perfect, first-person reminiscent testimony constitutes the best evidence available for Lincoln's early life. Two-time Lincoln Prize winner Douglas Wilson explained, "Virtually everything we know about Lincoln as a child and as a young man . . . comes exclusively from the recollections of people who knew him" so "the historian or biographer has no alternative but to find a way to work with it." In the late 1970s and early 1980s, psychohistorians turned to Herndon's work in particular as a source for new insights into the sixteenth president's psyche.[8] Simultaneously, documentary editors like Wilson edited, annotated, and published recollections of Lincoln's speeches and the oral testimonies gathered by Holland, Herndon, Nicolay, and Tarbell.[9] By placing oral testimony in the same "objective" and "value-neutral" format that their predecessors had used for Lincoln's letters and speeches, this new generation of Lincoln scholars again made Herndon's notes "safe" in much the same way that Albert Beveridge had when he began calling them the "Weik Manuscripts." As a sort of cherry on the top of this transformation, historian John Y. Simon demonstrated in 1990 that sound contemporary evidence for the Rutledge relationship did exist and that the "professional consensus" against Herndon and his methods was as much collective agreement as scholarship.[10] As a result, the testimonies of "Best Witnesses" J. Edward Murr, Will Fortune, and Anna O'Flynn have once again turned up in citations, along with those few Lincoln Inquiry papers that were collected in the Evansville Public Library.[11]

A similar reversal occurred in connection with the grave of Lincoln's mother. The failure of the Indiana Lincoln Union to raise enough money before the stock market crash of 1929 dramatically delayed the state's effort to commemorate Nancy Hanks Lincoln as a pioneer mother. With George Wilson's report "The Lincoln Forest, Field, Flora, and Family" in hand, and having only the authority to pursue conservation, Richard Lieber enacted probably the greatest of all commemorative ironies by planting trees at the site, effectively reversing Lincoln's most tangible contribution to the state's history. Beginning in 1933, the Civilian Conservation Corps helped with landscaping and marking the site of the Lincoln family cabin. Frederick Olmsted Jr.'s complaints and the reluctance of Hoosier donors ultimately scuttled the plan for the large cathedral, but in 1944 a smaller structure was completed which did contain a Lincoln "chapel." In 1963, Indiana gave the site to the National Park Service, which today, in an effort to contextualize Lincoln's experience on the frontier, renamed it the Lincoln Boyhood National Memorial and operates it as a functioning living history farm. Nancy's grave remains preserved within the small pioneer cemetery, where visitors now regularly toss pennies around the base of her tombstone, but the entire site now hews more closely to the Lincoln Inquiry's desire to emphasize Lincoln on the frontier.[12]

Two other issues related to Nancy Hanks Lincoln remain unresolved. William Barton claimed, on the basis of one document that only he had seen and that appeared to have been lost, that Nancy's birth was illegitimate. Louis Warren vociferously contested the finding and when Barton died the reputedly "missing" document turned up in his Wigwam. When added to his role in the Lincoln/Rutledge forgery, this theft left Barton's reputation in tatters. The most thorough genealogical study completed since the 1930s could not identify Nancy's father, but the lack of irrefutable proof leaves the question open for some.[13]

The prospect of looking into the face of Nancy Lincoln likewise continues to appeal. In 1963, the National Park Service commissioned painter Lloyd Ostendorf to prepare a new portrait of Nancy that was based on "considerable research." After studying both previous portraits and "contemporary word descriptions," Ostendorf created an attractive young woman of smooth, white skin with straight, brown hair parted in the middle and pulled back in a pony tail. Her long nose, square jaw, and melancholy eyes help, in Ostendorf's words, to "emphasize the great resemblance between Lincoln and his mother." In 1976, the National

Cathedral in Washington, DC, installed a stained glass window of Nancy that looks down on a statue of her son. Dressed in blue, this Nancy is tall and thin, her somber face hidden in the shadows of her pioneer bonnet. In her hands she clutches a Bible while the white snakeroot plant creeps upward from below.[14]

Even Lincoln historian James G. Randall eventually came around to see the value of engaging the public in Lincoln studies. Two months before his death in 1953, Randall addressed the American Historical Association as president of the body before which he had, nearly twenty years before, called for the professionalization of Lincoln studies. In those intervening decades he had mentored doctoral students, nearly completed his own four-volume history of Lincoln's presidency, and researched in the papers bequeathed to the Library of Congress by Robert Todd Lincoln. After all that time, he remained convinced that there was a "lamentable gap" between the knowledge of historians and the general public and that a true scholar "confronts the public, which is in need of historical guidance." However, he had resigned himself to the fact—and he quoted himself in a new context—that "history is everybody's subject." History was "inescapable," it "intrudes upon us," and the work of a historian "is of no value in a vacuum or an ivory tower." The "many-sidedness of historical interpretation" gains its fullest strength when allowed to operate within a "free market of findings." In fact, the term "professional historian" had become "tiresome and overworked" and the time for "exclusiveness" had passed. In its place, Randall proposed the same conclusion that John Iglehart had reached in his last written work—the field of history requires "standards." Randall recommended objectivity, validity, and clarity; he encouraged discrimination, proportion, and cautious synthesis coupled with wariness of over-generalization; he also named the personal qualities of "historical sense," tolerance, and humility. The sum total of the standards constituted "Historianship," skills equally essential for citizenship.[15] After two decades of active work in the field of Lincoln studies, John Iglehart and James Randall came to share two conclusions: that the American public would and could participate in the field and that the best way to unite the work of the various participants would be to embrace common standards for historical work. The wide-ranging work of the Lincoln Inquiry allows for the expansion of Randall's concept to embrace a wider "Public Historianship."

History making is preeminently a social process. Historians discuss their research with archivists and colleagues, circulate drafts informally among friends, present their findings to conference attendees and students, submit their writings to editors and publishers. But historians also walk arm-in-arm with their audience, and history practiced in public is contentious, sprawling, energetic, competitive, rich, alive, and invigorating. Whereas Randall once saw the public as a pupil needing instruction, the Lincoln Inquiry saw a partner capable of immersive interaction. Where he recommended the "free market of findings" among scholars, the Lincoln Inquiry fought in a public arena that included scholars and state institutions, school teachers and sculptors, poets and preachers, filmmakers and family members. Precisely *because* Lincoln was everybody's subject and because Americans were interested in witnesses, stories, and immersion in the past, the Lincoln Inquiry succeeded in mobilizing hundreds of Americans to join its society, struggled to find a place in the crowded field of public history in Indiana, defended itself against challenges from both Lincoln biographers and civic leaders, and labored to synthesize its findings in an exhibit, a pageant, a pioneer village, and written essays and collections. The social networks of historical practice integrate contemporary friends and competitors with past witnesses and writers as well as public institutions and audiences. Tracing these networks reveals as much about the study of history as looking at fields, schools of thought, or historiographical issues because the Lincoln Inquiry combined local history with pageantry and politics while drawing evidence and models from Lincoln studies and the history of the frontier in the West. For better or for worse, knowledge about the past is produced by the social interactions of humans.

Public history also invariably rests on the shared interweaving of multiple domains of authority. Marveling at the way that the findings of the "best witnesses" had aligned with those of previous interviewers, Iglehart was reminded of the convergence of the engineers who dug the Hoosac Tunnel in western Massachusetts. Begun in 1851 and completed nearly twenty-five years later, the 4.75-mile-long tunnel became the second longest in the world and was renowned for that fact that while work crews began at each end, two more dug down to the center and began working outward until the four initiatives met within nine-sixteenths of an inch. However public historians enter the field of work, and whatever authority they bring or acquire—whether in life experience, or interviews, or classrooms, or archives—the entire enterprise benefits by identifying convergence from as many directions as possible. The experience of the Lincoln Inquiry also highlights the fact that the choices about methodology are bound up with definitions of authority, that broader schematic narratives shape the interpretations given to historic sites and findings, and that synthesis is essential in a process that welcomes contributions from wherever they may be found.[16]

Rigorous historical methodology can also connect with relevant human emotion. History is constructed through a variety of methods that extend from the encounter of sources, to the assessment of literature, to the selection and composition of a finished product. Participants in the Lincoln Inquiry looked for sources in local archives and local memories, read widely and critically and followed the *New York Times Book Review,* and practiced discriminating selection relevant to the written word or dramatic reenactment. Randall praised these practices and ultimately joined the Lincoln Inquiry in recognizing that the practice of history also involves human qualities of sense, proportion, humility, and tolerance. Esteem for family history and local heritage prompted the Lincoln Inquiry toward sound historical practice rather than away from it. Bess Ehrmann and George Honig wanted visitors to leave their productions having both learned and felt things about the past. Original costumes and accurate hinges led to impressions and unspoken understanding about character and the climate of the past.

The power of the past is most manifest through its presence. The Lincoln Inquiry motivated participation by viewing practitioners as standing on the edge of oblivion with access to parts of the residual past that would be lost to future generations. The "Best Witnesses" spoke with eyewitnesses to Lincoln's life but also turned into witnesses of their work in their own present. The Inquiry's tri-fold mission to collect relics, mark historic sites, and prepare biographies of ancestors connected the vanished past of Lincoln's Indiana frontier with the traces that survived within the grasp of the present. The photo exhibit, riverside pageant, and pioneer village all appealed to a sense of immersive encounter that served as gateway to a deeper experience with the past. Because the totality of the past has necessarily vanished, its reconstruction rests with those in the present who can combine tangible traces of it with compelling narratives and meaningful understanding. Presence avoids presentism that places all of the past in an eternal present at the same time that it eschews the view that considers the past an inscrutably "foreign" or "unnatural" place. Attention to presence, and to the sense of synchronization that arises when traces of the past are engaged in the present, helps historians reconstruct a past that is both accurate and relevant.

Historians then, as now, do history in a variety of places. They read manuscripts preserved in climate-controlled archives, but they also encounter sources in dusty courthouses and overstuffed attics. They digest the work of other historians privately in cozy armchairs and publicly on conference programs. They feel history at gravesites, river bends, and reconstructed villages. They contend for their interpretations in private conversations with friends, face-to-face encounters with competitors, and public meetings where friend and foe alike may respond within the principles of public historianship. Abraham Lincoln, John Iglehart, and James Randall are united in the recognition of the benefits that come when "a thousand minds" participate in the public study of "everybody's subject." Because history is everybody's subject, everybody's history matters.

⁂ Appendix A

Members of the Southwestern Indiana Historical Society, 1920–1939

T HE FOLLOWING persons have been identified as members, honorary
  members, guests, contributors to, or participants in the proceedings
of the Southwestern Indiana Historical Society.

Full names are given as listed in society records. Places of residence
include city and county (for Indiana cities) or state. Men and women
are identified. The "Status" column identifies as "Member" those who
were named on a handful of surviving membership lists; as "Honorary"
those who were noted in the society's meeting minutes; as "Guest" those
who were invited to give a keynote or lunch address; as "Contributor"
those who submitted papers but do not appear to have joined the society
or attended a meeting. Those names for which the "Status" column is blank
are people identified by name in the proceedings but not named on the
official membership lists.

The membership lists, minutes, and proceedings are all preserved in
the John E. Iglehart Collection, Willard Library, Evansville, IN.

Name	Place of Residence		M/F	Status
Abshier, Smith H.			M	
Abshire, Eugenia	Rockport	Spencer	F	Guest
Adams, William F.	Rockport	Spencer	M	Member
Agg, Rachel	Evansville	Vanderburgh	F	Member
Armstrong, Bertha Potts			F	
Armstrong, Ida D.	Rockport	Spencer	F	Member
Armstrong, Margaret R.	Rockport	Spencer	F	Member
Armstrong, Mary	Boonville	Warrick	F	Member
Armstrong, Mrs. J. Arlen	La Junta	CO	F	
Armstrong, Mrs. Robert A.	Cannelton	Perry	F	
Ashley, Jacob	Boonville	Warrick	M	Member

Name	Place of Residence		M/F	Status
Atchison, Louise	Rockport	Spencer	F	Member
Atkinson, Kenneth C.	Rockport	Spencer	M	Member
Bacon, Albion Fellows	Evansville	Vanderburgh	F	Member
Bacon, Hillary	Evansville	Vanderburgh	M	Member
Baker, Charles T.	Grandview	Spencer	M	Member
Baker, Mrs. C. T.	Grandview	Spencer	F	Member
Baker, Mrs. W. J.	Grandview	Spencer	F	Member
Barbour, Lillie	Evansville	Vanderburgh	F	
Barker, Levi B.	Boonville	Warrick	M	
Barker, William L.	Boonville	Warrick	M	Member
Barnett, Helen	Rockport	Spencer	F	
Bartrim, Mrs. James H.	Louisville	KY	F	Member
Bateman, Mrs. N. G.	Boonville	Warrick	F	Member
Baughman, Mrs. J. F.	Evansville	Vanderburgh	F	Member
Bayse, Taylor C.	Rockport	Spencer	M	Member
Beach, A. R.	Poseyville	Posey	M	Member
Beach, Mrs. A. R.	Poseyville	Posey	F	Member
Beach, Mrs. Alfred	Casper	WY	F	
Behrens, Anna	Huntingburg	Dubois	F	Member
Bergenroth, August	Troy	Perry	M	
Bergenroth, Mrs. Wm.	Troy	Perry	F	Member
Bergenroth, Mrs. Wm. M.	Cannelton	Perry	F	Member
Bergenroth, Sallie	Troy	Perry	F	
Berger, John G.	Fort Branch	Gibson	M	Member
Beveridge, Albert J.	Indianapolis	Marion	M	Guest
Biggs, Mrs. Clesh A.	Princeton	Gibson	F	Member
Bigney, Andrew Jackson	Evansville	Vanderburgh	M	
Bockstahler, William George			M	
Boehne, Mrs. James A.	Rockport	Spencer	F	
Boonshot, Daisy Anderson	Petersburg	Pike	F	Member
Bretz, Mrs. Addie	Rockport	Spencer	F	Member
Brewster, Paul G.	Oakland City	Gibson	M	
Brown, Mrs. Chas.	Rockport	Spencer	F	Member
Brown, Mrs. John	Rockport	Spencer	F	Member
Brownlee, Mrs. Chas.	Princeton	Gibson	F	Member
Buchanan, Charles J.	Indianapolis	Marion	M	
Bullcok, Arietta F.		Spencer	F	
Burns, J. P.		Knox	M	Member
Burns, T. J.	Vincennes	Knox		Member
Burr, Miss	Evansville	Vanderburgh	F	Member
Bush, E. M.	Evansville	Vanderburgh	M	Member
Bush, Mrs. E. M.	Evansville	Vanderburgh	F	Member
Butler, Amos W.	Indianapolis	Marion	M	
Butterfield, A. Sidney	Evansville	Vanderburgh	M	Member
Butterfield, Mrs. A. S.	Evansville	Vanderburgh	F	Member

Name	Place of Residence		M/F	Status
Buxton, Eva	Rockport	Spencer	F	Member
Caddick, Mrs. D. E.	Grandview	Spencer	F	Member
Carleton, William B.	Evansville	Vanderburgh	M	
Carr, Nana	Cannelton	Perry	F	Member
Chappell, John K.	Petersburg	Pike	M	
Chewning, John	Rockport	Spencer	M	Member
Clark, Jennie Latimer	Cannelton	Perry	F	Member
Clemens, Edward F.	Cannelton	Perry	M	
Clemens, Mrs. Frank	Cannelton	Perry	F	
Clemens, Mrs. H. M.	Cannelton	Perry	F	
Clements, Edward	Cannelton	Perry	M	Member
Clements, Herdis F.	Mt. Vernon	Posey	M	
Clifford, Emily Orr	Evansville	Vanderburgh	F	Member
Clifford, George S.	Evansville	Vanderburgh	M	Member
Clifford, Mrs. Samuel	Evansville	Vanderburgh	F	Member
Clifford, Samuel	Evansville	Vanderburgh	M	Member
Coleman, Christopher B.	Indianapolis	Marion	M	Guest
Collins, Herbert S.	Yankeetown	Warrick	M	
Conn, Virginia	Evansville	Vanderburgh	F	Member
Conway, Mary Irvin	Cannelton	Perry	F	Member
Conway, Mrs. M. C.	Cannelton	Perry	F	Member
Cook, Mina	Rockport	Spencer	F	Member
Cooper, Sarah Hunter	Jasper	Dubois	F	
Copeland, Mrs. Willis	Evansville	Vanderburgh	F	Member
Corin (?), Mrs. Nora A.	Cannelton	Perry	F	
Cotton, Miss	Evansville	Vanderburgh	F	Member
Coultas, Porter J.	Tell City	Perry	M	
Cowan, Elizabeth	Crawfordsville	Montgomery	F	Honorary
Cox, John E.	Evansville	Vanderburgh	M	
Crow, William Dixon	Petersburg	Pike	M	
Culbertson, D. Frank	Vincennes	Knox	M	Member
Cummings, Uriah Ballard	Tell City	Perry	M'	
Cutler, Mrs. Will	Evansville	Vanderburgh	F	Member
Cutler, Will	Evansville	Vanderburgh	M	Member
Cuttler, James	Mt. Auburn	Vanderburgh	M	Member
Cuttler, Mrs. James	Mt. Auburn	Vanderburgh	F	Member
Daniel, Walter V.			M	
Darby, Mrs.	Newburgh	Warrick	F	Member
Davidson, Helen M.	Evansville	Vanderburgh	F	Member
Davidson, Mrs. E. L.			F	
Davis, James F.			M	
Davis, Walter A.	Vincennes	Knox	M	
De Bruler, Eva			F	
De la Hunt, Thomas J.	Cannelton	Perry	M	Member
Dearing, William P.	Oakland City	Gibson	M	

Name	Place of Residence		M/F	Status
DeMott, Dr.		Pike	M	
Dennigan, William P.	Vincennes	Knox	M	
Deweese, Earl	Richland	Spencer	M	
Dixon, Matilda Morgan	Evansville	Vanderburgh	F	Member
Doll, Henry			M	
Donald, Mrs. D. W.	New Harmony	Posey	F	Member
Douglass, Oliver			M	
Downs, Dr. W. G.		Vanderburgh	M	
Downs, Thomas E.	Boonville	Warrick	M	Member
Dragoo, Ruth	Pittsburgh	KS	F	Member
Driver, Levi J.	Vincennes	Knox	M	
Dufendoll, Mrs. Ed. H.	Huntingburg	Dubois	F	Member
Dufendoll, Sadie	Huntingburg	Dubois	F	Member
Dunkerson, Laura C.	Evansville	Vanderburgh	F	
Dunlevy, Mabel DeBruler	Evansville	Vanderburgh	F	Member
Early, Mrs. L. J.	Cannelton	Perry	F	Member
Eckley, Winfield	Tell City	Perry	M	
Ehrman, Dorothy			F	
Ehrman, Mrs. Frederick J.	Evansville	Vanderburgh	F	
Ehrmann, Bess Virginia Hicks	Rockport	Spencer	F	Member
Ehrmann, Calder DeBruler	Rockport	Spencer	M	Member
Ehrmann, Eugenia DeBruler	Rockport	Spencer	F	Member
Elliott, Phoebe	New Harmony	Posey	F	Member
Embree, Louise	Princeton	Gibson	F	Member
Embree, Lucius C.	Princeton	Gibson	M	Member
Embree, Mrs. Lucius	Princeton	Gibson	F	Member
Enghof, Grace Adye			F	
Enlow, Pet Veatch	Rockport	Spencer	F	Member
Erlbacher, Irene	Evansville	Vanderburgh	F	Member
Erskine, Mrs. Levy	Evansville	Vanderburgh	F	Member
Erwin, Lotta Edson	Mt. Vernon	Posey	F	Member
Esarey, Logan	Bloomington	Monroe	M	Guest
Fauntleroy, Mary Emily	New Harmony	Posey	F	Member
Fenn, Roy	Tell City	Perry	M	
Fiebig, Mrs. Louise	Evansville	Vanderburgh	F	Member
Fiegel, J. R.	Rockport	Spencer	M	Member
Fiegel, Mrs. J. R.	Rockport	Spencer	F	Member
Fitton, Herbert Bolton	Mt. Vernon	Posey	M	
Fitton, Katherine F.	Mt. Vernon	Posey	F	Member
Fletcher, Mrs. C. L.	Northampton	MA	F	Member
Ford, Chas.	New Harmony	Posey	M	Member
Ford, George	New Harmony	Posey	M	Member
Ford, Mrs. Chas.	New Harmony	Posey	F	Member
Ford, Mrs. George	New Harmony	Posey	M	Member
Forsythe, Maud	Grandview	Spencer	F	Member

Name	Place of Residence		M/F	Status
Forsythe, Mrs. Harold	Newburgh	Warrick	F	
Fortune, William	Indianapolis	Marion	M	Honorary
Fretageot, Arthur E.	New Harmony	Posey	M	Member
Fretageot, Mary	New Harmony	Posey	F	
Fretageot, Nora Chadwick	New Harmony	Posey	F	Member
Fritsch, Dr. Wm. A.	Evansville	Vanderburgh	M	Member
Fuhrer, Mrs. Chas. W.	Evansville	Vanderburgh	F	Member
Fulling, Henry F.	Boonville	Warrick	M	Member
Funk, Mrs. Ed B.	Princeton	Gibson	F	Member
Garvin, Susan M.	Evansville	Vanderburgh	F	Member
Gasman (?), T. T.	Troy	Perry		
Gentry, Lizzie	Rockport	Spencer	F	Member
Gilchrist, Mrs. Alexander	Evansville	Vanderburgh	F	Member
Gillet, Mrs. Lowery	Evansville	Vanderburgh	F	Member
Glackman, Mrs. J. C.	Rockport	Spencer	F	Member
Goodge, George	Evansville	Vanderburgh	M	Member
Gough, Edward	Boonville	Warrick	M	Member
Gough, Ida M.	Boonville	Warrick	F	Member
Gough, Mrs. Edward	Boonville	Warrick	F	Member
Gough, Mrs. Eugene	Boonville	Warrick	F	Member
Gray, A. L.	Huntingburg	Dubois	M	Member
Gray, Beulah Brazelton	Otwell	Pike	F	
Gray, Mrs. A. L.	Huntingburg	Dubois	F	Member
Grigsby, Mrs. Ely			F	
Grill, Mrs. Mattie	Evansville	Vanderburgh	F	Member
Grimm, Mrs. John Gullick	Petersburg	Pike	F	
Gugemeyer, Louise E.	Huntingburg	Dubois	F	Member
Gunn, C. L.	Mt. Vernon	Posey	M	
Gwaltney, John	Midway	Spencer	M	
Haas, Grace Calkins	Princeton	Gibson	F	Member
Halbruge, Carrie V.	Rockport	Spencer	F	Member
Hale, Mrs. J. M.	Mt. Vernon	Posey	F	Member
Hanby, Alice L. Harper	Mt. Vernon	Posey	F	Member
Hargrave, Edward C.	Boonville	Warrick	M	Member
Harriman, Loudon A.	Princeton	Gibson	M	
Harris, Mrs. B. F.	Huntingburg	Dubois	F	
Hart, Mary Spencer	Mt. Vernon	Posey	F	Member
Hartigg, Alex	Evansville	Vanderburgh	M	Member
Hastings, Mrs.	Washington	Daviess	F	
Hatfield, Mr.			M	
Hatfield, Mrs. Frank H.	Evansville	Vanderburgh	F	
Hayford, Bertha		Lake	F	Member
Hayford, Elbert D.	Augusta	ME	M	Contributor
Haynes, Judith Montgomery		Spencer	F	
Hays, Will H.	Hollywood	CA	M	Contributor

Name	Place of Residence		M/F	Status
Heinspeter, Mrs. Wm.	Evansville	Vanderburgh	F	Member
Heinzle, Elizabeth Gautschi	Tell City	Perry	F	Member
Hemenway, James A.	Boonville	Warrick	M	Member
Hemer, H. W. A.	Huntingburg	Dubois	M	
Henner, Mrs. H. W. A.	Huntingburg	Dubois	F	Member
Herbert, Alice			F	
Heuring, Fred A.	Rockport	Spencer	M	Member
Heuring, Jessie Brandenburg	Rockport	Spencer	F	Member
Hill, Mary H.	Rockport	Spencer	F	Member
Hill, Mrs. Edward N.	Evansville	Vanderburgh	F	Member
Hohenberger, Frank M.	Martinsville	Morgan	M	Guest
Honig, Alda McCoy	Evansville	Vanderburgh	F	Member
Honig, George H.	Evansville	Vanderburgh	M	Member
Hooper, Susie	Cannelton	Perry	F	Member
Hoover, Mrs. J. Guy	Boonville	Warrick	F	Member
Hopkins, John S.	Evansville	Vanderburgh	M	Member
Hopkins, Mrs. A. J.	Boonville	Warrick	F	Member
Hopkins, Mrs. John S.	Evansville	Vanderburgh	F	Member
Hopkins, Mrs. Stuart	Evansville	Vanderburgh	F	
Houghland, Mrs. Robert	Boonville	Warrick	F	Member
Hovey, Charles J.			M	
Howe, J. Edwin	Cannelton	Perry	M	
Howe, Kaloolah	Evansville	Vanderburgh	F	Member
Howe, Mrs. J. Edwin	Cannelton	Perry	F	Member
Huddleston, Ann	Princeton	Gibson	F	
Hudson, Amelia Hall	Princeton	Gibson	F	Member
Huff, Aquila Colfax	Tell City	Perry	M	Member
Huffamn, Lemuel Q.			M	
Huffman, Ben F.	Rockport	Spencer	M	Member
Huffman, John Sr.	Huffman Mills	Spencer	M	Member
Huffman, Mollie	Rockport	Spencer	F	Member
Huffman, Mrs. Ben F.	Rockport	Spencer	F	Member
Hunter, Anna	Jasper	Dubois	F	Member
Husband, Louise	New Harmony	Posey	F	Member
Huthsteiner, Mrs. W. F.	Tell City	Perry	F	Member
Huthsteiner, Walter F.	Tell City	Perry	M	Member
Iglehart, E. H.	Indianapolis	Marion	M	Member
Iglehart, John Eugene	Evansville	Vanderburgh	M	Member
Iglehart, John L.	Evansville	Vanderburgh	M	Member
Iglehart, Joseph	Evansville	Vanderburgh	M	Member
Iglehart, Mrs. John L.	Evansville	Vanderburgh	F	Member
Iglehart, Mrs. Joseph	Evansville	Vanderburgh	F	Member
Iglehart, Mrs. William	Evansville	Vanderburgh	F	Member
Irwin, Mrs. Fred	Cannelton	Perry	F	Member
Jackson, Mrs. W. A.	Evansville	Vanderburgh	F	Member

Name	Place of Residence		M/F	Status
Jackson, W. A.	Evansville	Vanderburgh	M	Member
Jacques, Jonathan	Poseyville	Posey	M	
Jacquess, Mrs. Arthur E.	Poseyville	Posey	F	Member
Jacquess, Mrs. Jonathan	Poseyville	Posey	F	
Jaquess, William G.	Tunica	MS	M	
Johann, Mrs. Chas.	Evansville	Vanderburgh	F	Member
Johnson, Deidre Duff	Mt. Vernon	Posey	F	Member
Johnson, J. S.	Richland	Spencer	M	
Johnston, Juliet Alves	Henderson	KY	F	
Jolly, J. C.	Richland	Spencer	M	
Jones, Bonnie	Rockport	Spencer	F	Member
Jones, Mrs. Douglas	Mt. Vernon	Posey	F	Member
Kean, Horace M.	Jasper	Dubois	M	Member
Keck, Mrs. Andrew	Evansville	Vanderburgh	F	Member
Kellams, W. W.	Rockport	Spencer	M	Member
Keller, Helen	Evansville	Vanderburgh	F	Member
Kelley, Anna Hardy	New Albany	Floyd	F	Member
Kennedy, A. H.	Rockport	Spencer	M	Member
Kimball, Major	Mt. Vernon	Posey	M	
Kiper, Mrs. Roscoe	Boonville	Warrick	F	Member
Kiper, Roscoe	Boonville	Warrick	M	Member
Klein, Mrs. Otto	Mt. Vernon	Posey	F	Member
Knapp, Mrs. H. C.	Huntingburg	Dubois	F	Member
Kniblock, Otto N.			M	
Kohlmeier, Albert L.	Bloomington	Monroe	M	
Kolmeyer, John M.	Boonville	Warrick	M	Member
Lauenstein, Mrs. Fred	Evansville	Vanderburgh	F	Member
Laval, Mrs. Otto	Evansville	Vanderburgh	F	Member
Laval, Otto	Evansville	Vanderburgh	M	Member
Leaf, Kate	Rockport	Spencer	F	Member
Lehman, Mrs. William C.	Cannelton	Perry	F	Member
Lehman, William Charles	Cannelton	Perry	M	Member
Leich, Chester	Evansville	Vanderburgh	M	Member
Leich, Clarence	Evansville	Vanderburgh	M	Member
Leich, Mrs. Clarence	Evansville	Vanderburgh	F	Member
Lemond, Mrs. Milton	Huntingburg	Dubois	F	Member
Leonard, Esther Harrow	Mt. Vernon	Posey	F	Member
Lichtenberger, H.	New Harmony	Posey	M	Member
Lichtenberger, Mathilda	New Harmony	Posey	F	Member
Lieb, Charles	Rockport	Spencer	M	Member
Lieb, Mrs. Charles	Rockport	Spencer	F	Member
Lincoln, Edmund S.	Cannelton	Perry	M	Member
Lindley, Harlow	Indianapolis	Marion	M	
Lindsay, U. S.	Rockport	Spencer	M	Member
Lindsey, Caleb J.	Boonville	Warrick	M	Guest

Name	Place of Residence		M/F	Status
Little, Andrew C.	Cannelton	Perry	M	Member
Lockridge, Ross F.	Bloomington	Monroe	M	
Lockyear, Elmer Q.	Evansville	Vanderburgh	M	
Logsdon, Mrs. Hiram M.	Evansville	Vanderburgh	F	Member
Lucas, Harvey	Vincennes	Knox	M	Member
Lynch, William O.	Bloomington	Monroe	M	Guest
Maas, Grace Jeanette Bullock	Gentryville	Spencer	F	
Markland, Jessie	Rockport	Spencer	F	Member
Marlett, Bessie Starr	Evansville	Vanderburgh	F	Member
Marlett, Francis Bartlett	Evansville	Vanderburgh	F	Member
Marlette, John J.	Evansville	Vanderburgh	M	Member
Martin, Mrs. P. Aiken	Evansville	Vanderburgh	F	Member
Mason, Mrs.	Vincennes	Knox	F	
Mason, Mrs. W. C.	Rockport	Spencer	F	Member
Mason, William C.	Vincennes	Knox	M	Member
Masterson, T. Hardy	Kennett	MO	M	
Mattingly, Mrs. Ray	Rockport	Spencer	F	Member
May, Mrs. Samuel	Evansville	Vanderburgh	F	Member
May, Samuel L.	Evansville	Vanderburgh	M	Member
McAnnis, Mrs. C. C.	Harrisville	KY	F	
McCulla, Fannie E.	Boonville	Warrick	F	Member
McCullough, Ethel Farquhar	Evansville	Vanderburgh	F	Member
McNeely, Mrs.	Evansville	Vanderburgh	F	Member
Meeks, Aaron				
Meeks, Atha			M	
Miller, Leonora P.	Princeton	Gibson	F	
Minor, Mrs. A C (?)	Cannelton	Perry	F	
Minor, Mrs. William G.	Cannelton	Perry	F	
Minor, William G.	Cannelton	Perry	M	
M'Laughlin, Mabel Nisbet	Henderson	KY	F	
Montgomery, Judith Hazen	Rockport	Spencer	F	
Moore, W. W.	Rockport	Spencer	M	Member
Morgan, David H.	Pittsburg	KS	M	Member
Morrison, George W.			M	
Moutschka, John Paul	Tell City	Perry	M	
Mullen, Lee	Cannelton	Perry	M	Member
Munford, Thomas	New Harmony	Posey	M	Member
Murr, J. Edward	Princeton	Gibson	M	Member
Nesbit, Rose Blount	Kalamazoo	MI	F	Member
Nester, Mrs. Chas. J.	Boonville	Warrick	F	Member
Nolte, Lola	Mt. Vernon	Posey	F	Member
Odell, Helen H.	Cannelton	Perry	F	Member
O'Flynn, Anna C.	Vincennes	Knox	F	Member
Oliver, John W.	Indianapolis	Marion	M	Honorary
Olmsted, Ella	Evansville	Vanderburgh	F	Member

Name	Place of Residence		M/F	Status
Orr, Louise Dunkerson	Evansville	Vanderburgh	F	Member
Orr, Samuel Lowry	Evansville	Vanderburgh	M	Member
Ortmeyer, Daniel	Evansville	Vanderburgh	M	Member
Ortmeyer, Mrs. Daniel	Evansville	Vanderburgh	F	Member
Osborne, Mrs. Lane		Spencer	F	
Page, Ann	Evansville	Vanderburgh	F	Member
Parson, Major Byron	Evansville	Vanderburgh	M	Member
Parson, Mrs. Bryon	Evansville	Vanderburgh	F	Member
Pattie, Grace	Rockport	Spencer	F	Member
Paxton, Thomas R.	Princeton	Gibson	M	Member
Payne, Addie Polk Miller	Tobinsport	Perry	F	Member
Payne, Mollie	Rockport	Spencer	F	Member
Pelham, Carolyn	New Harmony	Posey	F	Member
Pennington, Spencer	Rockport	Spencer	M	
Pickhart, E. W.	Huntingburg	Dubois	M	Member
Polk, Edwin	Rockport	Spencer	M	Member
Polk, Lester	Rockport	Spencer	M	Member
Polk, Mrs. Edwin	Rockport	Spencer	F	Member
Polk, Mrs. Lester	Rockport	Spencer	F	Member
Poor, Mrs. M. J.	Newburgh	Warrick	F	Member
Posey, Myrtle	Rockport	Spencer	F	Member
Potter, Alice Cauthorn	Princeton	Gibson	F	
Potter, Mildred	Princeton	Gibson	F	
Powell, E. Ainger	Evansville	Vanderburgh	M	
Powell, Eugene	Evansville	Vanderburgh	M	
Powell, Harriet	Lamar	Spencer	F	
Prosser, Hamline R.	Minneapolis	MN	M	
Rabb, Kate Milner	Indianapolis	Marion	F	Member
Raleigh, Eldora Minor	Newburgh	Warrick	F	Member
Ray, Jeff	Rockport	Spencer	M	Member
Reed, Mrs. D.	Boonville	Warrick	F	Member
Reed, Virginia	Evansville	Vanderburgh	F	Member
Reilly, Anne Hazelton	Evansville	Vanderburgh	F	Member
Reis, Henry	Evansville	Vanderburgh	M	
Reynolds, Mary F.	Evansville	Vanderburgh	F	Member
Rhoades, J. Helen	Rockport	Spencer	F	Member
Rhodes, Ada	Rockport	Spencer	F	Member
Richardson, Dora V. Hall		Perry	F	
Richardson, Isaiah	Rockport	Spencer	M	Member
Richardson, Mrs. Isaiah	Rockport	Spencer	F	Member
Richrich, T. H.	Lynnville	Warrick	M	Member
Riker, Dorothy	Indianapolis	Marion	F	
Roberts, Alice	Rockport	Spencer	F	Member
Roberts, R.	Rockport	Spencer	M	Member
Robinson, Ivor J.	Boonville	Warrick	M	Member

Name	Place of Residence		M/F	Status
Robinson, Mrs. W. D.	Evansville	Vanderburgh	F	Member
Robinson, W. D.	Evansville	Vanderburgh	M	Member
Rodeheffer, Rev.			M	
Roetzel, Mrs. C. F.	Boonville	Warrick	F	Member
Rose, Helen	Ireland	Dubois	F	Member
Rose, Mrs. B. S.		Vanderburgh	F	
Ross, William W.	Evansville	Vanderburgh	M	Member
Roth, Emma	Boonville	Warrick	F	Member
Roth, H. C.	Huntingburg	Dubois	M	Member
Roth, Mrs. Gus.	Boonville	Warrick	F	Member
Roth, Mrs. H. C.	Huntingburg	Dubois	F	Member
Rothert, Hugo C.	Huntingburg	Dubois	M	Member
Rothert, Otto A.	Louisville	KY	M	Member
Rothert, Willa MacMahon	Huntingburg	Dubois	F	Member
Rowland, Mrs. Jacob	Cannelton	Perry	F	Member
Rucker, Mrs. James B.	Lebanon	TN	F	
Rugledge, Mrs. L. S.	Newburgh	Warrick	F	Member
Runcie, Anna	Evansville	Vanderburgh	F	Member
Runcie, Ella	Evansville	Vanderburgh	F	Member
Sager, Ben F.	Vincennes	Knox	M	Member
Salm, Mrs. Charles H.		Spencer	F	
Sanders, Edna Brown	Evansville	Vanderburgh	F	Member
Sapp, Mildred			F	
Saunders, Elizabeth M.	Evansville	Vanderburgh	F	Member
Saunders, Jas D.	Evansville	Vanderburgh	M	Member
Savage, L. N.	Rockport	Spencer	M	Member
Savage, Mrs. L. N.	Rockport	Spencer	F	Member
Scales, Earl	Boonville	Warrick	M	Member
Scales, Mrs. Earl	Boonville	Warrick	F	Member
Schemenhorn, Ola	Rockport	Spencer	F	Member
Schmidt, Paul	Evansville	Vanderburgh	M	Guest
Schoenfield, Mrs. Louis	Rockport	Spencer	F	Member
Schreeder, C. C.	Evansville	Vanderburgh	M	
Schreiber, Anna Dhonau	Tell City	Perry	F	
Schreiber, Charles D.	Tell City	Perry	M	Member
Schreiber, Darwin		Perry	M	
Schreiber, Mrs. C. D.	Tell City	Perry	F	Member
Schultz, Ed	Tell City	Perry	M	
Schultz, Kate Pitcher Whitworth	Mt. Vernon	Posey	F	Member
Schumaker, Mrs. Sam	Rockport	Spencer	F	Member
Schurmeier, Clyde	Boonville	Warrick	F	
Seasongood, Ed. F.	Evansville	Vanderburgh	M	Member
Seay, Don	Rockport	Spencer	M	
Sexton, Jean	Gibson	Member		
Shake, Curtis G.	Vincennes	Knox	M	

Name	Place of Residence		M/F	Status
Shaller (?), James C.	Cannelton	Perry	M	
Shaller (?), Mrs. James C.	Cannelton	Perry	F	
Shrode, Mrs. J. R.	Rockport	Spencer	F	Member
Shrode, Roy	Rockport	Spencer	M	Member
Skiles, Mrs. Henry	Evansville	Vanderburgh	F	Member
Slackman, Mrs. Clay	Rockport	Spencer	F	Member
Smith, George A.	Cannelton	Perry	M	
Smith, Mrs. Robt.	Evansville	Vanderburgh	F	Member
Snepp, Daniel Webster	Evansville	Vanderburgh	M	
Snyder, Minnie D.	Rockport	Spencer	F	
Somes, J. H. Vanderburg			M	
Sonntag, Marcus S.	Evansville	Vanderburgh	M	
Spayd, Bettie Veatch	Alderwood Manor	WA	F	Contributor
Spencer, Mary Nolte	Mt. Vernon	Posey	F	Member
Springer, Cora M.	Princeton	Gibson	F	Member
Standley, Mrs. G. O.	Cannelton	Perry	F	
Steitler, Mrs. George	Rockport	Spencer	F	Member
Stevenson, Eva	Rockport	Spencer	F	Member
Stevenson, Mrs. Arch	Rockport	Spencer	F	Member
Stevenson, William	Rockport	Spencer	M	
Stewart, Clare E.	Princeton	Gibson	F	Member
Stewart, Samuel A.	Princeton	Gibson	M	Member
Stoops, Alice Parry	Petersburg	Pike	F	Member
Stoops, Marmaduke McClellan	Petersburg	Pike	M	
Stork, W. F.	Huntingburg	Dubois		Member
Stormont, Gil. R.	Princeton	Gibson	M	Member
Strickland, J. Roy	Owensville	Gibson	M	Member
Strong, Mrs. Rose J.	Evansville	Vanderburgh	F	Member
Sweeney, Luella	Tell City	Perry	F	
Sweeny, Andrew			M	
Sweet, William Warren	Greencastle	Putnam	M	
Tarbell, Ida	New York	NY	F	Honorary
Taylor, Anna Stevenson	Mt. Zion	Wells	F	Member
Taylor, Arthur H.	Petersburg	Pike	M	Member
Taylor, Charles H.	Boonville	Warrick	M	
Taylor, Lizzie Graham	Rockport	Spencer	F	
Taylor, Mrs. Lewis	Yankeetown	Warrick	F	
Thixton, Lillian Walker	Henderson	KY	F	Guest
Thomas, Agnes Haas	Princeton	Gibson	F	Member
Thomas, Anna L.	Princeton	Gibson	F	Member
Thomas, Mrs. A. J.	New Harmony	Posey	F	Member
Thompson, Charles M.		IL		
Thorpe, Edith	Rockport	Spencer	F	
Tillman, Mabel		Warrick	F	
Torance, Mrs. Wm. J.	Evansville	Vanderburgh	F	Member

Name	Place of Residence		M/F	Status
Torbet, Chas.	Evansville	Vanderburgh	M	Member
Torrance, Theodora Hazen McGill	Evansville	Vanderburgh	F	Member
Towles, Susan Starling	Henderson	KY	F	Guest
Townsend, Clay J.	Osgood	Riley	M	Member
Tracewell, Robert	Evansville	Vanderburgh	M	
Traylor, Bomar	Jasper	Dubois	M	Member
Trimble, Eliza Scott	Evansville	Vanderburgh	F	Member
Truempy, Mrs. T. J.	Cannelton	Perry	F	
Turnham, G. W.	Evansville	Vanderburgh	M	Member
Turnham, Mrs. G. W.	Evansville	Vanderburgh	F	Member
Twigg, Virginia	Los Angeles	CA	F	Contributor
Twineham, Agnes L.	Princeton	Gibson	F	Member
Uler, Helen	Petersburg	Pike	F	
Vannest, Charles Garrett			M	
Veatch, Mrs. Henry			F	
Vogel, Mrs. M. P.	Detroit	MI	F	Member
Wagner, Louis	Huntingburg	Dubois	M	Member
Walker, Elinor	Rockport	Spencer	F	Member
Walker, Mrs. Guy H.	Rockport	Spencer	F	Member
Walker, Mrs. J. H.	Rockport	Spencer	F	Member
Walschmidt, William M.	Cannelton	Perry	M	
Warren, Louis A.	Ft. Wayne	Allen	M	Honorary
Warren, Mrs. William	Newburgh	Warrick	F	Member
Warren, William	Newburgh	Warrick	M	Member
Wartman, Sara	Los Angeles	CA	F	Member
Waters, George J.	Poseyville	Posey	M	Member
Waters, Mrs. George	Poseyville	Posey	F	Member
Watts, Edwyn E.	Princeton	Gibson	M	
Weatherholt, Jacob			M	
Weatherholt, Wallace	Tobinsport	Perry	M	
Wedeking, Albert J.	Dale	Spencer	M	Member
Weil, Mrs. M.	Rockport	Spencer	F	Member
Weiner, Nelle	Rockport	Spencer	F	Member
Weisinger, Mrs. M. A.	Mt. Vernon	Posey	F	Member
Welborn, Anne Acton	Evansville	Vanderburgh	F	Member
Welborn, J.	Princeton	Gibson	M	Member
Welborn, Mary	Princeton	Gibson	F	Member
Welborn, Mrs. Oscar M.	Princeton	Gibson	F	Member
Welborn, Oscar M.	Princeton	Gibson	M	Member
Weyerbacher, Kenneth H.	Boonville	Warrick	M	Member
Wheatley, Ella Cockrum	Oakland City	Gibson	F	Member
Wheeler, Lawrence	Princeton	Gibson	M	Member
Wheeler, Mary	Evansville	Vanderburgh	F	Member
Wheeler, Walton M.	Evansville	Vanderburgh	M	
White, Della		Lake	F	Member

Name	Place of Residence		M/F	Status
White, Hettie	Rockport	Spencer	F	Member
White, Mary	Evansville	Vanderburgh	F	Member
Whitelock, Mrs.		Pike	F	
Wilbur, Mrs. Agnes I.	Cannelton	Perry	F	Member
Wilkinson, Laura	Rockport	Spencer	F	Member
Wilkinson, Mrs. Lottie	Rockport	Spencer	F	Member
Williams, Alla	Evansville	Vanderburgh	F	Member
Williams, Genevieve MacDonald	Huntingburg	Dubois	F	Member
Wilson, George R.	Indianapolis	Marion	M	Member
Wilson, Margaret Ann	Jasper	Dubois	F	Member
Wilson, Miles			M	
Wilson, Mrs. Robert Ernest	Mt. Vernon	Posey	F	Member
Wilson, Mrs. Robert R.	Boonville	Warrick	F	
Wilson, Mrs. William A.	Jasper	Dubois	F	Member
Wilson, Roberta Georgine			F	
Wilson, Sadye Anderson	Newburgh	Warrick	F	
Wilson, Thomas J.	Corydon	Harrison	M	Member
Wilson, Wesley		Warrick	M	
Winterhalter, Herbert F.	Boonville	Warrick	M	
Wolfe, Clarence P.	New Harmony	Posey	M	
Woodburn, James A.	Bloomington	Monroe	M	
Woods, John Hall	Princeton	Gibson	M	
Woods, Mrs. Robert A.	Princeton	Gibson	F	Member
Woods, Robert A.	Princeton	Gibson	M	
Woolfolk, Myrtle Ray	Grandview	Spencer	F	Member
Wright, Amos	Rockport	Spencer	F	Member
Wright, Fannie	Rockport	Spencer	F	Member
Wright, Grace	Evansville	Vanderburgh	F	Member
Wright, Laura Mercy	Rockport	Spencer	F	Member
Wright, Lizzie B.	Rockport	Spencer	F	Member
Wright, Margaret	Rockport	Spencer	F	
Wright, Mrs. Amos	Rockport	Spencer	F	Member
Wulkap, Helen	Evansville	Vanderburgh	F	Member
Young, Otis E.	South Bend	St. Joseph	M	

ළ Appendix B

Papers, Publications, and Works of the Lincoln Inquiry

T HIS BIBLIOGRAPHY attempts to identify all of the conference papers, publications, and works created by the Southwestern Indiana Historical Society during the 1920s and 1930s. If an item was presented or announced at a society meeting, the date is given in square brackets. "BE" refers to the identification number provided by Bess V. Ehrmann in *The Missing Chapter in the Life of Abraham Lincoln* (Chicago, 1938), 23–60. "EVPL" identifies the pages on which the item or a summary of the item is recorded in the four-volume "Annals of the Southwestern Indiana Historical Society" that is preserved in the Evansville Public Library. For Iglehart Papers, "Proceedings," and SWIHS Collection see Abbreviations.

Adams, Will. "Biographical Sketch of Josiah and Elizabeth (Anderson) Crawford." Bess V. Ehrmann Scrapbooks, D-1, letters. Spencer County Historical Society. [November 17, 1925; BE 38; EVPL 2:1–9]

Armstrong, Bertha Potts. Davidson Library of 60 volumes. [February 10, 1927]

Armstrong, Ida D. "The Lincolns in Spencer County." *Indiana Historical Commission Bulletin* No. 18, *Proceedings of the Southwestern Indiana Historical Society* (October 1923): 54–62. [February 28, 1923; BE 17]

———. "Rockport," *Evansville Courier,* December 25, 1921, SWIHS Collection.

Bacon, Albion Fellows. "Lincoln." *Indiana Magazine of History* 21, no. 1 (March 1925): 1–2. [October 14, 1924]

———. "At the Landing." *Indiana Historical Commission Bulletin* No. 18, *Proceedings of the Southwestern Indiana Historical Society* (October 1923): 132–35. [February 28, 1923, February 6, 1925]

———. "Word Pictures of Pioneer Families and Lincoln Contemporaries." *Indiana History Bulletin,* Vol. 6, Extra No. 3, *Proceedings of the Southwestern Indiana Historical Society during its Ninth Year* (August 1929): 122. [October 30, 1928; BE 59]

———. "Old Daddy Hight." [February 19, 1929]

Baker, Charles T. "How Abe Saved the Farm." *Grandview Monitor,* August 26, 1920. [BE 1]

———. Article about Lincoln and Crawford. *Grandview Monitor,* August 26, 1920. [BE 2]

———. "Proceedings of the Grandview Lincoln Markers' Dedication, February 12, 1928." [February 23, 1928; BE 71]

———. "The Lincoln Family in Spencer County: Interesting Facts and Stories Gleaned from Descendants of the Earliest Pioneers and Neighbors of the Greatest President." 1928. [EVPL 3:10–21]

———. "Literacy of the Lincoln Neighbors." SWIHS Collection. [June 5, 1930; BE 81]

———. "The Disposal of the Lincoln Farm." 1934. [EVPL 3: 22–24]

———. "Facts Concerning Yellow Banks." N.d.

———. Lincoln Play. N.d. [BE 134]

Barbour, Lillie. "Dennys and Hudspeths." [December 4, 1931]

Barker, Levi B. "Warrick County Neighbors of the Lincoln Family." SWIHS Collection. [June 5, 1930]

Barker, William L. "Ratliff Boon." *Indiana Historical Commission Bulletin* No. 16, *Proceedings of the Southwestern Indiana Historical Society* (October 1922): 72–78. [January 31, 1922; BE 13]

———. "History of the Lincoln Route." *Indiana History Bulletin,* Vol. 4, Extra No. 1, *Proceedings of the Southwestern Indiana Historical Society during its Seventh Year* (December 1926): 43–70. [June 24, 1926; BE 39]

———. "Warrick County and the Northwest Territory." *Indiana Magazine of History* 24, no. 2 (June 1928): 121–29. [June 14, 1927]

———. "The Lincoln Country." SWIHS Collection. [October 22, 1930; EVPL 3:25–28]

———. "Resume of 1929 and 1930." SWIHS Collection. [February 12, 1931]

———. "The Lincoln Route," *The Winslow Dispatch,* August 7, 1931.

———. "Personal Reminiscence of Judge John Hanby." [December 4, 1931]

———. "Some Barker Family History." *Indiana Magazine of History* 37 (March 1941): 50–56. [March 11, 1932]

Barker, William, Philip Lutz, and Union Youngblood, comps. *Brief of The Warrick County Lincoln Route Association.* Booneville, IN, 1931.

Barnett, Helen. "Barnetts of Spencer County." [October 26, 1934; BE 136]

Beach, A. R. "A Bit of Half-Forgotten History: A Battle of the War of the American Revolution fought on Indiana Soil." [September 28, 1920; EVPL 74–79]

Beach, Mrs. Alfred. "Data on Hall and Hanks Families." [BE 20]

Bergenroth, Sallie. "Some Early Troy History." [June 1, 1928; BE 56; EVPL 3:29–33]

Bigney, A. J. "How the Colleges Can Co-operate with the Historical Societies." *Indiana History Bulletin,* Vol. 1, Extra No., *Proceedings of the Fifth Annual Meeting of the Southwestern Indiana Historical Society* (June 1924): 49–51. [February 12, 1924]

Bockstahler, William George. "Pioneer Work and Growth of the German Methodist Church in Southern Indiana." [March 9, 1934]

Boonville Press Club. Annual Services at the Grave of Nancy Hanks Lincoln. [BE 125]

Brewster, Paul G. "Indiana's Heritage of Song: Its Historical and Cultural Significance." [October 6, 1936]

Buchanan, Charles J. "Address." "Proceedings," 16–18. [October 14, 1924]

Bullcok, Arietta F. "Old Time Tales Told of Jonesboro." [BE 106]

Butler, Amos W. "Indiana Public Charities."

Carleton, William B., "The Lincoln Atmosphere." SWIHS Collection. [June 5, 1930]

Clark, Jennie Latimer. "Sketch of George Ewing." [May 24, 1921]

————. "Early Literary Clubs in Cannelton and the Woman's Travel Club." [Sep-
tember 29, 1922]

————. "The Cannelton Potteries." SWIHS Collection. [October 22, 1930]

Clements, Herdis F. "Early Courts of Posey County." [November 1, 1929]

Clifford, George S. "Life of George Clifford."

Clifford, Mrs. George S. (Emily Orr). "Private Schools in Evansville from 1842 to
1853." *Indiana Historical Commission Bulletin* No. 18, *Proceedings of the Southwestern Indiana Historical Society* (October 1923): 32–54. [February 28, 1923]

————. "Judge Matthew Foster." [October 25, 1927]

————. "First Church of Evansville."

Coleman, Christopher B. "Historical Work in Indiana." *Indiana History Bulletin,*
Vol. 3, Extra No. 1, *Proceedings of the Southwestern Indiana Historical Society: Papers Read Before the Society at Various Meetings, 1920–1925* (December
1925): 64–66. [October 14, 1924]

————. "Emphasis in the Work of Historical Societies." *Indiana History Bulletin,*
Vol. 6, Extra No. 3, *Proceedings of the Southwestern Indiana Historical Society
during its Ninth Year* (August 1929): 9–16. [November 17, 1925; EVPL
2:10–20]

————. "John Hay, The Son of Pioneers." *The Undying Past and Other Addresses.*
Indianapolis, 1946, 112–26. [October 25, 1927]

————. "Judge John Law." *The Undying Past and Other Addresses.* Indianapolis,
1946, 89–111. [February 6, 1930; BE 77]

————. "Historical Societies and Schools." [February 12, 1931]

————. "Washington and the West." [March 11, 1932]

————. "First State Constitution and First State Capitol." SWIHS Collection.
[March 17, 1933]

————. "The Lincoln Legend." *Indiana Magazine of History* 29 (Dec 1933): 277–86.

————. "Indiana Its Evolution and Its Distinctive Features." [October 6, 1936]

Collins, Herbert S. "Items of Warrick County History." SWIHS Collection. [Sep-
tember 29, 1922]

Cook, Mina. "History of Early Schools in Spencer County." SWIHS Collection.
[October 8, 1926]

————. "Early Interests in Spencer County." SWIHS Collection. [October 30, 1928]

————. "History of the First Public Schools in Evansville." [February 19, 1929]

Cooper, Sarah Hunter. "Pioneers and School Experiences." SWIHS Collection.
[October 12, 1923]

Cox, John E. "Judge John Pitcher." *Indiana Historical Commission Bulletin* No.
18, *Proceedings of the Southwestern Indiana Historical Society* (October 1923):
93–94. [February 28, 1923; BE 29]

————. "General Thomas Pitcher." "Proceedings," 29–30. [June 15, 1923]

————. "Recollection." "Proceedings," 49–52. [June 15, 1923]

Crow, William Dixon. "Goodlett Morgan." [November 17, 1925]

Culbertson, D. Frank. "One Hundred and Fiftieth Centennial Plans for 1929." [February 25, 1926]

————. "[George Rogers] Clark Monument." [June 14, 1927]

————. "The Clark Memorial and Its Development." SWIHS Collection. [June 5, 1931]

Cummings, Uriah Ballard. "The Cummings Family, Perry County Pioneers." [October 12, 1923]

Daniel, Walter V. "Remarkable Incidents in the Life of Captain W. H. Daniel." [June 8, 1933]

Davidson, Helen M. "James Cawson's Library, 1818–1840." SWIHS Collection. [February 10, 1927; BE 50; EVPL 3:44–49]

————. "Letters relating to the English Newspaper Notice and the Death, also the Diary of James Cawson." [February 6, 1930]

————. "A Diary and Some Letters Written by James Cawson." SWIHS Collection. [February 12, 1931; BE 88; EVPL 3:34–43]

Davidson, Mrs. E. L. "Nancy Hanks Lincoln," Springfield [Washington County, KY] newspaper clipping, 1909. SWIHS Collection. [October 30, 1928; BE 55; EVPL 50–54]

Davis, James F. "Abraham Lincoln Makes a Speech in Posey County." [November 1, 1929]

Davis, Walter A. "Old Vincennes." [September 16, 1932]

De Bruler, Eva. "Hargrave Families."

de la Hunt, Thomas J. Perry County: A History. Indianapolis: W. K. Stewart, 1916. [BE 32]

————. "The Pocket in Indiana History." Indiana Magazine of History 16 (Dec 1920): 308–16. [February 23, 1920]

————. "Review of Lincoln Information," Evansville Courier, February 12, 1921. [BE 22]

————. "Cannelton Scene" from The Pageant of Perry County, 1814–1916. Tell City, 1916. [May 24, 1921]

————. "Old Gilead Church and Its Founder, the Reverend Charles Polk." Indiana Historical Commission Bulletin No. 16, Proceedings of the Southwestern Indiana Historical Society (October 1922): 96–104. [October 11, 1921]

————. "Publicity in Newspapers." Indiana Historical Commission Bulletin No. 16, Proceedings of the Southwestern Indiana Historical Society (October 1922): 29–31. [January 31, 1922]

————. "A Personal Letter Written in 1849 by Huntington." "Proceedings," October 12, 1923, 18–26. [October 12, 1923]

————. "Mistletoe Lodge and Tell City Pioneers." Tell City Historical Society Museum, Tell City, IN. [October 12, 1923]

————. "President's Address." Indiana History Bulletin, Vol. 1, Extra No., Proceedings of the Fifth Annual Meeting of the Southwestern Indiana Historical Society (June 1924): 11–14. [February 12, 1924]

————. "President's Address." "Proceedings," June 10, 1924 7–10. [June 10, 1924]

———. "Address." "Proceedings," October 14, 1924 3–6. [October 14, 1924]
———. "Mann Butler's Account of the George Rogers Clark Expedition." [February 25, 1926]
———. "Judge Elisha Mills Huntington" *Indiana Magazine of History* 23, no. 2 (June 1927): 115–29. [February 10, 1927]
———. "Joshua Brannon Huckeby, Perry County Pioneer." *Indiana History Bulletin*, Vol. 6, Extra No. 3, *Proceedings of the Southwestern Indiana Historical Society during its Ninth Year* (August 1929): 46–55. [February 23, 1928; BE 69; EVPL 55–68]
———. "The Lincolns' Eastward Environment." *Indiana History Bulletin*, Vol. 6, Extra No. 3, *Proceedings of the Southwestern Indiana Historical Society during its Ninth Year* (August 1929): 114–18. [October 30, 1928; BE 48; EVPL 3:69–76]
———. "Prologue" to *The Pageant of Perry County, 1814–1916*. Tell City, 1916. [October 22, 1930]
Dearing, W. P. "History and Youth." *Indiana History Bulletin*, Vol. 5, Extra No. 1, *Proceedings of the Southwestern Indiana Historical Society during its Eighth Year* (March 1928): 32–44. [October 8, 1926]
———. "Remarks Endorsing Lincoln Memorial." "Proceedings," October 25, 1927, 31–33. [October 25, 1927]
———. "Early Culture of the Pioneers of Southwestern Indiana." SWIHS Collection. [September 16, 1932; BE 104]
Deweese, Earl. "Abe Lincoln." SWIHS Collection. [June 5, 1929; BE 62; EVPL 3:77–79]
———. "Descendants in Spencer County of Sweeney, Pioneer Gentryville School Teacher of Abraham Lincoln." [June 5, 1929; BE 62]
Doll, Henry. "St. Francis Xavier Church at Vincennes." [September 16, 1932]
Douglass, Oliver. "Life of Captain John James." [October 11, 1921]
Eckley, Winfield. "The History of the Clay Industry in Tell City, Indiana." *Tell City News*, October 24, 1930. SWIHS Collection. [October 22, 1930]
Ehrman, Mrs. Frederick J. "Sketch of Dr. Ehrman." "Proceedings," June 10, 1924, 16–17. [June 10, 1924]
Ehrmann, Bess Virginia Hicks. "Museum Collections." *Indiana Historical Commission Bulletin* No. 16, *Proceedings of the Southwestern Indiana Historical Society* (October 1922): 78–81. [January 31, 1922]
———. "The Grigsbys." *Indiana Historical Commission Bulletin* No. 18, *Proceedings of the Southwestern Indiana Historical Society* (October 1923): 89–90. [February 28, 1923; BE 8]
———. "The Lincoln Inquiry." *Indiana Magazine of History* 21 (March 1925): 3–17. [October 14, 1924]
———. "Lincoln's Indiana Neighbors." *Indiana History Bulletin* 5, Extra No. 2, *Proceedings of the Ninth Annual Indiana History Conference* (April 1928): 65–75. [November 17, 1925; BE 82; EVPL 3:89–99]
———. "When Lincoln Went Flatboating from Rockport." September 16, 1926 (pageant). [BE 116]
———. "Origins of Rockport Pageant." "Proceedings," October 8, 1926, 14–15. [October 8, 1926]

————. "Prologue to Pageant—When Lincoln Went Flatboating from Rockport." *Indiana History Bulletin,* Vol. 5, Extra No. 1, *Proceedings of . . . its Eighth Year* (March 1928): 30–31. [October 8, 1926]

————. "New Letters, Lincoln Data." "Proceedings," October 8, 1926, 16. [October 8, 1926]

————. "Thomas Pindal Britton." *Indiana History Bulletin,* Vol. 5, Extra No. 1, *Proceedings of the Southwestern Indiana Historical Society during its Eighth Year* (March 1928): 63–68. [February 10, 1927; BE 58; EVPL 3:80–88]

————. "Work of the Society." "Proceedings," October 25, 1927, 7–13. [October 25, 1927]

————. "When Lincoln Went Flatboating from Rockport." July 4, 1928 (pageant). [BE 116]

————. "Word Pictures of Pioneer Families and Lincoln Contemporaries." *Indiana History Bulletin,* Vol. 6, Extra No. 3, *Proceedings of the Southwestern Indiana Historical Society during its Ninth Year* (August 1929): 119–21. [October 30, 1928; BE 59]

————. "Resume of Activities for 1927 and 1928." [February 19, 1929]

————. "Review of Anne Fellows Johnston's *Autobiography* and Albion Fellows Bacon's *The Charm String.*" [November 1, 1929]

————. "The Lincoln Pageant." *Indiana Club Woman* 9, no. 4 (May–June 1930): 7–8. [BE 118]

————. "When Lincoln Went Flatboating from Rockport." July 4, 1930 (pageant). [BE 116]

————. "Lincoln's Spencer County Friends and Neighbors." *Indianapolis Sunday Star,* February 8, 1931. [BE 83]

————. "When Lincoln Went Flatboating from Rockport." 1931 (film). [BE 117]

————. "Lincoln's Early Indiana Life." [February 12, 1931; BE 117]

————. "Memorial Unveilings at Boonville." SWIHS Collection. [March 17, 1933]

————. "The Lincoln Inquiry." [June 8, 1933]

————. *The Missing Chapter in the Life of Abraham Lincoln; a Number of Articles, Episodes, Photographs, Pen and Ink Sketches Concerning the Life of Abraham Lincoln in Spencer County, Indiana, Between 1816–1830 and 1844.* Chicago. 1938.

————. "What Indiana did for Lincoln." SWIHS Collection. [BE 111; EVPL 3: 113–35]

————. Correspondence regarding the grave of Nancy Hanks Lincoln. [BE 36]

Ehrmann, Eugenia. "Judge Lemuel Quincy DeBruler," 171–75, in John E. Iglehart and Eugenia Ehrmann. *The Environment of Abraham Lincoln in Indiana with an Account of the DeBruler Family* (IHS Publications, Vol. 8, No. 3; Indianapolis, 1925). [October 11, 1921; February 6, 1925; BE 66; EVPL 1:17–22]

Elliott, Phoebe. "John Corbin." *Indiana History Bulletin,* Vol. 3, Extra No. 1, *Proceedings of the Southwestern Indiana Historical Society: Papers Read Before the Society at Various Meetings, 1920–1925* (December 1925): 33–37. [June 15, 1923]

Embree, Louise. "David Robb (1771–1844), Early Pioneer of Gibson County." [March 17, 1933; BE 99]

Embree, Lucius C. "Preservation of the Knowledge of Old People." *Indiana Historical Commission Bulletin* No. 16, *Proceedings of the Southwestern Indiana Historical Society* (October 1922): 66–72. [January 31, 1922]

———. "Morris Birckbeck's Estimate of the People of Princeton in 1817." *Indiana Magazine of History* 21 (Dec 1925): 289–99. [May 27, 1925; BE 42; EVPL 1:97–104]

———. "Address." [June 24, 1926]

———. "Address," "Proceedings," October 30, 1928, 32–37. [October 30, 1928]

Enghof, Grace Adye. "Lincoln Gleanings." [EVPL 3:163–174]

Erwin, Lotta Edson. "Eben Darwin Edson and Sons of the Early Bar of Posey County." *Indiana History Bulletin*, Vol. 1, Extra No. 1, *Proceedings of the Southwestern Indiana Historical Society* (December 1925): 42–50. [June 15, 1923]

Esarey, Logan, "The Sacredness of Documents." [May 25, 1920]

———. "Our Early Governors." SWIHS Collection. [June 10, 1924]

———. "Our Indiana Home." [June 9, 1932]

Fellinger, Cicero. "Road Traveled by the Lincolns to Illinois." Newspaper clipping, February 20, 1915. [BE 12]

Fenn, Roy. "Robert Fulton and His Interest in Southwestern Indiana." [March 17, 1933]

Fitton, Katherine F. "A Tribute to Alice Harper Hanby." Hanby File, Alexandrian Public Library. [June 8, 1933]

Fortune, William. *Warrick and its Prominent People: A History of Warrick County, Indiana from the Time of its Organization and Settlement, with Biographical Sketches of Some of its Prominent People of the Past and Present.* Evansville, IN: Courier Co., 1881.

———. "Lincoln in Indiana." *Indiana History Bulletin*, Vol. 3, Extra No. 1, *Proceedings of the Southwestern Indiana Historical Society during its Sixth Year: Papers Read Before the Society at Various Meetings, 1920–1925* (December 1925): 60–64. [October 14, 1924]

———. "The Environments of Abraham Lincoln in Indiana: The Best Witnesses." SWIHS Collection. [November 17, 1925; BE 37]

———. "George Rogers Clark Sesquicentennial." SWIHS Collection. [June 24, 1926]

———. "Sidelights on 'The Pocket' of Indiana." SWIHS Collection. [June 5, 1930]

Fretageot, Nora Chadwick. "New Harmony on the Wabash." SWIHS Papers. [June 1, 1922]

———. "The Robert Dale Owen Home in New Harmony." *Indiana History Bulletin*, Vol. 1, Extra No., *Proceedings of the Fifth Annual Meeting of the Southwestern Indiana Historical Society* (June 1924): 15–25. [February 12, 1924]

———. "Memories of Animal Life in Posey County." SWIHS Collection. [February 25, 1926]

———. "Hallowed Ground." [November 1, 1929]

———. "Evaluation of More Recently Issued Books in Indiana History." SWIHS Collection.

Garvin, Susan M. "The Southwestern Indiana Historical Society: Its Organization and Aims." *Indiana Historical Commission Bulletin* No. 13, *Proceedings of the Second Annual State History Conference* (May 1921): 40–45.

———. "The Garvin Family." *Indiana History Bulletin,* Vol. 1, Extra No., *Proceedings of the Fifth Annual Meeting of the Southwestern Indiana Historical Society* (June 1924): 27–37. [February 12, 1924]

Gough, Edward. "Canal Facts and Recollections." [September 29, 1922]

Gray, Beulah Brazelton. "Early History of Pike County." *Winslow Dispatch,* December 30, 1927. [October 25, 1927; BE 53; EVPL 3:198–200]

———. "Harbard P. DeBruler, Pioneer" and "Delectable Hill." [June 5, 1930; EVPL 181–97]

———. *The National Lincoln Memorial Highway over the Buffalo Trace.* Buffalo Trace Historical Association, 1931.

———. "Richard Hargrave, Pioneer and Circuit Rider." *Otwell Star,* July 14–September 29. [March 17, 1933; BE 100]

Gregory, Edward, comp. *At the End of the Trail: The Story of the Journey of Thomas Lincoln and his family through Hardin and Breckinridge Counties, Ky., to Indiana in 1816.* Cloverport, KY: Breckinridge-Perry County Lincoln Highway Association, 1938.

Grimm, Mrs. John Gullick. "History of the American Creed." "Proceedings," October 25, 1927, 17–19. [October 25, 1927]

Gunn, C. L., "History in the Modern School." [October 6, 1936]

Gwaltney, John. "History of the Town of Midway." SWIHS Collection. [October 8, 1926]

Halbruge, Carrie V. Daguerreotype and Portrait Exhibit of Spencer County Pioneers, March 11, 1929. [BE 115]

Hall, Arthur F., J. I. Holcomb, Richard Lieber, Jess Murden, and Curtis G. Shake. *The Lincoln Memorial Way through Indiana.* Indianapolis, 1932.

Hanby, Alice L. Harper. "John Pitcher." *Indiana Historical Commission Bulletin* No. 16, *Proceedings of the Southwestern Indiana Historical Society* (October 1922): 50–60. [January 31, 1922; BE 6; EVPL 4:1–9]

———. "The "Hoop-pole Fight'." [Mt. Vernon, IN] *Unafraid R__,* June __, 27, 1923. SWIHS Collection. [June 15, 1923]

———. "Private Life of Dann Lynn." [June 5, 1931]

Harris, Mrs. B. F. "First Settlers of Dubois County." [June 10, 1924]

Hatfield, Mr. "Early impressions of Perry County." [May 24, 1921]

Hayford, Elbert D. "The Environments of Abraham Lincoln in Indiana: The Best Witnesses: Early Days in Spencer County." [November 17, 1925; BE 37]

Hays, Will H. "John T. Hays." SWIHS Collection. [June 5, 1931]

Hemenway, James A. "Remarks." [September 29, 1922]

Hemer, H. W. A. "History of Maple Grove Camp Ground." SWIHS Collection. [June 10, 1924]

Herbert, Alice. "Lincoln's First Great Sorrow." [BE 140]

Historical Marker at Colonel Jones Residence in Gentryville. N.d. [BE 122]

Hohenberger, Frank M. "From Down in the Hills of Brown County." "Proceedings," February 23, 1928, 31–33. [February 23, 1928]

Honig, George H. "The Artist's Ideal of Lincoln." *Indiana History Bulletin,* Vol. 3, Extra No. 1, *Proceedings of the Southwestern Indiana Historical Society during its Sixth Year* (December 1925): 51–53. [October 14, 1924]

————. "The Environments of Abraham Lincoln in Indiana." "Proceedings," November 17, 1925, 27–29. [November 17, 1925; BE 37]

————. "An Interview with James Atlas Jones on the Lincoln Cabin in Spencer County." *Indiana History Bulletin,* Vol. 6, Extra No. 3, *Proceedings of the Southwestern Indiana Historical Society during its Ninth Year* (August 1929): 37–39. [February 23, 1928; BE 108]

————. "Research work, Clippings, and Data on the Last Lincoln Cabin from the Schreeder files." [June 5, 1929]

————. Monument to Abraham Lincoln in Henderson, KY. [November 1, 1929]

————. Lincoln Pioneer Village, Rockport, IN. July 4, 1935 (dedication).

————. "Postcard Map." [BE 114]

————. "Out-of-Town Markers." [EVPL 4:10–17]

Hopkins, John Sr. Letter, 1881. [September 28, 1920]

Hovey, Charles J. "Alvin Peterson Hovey." *Indiana History Bulletin,* Vol. 3, Extra No. 1, *Proceedings of the Southwestern Indiana Historical Society: Papers Read Before the Society at Various Meetings, 1920–1925* (December 1925): 29–33. [June 15, 1923; EVPL 1:80–84]

Howe, J. Edwin. "History of Perry County Baptist Association, 1821–1921." [September 29, 1922]

Howe, Kaloolah. "Address." [June 9, 1932]

Huddleston, Ann. "Captain Jacob Warrick, of Warrick County." [October 26, 1934]

Huffman, Lemuel Q. "Indiana Pioneer Life." [October 8, 1926; EVPL 2:113–15]

Husband, Louise. "A Chapter in the Life of the Old Fauntleroy Home." SWIHS Collection. [June 5, 1931]

Iglehart, John E. "The Coming of the English to Indiana in 1817 and their Hoosier Neighbors." *Indiana Magazine of History* 15 (Jun 1919): 89–178.

————. "Inaugural Address." *Indiana Historical Commission Bulletin* No. 16, *Proceedings of the Southwestern Indiana Historical Society* (October 1922): 85–94. [February 23, 1920]

————. Circular letter no. 1, April 26, 1920. SWIHS Collection.

————. "Future Work of the Historical Society." [January 31, 1921]

————. "Methodism in Southwestern Indiana." *Indiana Magazine of History* 17 (March 1921): 3–49 and *Indiana Magazine of History* 17 (June 1921): 117–49.

————. "Heroic Age in Indiana." SWIHS Collection. [October 11, 1921].

————. "Address of Judge John E. Iglehart." *Indiana Historical Commission Bulletin* No. 16, *Proceedings of the Southwestern Indiana Historical Society* (October 1922):10–21. [January 31, 1922]

————. "Thomas Posey." "Proceedings," June 1, 1922, 13–20. [June 1, 1922]

————. "Remarks." [September 29, 1922]

————. *An Account of Vanderburgh County from its Organization,* volume 3 of Logan Esarey, *History of Indiana from its Exploration to 1922.* Dayton, OH.: Dayton Historical Publishing Co., 1923. [BE 33]

————. "Correspondence between Lincoln Historians and this Society." *Indiana Historical Commission Bulletin* No. 18, *Proceedings of the Southwestern Indiana Historical Society* (October 1923): 63–88. [February 28, 1923; BE 24]

————. "Estimate of Francis Posey." *Indiana Historical Commission Bulletin* No. 18, *Proceedings of the Southwestern Indiana Historical Society* (October 1923):130–32. [February 28, 1923]

————. "Character Sketch of William Harrow." *Indiana History Bulletin*, Vol. 3, Extra No. 1, *Proceedings of the Southwestern Indiana Historical Society: Papers Read Before the Society at Various Meetings, 1920–1925* (December 1925): 25–28. [June 15, 1923]

————. "Address [to Evansville School Teachers], 1924." Iglehart Papers, box 8, folder 1, Indiana Historical Society.

————. "The DeBruler Family as Typical Pioneers," 176–82, in Iglehart and Eugenia Ehrmann, *The Environment of Abraham Lincoln in Indiana with an Account of the DeBruler Family* (IHS Publications, Vol. 8, No. 3; Indianapolis, 1925). [February 6, 1925; BE 66]

————. "Response." "Proceedings," May 27, 1925, 5–9. [May 27, 1925]

————. "The Environment of Abraham Lincoln in Indiana," 147–70, in Iglehart and Eugenia Ehrmann, *The Environment of Abraham Lincoln in Indiana with an Account of the DeBruler Family* (IHS Publications, Vol. 8, No. 3; Indianapolis, 1925). [November 17, 1925]

————. "The Historical Significance of the Conquest of George Rogers Clark of the Frontier of the Northwest." [June 24, 1926]

————. "Statement of George W. Morrison to Iglehart." [October 8, 1926]

————. "The Work of this Society for 1928." [February 23, 1928]

————. "Our Struggle for Life." [June 1, 1928]

————. "Reminiscences of the Life and Times of Horatio Q. Wheeler." SWIHS Collection. [February 19, 1929]

————. "Address." [November 1, 1929]

————. "Memorial to Mrs. Eldora Minor Raleigh." SWIHS Collection. [June 5, 1930; BE 85]

————. "The Spiritual Side of Historical Work." [October 22, 1930]

————. "Sketches of Grahams, Hudspiths, and Dennys." [February 12, 1931; BE 90]

————. "Grahams: Pioneers in the Mississippi Valley." Proceedings, December 4, 1931, 5–16. [December 4, 1931; BE 102]

————. "Significance of Frontier in American History." [June 9, 1932]

————. "Standards and Subjects of Historical Society Work." *Indiana History Bulletin*, Vol. 11, No. 8, *Proceedings of the Southwestern Indiana Historical Society, 1929–1933* (May 1934): 272–311.

————. "Environments and Opportunities of Lincoln in Indiana." SWIHS Collection.

Inco, Nancy Grigsby. "More Lincoln Memories." *Indiana Historical Commission Bulletin* No. 18, *Proceedings of the Southwestern Indiana Historical Society* (October 1923): 91–92. [February 28, 1923; BE 10]

Indiana Lincoln Union. Improvements, monument, and trail of stones in Nancy Hanks Lincoln Park. 1927–1944. [BE 123]

Jackson, John W. "Judge John W. Graham." [February 23, 1928; BE 97]

Jaquess, William G. "Narrative of Chickamauga and Chattanooga." *Indiana History Bulletin*, Vol. 6, Extra No. 3, *Proceedings of the Southwestern Indiana*

Historical Society during its Ninth Year (August 1929): 21–36. [May 27, 1925; EVPL 1:34–55]

Johnson, Mrs. Charles T. (Deidré Duff). "Moses Ashworth, Pioneer of Indiana Methodism, and His Times." *Indiana Historical Commission Bulletin* No. 18, *Proceedings of the Southwestern Indiana Historical Society* (October 1923): 94–118. [February 28, 1923]

———. "Word Pictures of Pioneer Families and Lincoln Contemporaries." *Indiana History Bulletin,* Vol. 6, Extra No. 3, *Proceedings of the Southwestern Indiana Historical Society during its Ninth Year* (August 1929): 122–27. [October 30, 1928; BE 59]

———. "Posey County Lore." [BE 74]

Johnson, J. S. "Early History of Richland and Baker Creek Baptist Church." [June 5, 1929]

Jolly, J. C. "Meeks Tragedy." [June 5, 1929]

Kennedy, A. H. "The Destiny of Man." [May 27, 1925]

———. "The Lincoln Tree." SWIHS Collection. [June 14, 1927]

———. "The Still Small Voice." [October 22, 1930]

Kiper, Roscoe. "Lincoln's Boyhood Days in Indiana," a paper read at Society of Indiana Pioneers, Indianapolis, December 1922. [BE 14]

———. "The Fame of Lincoln." "Proceedings," October 14, 1924, 10–15. [October 14, 1924]

———. "Lincoln's Environment in Indiana." *Indiana History Bulletin,* Vol. 3, Extra No. 1, *Proceedings of the Southwestern Indiana Historical Society: Papers Read Before the Society at Various Meetings, 1920–1925* (December 1925): 94–96. [May 27, 1925; BE 40; EVPL 23–27]

———. "President's Address." "Proceedings," November 17, 1925. [November 17, 1925]

———. "Address." "Proceedings," June 24, 1926, 16–18. [June 24, 1926]

———. "An Incident in Warrick County History." SWIHS Collection. [June 5, 1930; BE 86]

———. "Early newspapers of Warrick County." [October 26, 1934]

———. "An Address Delivered at Rockport, Indiana on the Occasion of the Dedication of the Lincoln Pioneer Village, July 4th, 1935." SWIHS Collection. [EVPL 4:29–39]

———. "Lincoln's Boyhood in Spencer County." [October 11, 1935; BE 137]

Klein, Mrs. Otto. "Judge George Gaybrook Green." [November 1, 1929]

———. "Brief Autobiography of General Thomas Posey." [March 17, 1933]

Knapp, Mrs. H. C., M.D. "Materia Medica of Pioneer Indiana." *Indiana History Bulletin,* Vol. 3, Extra No. 1, *Proceedings of the Southwestern Indiana Historical Society during its Sixth Year* (December 1925): 12–17. [June 10, 1924; BE 31; EVPL 4:40–47]

Kniblock, Otto N. "Early Navigation on St. Joseph River." *Indiana Historical Society Publications,* v. 8, no. 4 (1925).

Knight, Isaac. *Story of Isaac Knight, Indian Captive.* Evansville, IN: Journal Office, 1839. [June 1, 1928]

Kohlmeier, Albert L. "The Ohio Valley as the Keystone of the Arch of American Union." [March 9, 1934; BE 135]

Laval, Otto. "Indian Relics." *Indiana Historical Commission Bulletin* No. 18, *Proceedings of the Southwestern Indiana Historical Society* (October 1923): 135–37. [February 28, 1923]

Leonard, Mrs. Frederick Pierce. "General William Harrow." *Indiana History Bulletin*, Vol. 3, Extra No. 1, *Proceedings of the Southwestern Indiana Historical Society during its Sixth Year* (December 1925): 18–24. [June 15, 1923]

Lieb, Charles. "Remarks in the House of Representatives regarding the Dedication of Sarah Lincoln Grigsby's Grave." June 28, 1916. [BE 5]

Lincoln, Abraham. Poem, 1844. [June 1, 1928]

——. Letter to Nathaniel Grigsby, September 20, 1860. [February 28, 1923; BE 9]

——. Letter to David Turnham, October 23, 1860. [June 15, 1923; BE 3; EVPL 4:48]

——. Letter to John V. Dodge, May 31, 1862. [September 29, 1922]

Lincoln Trail Club. Markers in Hammond Township. N.d. [February 23, 1928; BE 120]

Lindley, Harlow. "Address." "Proceedings," June 10, 1924, 49–58. [June 10, 1924]

Lindsey, Caleb J. "Judge Zachariah Skelton." [June 5, 1930; BE 87]

Lockridge, Ross F., "Lincoln's Kentucky and Indiana Backgrounds." SWIHS Collection. [June 5, 1931; BE 91]

——. "George Rogers Clark." [June 8, 1933]

Lockwood, George. "The Pocket of Indiana." *Muncie Press*, Nov 1931. [June 9, 1932]

Lockyear, Elmer Q. "Francis B. Posey." *Indiana Historical Commission Bulletin* No. 18, *Proceedings of the Southwestern Indiana Historical Society* (October 1923): 126–30. [February 28, 1923]

Love, Robertus. "An Appreciation of Lincoln, 1909." "Proceedings," October 30, 1928, 9. [October 30, 1928]

Lucas, Harvey. "Recollections of a Teacher." [October 22, 1930]

Lutz, Philip. "The Fourth of July in Lincoln's Time and Today." SWIHS Collection. [October 11, 1935; BE 138]

Lynch, William O. "Trends in Indiana History." SWIHS Collection. [February 6, 1930]

Maas, Grace Jeanette Bullock. "Jonesboro." SWIHS Collection. [October 25, 1927; BE 52; EVPL 4:49–56]

——. "Group of Old Time Songs." [June 1, 1928]

Masterson, T. H. "Interviews with Spencer County Pioneers about 1895." *Indiana History Bulletin*, Vol. 6, Extra No. 3, *Proceedings of the Southwestern Indiana Historical Society during its Ninth Year* (August 1929): 56–59. [February 23, 1928; BE 70]

McCulla, Fannie E. "George W. and Mary Eleanor Brackenridge." [December 4, 1931; BE 94]

McCullough, Ethel Farquhar. "Card Indexing of Old Newspapers." *Indiana Historical Commission Bulletin* No. 16, *Proceedings of the Southwestern Indiana Historical Society* (October 1922): 32–37. [January 31, 1922]

——. "Work of the National Association for Historical Research." [March 9, 1934]

Meeks, Aaron. "The Atha Meeks Sr. Tragedy." SWIHS Collection. [October 11, 1921, June 24, 1926]

Miller, Lenora P. "The Princeton Male and Female Academy." *Indiana History Bulletin*, Vol. 5, Extra No. 1, *Proceedings of the Southwestern Indiana Historical Society during its Eighth Year* (March 1928): 18–29. [November 17, 1925]

M'Laughlin, Mabel Nisbet. "Nisbets, Journees, and Allied Families." [June 8, 1933]

Montgomery, Judith Hazen. "Early History of Luce Township, Spencer County, Indiana." SWIHS Collection. [October 8, 1926]

Morgan, David H. "Early Schools of Spencer County, Indiana." [June 24, 1926; EVPL 2:79–87]

———. "John Morgan, First Clerk of Spencer County." [June 24, 1926; BE 21]

———. "Early Agriculture in Indiana." SWIHS Collection. [June 24, 1926; EVPL 4:57–68]

———. "A View of Rockport from the River in 1856." SWIHS Collection. [October 8, 1926]

———. "Story of Buried Treasure in Spencer County." SWIHS Collection. [October 8, 1926]

———. "James Clifford Veatch." *Indiana History Bulletin*, Vol. 6, Extra No. 3, *Proceedings of the Southwestern Indiana Historical Society during its Ninth Year* (August 1929): 82–88. [October 30, 1928; BE 57]

Morlock, James E. "The Assassination of Lincoln." SWIHS Collection. [February 12, 1931; BE 89; EVPL 3:175–80]

Morrison, George W. "Boone Family and Brackenridge Family." [BE 112]

Moutschka, John Paul. "Ten Years in Early Tell City." [September 29, 1922]

Murr, J. Edward. "Lincoln in Indiana." *Indiana Magazine of History* 13 (Dec 1917): 307–48; *IMH* 14 (Mar 1918): 13–75; *IMH* 14 (Jun 1918): 148–82.

———. "Abraham Lincoln." [February 12, 1924; BE 19]

———. "The Environments of Abraham Lincoln in Indiana: The Best Witnesses." [November 17, 1925; BE 37]

O'Flynn, Anna C. "The Environments of Abraham Lincoln in Indiana: The Best Witnesses." [November 17, 1925; BE 37; EVPL 4:71–86]

———. "Reminiscences of Early Efforts for a Lincoln Memorial." "Proceedings," October 25, 1917, 27–30. [October 25, 1927]

———. "The Pumpkin Loup Garou." "Proceedings," February 6, 1930, 26–29. [February 6, 1930]

Oliver, John W. "Indiana War Records." [May 24, 1921]

———. "Progress of State Survey." [October 11, 1921]

———. "Remarks." *Indiana Historical Commission Bulletin* No. 16, *Proceedings of the Southwestern Indiana Historical Society* (October 1922): 37–40. [January 31, 1922]

———. "Greeting and Farewell." [June 15, 1923]

Olmsted, Ella, "Stringtown on the Red Banks Trail." SWIHS Collection. [June 5, 1931]

Orr, Louise Dunkerson. "The Casselberry Family." *Indiana History Bulletin*, Vol. 1, Extra No., *Proceedings of the Fifth Annual Meeting of the Southwestern Indiana Historical Society* (June 1924): 37–46. [February 12, 1924; BE 28]

Pelham, Carolyn. "Sketch of the Life of Joseph Neef." [November 1, 1929]

Perry County Historical Society and Spencer County Historical Society. Marker at Anderson Creek. N.d. [February 25, 1926; BE 119]

Potter, Alice Cauthorn. "Elihu Stout." [February 6, 1930; BE 75]

———. "Elihu Stout and His Descendants." [June 5, 1930]

Potter, Mildred. "Experience as a Radio Entertainer." [June 8, 1933]

Powell, E. Ainger. "Early Beginnings of Episcopacy in Southwestern Indiana." [February 6, 1930]

Powell, Eugene. "Mason Jones Howell." [October 30, 1928; BE 49]

Powell, Harriet. "The Powell Family." *Indiana History Bulletin,* Vol. 6, Extra No. 3, *Proceedings of the Southwestern Indiana Historical Society during its Ninth Year* (August 1929): 63–67. [June 1, 1928; BE 54; EVPL 4:93–100]

———. "Parrette Family." [EVPL 4:87–92]

Prosser, Hamline R. "Pioneer Families of Spencer County." [February 23, 1928; BE 68; EVPL 4:101–16]

Rabb, Kate Milner. "The Romance of Indiana History." [January 31, 1921]

———. "Rockport in 1857." [October 11, 1921]

———. "Indiana Lincoln Memorial Association." "Proceedings," October 12, 1923, 31–33. [October 12, 1923]

———. "The Value of Old Letters and Diaries." SWIHS Collection. [June 5, 1931]

Raleigh, Eldora Minor. "John A. Brackenridge." *Indiana Historical Commission Bulletin* No. 16, *Proceedings of the Southwestern Indiana Historical Society* (October 1922): 60–66. [January 31, 1922; BE 7; EVPL 4:117–25]

———. "The Early Days of Newburgh On-the-Ohio." *Indiana Historical Commission Bulletin* No. 18, *Proceedings of the Southwestern Indiana Historical Society* (October 1923): 9–31. [February 28, 1923]

———. "Graham Family." [June 24, 1926; BE 110]

———. "General Joseph E. Lane." *Indiana History Bulletin,* Vol. 4, Extra No. 1, *Proceedings of the Southwestern Indiana Historical Society during its Seventh Year* (December 1926): 71–82. [October 8, 1926; BE 46]

———. "Little Sketches of Early Warrick County Pioneers." [February 10, 1927]

Reilly, Anne Hazelton. "William Reilly." [October 8, 1926]

Reilly, Mary French Wilson. "Early Times in Evansville." [September 29, 1922; EVPL 2:74–78]

Rhoades, J. Helen. "Life of James Gentry, Jr." [June 24, 1926; BE 4; EVPL 4:126–30]

Richardson, Dora V. Hall. "Connor and Hall Families of Perry County." [September 29, 1922]

Riker, Dorothy L. "Jonathan Jennings." *Indiana Magazine of History* 28 (December 1932): 223–39. [December 4, 1931]

Robb, Henry. "Letter by Henry Robb, February 5, 1854." [September 28, 1920; EVPL 1:63–67]

Robinson, I. J. *The Lincoln Country of Southwestern Indiana.* Evansville: Southwestern Indiana Civic Association, c. 1935. [BE 141]

Robinson, W. D. "Henry Van Der Burgh." *Indiana History Bulletin,* Vol. 3, Extra No. 1, *Proceedings of the Southwestern Indiana Historical Society: Papers Read Before the Society at Various Meetings, 1920–1925* (December 1925): 76–88. [February 6, 1925; BE 67; EVPL 1:1–16]

Rockport Business and Professional Women's Club. Marker at Rockport Tavern. N.d. [February 10, 1927; BE 121]

Rodeheffer, Rev. "History of Santa Claus Campground." [October 14, 1924]

Ross, William W. "Romance of Ohio River Transportation." *Indiana History Bulletin,* Vol. 3, Extra No. 1, *Proceedings of the Southwestern Indiana Historical Society: Papers Read Before the Society at Various Meetings, 1920–1925* (December 1925): 67–75. [February 6, 1925; EVPL 1:85–96]

Rothert, Otto A. "Dubois County Writers." "Proceedings," June 10, 1924, 32–38. [June 10, 1924]

Rothert, Willa MacMahon. "Sketch of Col. Jacob Geiger." [June 10, 1924]

Rucker, Mrs. James B. "The Parette Family." *Indiana History Bulletin,* Vol. 6, Extra No. 3, *Proceedings of the Southwestern Indiana Historical Society during its Ninth Year* (August 1929): 17–20. [May 27, 1925]

Sager, Ben F. "Indiana's First Soldiers." *Indiana History Bulletin,* Vol. 5, Extra No. 1, *Proceedings of the Southwestern Indiana Historical Society during its Eighth Year* (March 1928): 45–49. [October 8, 1926]

———. "Clark's Victory as a Military Venture and the French Contributions to its Success." *Indiana History Bulletin,* Vol. 5, Extra No. 1, *Proceedings of the Southwestern Indiana Historical Society during its Eighth Year* (March 1928): 80–99. [June 14, 1927]

Sanders, Edna Brown. "James Clifford Veatch." *Indiana History Bulletin,* Vol. 6, Extra No. 3, *Proceedings of the Southwestern Indiana Historical Society during its Ninth Year* (August 1929): 68–81. [October 30, 1928; BE 57; EVPL 4: 137–56]

———. "Old French Quarters, New Orleans." [June 5, 1929]

Schmidt, Paul. "Society of Fine Arts and History." "Proceedings," June 9, 1932, 16–18. [June 9, 1932]

Schools. Annual Visits to Nancy Hanks Lincoln Park. [BE 132]

Schreeder, C. C., "Vanderburgh County in the Mexican War." SWIHS Collection. [February 10, 1927]

———. "The Lincolns and Their Home in Spencer County, Indiana." [June 5, 1929; BE 63; EVPL 4:157–69]

———. "One Log of the Lincolns' Indiana Cabin." [BE 64]

Schreiber, Charles D. "Some Historical Facts Concerning Tell City, Indiana by C. D. Schreiber." [October 12, 1923; EVPL 2:92–102]

Schultz, Kate Pitcher Whitworth "General Thomas Gamble Pitcher." *Indiana History Bulletin,* Vol. 3, Extra No. 1, *Proceedings of the Southwestern Indiana Historical Society: Papers Read Before the Society at Various Meetings* (December 1925): 37–42. [June 15, 1923]

Seay, Don. "Early History of Oak Grove." [October 8, 1926]

Shake, Curtis G. "Report on Celebration of Lincoln Migration." [February 6, 1930]

———. "Conservation and Development of our Historical Resources." [February 12, 1931]

Snepp, Daniel Webster. "Evansville's Commercial History between 1850 and 1865." [February 10, 1927]

Snyder, Minnie D. "History of Rockport Indiana." Bess V. Ehrmann, Scrapbooks, D-1, Letters, Spencer County Public Library. [October 8, 1926]

Somes, Joseph H. Van Der Burgh. "Henry Van Der Burgh and His Family." *Indiana History Bulletin,* Vol. 3, Extra No. 1, *Proceedings of the Southwestern Indiana Historical Society: Papers Read Before the Society at Various Meetings* (December 1925): 89–93. [February 6, 1925; BE 66; EVPL 4:170–76]

Sonntag, Marcus S. "Indiana's World War Memorial." "Proceedings," February 6, 1925, 23–27. [February 6, 1925]

Spayd, Bettie Veatch. "The Veatch Family." *Indiana History Bulletin,* Vol. 6, Extra No. 3, *Proceedings of the Southwestern Indiana Historical Society during its Ninth Year* (August 1929): 40–45. [February 23, 1928; BE 57]

Spencer County Historical Society. Photograph of James Grigsby. N.d. [BE 9]

Stevenson, William. "A Race to the Land Office." SWIHS Collection. [October 8, 1926]

Stewart, J. L. "Rockport Tavern Where Lincoln Stopped," *Rockport Journal,* n.d. [June 1, 1928; BE 23]

Stoops, Alice Parry. *The Pageant of Petersburg and Pike County: The Historical Development of Pike County.* Petersburg, IN: Democrat Printery, 1916. [October 25, 1927]

Stormont, Gil. R. "Judge William Prince." *Indiana Historical Commission Bulletin* No. 18, *Proceedings of the Southwestern Indiana Historical Society* (October 1923): 119–25. [February 28, 1923; BE 30]

Sweeney, Luella. "Early Potteries in Troy." SWIHS Collection. [October 22, 1930]

Sweeny, Andrew. Article on Lincoln in the *Indianapolis Star.* [March 17, 1933]

Sweet, William Warren. "Why Do We Study History?" SWIHS Collection. [February 10, 1927]

Tarbell, Ida M. "The Boy Lincoln." *New York Herald Tribune,* 1928, 12. [BE 129]

Taylor, Anna Stevenson. "History of Christian Churches, Spencer County." [October 11, 1921; EVPL 2:88–91]

Taylor, Charles H. "Diary of Robert Taylor on his Trip to California, via Panama in 1850." Evansville Public Library, Indiana Room. [June 5, 1929]

Taylor, Lizzie Graham. "Christopher Columbus Graham." [December 4, 1931; BE98]

———. "Mary Graham." [December 4, 1931]

Taylor, Mrs. Lewis. "Early Reminiscences of Anderson Township." [May 27, 1925; BE 43]

Thixton, Lillian Walker. "Celebration at Henderson." [November 1, 1929]

———. "Audubon Memorial." [February 6, 1930]

Thorpe, Edith. "Captain Spier Spencer and the County Named for Him." SWIHS Collection. [October 30, 1928]

Torrance, Theodora Hazen McGill. "Lincoln Memorial Commission." "Proceedings," October 14, 1924, 19–21. [October 14, 1924]

———. "Gaines Head Roberts and the McGill Family." *Indiana History Bulletin,* Vol. 5, Extra No. 1, *Proceedings of the Southwestern Indiana Historical Society during its Eighth Year* (March 1928): 11–17. (May 27, 1925; BE 47; EVPL 4: 177–85]

Towles, Susan Starling. *John James Audubon in Henderson, Kentucky.* Louisville, KY: John P. Morton & Co., Inc., 1925. [February 12, 1924]

———. "Aims and Purposes of the Transylvania Society." "Proceedings," November 1, 1929, 7–12. [November 1, 1929]

———. "Audubon Memorial." [February 6, 1930]

Twigg, Virginia. "St. Stephen's, the First Church in New Harmony." *Indiana History Bulletin,* Vol. 5, Extra No. 1, *Proceedings of the Southwestern Indiana Historical Society during its Eighth Year* (March 1928): 7–10. [June 1, 1922; EVPL 1:28–33]

Uler, Helen. "Sketch of Hosea Smith and Early Pike County History." [June 10, 1924]

Vannest, Charles Garrett. *Lincoln the Hoosier: Abraham Lincoln's Life in Indiana.* St. Louis: Eden Publishing House, 1928. [BE 128]

Veatch, James C. "Commander and Company." Bess V. Ehrmann, Scrapbooks, D-1, Spencer County Public Library. [October 8, 1926]

Veatch, Pet Enlow. "Papers of General James C. Veatch relating to Funds Raised by Rockport Citizens for the Fence Erected around Nancy Hanks' Grave." [February 6, 1930; BE 78]

Warren, Louis A. Visit to Spencer County, 1923. [BE 18]

———. "The Mystery of Lincoln's Melancholy." *Indiana History Bulletin,* Vol. 3, Extra No. 1, *Proceedings of the Southwestern Indiana Historical Society: Papers Read Before the Society at Various Meetings, 1920–1925* (December 1925): 53–60. [October 14, 1924; BE 133; EVPL 2:103–12].

Warrick County Historical Society. Monument commemorating Lincoln's visits to the Brackenridge home. Boonville, IN. N.d. [BE 126]

Waters, George J. "Portraits of Mr. and Mrs. Jonathan Jacques." [September 28, 1920]

Watts, Edwyn E. "General John Gibson, Secretary of Indiana Territory." [March 11, 1932]

Weatherholt, Jacob. "Memory of Jacob Weatherholt, Jr., August 20, 1866." Deed Record Book A, Perry County Recorder's Office, Cannelton, IN. SWIHS Papers. [June 1, 1928; EVPL 186–87]

Wedeking, Albert J. "Plans for Lincoln City Memorial." "Proceedings," October 12, 1923. [October 12, 1923]

Weik, Jesse. "Lincoln and the Wool Carder's Niece." *Success Magazine,* December 1902. [May 27, 1925; BE 41; EVPL 1:56–62]

Wheatley, Ella Cockrum. "A Son of a Pioneer Family." [February 6, 1925; BE 65]

Wheeler, Walton M. "English Settlement." Alexandrian Public Library, Mount Vernon, IN. [February 6, 1930; BE 76]

Williams, Genevieve Macdonald. *The Pageant of Dubois County.* Huntingburg, IN: E. W. Pickhardt Ptg. Co., 1916. [June 14, 1927]

Wilson, George R., ed. "Hindostan, Greenwich and Mt. Pleasant. The Pioneer Towns of Martin County.—Memoirs of Thomas Jefferson Brooks." *Indiana Magazine of History* 16 (Dec 1920): 285–302.

———. "The Birth of a State." *Indiana Historical Commission Bulletin* No. 16, *Proceedings of the Southwestern Indiana Historical Society* (October 1922): 41–50. [January 31, 1922; BE 25]

———. "George H. Proffit: His Day and Generation." *Indiana Magazine of History* 18, no. 1 (March 1922): 1–46. [BE 27; EVPL 4:188–225]

———. Judge James Lockhart. *Indiana Historical Society Publications,* Vol. 8, No. 1 (Indianapolis: Wm. B. Burford, 1923): 1–69. [February 28, 1923; BE 26]

———. "General Washington Johnston." *Indiana Magazine of History* 20 (June 1924): 123–53. [February 12, 1924; BE 24]

———. "Senator Benjamin Rose Edmonston." *Indiana History Bulletin,* Vol. 4, Extra No. 1, *Proceedings of the Southwestern Indiana Historical Society during its Seventh Year* (December 1926): 7–42. [May 27, 1925; BE 45; EVPL 2: 21–73]

———. "The Lincoln Forest, Field, Flora and Family, 1816–1830: Report of Committee," January 12, 1928. Spencer County Public Library, Rockport, Indiana. [February 23, 1928; BE 35]

Wilson, Margaret A. "The Buffalo Trail—the Great Wilderness Road of Southern Indiana—and its Maker." *Indiana History Bulletin,* Vol. 5, Extra No. 1, *Proceedings of the Southwestern Indiana Historical Society during its Eighth Year* (March 1928): 50–62. [February 10, 1927; BE 51]

———. "Notes on 'The Narrative of the Captivity and Sufferings of Isaac Knight from Indian Barbarity.'" *Indiana History Bulletin,* Vol. 6, Extra No. 3, *Proceedings of the Southwestern Indiana Historical Society during its Ninth Year* (August 1929): 60–62. [June 1, 1928]

———. "Reverend Andrew Jackson Strain." George Wilson, "Historical Notes on Dubois County," Vol. 9 (1929), 455–76, G R Wilson Mss, Lilly Library. [February 19, 1929; BE 61]

Wilson, Miles. "Recollection." "Proceedings," June 15, 1923, 52–54. [June 15, 1923]

Wilson, Mrs. Robert R. "Sketch of Dr. Christopher Columbus Graham." [December 4, 1931]

———. "Robert A. Smith." [December 4, 1931]

———. "Thomas B. Graham." [March 11, 1932; BE 96]

———. "Bethel Family of Warrick County." [June 9, 1932; BE 105]

Wilson, Mrs. William A. "Poem." [October 11, 1921]

———. "Dubois County." [BE 113]

Wilson, Sadye Anderson. "Bailey Anderson the First." [BE 44]

Wilson, Thomas. "Distinctive Features of Indiana's First Constitution." *Indiana History Bulletin,* Vol. 5, Extra No. 1, *Proceedings of the Southwestern Indiana Historical Society during its Eighth Year* (March 1928): 69–79. [June 14, 1927]

Winterhalter, Herbert F. "History of St. Meinrad." [February 6, 1930]

Wolfe, Clarence P. "Steamboat Days." SWIHS Collection. [February 12, 1931]

———. "The American Guide: A WPA Writers Project." [October 6, 1936]

Woodburn, James A. "Address." SWIHS Collection. [February 12, 1924]

Woods, John Hall. "Indiana from 1816 to 1826." [June 5, 1931; BE 93]

Woods, Robert Archer. "Early Freemasonry in Vincennes and Princeton." [June 5, 1929; BE 73]

———. "Presbyterianism in Princeton, Indiana, from 1810–1930." *Indiana Magazine of History* 26 (June 1930): 93–125. [November 1, 1929]

———. "President's Address." SWIHS Collection. [June 5, 1931]

———. "Early Princeton and Gibson County." [December 4, 1931; BE 101]

———. "Judge Samuel Hall of Gibson County." [March 11, 1932; BE 103]

———. "Hoosier Beginnings." SWIHS Collection. [September 16, 1932]

———. "Was General Washington Johnston the Father of Indiana Free Masonry?" [March 17, 1933]

———. "The Relation of Southwestern Indiana Pioneers to those of other Pioneer Sections." [BE 92]

Woolfolk, Myrtle Ray. "Early History of Hammond Township." SWIHS Collection. [October 8, 1926]

Wright, Laura Mercy. "Daniel Grass." *Indiana History Bulletin,* Vol. 3, Extra No. 1, *Proceedings of the Southwestern Indiana Historical Society during its Sixth Year: Papers Read Before the Society at Various Meetings, 1920–1925* (December 1925): 7–11. [September 28, 1920; BE 15; EVPL 1:68–73]

———. "William Smither." [December 4, 1931; BE 95]

———. "Pioneer Mother." [BE 139]

Yale University Press Film Service. *Vincennes.* 1923. [February 25, 1926]

Young, Otis E. "Development of Public Education in Southwestern Indiana, 1816–1880." *Indiana History Bulletin,* Vol. 6, Extra No. 3, *Proceedings of the Southwestern Indiana Historical Society during its Ninth Year* (August 1929): 89–113. [October 30, 1928]

———. "Technique of Historical Research." [October 6, 1936]

Abbreviations

Beveridge Correspondence	Albert J. Beveridge Correspondence, 1924–1928, Abraham Lincoln Presidential Library, Springfield, IL
Beveridge Papers	Albert Jeremiah Beveridge Papers, Manuscript Division, Library of Congress, Washington, DC
Director's Correspondence	Director's Correspondence with Collectors, Lincoln Financial Foundation Collection at the Allen County Public Library, Fort Wayne, IN, courtesy of the State of Indiana
Embree Papers	Lucius C. Embree Papers, 1786–1933, Manuscripts Section, Indiana State Library, Indianapolis, IN
Iglehart Papers	John E. Iglehart Papers, 1853–1953, Indiana Historical Society, Indianapolis, IN
"Minute Book 1"	"Southwestern Indiana Historical Society Minute Book 1, 1920–1924," reel 6, item 10, John E. Iglehart Collection, Willard Library, Evansville, IN
"Minute Book 2"	"Southwestern Indiana Historical Society Minute Book 2, 1925–1936," reel 6, item 11, John E. Iglehart Collection, Willard Library, Evansville, IN
"Proceedings"	"Proceedings of the Southwestern Indiana Historical Society," reel 6, item 13, John E. Iglehart Collection, Willard Library, Evansville, IN
SWIHS Collection	Southwestern Indiana Historical Society Collection, Willard Library, Evansville, IN
Tarbell Collection	Ida M. Tarbell Collection, Pelletier Library, Allegheny College, Meadville, PA
Turner Collection	Frederick Jackson Turner Collection, 1862–1963, Manuscripts Department, Huntington Library, San Marino, CA
Weik Papers	Jesse Weik Papers, 1833–1939, Abraham Lincoln Presidential Library, Springfield, IL

Notes

Introduction: "Lincoln Is Everybody's Subject"

1. Sam Wineburg, "Crazy for History," *Journal of American History* 90, no. 4 (March 2004): 1401–14; Roy Rosenzweig and David Thelen, *The Presence of the Past: Popular Uses of History in American Life* (New York: Columbia University Press, 1998), 31.

2. "Lincoln Ranked Best President in C-SPAN Poll of Historians," *Washington Times*, February 16, 2009; Lydia Saad, "Lincoln Resumes Position as Americans' Top-Rated President," *Gallup.com*, February 19, 2007; Ula Ilnytzky, "Lincoln 1864 Manuscript sets Record at NYC Auction," *Associated Press*, February 12, 2009; "Student Finds Rare Lincoln Fingerprint," Miami University News Release, February 9, 2009; Online Computer Library Center, Inc., *WorldCat Identities*, www.worldcat.org/identities/; John O'Connor, "From Kids to Obama, Nation Marks Lincoln's 200th," *Associated Press*, February 12, 2009; Kristen Wyatt, "Western States Remembering Abe Lincoln, Too," *Associated Press*, February 7, 2009; Vernon Burton, "Abraham Lincoln at Two Hundred," *OAH Newsletter* 37 (November 2009).

3. J. G. Randall, "Has the Lincoln Theme Been Exhausted?" *American Historical Review* 41, no. 2 (January 1936): 270–94. For distinctions between amateur and professional see David Lowenthal, *The Heritage Crusade and the Spoils of History* (London: Viking, 1997); Michael Kammen, "History Is Our Heritage: The Past in Contemporary American Culture," *In the Past Lane: Historical Perspectives on American Culture* (New York: Oxford University Press, 1997), 214–22; Margaret MacMillan, *Dangerous Games: The Uses and Abuses of History* (New York: Modern Library, 2009); Jerome De Groot, "Historians No Longer Own History," *History News Network*, April 13, 2009, http://hnn.us/articles/73272.html.

4. Richard S. Taylor, "Telling Lincoln's Story," *Journal of The Abraham Lincoln Association* 21, no. 2 (Summer 2000): 44.

5. Barry Schwartz, *Abraham Lincoln in the Post-Heroic Era: History and Memory in Late Twentieth-Century America* (Chicago: University of Chicago Press, 2008), 3.

6. Rosenzweig and Thelen, *The Presence of the Past*, 3; Michael Frisch, *A Shared Authority: Essays on the Craft and Meaning of Oral and Public History*

(Albany: State University of New York Press, 1990), 262; Terry Fife, quoted in Catherine M. Lewis, *The Changing Face of Public History: The Chicago Historical Society and the Transformation of an American Museum* (DeKalb: Northern Illinois University Press, 2005), 71.

7. Josiah Holland, *Life of Abraham Lincoln* (Springfield, MA: Gurdon Bill, 1866); William H. Herndon and Jesse W. Weik, *Herndon's Lincoln,* ed. Douglas L. Wilson and Rodney O. Davis (Urbana: University of Illinois Press, 2006), 4; Chauncey Black to Ward Hill Lamon, cited in Benjamin Thomas, *Portrait for Posterity: Lincoln and His Biographers* (New Brunswick, NJ: Rutgers University Press, 1947), 36–37.

8. "A Foundation for the Study of Lincoln," *Indiana History Bulletin* 5, no. 8 (May 1928), 141–43; Christopher B. Coleman, "Emphasis in the Work of Historical Societies," *Indiana History Bulletin,* Vol. 6, Extra No. 3, *Proceedings of the Southwestern Indiana Historical Society during its Ninth Year* (August 1929): 16. See also "Notes and Comments," *Mississippi Valley Historical Review* 11, no. 1 (June 1924), 157–85.

9. Clifford Geertz, "Thick Description: Toward an Interpretive Theory of Culture," *The Interpretation of Cultures: Selected Essays by Clifford Geertz* (New York: Basic Books, 1973), 3–30; David D. Hall, ed., *Lived Religion in America: Toward a History of Practice* (Princeton: Princeton University Press, 1997); Grant Wacker, *Heaven Below: Early Pentecostals and American Culture* (Cambridge, MA: Harvard University Press, 2001).

10. Ian Tyrrell, *Historians in Public: The Practice of American History, 1890–1970* (Chicago: University of Chicago Press, 2005); Ian Tyrrell, "Public at the Creation: Place, Memory, and Historical Practice in the Mississippi Valley Historical Association, 1907–1950," *Journal of American History* 94, no. 1 (June 2007): 19–46.

11. Eelco Runia, "Presence," *History and Theory* 45 (February 2006): 5.

12. Merrill D. Peterson, *Lincoln in American Memory* (New York: Oxford University Press, 1994); Schwartz, *Abraham Lincoln in the Post-Heroic Era;* David W. Blight, *Race and Reunion: The Civil War in American Memory* (Cambridge, Mass.: Belknap Press, 2001); Foner, McPherson, and Blight, in Eric Foner, ed., *Our Lincoln New Perspectives on Lincoln and His World* (New York: W. W. Norton, 2008), 11–18, 19–36, 269–82.

1. The Lincoln Inquiry

1. John E. Iglehart to Juliet Von Behren and Deidré Duff Johnson, September 13, 1928, box 5, folder 10, John E. Iglehart Papers (Indiana Historical Society, Indianapolis), hereafter Iglehart Papers; John E. Iglehart, "Remarks," "Proceedings of the Southwestern Indiana Historical Society," September 29, 1922, 11 (Willard Library, Evansville, IN), hereafter "Proceedings"; "John E. Iglehart Dead," *Evansville Press,* April 18, 1934; John E. Iglehart to Deidré Johnson, October 10, 1924, box 5, folder 7, Iglehart Papers; J. Edward Murr to Albert J. Beveridge, November 21, 1924, carton 290, Albert Jeremiah Beveridge Papers, Manuscript Division (Library of Congress, Washington, DC); hereafter Beveridge Papers.

2. John E. Iglehart, "The Coming of the English to Indiana in 1817 and Their Hoosier Neighbors," *Indiana Magazine of History* 15, no. 2 (June 1919): 89–178;

John E. Iglehart, "The Life and Times of John Shrader, Including the Introduction and Progress of Methodism in Southwestern Indiana," *Indiana Magazine of History* 17, no. 1 (March 1921): 3–49, and 17, no. 2 (June 1921): 117–49; John E. Iglehart, *An Account of Vanderburgh County from Its Organization,* volume 3 of Logan Esarey, *History of Indiana from Its Organization to 1922,* 3 vols. (Dayton, OH: Dayton Historical Publishing Company, 1922).

3. Monroe's work was utilized in Joanna L. Stratton, *Pioneer Women: Voices from the Kansas Frontier* (New York: Simon & Schuster, 1981); Meeker wrote *The Ox Team: or the Old Oregon Trail* (1906), *Ventures and Adventures of Ezra Meeker* (1908), and *Story of the Lost Trail to Oregon* (1915); Marguerite Miller, *Home Folks: A Series of Stories by Old Settlers of Fulton County,* 2 vols. (Rochester, IN: by the author, [c. 1910]); David J. Russo, *Keepers of Our Past: Local Historical Writing in the United States, 1820s–1930s* (Westport, CT: Greenwood Press, 1988), 5.

4. "Old Settler's Meeting" and "What They Are Doing in Iowa," *Indiana Magazine of History* 2, no. 1 (March 1906), 28, 50–51; James H. Madison, *Indiana through Tradition and Change: A History of the Hoosier State and Its People, 1920–1945* (Indianapolis: Indiana Historical Society, 1982), 345–47; Arthur M. Schlesinger, "Biography of a Nation of Joiners," *American Historical Review* 50, no. 1 (October 1944): 1–25.

5. "Articles of Incorporation," November 29, 1919 (signed) and January 2, 1920 (notarized), in "Southwestern Indiana Historical Society Minute Book 1, 1920–1924," reel 6, item 10, Southwestern Indiana Historical Society Collection (Willard Library, Evansville, IN), hereafter "Minute Book 1"; "Bylaws," reel 6, item 9, Southwestern Indiana Historical Society Collection (Willard Library, Evansville, IN), hereafter SWIHS Collection; Demarchus C. Brown to John E. Iglehart, October 27, 1919, Iglehart to James A. Woodburn, October 23, 1919, Harlow Lindley to Iglehart, October 25, October 31, 1919, reel 1, item 2, SWIHS Collection.

6. Russo, *Keepers of Our Past,* chaps, 1–3; Madison, *Indiana through Tradition and Change,* 5, 346; Michael Kammen, *Mystic Chords of Memory: The Transformation of Tradition in American Culture* (New York: Alfred A. Knopf, 1991), 40–61.

7. John E. Iglehart to Harlow Lindley, October 29, 1919, reel 1, item 2, SWIHS Collection; Thomas J. de la Hunt to Lucius Embree, February 6, 1923, box 11, folder 2, Lucius C. Embree Papers, 1786–1933 (Indiana State Library, Indianapolis), hereafter Embree Papers; William Barker, in "Proceedings," October 30, 1928, 3; de la Hunt to Iglehart, November 19, 1926, box 2, folder 15, Iglehart Papers.

8. John E. Iglehart, "Address," *Indiana Historical Commission Bulletin* no. 16, *Proceedings of the Southwestern Indiana Historical Society* (October 1922): 10; Iglehart to Frederick Jackson Turner, October 24, 1921, box 2, folder 13, Iglehart Papers.

9. William A. Barker, in "Proceedings," June 5, 1930, 12; Iglehart to Charles W. Moores, April 12, 1922, box 5, folder 1, Iglehart Papers; Lucius Embree, in *Indiana Historical Commission Bulletin* no. 16, *Proceedings of the Southwestern Indiana Historical Society* (October 1922): 21; John E. Iglehart, "Address," *Indiana Historical Commission Bulletin* No. 16, *Proceedings of the Southwestern Indiana*

Historical Society (October 1922): 11; Logan Esarey to Iglehart, September 22, 1922, box 1, folder 10, Iglehart Papers; George R. Wilson, "Historical Notes on Dubois County," 3 (1924): 256, Wilson GR Mss. (Lilly Library, Indiana University, Bloomington), hereafter identified by volume and year.

10. Ethel Farquhar McCullough, "Card Indexing of Old Newspapers," *Indiana Historical Commission Bulletin* no. 16, *Proceedings of the Southwestern Indiana Historical Society* (October 1922): 35; Bess Ehrmann, in "Proceedings," October 25, 1927, 46; George Robert Wilson, "The Birth of a State," *Indiana Historical Commission Bulletin* no. 16, *Proceedings of the Southwestern Indiana Historical Society* (October 1922): 41.

11. Bess Ehrmann, in "Proceedings," March 11, 1932; Deirdré Duff Johnson to John E. Iglehart, "Posey County Report," February 28, 1928, in "Minute Book 1"; A. J. Bigney, "How the Colleges Can Co-operate with the Historical Societies," *Indiana History Bulletin*, Vol. 1, Extra No., *Proceedings of the Fifth Annual Meeting of the Southwestern Indiana Historical Society* (June 1924): 51; Iglehart, in "Proceedings," June 1, 1922; John Oliver to Iglehart, January 13, 1930, box 5, folder 11, Iglehart Papers.

12. Robert N. Bellah, "Civil Religion in America," *Dædalus: Journal of the American Academy of Arts and Sciences* 96, no. 1 (Winter 1967): 1–21; Kammen, *Mystic Chords of Memory,* 194–227; Maurice Halbwachs, *On Collective Memory,* ed. and trans. Lewis A. Coser (Chicago: University of Chicago Press, 1992).

13. "Southwestern Indiana Historical Society Minute Book 2, 1925–1936," February 6, 1925, reel 6, item 11, SWIHS Collection (Willard Library, Evansville, IN), hereafter "Minute Book 2"; "Proceedings," September 29, 1922, 24–26, October 12, 1923, June 10, 1924, 21, May 27, 1925, 25, October 8, 1926, 8, June 14, 1927; Wilson, "Historical Notes on Dubois County," 3 (1924), 509; "Historical Body Has Big Function," *Evansville Journal,* March 1, 1923; Eldora Raleigh to John E. Iglehart, February 23, 1921, box 5, folder 4, Iglehart Papers.

14. Bess Ehrmann and Thomas J. de la Hunt, in *Indiana Historical Commission Bulletin* no. 16, *Proceedings of the Southwestern Indiana Historical Society* (October 1922): 22, 28–31; Thomas J. de la Hunt to John E. Iglehart, March 14, 1922, box 2, folder 15, Iglehart Papers. Marmaduke McClellan Stoops published the *Pike County Democrat* (1892–1925), Charles T. Baker edited and published the *Grandview Monitor,* U. B. Cummings owned a newspaper in Tell City, William B. Carleton edited and published the *Evansville Courier* (1896–1924) and the *Boonville Enquirer* (1924–44), Thomas E. Downs edited the *Boonville Republican,* Beulah Gray edited the *Otwell Star* (1929–45), W. W. Kellams edited the *Rockport Democrat,* and Gil R. Stormont published the *Princeton Clarion.*

15. Louise Dunkerson Orr, "The Casselberry Family," *Indiana History Bulletin,* Vol. 1, Extra No., *Proceedings of the Fifth Annual Meeting of the Southwestern Indiana Historical Society* (June 1924): 38. Demographic data compiled by author by comparing membership rolls against U.S. Census data, local histories and biographies, and local genealogical data. See Appendix A for information about specific individuals.

16. Lewis Atherton, *Main Street on the Middle Border* (Bloomington: Indiana University Press, 1954), 109. For characterizations of historical interest as the pastime of the elite, see Lewis Mumford, *The Culture of Cities* (New York: Harcourt,

Brace, 1938); Richard Hofstadter, *The Age of Reform: From Bryan to F.D.R.* (New York: Vintage Books, 1955); Arthur Mann, *Yankee Reformers in the Urban Age: Social Reform in Boston, 1880–1900* (New York: Harper & Row, 1966); E. Digby Baltzell, *The Protestant Establishment: Aristocracy and Caste in America* (New York: Random House, 1964); Michael D. Clark, *The American Discovery of Tradition, 1865–1942* (Baton Rouge: Louisiana State University Press, 2005), 16. For history as the means by which to Americanize ethnic minorities see John Higham, *Strangers in the Land: Patterns of American Nativism, 1860–1925* (New Brunswick, NJ: Rutgers University Press, 1955); John Bodnar, *Remaking America: Public Memory, Commemoration, and Patriotism in the Twentieth Century* (Princeton: Princeton University Press, 1992), chap. 3. For historical interest as a critique of modernity see T. J. Jackson Lears, *No Place of Grace: Antimodernism and the Transformation of American Culture, 1880–1920* (New York: Pantheon Books, 1981); Kammen, *Mystic Chords of Memory*, 163–93; David Lowenthal, *The Heritage Crusade and the Spoils of History* (London: Viking, 1997), 127–47.

17. Madison, *Indiana through Tradition and Change*, 6, 23; James M. Lindgren, *Preserving Historic New England: Preservation, Progressivism, and the Remaking of Memory* (New York: Oxford University Press, 1995), 6.

18. Thomas J. de la Hunt to John E. Iglehart, December 20, 1920, February 2, 1922, box 2, folder 15, Iglehart Papers.

19. Walter Muir Whitehill, "Preface," in Charles B. Hosmer Jr., *Presence of the Past: A History of the Preservation Movement in the United States Before Williamsburg* (New York: G. P. Putnam's Sons, 1965), 14; Rebecca Conard, *Benjamin Shambaugh and the Intellectual Foundations of Public History* (Iowa City: University of Iowa Press, 2002) 1.

20. John E. Iglehart, in "Proceedings," February, June 1, 1922; William L. Barker, in "Proceedings," November 1, 1929, 3; George R. Wilson, "Historical Notes on Dubois County," 2 (1926), 601.

21. Christopher B. Coleman, "Historical Work in Indiana," *Indiana History Bulletin*, Vol. 3, Extra No. 1, *Proceedings of the Southwestern Indiana Historical Society during its Sixth Year: Papers Read Before the Society at Various Meetings, 1920–1925* (December 1925): 66; Philip Lutz, "The Fourth of July in Lincoln's Time and Today," July 4, 1935, 1, SWIHS Collection; Harriett Powell, in "Proceedings," June 1, 1928, 13; Roscoe Kiper, "Address of Welcome," in "Proceedings," September 29, 1922, 2; William L. Barker, "Resume of 1929 and 1930," February 12, 1931, 5, reel 7, item 1, SWIHS Collection; Robert A. Woods, in "Proceedings," November 1, 1929.

22. Arthur Taylor, *Indiana Historical Commission Bulletin* no. 16, *Proceedings of the Southwestern Indiana Historical Society* (October 1922), 26–28; Iglehart, in "Proceedings," June 1, 1922.

23. John E. Iglehart, in "Proceedings," September 29, 1922, 18; Iglehart to Susan M. Garvin, February 24, 1921, box 4, folder 7, Iglehart Papers; Iglehart, "Address," *Indiana Historical Commission Bulletin* no. 16, *Proceedings of the Southwestern Indiana Historical Society* (October 1922): 13, 14.

24. John E. Iglehart, in "Proceedings," June 1, 1922; "Report of Committee on Reorganization," in "Minute Book 1," January 16, 1923; "Proceedings," February 28, 1923, 2–5; Iglehart, in "Proceedings," September 29, 1922, 31, February 28, 1923, 5.

25. Tony Horwitz, *Confederates in the Attic: Dispatches from the Unfinished Civil War* (New York: Pantheon Books, 1998), 11.

26. Christopher B. Coleman, "Editorial and Notes," *Indiana Magazine of History* 4, no. 2 (June 1908), 95; Walter Muir Whitehill, *Independent Historical Societies* (Boston: The Boston Athenaeum, 1962); Sally F. Griffith, *Serving History in a Changing World: The Historical Society of Pennsylvania in the Twentieth Century* (Philadelphia: University of Pennsylvania Press, 2001); Catherine M. Lewis, *The Changing Face of Public History: The Chicago Historical Society and the Transformation of an American Museum* (DeKalb: Northern Illinois University Press, 2005).

27. Iglehart, "Inaugural Address," 94; "Iglehart, "Address," *Indiana Historical Commission Bulletin* no. 16, *Proceedings of the Southwestern Indiana Historical Society* (October 1922): 20–21.

28. Josiah Holland, *Life of Abraham Lincoln* (Springfield, MA: Gurdon Bill, 1866); William H. Herndon and Jesse W. Weik, *Herndon's Lincoln*, ed. Douglas L. Wilson and Rodney O. Davis (Urbana: University of Illinois Press, 2006), 4; Chauncey Black to Ward Hill Lamon, cited in Benjamin Thomas, *Portrait for Posterity: Lincoln and His Biographers* (New Brunswick, NJ: Rutgers University Press, 1947), 36–37.

29. Iglehart, "The Heroic Age in Indiana," 4; Iglehart, "Address" [to Evansville School Teachers], 1924, 2–3; see also Iglehart, "Inaugural Address," *Indiana Historical Commission Bulletin* no. 16, *Proceedings of the Southwestern Indiana Historical Society* (October 1922): 85–94, and Iglehart, "Correspondence between Lincoln Historians and This Society," *Indiana Historical Commission Bulletin* no. 18, *Proceedings of the Southwestern Indiana Historical Society* (October 1923): 63–88.

30. Iglehart, "Correspondence between Lincoln Historians and This Society," 69; see also Iglehart, "The Coming of the English to Indiana in 1817 and Their Hoosier Neighbors," 135–36, and Iglehart, "Inaugural Address," 92–93.

31. Iglehart, "Inaugural Address," 92; Iglehart, "Correspondence between Lincoln Historians and This Society," 70; Iglehart to Phoebe Hamlin, November 22, 1918, Iglehart Papers, box 4, folder 8, (IHS); See also Iglehart, "The Heroic Age in Indiana," 4.

32. John E. Iglehart to Frederick Jackson Turner, October 24, 1921, Frederick Jackson Turner Collection, 1862–1963 (The Huntington Library, San Marino, CA), hereafter Turner Collection; "Proceedings," June 1, 1922, 13–20; "Minute Book 1," September 28, 1920.

33. Logan Esarey, "The Pioneer Aristocracy," *Indiana Magazine of History* 14, no. 3 (September 1918): 270–87. Iglehart, "The Coming of the English to Indiana in 1817 and Their Hoosier Neighbors," 137, 91–92; see also Iglehart, "Inaugural Address," 88, and Iglehart, "Correspondence between Lincoln Historians and This Society," 68; Esarey to Iglehart, January 7, 1919, box 1, folder 10, Iglehart Papers. In 1927 the society passed a resolution calling for the reprinting of Esarey's article, "Proceedings," October 25, 1927.

34. William Cronon, "Turner's First Stand: The Significance of Significance in American History," in *Writing Western History: Essays on Major Western Historians,* ed. Richard W. Etulain (Albuquerque: University of New Mexico Press, 1991), 73–101.

35. James. G. Randall to Frederick Jackson Turner, July 7, 1907, Turner Collection; for contrast see the correspondence with Reuben Gold Thwaites, Mark Anthony DeWolf Howe, Archibald Henderson, and Guy Emerson.

36. John E. Iglehart to Frederick Jackson Turner, October 24, 1921, Turner to Iglehart, October 26, 1921, Turner Collection.

37. Ian Tyrrell, *Historians in Public: The Practice of American History, 1890–1970* (Chicago: University of Chicago Press, 2005), 216.

38. John E. Iglehart, Circular letter no. 1, April 26, 1920, reel 6, item 9, SWIHS Collection. See also Bess V. Ehrmann, *The Missing Chapter in the Life of Abraham Lincoln; A Number of Articles, Episodes, Photographs, Pen and Ink Sketches Concerning the Life of Abraham Lincoln in Spencer County, Indiana, between 1816–1830 and 1844* (Chicago: Walter M. Hill, 1938), 23–60. See Appendix B.

39. John E. Iglehart to Carl Sandburg, February 15, 1927, box 2, folder 7, Iglehart Papers; William Barker, in "Proceedings," March 11, 1932, 16–17. Some of the more notable assignments include Lucius C. Embree, "Morris Birckbeck's Estimate of the People of Princeton in 1817," *Indiana Magazine of History* 21, no. 4 (December 1925): 289–99; Deidré Johnson, "Moses Ashworth, Pioneer of Indiana Methodism"; Albion Fellows Bacon, "At the Landing," *Indiana Historical Commission Bulletin* no. 18, *Proceedings of the Southwestern Indiana Historical Society* (October 1923): 132–35; George R. Wilson, *Judge James Lockhart* (Indiana Historical Society Publications, Vol. 8, No. 1; Indianapolis: Wm. B. Burford, 1923): 1–69. A complete listing of conference papers, publications, and works is contained in Appendix B.

40. Albion Fellows Bacon in "Proceedings," February 12, 1924, 4–5; Thomas J. de la Hunt, in "Proceedings," June 10, 1924.

41. Alan Taylor, *William Cooper's Town: Power and Persuasion on the Frontier of the Early American Republic* (New York: Alfred A. Knopf, 1995), 8; John E. Iglehart to Frederick Jackson Turner, October 24, 1921, 1, Turner Collection; John E. Iglehart, "Address," *Indiana Historical Commission Bulletin* no. 16, *Proceedings of the Southwestern Indiana Historical Society* (October 1922): 13, 14; Iglehart, "Inaugural Address," 85–86.

42. Wilson, "Historical Notes on Dubois County," 2 (1926): 442; Lucius Embree, "Report," May 25, 1920, Embree Papers; Ehrmann, "The Lincoln Inquiry," 4; Emily Orr Clifford, "Private Schools in Evansville from 1842 to 1853," *Indiana Historical Commission Bulletin* no. 18, *Proceedings of the Southwestern Indiana Historical Society* (October 1923): 54.

43. Iglehart, "Inaugural Address," 94.

44. Mark Salber Phillips, "History, Memory, and Historical Distance," in *Theorizing Historical Consciousness,* ed. Peter Seixas (Toronto: University of Toronto Press, 2004), 89; Roger I. Simon, "The Pedagogical Insistence of Public Memory," in *Theorizing Historical Consciousness,* 183–201; Wilson, "Historical Notes on Dubois County," 4 (1925): 237; Thomas J. de la Hunt, in "Proceedings," June 10, 1924, 10; Dearing, "History and Youth," 32–44.

45. Christopher B. Coleman, "Historical Work in Indiana," *Indiana History Bulletin,* Vol. 3, Extra No. 1, *Proceedings of the Southwestern Indiana Historical Society during its Sixth Year: Papers Read Before the Society at Various Meetings, 1920–1925* (December 1925): 65; Wilson, "Commonplace Book, 1925," 178;

Wilson, "Historical Notes on Dubois County," 2 (1926): 28; 6 (1926): 345; 11 (1930): 453; 4 (1925): 330; 2 (1926): 177, 309–10, 500, 600.

46. George Wilson to John E. Iglehart, December 22, 1928, box 5, folder 16, Iglehart Papers; William P. Dearing, "Early Culture of the Pioneers of Southwestern Indiana," September 16, 1932, 3–4, SWIHS Collection; Logan Esarey to Lucius Embree, June 20, 1925, box 11, folder 3, Embree Papers.

47. Wilson to Iglehart, August 19, 1925, box 5, folder 14, Iglehart Papers; Merrill D. Peterson, *Lincoln in American Memory* (New York: Oxford University Press, 1994), 266; Iglehart, "Inaugural Address," 86, 88; Coleman, "Historical Work in Indiana," 65; "State History Never Written, Society Is Told," *Evansville Courier,* March 1, 1923; "Historical Body Has Big Function," *Evansville Journal,* March 1, 1923.

48. James L. Baughman, *Henry R. Luce and the Rise of the American News Media* (Baltimore: Johns Hopkins University Press, 2001), 201; Barry Schwartz, *Abraham Lincoln in the Post-Heroic Era: History and Memory in Late Twentieth-Century America* (Chicago: University of Chicago Press, 2008), 115–45.

49. Logan Esarey to John E. Iglehart, October 31, 1919, box 1, folder 10, Iglehart Papers; Esarey, quoted in "Preserving History," *Evansville Courier,* May 30, 1920; Iglehart, "Remarks," in "Proceedings," September 29, 1922, 4.

50. Frank E. Vandiver, *Black Jack: The Life and Times of John J. Pershing,* 2 vols. (College Station: Texas A&M University Press, 1977), 2:724.

51. "Minute Book 1," May 24, 1921.

52. "Lafayette, We are Here!" [unrecorded], May 24, 1921, in "Scrapbook No. 31," SWIHS Collection; Logan Esarey, "Historical News," *Indiana Magazine of History* 17, no. 3 (September 1921): 298; John W. Oliver to John E. Iglehart, July 28, 1921, box 5, folder 11, Iglehart Papers.

2. A Crowded Field

1. "Memorandum of a Smoker held Tuesday Night, February 12, 1924, at Evansville, from 7:30 to 9:30," 2, 5, box 3, folder 6, Iglehart Papers.

2. Ida M. Tarbell, *The Life of Abraham Lincoln,* 2 vols. (New York, Lincoln Memorial Association, 1900); John Drinkwater, *Abraham Lincoln: A Play* (Boston: Houghton Mifflin, 1919); Barry Schwartz, *Abraham Lincoln and the Forge of National Memory* (Chicago: University of Chicago Press, 2000); Merrill D. Peterson, *Lincoln in American Memory* (New York: Oxford University Press, 1994), 144–55, 175–90, 200–204.

3. William E. Barton, *The Soul of Abraham Lincoln* (New York: George H. Doran, 1920); Barton, *The Paternity of Lincoln* (New York: George H. Doran, 1920); Ida M. Tarbell, *Boy Scouts' Life of Lincoln* (New York: Macmillan, 1921); Jesse W. Weik, The Real Lincoln: A Portrait (Boston: Houghton Mifflin, 1922); Waldo Lincoln, *History of the Lincoln Family: An Account of the Descendants of Samuel Lincoln of Hingham, Massachusetts, 1637–1920* (Worchester, MA: Commonwealth Press, 1923); Thomas F. Schwartz, "James Jay Monaghan's *Lincoln Bibliography, 1839–1939:* A History," *Journal of the Abraham Lincoln Association* 14, no. 2 (Winter 1993): 55–59; Christopher A. Thomas, *The Lincoln Memorial and American Life* (Princeton: Princeton University Press, 2002).

4. John E. Iglehart to Ida M. Tarbell, May 1, 1925, Ida M. Tarbell Collection (Pelletier Library, Allegheny College, Meadville, PA); hereafter Tarbell Collection.

5. D. E. Fehrenbacher, *The Changing Image of Lincoln in American Historiography: An Inaugural Lecture delivered before the University of Oxford on 21 May 1968* (Oxford: Clarendon Press, 1968), 7; William E. Barton to John E. Iglehart, May 26, 1922, Iglehart Papers. On Barton see *The Autobiography of William E. Barton* (Indianapolis: Bobbs-Merrill, 1932); Robert Barton, *William E. Barton: Biographer* (Springfield, IL: [n.p.], 1946); Benjamin Thomas, *Portrait for Posterity: Lincoln and His Biographers* (New Brunswick, NJ: Rutgers University Press, 1947), 214–42.

6. Iglehart to Barton, June 3, 1922, box 1, folder 2, Iglehart Papers.

7. Ida M. Tarbell and J. McCan Davis, *The Early Life of Abraham Lincoln: Containing Many Unpublished Documents and Unpublished Reminiscences of Lincoln's Early Friends, With 160 Illustrations, including 20 Portraits of Lincoln* (New York: S. S. McClure, 1896); Ida M. Tarbell, *Life of Abraham Lincoln: Drawn from Original Sources and Containing many Speeches, Letters and Telegraphs Hitherto Unpublished,* 2 vols. (New York: Lincoln Memorial Association, 1900); Ida M. Tarbell, *All in the Day's Work: An Autobiography* (New York: Macmillan, 1939), 174.

8. Tarbell, *All in the Day's Work,* 163; Thomas, *Portrait for Posterity,* 183; Peterson, *Lincoln in American Memory,* 155.

9. Tarbell to Iglehart, November 16, 1922, Iglehart to Tarbell, November 17, 1922, Tarbell to Iglehart, November 20, 1922, Tarbell Collection; Iglehart, "Correspondence between Lincoln Historians and This Society," *Indiana Historical Commission Bulletin* no. 18, *Proceedings of the Southwestern Indiana Historical Society* (October 1923): 71.

10. John Braeman, *Albert J. Beveridge: American Nationalist* (Chicago: University of Chicago Press, 1971), 13, 36–37, 280–83.

11. Albert J. Beveridge to Iglehart, January 16, February 24, 27, 1923, box 1, folder 5, Iglehart Papers.

12. Iglehart, "Correspondence between Lincoln Historians and This Society," 65, 87; Iglehart, in "Proceedings," February 28, 1923, 7.

13. Lana Ruegamer, *A History of the Indiana Historical Society, 1830–1980* (Indianapolis: Indiana Historical Society, 1980), 77–97; George S. Cottman, "Local Historical Societies," *Indiana Magazine of History* 1, no. 2 (1905): 98–103; Lorna Lutes Sylvester, "Introduction," *"No Cheap Padding": Seventy-five Years of the Indiana Magazine of History, 1904–1979* (Indianapolis: Indiana Historical Bureau, 1980), vii–xviii; Murray Holliday, *A History of the Society of Indiana Pioneers, 1916–2005,* rev. ed. (Indianapolis: Society of Indiana Pioneers, 2005); Kate Milner Rabb, "Indiana Historical Commission," *Indiana Historical Bulletin* 2, no. 8 (1925): 163–69; James H. Madison, "Celebrating Indiana: 1816, 1916, 2016," in *The State of Indiana History 2000: Papers Presented at the Indiana Historical Society's Grand Opening,* ed. Robert M. Taylor Jr. (Indianapolis: Indiana Historical Society, 2001), 273–96; David Vanderstel, "History in the Public's Interest: The State of Public History in Indiana," in *The State of Indiana History 2000,* 541–44.

14. Ruegamer, *A History of the Indiana Historical Society, 1830–1980,* 114–15.

15. John W. Oliver, "Remarks," and Iglehart, in *Indiana Historical Commission Bulletin* no. 16, *Proceedings of the Southwestern Indiana Historical Society* (October

1922): 37–40; John E. Iglehart to Charles W. Moores, April 12, 1922, box 5, folder 1, Iglehart Papers; Iglehart, "Correspondence between Lincoln Historians and This Society," 68; Iglehart, "Remarks," in "Proceedings," September 29, 1922, 3–15.

16. "Society Urges Change in Road," Evansville *Courier,* February 1921; John E. Iglehart and Susan M. Garvin to [Governor] Warren McCray, April 22, 1921; McCray to Iglehart, May 2, 1921, in "Minute Book 1," May 24, 1921; John E. Iglehart, in "Proceedings," June 1, 1922; Ethel Farquhar McCullough, "Card Indexing of Old Newspapers," *Indiana Historical Commission Bulletin* no. 16, *Proceedings of the Southwestern Indiana Historical Society* (October 1922): 36; "Proceedings," June 10, 1924, 21, 47, February 6, 1925, 45–61.

17. Logan Esarey to John E. Iglehart, February 3, 1919, box 1, folder 10, Iglehart Papers; Judge Gough in "Minute Book 1," September 28, 1920; George R. Wilson to Iglehart, January 13, 1921, box 5, folder 14, Iglehart Papers.

18. John W. Oliver to John E. Iglehart, August 4, August 8, 1922, Oliver to Iglehart, November 17, 1922, box 5, folder 11, Iglehart Papers; John W. Oliver, in *Indiana Historical Commission Bulletin* no. 16, *Proceedings of the Southwestern Indiana Historical Society* (October 1922): 3.

19. Thomas J. de la Hunt to John E. Iglehart, August 22, September 19, 1922; Iglehart to de la Hunt, August 23, 1922, box 2, folder 15, Iglehart Papers; "Minute Book 1," February 23, 1920; James A. Woodburn in the editor's note to Thomas J. de la Hunt, "The Pocket in Indiana History," *Indiana Magazine of History* 16, no. 4 (December 1920): 308.

20. John E. Iglehart to Deidré Duff Johnson, July 5, 1923; Deidré Duff Johnson to John E. Iglehart, August 25, 1923; Iglehart, dictation, August 31, 1923, box 5, folder 7, Iglehart Papers.

21. Harlow Lindley, in *Indiana Historical Commission Bulletin* no. 18, *Proceedings of the Southwestern Indiana Historical Society* (October 1923): 3; John E. Iglehart to Thomas J. de la Hunt, April 29, 1924, box 2, folder 15, Iglehart Papers.

22. John E. Iglehart to George Wilson, January 10, 1924, box 5, folder 14, Iglehart Papers.

23. "Memorandum of a Smoker held Tuesday Night, February 12, 1924, at Evansville, from 7:30 to 9:30," box 3, folder 6, Iglehart Papers.

24. John E. Iglehart to Lucius Embree, February 25, 1924, box 11, folder 2, Embree Papers; Iglehart to Thomas J. de la Hunt, April 29, May 9, 1924, box 2, folder 15, Iglehart Papers; "Minute Book 1," May 16, 1924; Iglehart to Genevieve Williams and Lucius Embree, May 13, 1924, June 2, 1924, box 11, folder 2, Embree Papers; Iglehart to Bess Ehrmann, July 17, 1924, box 3, folder 14, Iglehart Papers.

25. Thomas J. de la Hunt and Harlow Lindley in "Proceedings," June 10, 1924, 7–10, 49–58; John E. Iglehart to Christopher B. Coleman, October 17, 1924, box 3, folder 6, Iglehart Papers. Iglehart refers to *Indiana History Bulletin,* Vol. 1, Extra No., *Proceedings of the Fifth Annual Meeting of the Southwestern Indiana Historical Society* (June 1924); Logan Esarey to John E. Iglehart, October 7, 1924, box 1, folder 10, Iglehart Papers.

26. John E. Iglehart to Bess Ehrmann, July 17, 1924, box 3, folder 14, Iglehart Papers.

27. Ruegamer, *A History of the Indiana Historical Society,* 135–39; George Wilson to John E. Iglehart, October 6, 1924, box 5, folder 14, Iglehart Papers.

28. Thomas J. de la Hunt, in "Proceedings," October 14, 1924.

29. Louis A. Warren, "The Mystery of Lincoln's Melancholy," *Indiana History Bulletin*, Vol. 3, Extra No. 1, *Proceedings of the Southwestern Indiana Historical Society during its Sixth Year: Papers Read Before the Society at Various Meetings, 1920–1925* (December 1925): 59–60.

30. Albion Fellows Bacon, "Lincoln," *Indiana Magazine of History* 21, no. 1 (March 1925): 1–2; George H. Honig, "The Artist's Ideal of Lincoln," *Indiana History Bulletin*, Vol. 3, Extra No. 1, *Proceedings of the Southwestern Indiana Historical Society during its Sixth Year: Papers Read Before the Society at Various Meetings, 1920–1925* (December 1925): 51–53.

31. Christopher B. Coleman, "Historical Work in Indiana," *Indiana History Bulletin*, Vol. 3, Extra No. 1, *Proceedings of the Southwestern Indiana Historical Society during its Sixth Year: Papers Read Before the Society at Various Meetings, 1920–1925* (December 1925): 64–66.

32. Bess V. Ehrmann, "The Lincoln Inquiry," *Indiana Magazine of History* 21, no. 1 (March 1925): 3–4.

33. Ida M. Tarbell, *In the Footsteps of the Lincolns* (New York: Harper and Brothers, 1924), 150; Roscoe Kiper, in "Proceedings," October 14, 1924, 43.

34. John E. Iglehart to Christopher B. Coleman, October 17, 1924, Coleman to Iglehart, October 20, 1924, box 3, folder 6, Iglehart Papers; Christopher B. Coleman, "Historical Work in Indiana," *Indiana History Bulletin*, Vol. 3, Extra No. 1, *Proceedings of the Southwestern Indiana Historical Society during its Sixth Year: Papers Read Before the Society at Various Meetings, 1920–1925* (December 1925): 64–66; John E. Iglehart to the members of the Executive Committee of the Southwestern Indiana Historical Society, December 9, 1924, in "Minute Book 1."

35. Ruegamer, *A History of the Indiana Historical Society*, 140–41; John E. Iglehart to Logan Esarey, January 24, 1927, box 1, folder 10, Iglehart Papers.

36. "Minute book 2," January 23, 1925; "Proceedings," February 6, 1925, 30–31, 43–46; Christopher B. Coleman to John E. Iglehart, February 5, 6, 1925, Iglehart to Hon. Ed Jackson, February 6, 1925, box 3, folder 6, Iglehart Papers.

37. Christopher B. Coleman to John E. Iglehart, January 24, March 4, 1925, box 3, folder 6, Iglehart Papers; Ruegamer, *A History of the Indiana Historical Society*, 140–41, 139.

38. Iglehart to the members of the Executive Committee of the Southwestern Indiana Historical Society, December 9, 1924, in "Minute Book 1"; Coleman to Iglehart, January 24, March 4, 1925, box 3, folder 6, Iglehart Papers; Christopher B. Coleman in "Proceedings," June 1, 1928, 37.

3. The Best Witnesses

1. John E. Iglehart, "Dictation," September 20, 1929, box 4, folder 11, Iglehart Papers.

2. A. R. Beach, "A Bit of Half-Forgotten History: A Battle of the War of the American Revolution fought on Indiana Soil," Annals of the Southwestern Indiana Historical Society, 81–86 (Indiana State Library, Indianapolis).

3. Merrill D. Peterson, *Lincoln in American Memory* (New York: Oxford University Press, 1994), 85.

4. Josiah Holland, *The Life of Abraham Lincoln* (Springfield, MA: Gurdon Bill, 1866), 542; Charles T. Morrissey, "The Perils of Instant History: Josiah G. Holland's Biography of Abraham Lincoln," *Journal of Popular Culture* 7 (Fall 1973): 347–50; Benjamin P. Thomas, *Portrait for Posterity: Lincoln and His Biographers* (New Brunswick, NJ: Rutgers University Press, 1947), 3–6.

5. William H. Herndon to Isaac N. Arnold, December 27, 1882, quoted in David Donald, *Lincoln's Herndon* (New York: Alfred A. Knopf, 1948), 212–13; Allen C. Guelzo, "Holland's Informants: The Construction of Josiah Holland's 'Life of Abraham Lincoln,'" *Journal of the Abraham Lincoln Association* 23, no. 1 (Winter 2002): 1–53.

6. William H. Herndon to Josiah Holland, June 8, 1865, William H. Herndon to Caroline H. Dall, December 20, 1866, cited in Donald, *Lincoln's Herndon,* 169, 181; Thomas, *Portrait for Posterity,* 8.

7. Herndon, notes from interview with Sarah Bush Lincoln, September 8, 1865, in *Herndon's Informants: Letters, Interviews, and Statements about Abraham Lincoln,* ed. Douglas L. Wilson and Rodney O. Davis (Urbana: University of Illinois Press, 1998), 106–7, 109.

8. For articulations of the position see Charles B. Strozier, *Lincoln's Quest for Union: Public and Private Meanings* (New York: Basic Books, 1982), xvi; Douglas L. Wilson, "Abraham Lincoln, Ann Rutledge, and the Evidence of Herndon's Informants," *Civil War History* 36 (1990): 301–23; Douglas L. Wilson, "William H. Herndon and His Lincoln Informants," *Journal of the Abraham Lincoln Association* 14, no. 1 (Winter 1993): 15–34; Rodney O. Davis, "William Herndon's Indiana Oral History Project, 1865," *Indiana Magazine of History* 89, no. 2 (June 1993): 136–47. The claim has been challenged by Richard S. Taylor, "Telling Lincoln's Story," *Journal of The Abraham Lincoln Association* 21, no. 2 (Summer 2000): 44–68; C. A. Tripp, "The Strange Case of Isaac Cogdal," *Journal of the Abraham Lincoln Association* 23, no. 1 (Winter 2002): 69–77. The quote is from Taylor, 56.

9. William H. Herndon to Jesse Weik, December 13, 1888, quoted in Wilson and Davis, *Lincoln's Informants,* xxi; Donald, *Lincoln's Herndon,* 172.

10. Donald, *Lincoln's Herndon,* 343; William H. Herndon and Jesse W. Weik, *Herndon's Lincoln: The True Story of a Great Life* (Chicago: Belford, Clark, 1889).

11. Michael Frisch, *A Shared Authority: Essays on the Craft and Meaning of Oral and Public History* (Albany: State University of New York Press, 1990), 8–10, 187; Nigel Hamilton, *Biography: A Brief History* (Cambridge, MA: Harvard University Press, 2007), 100–128.

12. John Nicolay and John Hay, *Abraham Lincoln: A History,* 10 vols. (New York: Century, 1890). The work is assessed in Michael Burlingame, "Nicolay and Hay: Court Historians," *Journal of the Abraham Lincoln Association* 19, no. 1 (Winter 1998): 1–20. The interview notes are compiled in Burlingame, ed., *An Oral History of Abraham Lincoln: John G. Nicolay's Interviews and Essays* (Carbondale: Southern Illinois University Press, 1996), quotations from xv–xvi.

13. Osborn H. Oldroyd, ed., *The Lincoln Memorial: Album-Immortelles* (New York: G. W. Carleton, 1882); Allen Thorndike Rice, ed., *Reminiscences of Abraham Lincoln by Distinguished Men of His Time* (New York: Harper and Brothers, 1885); Francis F. Browne, ed., *The Every-day Life of Abraham Lincoln* (New York:

N. D. Thompson, 1886); William Hayes Ward, ed., *Abraham Lincoln: Tributes from his Associates, Reminiscences of Soldiers, Statesmen, and Citizens* (New York: Thomas Y. Crowell, 1895); Henry B. Rankin, *Personal Recollections of Abraham Lincoln* (New York: G. P. Putnam's Sons, 1916); Ervin S. Chapman, ed., *Latest Light on Abraham Lincoln and War-Time Memories*, 2 vols. (New York: Fleming H. Revell, 1917); Henry B. Rankin, ed., *Intimate Character Sketches of Abraham Lincoln* (Philadelphia: J. B. Lippincott, 1924); John E. Washington, *They Knew Lincoln* (New York: E. P. Dutton, 1942); Rufus R. Wilson, ed., *Intimate Memories of Lincoln* (Elmira, NY: Primavera Press, 1945).

14. Madison Hemings, interviewed in *Pike County* [Waverly, OH] *Republican*, March 13, 1873, reprinted in Annette Gordon-Reed, *Thomas Jefferson and Sally Hemings: An American Controversy* (Charlottesville: University Press of Virginia, 1997), 245–48.

15. Ida M. Tarbell, *He Knew Lincoln* (New York: McClure, Phillips, 1907), 3, 19, 24. This and other stories were collected in Tarbell, *He Knew Lincoln, and Other Billy Brown Stories* (New York: Macmillan, 1922). J. Rogers Gore less successfully "dramatized" the testimony of Austin Gollaher in *The Boyhood of Abraham Lincoln from the Spoken Narratives of Austin Gollaher* (Indianapolis: Bobbs-Merrill, 1921).

16. George P. Hambrecht Manuscripts, Lilly Library, Indiana University, Bloomington; J. T. Hobson, *Footprints of Abraham Lincoln: Presenting Many Interesting Facts, Reminiscences and Illustrations Never Before Published* (Dayton, OH: Otterbein Press, 1909); Arthur E. Morgan, "New Light on Lincoln's Boyhood," *Atlantic Monthly* 125 (February 1920): 214. Newspapers that regularly ran Lincoln reminiscences include the *Charleston* [IL] *Courier; Chicago Tribune; Evansville* [IN] *Courier; Louisville* [KY] *Courier-Journal; Rockport* [IN] *Journal; Shelby County* [IL] *Leader;* and *St. Louis Globe-Democrat.*

17. Albion Fellows Bacon, "Lincoln," *Indiana Magazine of History* 21, no. 1 (March 1925), 2.

18. William Fortune, "Lincoln in Indiana," *Indiana History Bulletin*, Vol. 3, Extra No. 1, *Proceedings of the Southwestern Indiana Historical Society during its Sixth Year: Papers Read Before the Society at Various Meetings, 1920–1925* (December 1925): 62; William Fortune to Ida M. Tarbell, October 19, 1925, Tarbell Collection; William Fortune, "An Indiana Investigator," in *The Missing Chapter in the Life of Abraham Lincoln: A Number of Articles, Episodes, Photographs, Pen and Ink Sketches Concerning the Life of Abraham Lincoln in Spencer County, Indiana, between 1816–1830 and 1844,* ed. Bess V. Ehrmann (Chicago: Walter M. Hill, 1938), 64, 70, 73.

19. Alice L. Harper Hanby, "John Pitcher," *Indiana Historical Commission Bulletin* no. 16, *Proceedings of the Southwestern Indiana Historical Society* (October 1922): 55.

20. Allesandro Portelli, "What Makes Oral History Different?" in *The Death of Luigi Trastulli and Other Stories: Form and Meaning in Oral History* (Albany: SUNY Press, 1991), 45–58.

21. The interviews were conducted by Kate Armstrong in 1887 and reported in Ida D. Armstrong, "The Lincolns in Spencer County," *Indiana Historical Commission Bulletin* no. 18, *Proceedings of the Southwestern Indiana Historical Society* (October 1923): 59.

22. Logan Esarey, "Pioneer Aristocracy," *Indiana Magazine of History* 13 (September 1917): 270–87.

23. James E. Morlock, "The Assassination of Lincoln," 1–2, SWIHS Collection, is the report of an interview with John Shanklin Ramsay conducted April 18, 1930, read by Morlock to the Posey County Historical Society, April 19, 1930, and then read by Katherine F. Fitton to the Southwestern, February 12, 1931.

24. Della Pollack, ed., *Remembering: Oral History Performance* (New York: Palgrave Macmillan, 2005), 1.

25. Wilson, "Historical Notes on Dubois County," 3 (1924): 523–29; "Historical Notes on Dubois County," 15 (1933): 196; Lucius C. Embree, "Preservation of the Knowledge of Old People," *Indiana Historical Commission Bulletin* no. 16, *Proceedings of the Southwestern Indiana Historical Society* (October 1922): 69–72. Compare Allesandro Portelli, "Response to Commentaries," *Oral History Review* 32, no. 1 (Winter–Spring 2005): 33; Douglas J. Wilson, *Honor's Voice: The Transformation of Abraham Lincoln* (New York: Alfred A. Knopf, 1998), 10.

26. On the modern movement see Donald Ritchie, *Doing Oral History,* 2d ed. (New York: Oxford University Press, 2003); Ronald J. Grele, ed., *Envelopes of Sound: The Art of Oral History,* revised ed. (Westport, CT: Meckler, 1990); David Stricklin and Rebecca Sharpless, eds., *The Past Meets the Present: Essays on Oral History* (Lanham, MD: University Press of America, 1988).

27. John Braeman, *Albert J. Beveridge: American Nationalist* (Chicago: University of Chicago Press, 1971), 298–303; "Memorandum of Interview with Senator Beveridge," c. January 1925, 6, box 1, folder 5, Iglehart Papers.

28. Albert J. Beveridge to J. Franklin Jameson, April 21, 1924, reprinted in Elizabeth Donnan and Leo F. Stock, "Senator Beveridge, J. Franklin Jameson, and Abraham Lincoln," *Mississippi Valley Historical Review* 35, no. 4 (March 1949), 646; Albert J. Beveridge to Charles A. Beard, June 20, 1924, container 285, Beveridge Papers.

29. Beveridge quotations as cited in Braeman, *Albert J. Beveridge,* 294; Beveridge to Beard, July 26, 1924, container 285, Beveridge Papers.

30. Peter Novick, *That Noble Dream: The "Objectivity Question" and the American Historical Profession* (Cambridge: Cambridge University Press, 1988), 21–61.

31. See Nicolay and Hay, *Complete Works of Abraham Lincoln,* 2 vols. (New York: Century, 1894); Nicolay and Hay, *Complete Works of Abraham Lincoln,* 12 vols. (New York: Francis D. Tandy Co., 1905); Gilbert A. Tracy, *Uncollected Letters of Abraham Lincoln* (New York: Houghton Mifflin, 1917).

32. Beveridge to Worthington C. Ford, February 14, 1923, container F6, Beveridge Papers; Beveridge to Jesse W. Weik, February 24, 1927, Albert Jeremiah Beveridge Correspondence, 1924–1928, folder 4 (Abraham Lincoln Presidential Library, Springfield, IL), hereafter Beveridge Correspondence.

33. See Beveridge to Weik, July 18, August 4, September 13, 1921, December 22, 1922, January 10, March 1, March 17, June 29, 1923; Houghton Mifflin Company to Weik, February 23, 1923, Jesse Weik, Papers, 1833–1939, box 2 (Abraham Lincoln Presidential Library, Springfield, IL).

34. Braeman, *Albert J. Beveridge,* 293–94; Beveridge to Jameson, May 28, 1923, in *Mississippi Valley Historical Review* 35, no. 4 (March 1949), 644; Beveridge to Paul Angle, October 14, 1926, container 285, Beveridge Papers; Beveridge to Weik,

May 26, 1926, Jesse Weik Papers, 1833–1939 (Abraham Lincoln Presidential Library, Springfield, IL), hereafter Weik Papers.

35. Beveridge to Archibald Henderson, April 14, 1925, container 289, Beveridge Papers; Beveridge to Louis A. Warren, May 17, 1924, Beveridge to George F. Parker, February 27, 1923, box 2, Director's Correspondence with Collectors (Lincoln Financial Foundation Collection at the Allen County Public Library, Fort Wayne, IN, courtesy of the State of Indiana), hereafter Director's Correspondence; Beveridge to Jameson, October 21, 1924, *Mississippi Valley Historical Review* 35, no. 4 (March 1949), 649; Braeman, *Albert J. Beveridge,* 301–2.

36. Beveridge to Weik, August 5, 1924, folder 4, Beveridge Correspondence; Beveridge to Jameson, October 21, 1924, *Mississippi Valley Historical Review* 35, no. 4 (March 1949), 648–49. See also Beveridge to Iglehart, October 21, 1924, box 1, folder 5, Iglehart Papers; Beveridge to William E. Connelley, November 10, 1924, folder 1, Beveridge Correspondence.

37. Jameson to Beveridge, October 10, December 17, 1924, Container 289; Beard to Beveridge, September 17, 1924, container 285; James A. Woodburn to Beveridge, November 19, 1924, container 296, Stephenson to Beveridge, November 23, 1924, container 294, Beveridge Papers; William E. Connelley to Beveridge, January 21, 1925, folder 1, Beveridge Correspondence.

38. Bess Ehrmann to Beveridge, December 29, 1924, container 288, Roscoe Kiper to Beveridge, January, container 290; Will F. Adams to Beveridge, December 18, 1924, container 285; J. Edward Murr to Beveridge, November 21, 1924, container 290, Beveridge Papers.

39. John E. Iglehart to Albert J. Beveridge, August 23, October 27, November 6, 1924, Beveridge to Iglehart, November 6, 12, 1924, container 289, Beveridge Papers.

40. Woodburn to Beveridge, November 19, 1924; Beveridge to Woodburn, November 22, 1924, container 296, Beveridge Papers.

41. D. E. Fehrenbacher, *The Changing Image of Lincoln in American Historiography: An Inaugural Lecture delivered before the University of Oxford on 21 May 1968* (Oxford: Clarendon Press, 1968), 8; Barton to Tarbell, April 19, 1920, March 30, 1923; Tarbell to Barton, February 17, 1923; Barton to Tarbell, February 18, 19, 1924, Ida M. Tarbell Collection.

42. Warren to Barton, March 13, 1922, Barton to Warren, March 16, 1922, see also their correspondence between 1919 and 1923, box 2, Director's Correspondence.

43. Beveridge to Barton, May 30, July 29, November 25, 1924, container 286; Beveridge to Warren, July 28, 1924, container 295, Beveridge Papers; Warren to Beveridge, September 9, 1924; Beveridge to Warren, November 11, 1924, box 2, Director's Correspondence. Warren alluded to Barton's betrayal in a letter to Beveridge, but did not send the item: Warren to Beveridge, July 23, 1924, box 2, Director's Correspondence.

44. Louis A. Warren, "Unused Sources for Modern Historians," *Indiana History Bulletin,* Vol. 2, Extra Number, *Proceedings of the Sixth Annual Indiana History Conference, December 5–6, 1924* (February 1925): 30, 37.

45. Beveridge to Bess Ehrmann, January 2, 1925, Container 288, Beveridge Papers; Albert J. Beveridge, *Indiana History Bulletin,* Vol. 2, Extra Number (February 1925): 28.

46. Albert J. Beveridge, "Lincoln as His Partner Knew Him," *Literary Digest International Book Review* 1 (September 1923): 33.

47. Beveridge to James A. Woodburn, April 16, 1926, container 296, Beveridge Papers.

48. John E. Iglehart to George Wilson, August 18, 1925, box 5, folder 14, Iglehart Papers.

49. John E. Iglehart, dictation, November 17, 1925, SWIHS Collection; Iglehart to J. Edward Murr, October 2, 1925, box 2, folder 4, Iglehart Papers.

50. Jerrold Hirsch, *Portrait of America: A Cultural History of the Federal Writers' Project* (Chapel Hill: University of North Carolina Press, 2003), 160.

51. J. Edward Murr, quoted in Ehrmann, *Missing Chapter in the Life of Abraham Lincoln,* 88; Anna O'Flynn, "Proceedings," November 17, 1925. Murr's previous published work relied only generally on his interviews. J. Edward Murr, "Lincoln in Indiana," *Indiana Magazine of History* 13, no. 4 (December 1917): 307–48; 14, no. 1 (March 1918): 13–75; 14, no. 2 (June 1918): 148–82.

52. Phoebe Elliott, "John Corbin," *Indiana History Bulletin,* Vol. 3, Extra No. 1, *Proceedings of the Southwestern Indiana Historical Society during its Sixth Year: Papers Read Before the Society at Various Meetings, 1920–1925* (December 1925): 33; Ehrmann, "The Lincoln Inquiry," 3–4; James Axtell, "The Pleasures of Teaching History," *The History Teacher* 34, no. 4 (August 2001): 433.

53. John E. Iglehart, "Address [to Evansville School Teachers]," 1924, 7–8, box 8, folder 1, Iglehart Papers; John E. Iglehart to Henry Hazlitt, July 27, 1927, box 2, folder 1, Iglehart Papers; Iglehart to W. H. McCurdy, January 3, 1920, Esarey to Iglehart, November 30, 1926, Iglehart Papers.

54. Havelock Ellis, *The Dance of Life* (New York: Houghton Mifflin, 1923), 259; Vilhjalmur Stefansson, *The Standardization of Error* (New York: W. W. Norton, 1927); see also Richard S. Taylor, "Telling Lincoln's Story." *Journal of the Abraham Lincoln Association* 21 (Summer 2000): 44–68; Jo Blatti, "Public History and Oral History," *Journal of American History* 77, no. 2 (September 1990): 615.

55. Novick, *That Noble Dream,* 220; Iglehart, "Response," in "Proceedings," May 27, 1925, 5–9.

56. Frisch, *A Shared Authority;* Michael Frisch, "Sharing Authority: Oral History and the Collaborative Process," *Oral History Review* 30, no. 1 (2003): 111–13; Rebecca Jones, "Blended Voices: Crafting a Narrative from Oral History Interviews," *Oral History Review* 31, no. 1 (Spring 2004): 23–42; Rebecca Conard, "Public History as Reflective Practice: An Introduction," *Public Historian* 28, no. 1 (Winter 2006), 11. For a zero-sum application in the museum field see Catherine M. Lewis, *The Changing Face of Public History: The Chicago Historical Society and the Transformation of an American Museum* (DeKalb: Northern Illinois University Press, 2005), 120.

57. John E. Iglehart to William Fortune, January 12, February 13, 1926, box 3, folder 12; Iglehart to Bess Ehrmann, October 23, 1925, box 3, folder 14; Logan Esarey to Iglehart, November 24, 1927, box 1, folder 11, Iglehart Papers.

58. Christopher B. Coleman, "Emphasis in the Work of Historical Societies," *Indiana History Bulletin,* Vol. 6, Extra No. 3, *Proceedings of the Southwestern Indiana Historical Society during its Ninth Year* (August 1929): 16; Coleman to Iglehart, November 23, December 16, 1925, January 14, 1926, box 3, folder 7, Iglehart Papers;

Iglehart to William Fortune, August 18, 1927, box 3, folder 12, Iglehart Papers; Minutes of Executive Committee Meeting, January 12, 1927, "Minute Book 2."

59. Iglehart to Coleman, January 19, 1926, box 3, folder 7; Iglehart to Ehrmann, November 12, 1926, box 3, folder 4; Iglehart to Ehrmann, March 31, 1928, box 3, folder 15; Iglehart to Johnson, September 17, 1926, box 5, folder 8, Iglehart Papers.

60. Albert J. Beveridge to Paul M. Angle, October 25, November 27, 1926; Beveridge to Thomas Adams, July 10, 1924, container 285; Albert J. Beveridge to Roscoe Kiper, January 9, 1925, container 290, Beveridge Papers; Braeman, *Albert J. Beveridge,* 304–11.

4. Lincoln's Indiana Environment

1. Deidré Dorothy Duff Johnson, "Key to Hovey Material," Hovey Mss. Lilly Library, Indiana University, Bloomington.

2. Deidré Duff Johnson, "Moses Ashworth, Pioneer of Indiana Methodism, and his Times," *Indiana Historical Commission Bulletin* no. 18, *Proceedings of the Southwestern Indiana Historical Society* (October 1923): 95; Deidré Duff Johnson to John E. Iglehart, November 2, 1927, box 5, folder 8, Iglehart Papers.

3. Deidré Duff Johnson, in "Proceedings," November 1, 1929, 20–21.

4. Tarbell to Iglehart, April 15, 1924, Iglehart Papers.

5. Mark E. Neely Jr., *Escape from the Frontier: Lincoln's Peculiar Relationship with Indiana* (Fort Wayne, IN: The Lincoln National Life Insurance Company, 1980); Chauncey Black, cited in Benjamin Thomas, *Portrait for Posterity: Lincoln and His Biographers* (New Brunswick, NJ: Rutgers University Press, 1947), 36–37; Ida M. Tarbell, *In the Footsteps of the Lincolns* (New York: Harper & Brothers, 1924), 137.

6. Albert J. Beveridge, *Abraham Lincoln, 1809–1858,* 2 vols. (Boston: Houghton Mifflin, 1928), 1:40–45; Louis A. Warren, *Lincoln's Youth, 1816–1830* (1959; Indianapolis: Indiana Historical Society Press, 2002), 23; for the intricacies of the paternity debate see Merrill D. Peterson, *Lincoln in American Memory* (New York: Oxford University Press, 1994), 232–43.

7. Tarbell, *In the Footsteps of the Lincolns,* preface, 30, 53; Iglehart to Tarbell, December 18, 1296, Tarbell Collection; Christopher B. Coleman, "The Lincoln Legend," *Indiana Magazine of History* 29 (December 1933): 281–82.

8. Peterson, *Lincoln in American Memory,* 267–68; Neely, *Escape from the Frontier,* 4–8. Neely is followed in his line of reasoning by David Herbert Donald, *Lincoln* (New York: Simon & Schuster, 1995), 33, and William Lee Miller, *Lincoln's Virtues: An Ethical Biography* (New York: Knopf, 2002), 60.

9. Copies of the correspondence between the pair are housed in both the Iglehart Papers and the Turner Collection.

10. Iglehart, "Inaugural Address," 85–94; Iglehart, "Address," *Indiana Historical Commission Bulletin* no. 16, *Proceedings of the Southwestern Indiana Historical Society* (October 1922): 10–21; Iglehart, "Correspondence between Lincoln Historians and This Society," *Indiana Historical Commission Bulletin, No. 18, Proceedings of the Southwestern Indiana Historical Society* (October 1923): 63–88; Iglehart, Dictation, September 10, 1928, SWIHS Collection; Iglehart, "The Coming of the English to Indiana in 1817 and Their Hoosier Neighbors," *Indiana Magazine of*

History 15, no. 2 (June 1919): 92, 149; Iglehart, "Methodism in Southwestern Indiana," *Indiana Magazine of History* 17, no. 2 (June 1921): 135–40; Iglehart, "The Environment of Abraham Lincoln in Indiana," In *The Environment of Abraham Lincoln in Indiana with an Account of the DeBruler Family,* by John E. Iglehart and Eugenia Ehrmann, *Indiana Historical Society Publications,* Vol. 8, No. 3; Indianapolis, 1925, 147–70.

11. Roscoe Kiper, "Lincoln's Environment in Indiana," *Indiana History Bulletin,* Vol. 3, Extra No. 1, *Proceedings of the Southwestern Indiana Historical Society during its Sixth Year: Papers Read Before the Society at Various Meetings, 1920–1925* (December 1925): 96; Iglehart to Wilson, January 5, 1927, box 5, folder 15, Iglehart Papers; Theodore Roosevelt, *The Winning of the West,* 4 vols. (1889–1896), 1:101, 4:194.

12. Christopher B. Coleman, "The Lincoln Legend," *Indiana Magazine of History* 29 (December 1933): 285; Wilson, "Historical Notes on Dubois County," 20 (1938): 369. See also Iglehart in "Proceedings," June 1, 1922, 13–20; Robert A. Woods, "President's Address," reel 7, item 1, SWIHS Collection.

13. Iglehart to Will Fortune, May 22, 1933, box 3, folder 13, Iglehart Papers; Iglehart, Dictation, April 22, 1930, p. 3, box 1, folder 2, Iglehart Papers; Iglehart, "Address [to Evansville School Teachers]," 1924, box 8, folder 1, Iglehart Papers.

14. Emily Orr Clifford, "Private Schools in Evansville from 1842 to 1853," *Indiana Historical Commission Bulletin* no. 18, *Proceedings of the Southwestern Indiana Historical Society* (October 1923): 32; Iglehart to Tarbell, December 18, 1926, Tarbell Collection; Albion Fellows Bacon, in "Proceedings," February 12, 1924; Austin Corbin, "Welcome," and Albion Fellows Bacon, "Response," in "Proceedings," October 12, 1923, 5.

15. Thomas J. de la Hunt to John E. Iglehart, May 21, 1925, box 2, folder 15, Iglehart Papers; see Wilson, "Commonplace Book, 1925," 187; Wilson, "Historical Notes on Dubois County," 4 (1925): 56; Logan Esarey and Otto Rothert, in "Proceedings," June 10, 1924, 27–28; John E. Iglehart, in "Proceedings," June 1, 1922, 19; David H. Morgan, "James Clifford Veatch," *Indiana History Bulletin,* Vol. 6, Extra No. 3, *Proceedings of the Southwestern Indiana Historical Society during its Ninth Year* (August 1929): 82.

16. Logan Esarey, "Our Early Governors," 1, SWIHS Collection; Wilson, "Historical Notes on Dubois County," 13 (1931): 567; George Robert Wilson, "The Birth of a State," *Indiana Historical Commission Bulletin* no. 16, *Proceedings of the Southwestern Indiana Historical Society* (October 1922): 50.

17. Ida D. Armstrong, "The Lincolns in Spencer County," *Indiana Historical Commission Bulletin* no. 18, *Proceedings of the Southwestern Indiana Historical Society* (October 1923): 59. On corroboration see Wilson, "Historical Notes on Dubois County," 3 (1924): 535; 15 (1933): 196; John E. Iglehart to Logan Esarey, February 6, 1919, box 1, folder 10, Iglehart Papers.

18. Robert A. Woods, "Response," in "Proceedings," June 5, 1930, 5; Thomas J. de la Hunt to John E. Iglehart, January 14, 1922, box 2, folder 15, Iglehart Papers; Iglehart, "Address," *Indiana Historical Commission Bulletin* no. 16, *Proceedings of the Southwestern Indiana Historical Society* (October 1922): 13; Albion Fellows Bacon, in "Proceedings," February 12, 1924, 4; de la Hunt, "Publicity in Newspapers," *Indiana Historical Commission Bulletin,* No. 16, *Proceedings of the*

Southwestern Indiana Historical Society (October 1922): 31; Ehrmann, in "Proceedings," February 28, 1923, 13; Wilson, "Historical Notes on Dubois County," 4 (1925): 19; Ehrmann to Iglehart, May 21, 1929, box 4, folder 1, Iglehart to Wilson, January 30, 1929, box 5, folder 16, Iglehart Papers; Rabb, "The Listening Post," *Indianapolis Star,* April 10–11, 1924.

19. George Wilson to Bess Ehrmann, April 16, 1925, box 5, folder 14, Iglehart Papers; Nora C. Fretageot, "Memories of Animal Life in Posey County" and David H. Morgan, "A View of Rockport from the River in 1856," SWIHS Collection; Thomas J. de la Hunt, "The Pocket in Indiana History," *Indiana Magazine of History* 16 (December 1920): 308–16; George Wilson, "Commonplace Book, 1925," 161; William B. Carleton, "The Lincoln Atmosphere," SWIHS Collection; Roscoe Kiper, "Lincoln's Environment in Indiana," *Indiana History Bulletin,* Vol. 3, Extra No. 1, *Proceedings of the Southwestern Indiana Historical Society during its Sixth Year: Papers Read Before the Society at Various Meetings, 1920–1925* (December 1925): 94–96; Iglehart, "Correspondence between Lincoln Historians and This Society," 72.

20. Iglehart, "Inaugural Address," 94; Executive Committee Meeting, March 14, 1920, "Minute Book 1"; "Circular Letter no. 1," April 26, 1920, reel 6, item 9, SWIHS Collection; Iglehart, "Remarks," in "Proceedings," September 29, 1922; Roscoe Kiper, "President's Address," in "Proceedings," November 17, 1925; Executive Committee Meeting, March 15, 1927, "Minute Book 2"; Ehrmann, "Address," in "Proceedings," October 25, 1927; Executive Committee Meeting, January 19, 1928, "Minute Book 2"; Ehrmann, "President's Address," in "Proceedings," February 23, 1928; John E. Iglehart and Eugenia Ehrmann, *The Environment of Abraham Lincoln in Indiana with an Account of the De Bruler Family.* Indiana Historical Society Publications, vol. 8, no. 3. Indianapolis, 1925.

21. Kate Milner Rabb, "The Value of Old Letters and Diaries," June 5, 1931, 1, SWIHS Collection; John E. Iglehart to Logan Esarey, February 6, 1919, box 1, folder 10, Iglehart Papers; Wilson, "Historical Notes on Dubois County," 4 (1925): 134, 175; 8 (1928): 544; 5 (1926): 128; 14 (1932): 425.

22. Wilson, "Historical Notes on Dubois County," 2 (1926): 293; 3 (1924): 188, 438; 4 (1925): 133; 5 (1926): 214; 11 (1930): 364; 14 (1932): 425; for one particularly relic-filled meeting see "Minute Book 2," June 1, 1928.

23. Surviving markers include one at Anderson Creek where Lincoln operated a ferry boat in 1826, and one at the Sargent House in Rockport where Lincoln stayed in 1844.

24. William Roscoe Thayer, *The Art of Biography* (New York: Charles Scribner's Sons, 1920), 16–17, 53, 60–61.

25. John E. Iglehart, "Memorandum of Unfinished Work of the Southwestern Indiana Historical Society," February 16, 1926, Willard Library, JEI Papers, reel 7, item 1f.

26. Lincoln to Jesse W. Fell, December 20, 1859, in *The Collected Works of Abraham Lincoln,* ed. Roy P. Basler, 8 vols. (New Brunswick, NJ: Rutgers University Press, 1953), 3:511–12; Abraham Lincoln, "Autobiography Written for John L. Scripps," [c. June 1860], *Collected Works of Abraham Lincoln,* 4:60–67.

27. Charles T. Baker, "Lincoln Markers," in "Proceedings," February 23, 1928, 44; C. C. Schreeder, "The Lincolns and Their Home in Spencer County, Indiana,"

226 NOTES TO PAGES 96–97

Bess V. Ehrmann Scrapbooks, D-1, Lincoln folder (Spencer County Public Library, Rockport, IN).

28. Ida D. Armstrong, "The Lincolns in Spencer County," *Indiana Historical Commission Bulletin* no. 18, *Proceedings of the Southwestern Indiana Historical Society* (October 1923): 59; Warren, *Lincoln's Youth*, 248 n9.

29. Lincoln to David Turnham, October 23, 1860, in *Collected Works of Abraham Lincoln*, 4:130–31. The society also displayed copies of Lincoln to Nathaniel Grigsby, September 20, 1860, in *Collected Works of Abraham Lincoln*, 4:116. Lincoln to Simon Cameron, June 17, 1861, was published in Iglehart and Ehrmann, *The Environment of Abraham Lincoln in Indiana with an Account of the De Bruler Family*, part 1; see also *Collected Works of Abraham Lincoln*, 4:409.

30. "Proceedings," September 29, 1922, June 15, 1923, 49–54, February 12, 1924, 18, June 10, 1924, 21, June 1, 1928, 7–8, 48–52; Bess Ehrmann, "Museum Collections," *Indiana Historical Commission Bulletin* no. 16, *Proceedings of the Southwestern Indiana Historical Society* (October 1922): 78–81; Otto Laval, "Indian Relics," *Indiana Historical Commission Bulletin* no. 18, *Proceedings of the Southwestern Indiana Historical Society* (October 1923): 135–37.

31. Herndon identified Lincoln's half-sister Matilda Johnston and Ann Roby: William H. Herndon and Jesse W. Weik, *Herndon's Lincoln*, ed. Douglas L. Wilson and Rodney O. Davis (Urbana: University of Illinois Press, 2006), 34, 37; his research notes also identify Elizabeth Wood: Douglas L. Wilson and Rodney O. Davis, eds., *Herndon's Informants: Letters, Interviews, and Statements about Abraham Lincoln* (Urbana: University of Illinois Press, 1998), 334; Tarbell cited an unidentified girl whose wagon broke down while passing through: *Life of Abraham Lincoln: Drawn from Original Sources and Containing many Speeches, Letters and Telegraphs Hitherto Unpublished*, 2 vols. (New York: Doubleday & McClure, 1900), 1:26–27 and *In the Footsteps of the Lincolns*, 152–53; Weik named Julia Evans in "The Wool Carder's Niece," *Success Magazine* (1902).

32. T. H. Masterson and John O. Chewning spoke with Elizabeth Tully in 1894: T. H. Masterson, "Interviews with Spencer County Pioneers about 1895," *Indiana History Bulletin*, Vol. 6, Extra No. 3, *Proceedings of the Southwestern Indiana Historical Society during its Ninth Year* (August 1929): 56–59; J. Edward Murr, "Lincoln in Indiana," *Indiana Magazine of History* 14, no. 1 (March 1918): 53–58; Anna C. O'Flynn Papers (Lewis Historical Library, Vincennes University, Vincennes, IN); Elizabeth Ray was named in Grandview *Monitor*, April 19, 1935. In 1887–1888 Kate Evelyn Armstrong interviewed Mrs. Oskins and Sarah Lukins, both of whom were revealed to be stretching the truth in Ida D. Armstrong, "The Lincolns in Spencer County," *Indiana Historical Commission Bulletin* no. 18, *Proceedings of the Southwestern Indiana Historical Society* (October 1923): 59.

33. Warren, *Lincoln's Youth*, 155–58; Beveridge, *Abraham Lincoln*, 1:80–81. Michael Burlingame comments on Polly Richardson (Murr), Elizabeth Wood (Herndon/O'Flynn), Elizabeth Tully (Masterson and Chewning), and Anna Roby (Herndon) in *Abraham Lincoln: A Life* (Baltimore: Johns Hopkins University Press, 2008), 1:41–42.

34. Wilson and Davis, *Herndon's Lincoln*, 52; Alice L. Harper Hanby, "John Pitcher," *Indiana Historical Commission Bulletin* no. 16, *Proceedings of the Southwestern Indiana Historical Society* (October 1922): 50–60; see also Charles

Moores to Iglehart, February 18, 1922, box 5, folder 1, Iglehart Papers, and Robert Bray, "What Lincoln Read—An Evaluative and Annotated List," *Journal of the Abraham Lincoln Association* 28, no. 2 (Summer 2007): 39. For a reminiscence about Pitcher from later in life see also John E. Cox, "Judge John Pitcher," *Indiana Historical Commission Bulletin* no. 18, *Proceedings of the Southwestern Indiana Historical Society* (October 1923): 93–94.

35. Wilson and Davis, *Herndon's Lincoln,* 50; Eldora Minor Raleigh, "John A. Brackenridge," *Indiana Historical Commission Bulletin* no. 16, *Proceedings of the Southwestern Indiana Historical Society* (October 1922): 62–63; Eldora Raleigh to Iglehart, October 9, 192; deposition handwritten on Iglehart to Raleigh, April 10, 1935, box 5, folder 4, Iglehart Papers.

36. Jesse W. Weik, *The Real Lincoln: A Portrait* (Boston: Houghton Mifflin, 1922), 130; Ida M. Tarbell, *The Life of Abraham Lincoln,* 2 vols. (New York, Lincoln Memorial Association, 1900), 1:34; Tarbell, *In the Footsteps of the Lincolns,* 149.

37. Beveridge, *Abraham Lincoln,* 1:77; Beveridge to Kiper, January 9, 1925, container 290, and Beveridge to Iglehart, August 26, 1924, container 289, Beveridge Papers; Warren, *Lincoln's Youth,* 198–99.

38. Fortune correspondence with Tarbell, 1922, Tarbell Collection; Fortune correspondence with Beveridge, 1924, container 288, Beveridge Papers; Beveridge, *Abraham Lincoln,* 1:83–84; Warren, *Lincoln's Youth,* 195. See also Benjamin P. Thomas, "Lincoln's Humor: An Analysis," *Journal of the Abraham Lincoln Association* 3 (1981): 28–47, note 2; Bray, "What Lincoln Read," 71.

39. Wilson and Davis, *Herndon's Lincoln,* 44–45; Iglehart, "Correspondence between Lincoln Historians and This Society," 83–86; Warren, *Lincoln's Youth,* 152, 251 n. 13; Iglehart to Sandburg, November 20, 1926, box 2, folder 7, Iglehart Papers.

40. Wilson and Davis, *Herndon's Lincoln,* 42; Tarbell, *Life of Lincoln,* 1:33–34; Tarbell, *In the Footsteps of the Lincolns,* 146; Beveridge, *Abraham Lincoln,* 1:74–75; Warren, *Lincoln's Youth,* 201–2; Frederick Trevor Hill, *Lincoln the Lawyer* (1906; reprint, New York: Century, 1913), 11–12. Murr, "Lincoln in Indiana," *Indiana Magazine of History* 14, no. 2 (June 1918): 153, held that Lincoln had memorized the Declaration and Constitution; Bray, "What Lincoln Read," 58, concludes that Lincoln only read the front matter; see also Ward Hill Lamon, *The Life of Abraham Lincoln, from His birth to His Inauguration as President* (Lincoln: University of Nebraska Press, 1999), 37–38, 67.

41. Iglehart, "Memorandum upon reading volume 1, Life of Abraham Lincoln [by Barton]," April 9, 1925, box 1, folder 2, Iglehart Papers; Lincoln, "Communication to the People of Sangamo County," March 9, 1832, in *Collected Works,* 1:5–9; see also Hanby, "John Pitcher," 51–53. For earlier views see Iglehart, "Methodism in Southwestern Indiana," *Indiana Magazine of History* 17, no. 2 (June 1921), 144–45; Iglehart, "Address [to Evansville School Teachers]," 1924, 24–26, box 8, folder 1, Iglehart Papers. Mark Neely connected the platform simply to Lincoln's experience in Indiana: *Escape from the Frontier,* 7–8.

42. De la Hunt, in "Proceedings," June 1, 1928, 26–29; Executive Committee Meeting Minutes, September 10, 1928, "Minute Book 2"; R. Gerald McMurtry, "The Lincoln Migration from Kentucky to Indiana," *Indiana Magazine of History* 33, no. 4 (December 1937): 409–12 and n. 79; Warren, *Lincoln's Youth,* 221 n. 9.

43. R. Gerald McMurtry, "The Lincoln Migration from Kentucky to Indiana," *Indiana Magazine of History* 33, no. 4 (December 1937): 385–421; John F. Cady, "The Religious Environment of Lincoln's Youth," *Indiana Magazine of History* 37, no. 1 (March 1941): 16–30; Reinhard H. Luthin, "Indiana and Lincoln's Rise to the Presidency," *Indiana Magazine of History* 48, no. 4 (December 1942): 384 n. 1; Maurine Whorton Redway and Dorothy Kendall Bracken, *Marks of Lincoln on Our Land* (New York: Hastings House, 1957), 31–34; Carl and Rosalie Frazier, *The Lincoln Country in Pictures* (New York: Hastings House, 1963), 15–17; Warren, *Lincoln's Youth*, 76, 97, 100, 155–58, 173, 188, 238, 245–51, 262–64, 266.

44. Leonard Swett, in *Reminiscences of Abraham Lincoln by Distinguished Men of His Time,* ed. Allen Thorndike Rice (New York: Harper and Brothers, 1885), 459; *History of Warrick, Spencer and Perry Counties, Indiana* (Chicago: Goodspeed Brothers, 1885), 273; Lucius C. Embree, "Morris Birkbeck's Estimate of the People of Princeton in 1817," *Indiana Magazine of History* 21 (December 1925): 292; Iglehart, "Correspondence between Lincoln Historians and This Society," 73. Recently, William Bartelt confirmed Iglehart's characterization by documenting the "community's fluidity" through a comparison of names on the 1820 and 1830 censuses: William E. Bartelt, *"There I Grew Up": Remembering Abraham Lincoln's Indiana Youth* (Indianapolis: Indiana Historical Society, 2008), 107; he identifies the inhabitants of Pigeon Creek on 103–6.

45. Malcolm J. Rohrbough, *Trans-Appalachian Frontier: People, Societies, and Institutions, 1775–1850* (1978; Bloomington: Indiana University Press, 2008); Nicole Etcheson, *The Emerging Midwest: Upland Southerners and the Political Culture of the Old Northwest, 1787–1861* (Bloomington: Indiana University Press, 1996); Andrew Cayton, *Frontier Indiana* (Bloomington: Indiana University Press, 1998); Richard F. Nation, *At Home in the Hoosier Hills: Agriculture, Politics, and Religion in Southern Indiana, 1810–1870* (Bloomington: Indiana University Press, 2005).

46. J. Helen Rhoades, "Life of James Gentry, Jr.," Will Adams, "Biographical Sketch of Josiah and Elizabeth (Anderson) Crawford," Ehrmann Scrapbooks, D-1, Letters; Bess V. Ehrmann, "The Grigsbys," *Indiana Historical Commission Bulletin* no. 18, *Proceedings of the Southwestern Indiana Historical Society* (October 1923): 89–90; Nancy Grigsby Inco, "More Lincoln Memories," *Indiana Historical Commission Bulletin* no. 18, *Proceedings of the Southwestern Indiana Historical Society* (October 1923): 91–92; Laura Mercy Wright, "Daniel Grass," *Indiana History Bulletin,* Vol. 3, Extra No. 1, *Proceedings of the Southwestern Indiana Historical Society during its Sixth Year: Papers Read Before the Society at Various Meetings, 1920–1925* (December 1925): 7–11; Louise Dunkerson Orr, "The Casselberry Family," *Indiana History Bulletin,* Vol. 1, Extra No., *Proceedings of the Fifth Annual Meeting of the Southwestern Indiana Historical Society* (June 1924): 37–46; Christopher Bush Coleman, "John Law," in *The Undying Past and Other Addresses* (Indianapolis: Indiana State Library, 1946), 89–111.

47. *Lincoln Day-by-Day: A Chronology* (Washington, DC: Government Printing Office, 1960), now online at www.thelincolnlog.org. Published lists are found in Bess V. Ehrmann, "The Lincoln Inquiry," *Indiana Magazine of History* 21 (March 1925): 3–17; Ehrmann, *Missing Chapter in the Life of Abraham Lincoln* (1938), 23–60, quote from 23; Iglehart and Ehrmann, *The Environment of Abraham Lincoln in Indiana with an Account of the De Bruler Family;* 155–70.

48. Lowell H. Harrison, *Lincoln of Kentucky* (Lexington: University Press of Kentucky, 2000), 29. One sample observation is Levi B. Barker, "Warrick County Neighbors of the Lincoln Family," SWIHS Collection; for explorations of New England influences see Kate Pitcher Whitworth Schultz, "General Thomas Gamble Pitcher," *Indiana History Bulletin*, Vol. 3, Extra No. 1, *Proceedings of the Southwestern Indiana Historical Society during its Sixth Year: Papers Read Before the Society at Various Meetings, 1920–1925* (December 1925): 37–42; Thomas J. de la Hunt, "Judge Elisha Mills Huntington," *Indiana Magazine of History* 23 (June 1927): 115–29. See also William E. Barton, *The Life of Abraham Lincoln,* 2 vols. (Indianapolis: Bobbs-Merrill, 1925), 1:119; Beveridge, *Abraham Lincoln,* 1:39.

49. Grace Jeanette Bullock Maas, "Jonesboro," June 14, 1927, SWIHS Collection. William Bartelt later confirmed the same in "The Land Dealings of Spencer County, Indiana, Pioneer Thomas Lincoln," *Indiana Magazine of History* 87, no. 3 (September 1991): 211–23.

50. Deidré Duff Johnson, "Moses Ashworth, Pioneer of Indiana Methodism"; Margaret Ann Wilson, "Reverend Andrew Jackson Strain," in Wilson, "Historical Notes on Dubois County," 9 (1929): 455–76.

51. Robert Archer Wood, "The Relation of Southwestern Indiana Pioneers to those of other Pioneer Sections," cited in Ehrmann, *Missing Chapter,* 52; Helen M. Davidson, "James Cawson's Library, 1818–1840," SWIHS Collection; C. T. Baker, "Literacy of the Lincoln Neighbors," clipping, June 5, 1930, SWIHS Collection; Thomas James de la Hunt, "The Lincolns' Eastward Environment," *Indiana History Bulletin*, Vol. 6, Extra No. 3, *Proceedings of the Southwestern Indiana Historical Society during its Ninth Year* (August 1929): 114–18, advertisement cited on 117; Rockport Public Library holdings listed at several hundred by 1820 in *History of Warrick, Spencer and Perry Counties,* 273. Michael H. Harris finds many books available in "The Frontier Lawyer's Library; Southern Indiana, 1800–1850, as a Test Case," *American Journal of Legal History* 16, no. 3 (July 1972): 239–51.

52. Mrs. H. C. Knapp (M.D.), "Materia Medica of Pioneer Indiana," *Indiana History Bulletin*, Vol. 3, Extra No. 1, *Proceedings of the Southwestern Indiana Historical Society during its Sixth Year: Papers Read Before the Society at Various Meetings, 1920–1925* (December 1925): 12–17. Superstitions are listed without context in Wilson and Davis, *Herndon's Lincoln,* 54; Murr, "Lincoln in Indiana," *Indiana Magazine of History* 13, no. 4 (December 1917): 335–39; Beveridge, *Abraham Lincoln,* 1:50; Michael Burlingame, *Abraham Lincoln: A Life* (Baltimore: Johns Hopkins University Press, 2008), 23–24. On the blending of Christianity and folk belief from colonial times through the Early Republic, see Jon Butler, *Awash in a Sea of Faith: Christianizing the American People* (Cambridge: Harvard University Press, 1990).

53. Roscoe Kiper, "Address," Proceedings, October 14, 1924, 12.

54. Kenneth J. Winkle, *The Young Eagle: The Rise of Abraham Lincoln* (Dallas, TX: Taylor Trade, 2001); Allen C. Guelzo, "Review of *The Young Eagle* by Kenneth J. Winkle," *American Historical Review* 109, no.5 (December 2004): 1569; Matthew Pinsker, "Lincoln Theme 2.0," *Journal of American History* 96, no. 2 (September 2009): 425. Reviewing the book for the *Journal of American History,* Stephen Hansen praised "the originality of its insights" and "fresh perspective": "Review of

Winkle, *The Young Eagle: The Rise of Abraham Lincoln," Journal of American History* 91, no .2 (September 2004): 633.

55. Neely, *Escape from the Frontier,* 5–8; William C. Harris, *Lincoln's Rise to the Presidency* (Lawrence: University Press of Kansas, 2007), 7.

56. Bacon, "Lincoln," *Indiana Magazine of History* 21 (March 1925): 1–2.

57. Tarbell to Iglehart, May 13, 1925, Tarbell Collection; Christopher B. Coleman, "Emphasis in the Work of Historical Societies," *Indiana History Bulletin,* Vol. 6, Extra No. 3, *Proceedings of the Southwestern Indiana Historical Society during its Ninth Year* (August 1929), 16; Oliver to Iglehart, April 9, 1926, box 5, folder 11, Iglehart Papers; [Milo Quaife], "Historical News and Comments," *Mississippi Valley Historical Review* 14, no. 3 (December 1927): 436–37.

58. Bess Ehrmann, "What Indiana did for Lincoln," SWIHS Collection; Ellery Sedgwick to Bess Ehrmann, February 11, 1927, Ehrmann to Iglehart, March 27, 1927, box 3, folder 14, Iglehart Papers.

5. The Klan and a Conspiracy

1. William Herndon, in Douglas L. Wilson and Rodney O. Davis, eds., *Herndon's Informants: Letters, Interviews, and Statements about Abraham Lincoln* (Urbana: University of Illinois Press, 1998), 116–17.

2. Thomas J. de la Hunt, "Address," in "Proceedings," October 14, 1924, 4–5.

3. "Women Invited to Move for Nancy Hanks Lincoln Shrine," *Indianapolis Star,* March 6, 1927.

4. Hayden White, *Metahistory: The Historical Imagination in Nineteenth-Century Europe* (Baltimore: Johns Hopkins University Press, 1973); James V. Wertsch, "Specific Narratives and Schematic Narrative Templates," in *Theorizing Historical Consciousness,* ed. Peter Seixas (Toronto: University of Toronto Press, 2004), 49–62; Sam Wineburg, *Historical Thinking and Other Unnatural Acts* (Philadelphia: Temple University Press, 2001), 232–55; Andrew C. Butler, Franklin M. Zaromb, Keith B. Lyle, and Henry L. Roediger, III, "Using Popular Films to Enhance Classroom Learning: The Good, the Bad, and the Interesting," *Psychological Science* 20, no. 9 (September 1, 2009): 1161–68.

5. Wilson, "Historical Notes on Dubois County," 4 (1925): 56.

6. [J. C. Jolly, of Richland, Spencer County,] "Scalp Lieber," *Rockport Journal,* August 21, 1925.

7. Jill York O'Bright, *"There I Grew Up": A History of the Administration of Abraham Lincoln's Boyhood Home* ([Washington, DC:] National Park Service, 1987), chap. 1; Indiana Lincoln Memorial Association, Papers, 1922–1928, and Margaret M. Scott, Papers, 1873–1950, Manuscripts Section (Indiana State Library, Indianapolis); Anna C. O'Flynn, "Reminiscences of Early Efforts for a Lincoln Memorial," in "Proceedings," October 25, 1927, 27–30; reports of the various activities are recorded in "Proceedings," by Thomas J. de la Hunt, September 29, 1922, 23; Roscoe Kiper, June 15, 1923, 33; Kate Milner Rabb, October 12, 1923, 31–33; Albert J. Wedeking, October 12, 1923, 35–38; Thomas J. de la Hunt, October 14, 1924, 3–6, 15–16.

8. "Historical News," *Indiana Magazine of History* 19, no. 2 (June 1923): 203–4. The nine-member commission included four members of the Lincoln Inquiry:

former state representative and future society president Roscoe Kiper, current state representative Albert J. Wedeking, current state senator Charles J. Buchanan, and society parliamentarian Theodora Torrance.

9. Emma Rappaport Lieber, *Richard Lieber, by His Wife, Emma* (Indianapolis, 1947), 2–7, 53; Robert Allen Frederick, "Colonel Richard Lieber, Conservationist and Park Builder: The Indiana Years" (Ph.D. diss., Indiana University, 1960), pp. 246–52 for the Lincoln Park. On Lieber's vision and development of the state parks see Charles B. Hosmer, Jr., *Preservation Comes of Age: From Williamsburg to the National Trust, 1926–1949*, 2 vols. (Charlottesville: University Press of Virginia, 1981), 1:384–97; Charles B. Hosmer, Jr., "The Roots of AASLH," in *Local History, National Heritage: Reflections on the History of AASLH* (Nashville, TN.: American Association for State and Local History, 1991), 16–20.

10. "Lincoln City Objects to State Auto Ruling," *Terre Haute Star*, August 11, 1925; "Nancy Hanks Lincoln Park," *Huntingburg Signal*, August 21, 1925; "Indiana Lincoln Memorials," *Indianapolis News*, August 25, 1925; "Spencer County Folks to Go Over Lieber's Head," *Boonville Enquirer*, August 28, 1925; "Park to Be Enlarged," *Rockport Journal*, August 28, 1925; "Error in Park Deed," *Indianapolis News*, September 9, 1925. In 1907, Spencer County deeded some of the park to the state, but research on the 1925 transaction revealed that 16 1/2 acres of the property had not been properly deeded.

11. Leonard J. Moore, *Citizen Klansmen: The Ku Klux Klan in Indiana, 1921–1928* (Chapel Hill: University of North Carolina Press, 1991); James H. Madison, *The Indiana Way: A State History* (1986; Bloomington: Indiana University Press, 1990), 292.

12. Madison, *The Indiana Way*, 293–95; M. William Lutholtz, *Grand Dragon: D. C. Stephenson and the Ku Klux Klan in Indiana* (West Lafayette, IN: Purdue University Press, 1991).

13. O'Bright, *"Here I Grew Up,"* chap. 1; Frederick, "Colonel Richard Lieber," 246–52. On Hays see Stephen Vaughn, "The Devil's Advocate: Will H. Hays and the Campaign to Make Movies Respectable," *Indiana Magazine of History* 101, no. 2 (June 2005): 125–34.

14. Ed Jackson, "Proclamation," December 22, 1926, box 7, folder 18, Iglehart Papers; Ralph Hesler, "Laud Mother of Lincoln," *Indianapolis Star*, May 8, 1927; "Lincoln Shrine Plans Revealed," *Indianapolis Star*, June 10, 1927; "To Honor Lincoln as a Son of Indiana," *Indianapolis News*, June 9, 1927.

15. Ed Jackson, "A Proclamation," February 1, 1927, printed in *Indianapolis Star*, February 1, 1927; Richard Lieber to Christopher Coleman, March 2, 1927, box 3, folder 8, Iglehart Papers; "Lincoln Home Shrine Campaign Plan Ready," *Indianapolis News*, September 1, 1927; "$25,000 Gift to Aid Lincoln City Shrine," *Indianapolis News*, November 4, 1927; O'Bright, *"Here I Grew Up,"* chap. 1. Lieber's diary of 1927 contains clippings from around the state praising the plans, such as "Resolution Approves Lincoln Union Plan," *Indianapolis News*, January 14, 1927; "First Steps in Project Taken," *Kokomo Dispatch*, January 21, 1927; "Interest Growing in Proposed Nancy Hanks Lincoln Memorial," *Rockport Journal*, January 21, 1927; "Commemoration of Nancy Hanks Lincoln Grave Is Planned," *Richmond Item*, February 21, 1927; "Memorial to Abraham Lincoln and His Mother," *Corydon Democrat*, April 20, 1927.

16. William Fortune, "Lincoln in Indiana," *Indiana History Bulletin,* Vol. 3, Extra No. 1, *Proceedings of the Southwestern Indiana Historical Society during its Sixth Year: Papers Read Before the Society at Various Meetings, 1920–1925* (December 1925): 60–64; "Plan Shrine for Nancy Lincoln: State Plans to Buy More Land Near Grave," *Muncie Press,* May 17, 1926; "The Spirit of Lincoln," *Indianapolis News,* September 8, 1927; "Indiana to Honor Lincoln," Hancock, MI, *Copper Journal,* December 14, 1927; Indiana Lincoln Union, *Lincoln Memorials* (Indianapolis: Bookwalter, Ball, Greathouse Printing Co., 1927). On the advertisements see O'Bright, *"Here I Grew Up,"* chap. 1. Lieber levied the interstate rivalry spur in his first report to the Indiana Historical Commission, November 25, 1916, quoted in David M. Silver, ed., "Richard Lieber and Indiana's Forest Heritage," *Indiana Magazine of History* 67, no. 1 (March 1971): 45–55.

17. Ed Jackson, "A Proclamation," February 1, 1927; Anne Studebaker Carlisle, in "Women Invited to Move for Nancy Hanks Lincoln Shrine," *Indianapolis Star,* March 6, 1927. See also Charles Arthur Carlisle, "Nancy Hanks Shrine will be Great Tribute to Motherhood," newspaper clipping pasted into the Lieber diary, February 20, 1927; Ralph Hesler, "Laud Mother of Lincoln," *Indianapolis Star,* May 8, 1927.

18. For their part, the "friendly trees" became celebrities—they were rhapsodized about by the parachuting poet and photographed for the official state report detailing the memorial's construction. J. I. Holcomb to the Honorable Harry G. Leslie, Governor, and the directors and executive committee of the ILU, "Report of Inspection and Memorial Observance at Lincoln City," February 12, 1932, box 7, folder 18, Iglehart Papers; Indiana Lincoln Union, *The Indiana Lincoln Memorial* (Indianapolis: Indiana Lincoln Union, 1938), 49; Michael A. Capps, "Interpreting Lincoln–A Work in Progress: Lincoln Boyhood National Memorial as a Case Study," *Indiana Magazine of History* 105, no. 4 (December 2009), 330.

19. Hamlin Garland, *A Pioneer Mother* (Chicago: The Bookfellows, 1922); Fern Ioula Bauer, *The Historic Treasure Chest of the Madonna of the Trail* (Springfield, OH: J. McEnaney Printing, 1984); J. E. McCulloch, *Home: The Savior of Civilization* (Washington, DC: The Southern Co-operative League, 1924), 67–77.

20. Maureen Reed, "How Sacagawea Became a Pioneer Mother: Statues, Ethnicity, and Controversy in Oregon and New Mexico," a paper presented at the annual meeting of the American Studies Association, Albuquerque, NM, October 16, 2008.

21. Ida M. Tarbell, *The Life of Abraham Lincoln,* 2 vols. (New York, Lincoln Memorial Association, 1900), 1:21; Ida M. Tarbell, *In the Footsteps of the Lincolns* (New York: Harper & Brothers, 1924), 124, 126; Merrill D. Peterson, *Lincoln in American Memory* (New York: Oxford University Press, 1994), 232–43; see also James M. Martin, *A Defence of the Mother, Conversion, and Creed of Abraham Lincoln, Being an Open letter to the author of "The Soul of Abraham Lincoln,"* 2d ed. (Minneapolis, January 28, 1921).

22. F. L. Olmsted to Richard Lieber, March 24, 1927 (two letters), box 7, folder 16, Iglehart Papers. See also O'Bright, *"Here I Grew Up,"* chap. 1.

23. Ed Jackson, "A Proclamation," February 1, 1927, printed in *Indianapolis Star,* February 1, 1927; "Indiana Lincoln Memorials," *Indianapolis News,* August 25, 1925; "Plan Shrine for Nancy Lincoln: State Plans to Buy More Land Near

Grave," *Muncie Press,* May 17, 1926; "Lincoln Memorial Shrine," *Indianapolis Star,* June 7, 1927.

24. "Indiana the Playground," *Waterloo Press,* May 5, 1927.

25. Lieber's diaries—39 volumes treating the years 1890, 1891, 1895, 1909–1944—are maintained in the Lieber Mss., 1691–1945, Lilly Library, Bloomington, IN. Lieber's diaries for the 1920s contain brief notes about daily activities with very little commentary. The bulk of the diaries are composed of clippings gathered by the Central Press Clipping Service of Indianapolis and pasted on the dates of the activities described in the clippings.

26. James H. Madison, *Indiana through Tradition and Change: A History of the Hoosier State and Its People, 1920–1945,* vol. 5, *The History of Indiana* (Indianapolis: Indiana Historical Society, 1982), 44–72; Richard Lieber, Diary, 1927.

27. "Lieber Explains Aims of Lincoln Memorial," *Indianapolis News,* November 2, 1927; "Lincoln Shrine Has Coolidge Interest," *Indianapolis News,* December 3, 1927; "President Aids Lincoln Union," *Ft. Wayne News Sentinel,* December 24, 1927; "Open County Lincoln Shrine Drive Monday," February 11, 1928 (clipping from an unidentified newspaper pasted in Lieber's diary for February 6, 1928), emphasis added.

28. Karen L. Cox, *Dixie's Daughters: The United Daughters of the Confederacy and the Preservation of Confederate Culture* (Gainesville: University Press of Florida, 2003), 1–2; Patricia West, *Domesticating History: The Political Origins of America's House Museums* (Washington, DC: Smithsonian Institution Press, 1999), 94–99; W. Fitzhugh Brundage, *The Southern Past: A Clash of Race and Memory* (Cambridge, MA: The Belknap Press of Harvard University Press, 2005), 12–54; Barbara J. Howe, "Women in the Nineteenth-Century Preservation Movement," in *Restoring Women's History through Preservation,* ed. Gail Lee Dubrow and Jennifer B. Goodman (Baltimore: The Johns Hopkins University Press, 2003), 17–36; Scott E. Casper, *Sarah Johnson's Mount Vernon: The Forgotten History of an American Shrine* (New York: Hill and Wang, 2008), 69–75, 159–77.

29. Ehrmann to Iglehart, November 13, 1922, September 21, 1924, August 18, 1925, box 3, folder 14, Iglehart Papers; Kiper in "Proceedings," November 17, 1925, 3; Iglehart to Wilson, August 18, 1925, box 5, folder 15, and Iglehart to Embree, March 9, 1926, box 4, folder 6, Iglehart Papers; Bess Ehrmann to John E. Iglehart, September 19, 1926, box 3, folder 14, Iglehart Papers.

30. Ed Jackson to John E. Iglehart, April 20, 1927; Paul V. Brown to Iglehart, April 20, 1927; Frederick L. Olmsted Jr. to Iglehart, May 11, 1927; Anne Studebaker Carlisle to Iglehart, May 16, 1927; Richard Lieber to Iglehart, May 26, 1927, box 7, folder 16, Iglehart Papers.

31. Christopher Coleman to John E. Iglehart, June 2, 1927, box 3, folder 8, Iglehart Papers.

32. Louis A. Warren, "The Mystery of Lincoln's Melancholy," *Indiana History Bulletin,* Vol. 3, Extra No. 1, *Proceedings of the Southwestern Indiana Historical Society during its Sixth Year: Papers Read Before the Society at Various Meetings, 1920–1925* (December 1925): 55. On Warren and his Lincoln scholarship see Benjamin Thomas, *Portrait for Posterity: Lincoln and His Biographers* (New Brunswick, NJ: Rutgers University Press, 1947), 233–34; "Louis Austin Warren," *Lincoln*

Lore 1733 (July 1982), 1–4; 1734 (August 1982), 1–4; 1735 (September 1982), 1–4; 1736 (October 1982), 1–4.

33. Iglehart to Wilson, June 12, 1928, box 5, folder 16, Iglehart Papers. Stephen S. Visher, "Contrasts Among Indiana Counties in their Yield of Prominent Persons," *Proceedings of the Indiana Academy of Science* 38 (1929): 217–24; Visher, "Distribution of the Birthplaces of Indianians in 1870," *Indiana Magazine of History* 26, no. 2 (June 1930), 126–42; Visher, "Indiana's Population, 1850–1940, Sources and Dispersal," *Indiana Magazine of History* 38, no. 1 (March 1942): 51–59; Richard F. Nation, *At Home in the Hoosier Hills: Agriculture, Politics, and Religion in Southern Indiana, 1810–1870* (Bloomington: Indiana University Press, 2005); Alexandra Minna Stern, "'We Cannot Make a Silk Purse Out of a Sow's Ear': Eugenics in the Hoosier Heartland," *Indiana Magazine of History* 103, no. 1 (March 2007): 3–38.

34. John E. Iglehart to Christopher B. Coleman, June 23, 1927, box 3, folder 8, Iglehart Papers. William E. Barton, *The Life of Abraham Lincoln*, 2 vols. (Indianapolis: Bobbs-Merrill, 1925), 1:137.

35. Duff Johnson to Iglehart, June 4, 1927, box 5, folder 8; Bess Ehrmann to Iglehart, June 4, 1927, box 3, folder 14, emphasis in original; Coleman to Iglehart, July 5, 1927, box 3, folder 8; D. Frank Culbertson to Iglehart, June 2, 1927, box 7, folder 16, Iglehart Papers.

36. David W. Blight, *Race and Reunion: The Civil War in American Memory* (Cambridge, MA: The Belknap Press, 2001); Barry Schwartz, *Abraham Lincoln and the Forge of National Memory* (Chicago: University of Chicago Press, 2000).

37. Iglehart, in "Proceedings," June 14, 1927, 7–8; Tarbell to Iglehart, June 7, 1927, Tarbell Collection; Turner to Iglehart, May 20, 1927, Turner Collection.

38. Iglehart to Turner, May 28, 1927; Turner to Iglehart, May 31, 1927, Turner Collection.

39. Paul Brown to John E. Iglehart, August 20, 27, September 7, 8, 1927; Iglehart to Brown, September 4, 1927; Iglehart to Richard Lieber, Anne Studebaker Carlisle, Paul Brown, Thomas Taggart, and Frank Ball, September 15, 1927, box 7, folder 16, Iglehart Papers.

40. Beveridge to Weik, May 7, 1925, box 2, Jesse Weik Papers, 1833–1939 (Abraham Lincoln Presidential Library, Springfield, IL), hereafter Weik Papers; John Braeman, *Albert J. Beveridge: American Nationalist* (Chicago: University of Chicago Press, 1971), 291.

41. Barton to Weik, March 20, 1923; Beveridge to Weik, July 29, 1924, box 2, Weik Papers.

42. Beveridge to Warren, March 3, 1925, May 30, 1935, container 295, Beveridge Papers.

43. Beveridge to Paul Angle, February 23, 1926, container 285, Beveridge Papers.

44. Warren to Barton, March 5, 1926, April 13, 1926; Barton to Warren, March 12, April 9, 14, August 24, 1926, box 2, Director's Correspondence; Barton to Tarbell, December 10, 1923, Tarbell Collection; Barton to Paul Angle, May 18, 25, 1927, box 42, folder 6, Abraham Lincoln Association Papers, 1908–1983 (Abraham Lincoln Presidential Library, Springfield, IL).

45. Tarbell to Warren, October 29, November 29, 1922, June 23, 1925, November 19, 1926; Warren to Tarbell, January 17, 1923, Tarbell Collection.

46. Ehrmann to Iglehart, September 11, 1927, box 3, folder 14, Iglehart Papers; Coleman to John E. Iglehart, September 22, 1927, box 3, folder 8, Iglehart Papers.

47. Iglehart to Warren, September 22, 23, 1927, box 2, folder 8; Brown to Iglehart, September 23, 27, 1927, Iglehart to Brown, September 30, 1927, box 7, folder 16; Iglehart to Brown, October 3, 1927, box 7, folder 17, Iglehart Papers. O'Bright characterizes Iglehart's letter to Brown as being "irate," infers that Warren had criticized Ehrmann specifically, and assumes that Iglehart also objected to Ehrmann. O'Bright, *"Here I Grew Up,"* chap. 1.

48. Paul V. Brown, telegram to John E. Iglehart, October 4, 1927, box 7, folder 17; Christopher B. Coleman, telegram to Iglehart, October 4, October 4, 1927, box 3, folder 8, Iglehart Papers.

49. Louis Warren to John E. Iglehart, October 7, 1927, with an attached "Comments On 'Unused Sources for Modern Historians' by the Author Louis A. Warren," box 7, folder 17, Iglehart Papers.

50. John E. Iglehart to Christopher B. Coleman, October 19, 1927, box 3, folder 8, Iglehart Papers.

51. Will Fortune to Iglehart, September 7, 1927, box 2, folder 12; Iglehart to Christopher B. Coleman, October 6, 19, 1927, box 3, folder 8, Iglehart Papers; Iglehart correspondence with Worthington C. Ford, box 1, folders 15–16, Iglehart Papers.

52. "Proceedings," October 27, 1927, 21; "Special Meeting of the Historical Research and Reference Committee of the Indiana Lincoln Union," in SWIHS, "Proceedings," October 25, 1927; Logan Esarey to John E. Iglehart, October 29, 1927, box 1, folder 10; Coleman to Iglehart, November 4, 1927, Iglehart Papers.

53. Richard Lieber to Bess Ehrmann, November 7, 1927, box 3, folder 14, Iglehart Papers.

54. George Wilson, "The Lincoln Forest, Field, Flora and Family, 1816–1830," in Collection on Abraham Lincoln (S1170), Manuscripts Division (Indiana State Library, Indianapolis); Iglehart to Ehrmann, January 10, 1928, box 3, folder 15; Lieber to Ehrmann, January 26, 1928, box 7, folder 17, Iglehart Papers.

55. Reports of the speech are pasted throughout Lieber's diaries, Lieber Mss (Lilly Library). The first report to include the new paragraph is "Lieber Asks Aid for Lincoln Shrine Plan," *Indianapolis News,* December 17, 1927.

56. On the fundraising see "Campaign Started to Raise Funds for Hanks Memorial," *Indianapolis Star,* January 24, 1928; "Lincoln Fund Drive Gets Underway," *Bluffton News,* February 10, 1928; "In What Ways Will the Indiana Lincoln Union Memorial Benefit Indiana?" *Versailles Republican,* April 18, 1928; "Deplorable Is the Present Site of the Home of Abraham Lincoln in Indiana," *Union City, Ind., Times,* April 26, 1928; "Pig Sty Is on Sacred Ground," *Greenfield Reporter,* April 28, 1928. On site development see "Presentation of Tract for Lincoln Memorial," *Indianapolis News,* June 7, 1929; "Nancy Hanks Park Trees," *Indianapolis News,* January 20, 1930.

57. John E. Iglehart to Christopher B. Coleman, February 5, 1931, box 3, folder 3, Iglehart Papers.

58. Albert J. Beveridge, *Abraham Lincoln, 1809–1858,* 2 vols. (Boston: Houghton Mifflin, 1928), 1:41–42, 50–54, 77, 83–84.

59. Braeman summarizes the reviews in *Albert J. Beveridge,* 321–32 and "Albert J. Beveridge and Demythologizing Lincoln," *Journal of the Abraham Lincoln Association* 25, no. 2 (Summer 2004): 20–23. Richard Arnold Tilden, "Albert J. Beveridge: Biographer," *Indiana Magazine of History* 26, no. 2 (June 1930): 83, 85; John E. Iglehart to Bess Ehrmann, March 15, 1929, box 4, folder 1, Iglehart Papers.

6. In the Lincoln Atmosphere

1. "Our Pleasure!" *Evansville Courier,* section 2 "Sunday Journal," January 29, 1922.

2. Ehrmann, in "Proceedings," June 5, 1931, 3; Christopher B. Coleman, "Historical Work in Indiana," *Indiana History Bulletin,* Vol. 3, Extra No. 1, *Proceedings of the Southwestern Indiana Historical Society during its Sixth Year: Papers Read Before the Society at Various Meetings, 1920–1925* (December 1925): 65; Johnson to Iglehart, November 2, 1927, box 5, folder 8, Iglehart Papers; William B. Carleton, "The Lincoln Atmosphere," SWIHS Collection.

3. Coleman to Iglehart, October 21, 1931, box 3, folder 4, August 17, 1926, box 3, folder 8, Iglehart Papers. For reviews critical of source citations see [Unsigned,] "Review of *The Environment of Abraham Lincoln in Indiana* by John E. Iglehart and Eugenia Ehrmann," *Indiana Magazine of History* 22, no. 2 (June 1926): 226–27.

4. Charles Garrett Vannest, *Lincoln the Hoosier: Abraham Lincoln's Life in Indiana* (St. Louis: Eden Publishing House, 1928); John Oliver, "Review of *Lincoln the Hoosier* by Charles Garrett Vannest," *Mississippi Valley Historical Review* 15, no. 4 (March 1929): 553–57; William O. Lynch, "Review of *Lincoln the Hoosier* by Charles Garrett Vannest," *Indiana Magazine of History* 25, no. 2 (June 1929): 177–78.

5. Iglehart to Ehrmann, March 6, 10, 1928, box 3, folder 15, [unsigned] "In re Chapter 2, History of Lincoln," box 1, folder 6, Johnson to Iglehart, March 11, 1928, box 5, folder 9, Iglehart Papers.

6. Iglehart, "Memo," September 19, 1928; Albert J. Beveridge, *Abraham Lincoln, 1809–1858,* 2 vols. (Boston: Houghton Mifflin, 1928), 1:50–53.

7. Ehrmann, in "Proceedings," June 1, 1928, 18–19; Embree and Honig, in "Proceedings," October 30, 1928, 33, 39; Iglehart, "Re: Albert J. Beveridge on 'Lincoln'," September 28, 1928, 5–6, box 1, folder 6, Iglehart Papers; Iglehart to Johnson, November 19, 1928, box 5, folder 10, Iglehart Papers.

8. Bess V. Ehrmann, Albion Fellows Bacon, Mrs. Charles [Deidré Duff] T. Johnson, "Word Pictures of Pioneer Families and Lincoln Contemporaries," *Indiana History Bulletin,* Vol. 6, Extra No. 3, *Proceedings of the Southwestern Indiana Historical Society during its Ninth Year* (August 1929): 119–27; Ehrmann, Bacon, and Johnson, in "Proceedings," October 30, 1928, 43–56.

9. Ehrmann et al., "Word Pictures of Pioneer Families and Lincoln Contemporaries," 119–27, quoted material from 119; Ehrmann, in "Proceedings," October 20, 1928, 43.

10. Bess V. Ehrmann, *The Missing Chapter in the Life of Abraham Lincoln* (Chicago: Walter M. Hill, 1938), 28; Ehrmann to Iglehart, May 21, 1929, box 4,

folder 1, Iglehart Papers; Ehrmann, "Lincoln's Spencer County Friends and Neighbors," *Indianapolis Star,* February 8, 1931.

11. George H. Honig, "The Artist's Ideal of Lincoln," *Indiana History Bulletin,* Vol. 3, Extra No. 1, *Proceedings of the Southwestern Indiana Historical Society during its Sixth Year: Papers Read Before the Society at Various Meetings, 1920–1925* (December 1925): 51–52.

12. Susan Sontag, *On Photography* (New York: Farrar, Straus and Giroux, 1977), 154; Iglehart to Anna O'Flynn, July 22, 1926, Anna C. O'Flynn Papers (Lewis Historical Library, Vincennes University, Vincennes, IN).

13. Peter Burke, *Eyewitnessing: The Uses of Images as Historical Evidence* (Ithaca, NY: Cornell University Press, 2001), 10.

14. Harold Holzer, Gabor S. Borritt, and Mark Neely, Jr., *The Lincoln Image: Abraham Lincoln and the Popular Print* (Urbana: University of Illinois Press, 2001), 2–3.

15. Francis B. Carpenter, *Six Months at the White House with Abraham Lincoln: The Story of a Picture* (New York: Hurd and Houghton, 1866), 30; Allen Thorndike Rice, ed., *Reminiscences of Abraham Lincoln by Distinguished Men of His Time* (New York: Harper and Brothers, 1885), 5.

16. Ida M. Tarbell, *All in the Days' Work: An Autobiography* (New York: Macmillan, 1939), 167; Morse in Tarbell, *All in the Day's Work,* 167; Wilson, Cooley, and Walker in "The Earliest Portrait of Lincoln: Letters in Regard to the Frontispiece of the November *McClure's,*" *McClure's Magazine* 6, no. 1 (December 1895): 109, 111, 112.

17. Frank Luther Mott, *A History of American Magazines,* Vol. 4, *1885–1904* (Cambridge, MA: Harvard University Press, 1957), 5, 151, 589–91, 596; advertisement in Ida M. Tarbell and J. McCan Davis, *The Early Life of Abraham Lincoln: Containing Many Unpublished Documents and Unpublished Reminiscences of Lincoln's Early Friends, With 160 Illustrations, including 20 Portraits of Lincoln* (New York: S. S. McClure, 1896), inside back cover. Gregory M. Pfitzer, *Picturing the Past: Illustrated Histories and the American Imagination, 1840–1900* (Washington, DC: Smithsonian Institution Press, 2002), xv; Merrill Peterson cites Stefan Lorant's *Lincoln, His Life in Photographs* (1941) as "the first modern pictorial biography" of Lincoln in *Lincoln in American Memory* (New York: Oxford University Press, 1994), 341.

18. Ruth Painter Randall, *I Ruth: Autobiography of a Marriage* (Boston: Little, Brown, 1968), 95–96, 123; J. Rosenbaum, "Lincoln Centennial Memorial Press Clippings, Dec. 12, 1908–Feb. 13, 1909," 11 vols. (Abraham Lincoln Presidential Library, Springfield, IL).

19. Tarbell, *Early Life of Lincoln,* 35, 67; J. T. Hobson, *Footprints of Abraham Lincoln: Presenting Many Interesting Facts, Reminiscences and Illustrations Never Before Published* (Dayton, OH: Otterbein Press, 1909), 33, 49, 65.

20. Iglehart to Ehrmann, January 28, 1928, box 3, folder 15, Iglehart Papers; see also Iglehart to Ehrmann, February 7, 1928, box 3, folder 15, and Wilson to Johnson, January 19, 1928, box 5, folder 9, Iglehart Papers.

21. Iglehart, in "Proceedings," June 1, 1922, 19; Alexandra Minna Stern, "'We Cannot Make a Silk Purse Out of a Sow's Ear': Eugenics in the Hoosier Heartland," *Indiana Magazine of History* 103, no. 1 (March 2007): 3–38.

22. Peterson, *Lincoln in American Memory,* 234; Kenneth J. Winkle, "Introduction" to Ida M. Tarbell, *Abraham Lincoln and His Ancestors* (Lincoln: University of

Nebraska Press, 1997), xii; Ida M. Tarbell, *In the Footsteps of the Lincolns* (New York: Harper and Brothers, 1924), xix, 53, 128; Tarbell, *All in the Day's Work,* 385–86; Iglehart to Sandburg, February 22, 1927, box 2, folder 7, Iglehart Papers. See also William E. Barton, *The Paternity of Abraham Lincoln: Was He the Son of Thomas Lincoln?* (New York: George H. Doran, 1920); Peterson, *Lincoln in American Memory,* 232–43.

23. "Nancy Hanks Doll, Rockport Entry, Wins State Fidac Contest at Legion Convention," *Rockport Democrat,* September 1, 1933; see also "Nancy Hanks Doll Wins Fifth in National Contest," *Rockport Democrat,* October 13, 1933.

24. William B. Carleton, "The Lincoln Atmosphere," June 5, 1930, 1, 5, SWIHS Collection.

25. "Grand Opening of Rockport's New Park," July 26, 1923, Scrapbook no. 31, p. 34, Ehrmann Collection; "Historical Societies," *Indiana History Bulletin* 5, no. 3 (December 1927): 52; David Glassberg, *American Historical Pageantry: The Uses of Tradition in the Early Twentieth Century* (Chapel Hill: University of North Carolina Press, 1990)

26. Ehrmann, in "Proceedings," October 8, 1926, 14; Correspondence between Ehrmann and Tarbell, March–June 1928, Tarbell Collection; Ida M. Tarbell, "The Boy Lincoln," *New York Herald Tribune,* July 1, 1928, 12; Ehrmann to Iglehart, June 6, 1928, box 3, folder 15, Iglehart Papers; Mrs. Calder Ehrmann, "The Lincoln Pageant," *The Indiana Club Woman* 9, no. 4 (May–June 1930): 7–8.

27. Ehrmann, in "Proceedings," October 8, 1926, 14; "Pageants and Anniversary Celebrations," *Indiana History Bulletin* 4, no. 1 (October 1926): 17; Taylor Bayse, in "Proceedings," February 6, 1930, 6. The script is summarized in Ehrmann, *The Missing Chapter,* 128–38.

28. Ehrmann to Iglehart, September 19, 1926, box 3, folder 14, Iglehart Papers; Ehrmann, in "Proceedings," October 8, 1926, 14; Albion Fellows Bacon, "At the Landing," *Indiana Historical Commission Bulletin* no. 18, *Proceedings of the Southwestern Indiana Historical Society* (October 1923): 135; Roscoe Kiper, in "Proceedings," October 8, 1926, 7; William L. Barker, in "Proceedings," February 6, 1930.

29. Correspondence with Will Hays, 1928–1931, box 4, folders 4 and 10, and box 3, folders 2, 15, Iglehart Papers; criticism of Griffith may be found in "Historical Societies," *Indiana History Bulletin* 8, no. 10 (July 1931): 453; "Proceedings," February 12, 1931; Ehrmann, *Missing Chapter,* 128. Ehrmann filed copies of the film with a museum in Evansville and the Indiana State Library, but neither could be located as of 2006.

30. J. Ben Lieberman, "Lincoln Pioneer Village National Shrine," *Evansville Sunday Courier and Journal,* July 5, 1936; "Rockport Sculptor Builds Fame on Lincoln Legend," undated clipping in Naomi Joy Kirk Collection (Filson Historical Society, Louisville, KY). Raymond and Patricia Dawson maintain a comprehensive online archive of Honig's work at http://208.112.105.161/index.html.

31. Tarbell to Will Fortune, November 20, 1922, Tarbell Collection; John Oliver, in "Proceedings," February 23, 1928, 26; Richard S. Taylor and Mark L. Johnson, "The Spirit of the Place: Origins of the Movement to Reconstruct Lincoln's New Salem," *Journal of Illinois History* 7, no. 3 (Autumn 2004): 174–200; Keith A. Sculle, "The Howard Family Legacy at the Knob Creek Farm," *Journal of the Abraham Lincoln Association* 26, no. 2 (Summer 2005): 22–48.

32. "Lincoln Pioneer Village in Rockport Park near Completion," *Evansville Courier and Journal,* June 23, 1935; J. Ben Lieberman, "Vast Multitude Joins Rockport in Lincoln Rites," *Evansville Courier,* July 6, 1935; "Lincoln Pioneer Village Dedicated at Rockport," *Indiana History Bulletin* 12, no. 8 (June–July 1935): 250–51; "The New Rockport Lincoln Pioneer Village and Shrine to Be Enlarged by the WPA; The Plans Are Approved," *Rockport Democrat,* September 6, 1935; "Thousands Visit Rockport Pioneer Village Annually," *Evansville Courier and Journal,* June 28, 1936; "15,000 See 'Mr. and Mrs. Lincoln' in Program Dedicating Rockport Village," *Evansville Press,* July 5, 1936.

33. "Cabin Where Lincoln Memorized Shakespeare among 4 Buildings added to Pioneer Village," *Indianapolis News,* Friday, June 26, 1936; Raymond and Patricia Dawson maintain a comprehensive online archive about the Lincoln Pioneer Village at http://208.112.124.44/.

34. J. Ben Lieberman, "Vast Multitude Joins Rockport in Lincoln Rites," *Evansville Courier,* July 6, 1935; "Industrial School Planned for Lincoln Village," *Evansville Press,* April 28, 1935; W. E. Daniel, "Throng Attends Dedication of Lincoln Village," *Owensboro Messenger,* July 5, 1935.

35. See William J. Murtagh, *Keeping Time: The History and Theory of Preservation in America,* 3rd ed. (New York: John Wiley & Sons, 2006), 20–22, 75–86; Diane Barthel, *Historic Preservation: Collective Memory and Historical Identity* (New Brunswick, NJ: Rutgers University Press, 1996), 2–10. The Village is unmentioned in Charles B. Hosmer, Jr., *Preservation Comes of Age: From Williamsburg to the National Trust, 1926–1949,* 2 vols. (Charlottesville: University Press of Virginia, 1981), even though the volume contains a section devoted to Indiana (1:384–97).

36. Philip Lutz, "The Fourth of July in Lincoln's Time and Today," July 4, 1935, SWIHS Collection; Richard S. Taylor and Mark L. Johnson, "A Fragile Illusion: The Reconstruction of Lincoln's New Salem," *Journal of Illinois History* 7, no. 4 (Winter 2004): 274, 276; Mark Twain, *A Connecticut Yankee in King Arthur's Court* (New York: Oxford University Press, 1996), 71.

37. Coleman, "Emphasis in the Work of Historical Societies," *Indiana History Bulletin,* Vol. 6, Extra No. 3, *Proceedings of the Southwestern Indiana Historical Society during its Ninth Year* (August 1929): 16; James A. Woodburn, "Indiana and Her History," *Indiana Magazine of History* 27, no. 1 (March 1931): 3–4; Barton to Iglehart, May 9, 1930, box 1, folder 3, Iglehart Papers; Tarbell to Iglehart, December 5, 1933, Tarbell Collection.

38. George Wilson, "Historical Notes on Dubois County," 40 volumes, 6 (1926), 589; 4 (1925), 390; 7 (1927), 161; 2 (1926), 215 (Lilly Library, Bloomington, IN).

39. Wilson, "Historical Notes on Dubois County," 2 (1926), 29; "Proceedings," June 15, 1923, 7, February 12, 1924, 5; Bess Ehrmann, "Museum Collections," *Indiana Historical Commission Bulletin* no. 16, *Proceedings of the Southwestern Indiana Historical Society* (October 1922): 81.

40. Wilson, "Historical Notes on Dubois County," 2 (1926), 29; William L., Barker, "Resume of 1929 and 1930," February 12, 1931, reel 7, item 1j, SWIHS Collection; A. J. Bigney, "How the Colleges can Co-operate," *Indiana History Bulletin,* Vol. 1, Extra No., *Proceedings of the Fifth Annual Meeting of the Southwestern Indiana Historical Society* (June 1924): 49–51; Thomas James de la Hunt,

"Publicity in Newspapers," *Indiana Historical Commission Bulletin* no. 16, *Proceedings of the Southwestern Indiana Historical Society* (October 1922): 29; Edith Thorpe, "Captain Spier Spencer and the County Named for Him," SWIHS Collection.

41. John E. Iglehart to Robert A. Woods, May 31, 1932, box 5, folder 20, Iglehart Papers; Iglehart, "Standards and Subjects of Historical Society Work," *Indiana History Bulletin,* Vol. 11, No. 8, *Proceedings of the Southwestern Indiana Historical Society, 1929–1933* (May 1934): 272–311. The publication was noted in *Mississippi Valley Historical Review* 21, no. 2 (September 1934): 300, and *American Historical Review* 40, no. 2 (January 1935): 418–19.

42. William L. Barker, "History of the Lincoln Route," *Indiana History Bulletin,* Vol. 4, Extra No. 1, *Proceedings of the Southwestern Indiana Historical Society during its Seventh Year* (December 1926): 43–70; William Barker, Philip Lutz, and Union Youngblood, comps., *Brief of The Warrick County Lincoln Route Association* (Booneville, Ind., 1931); Coleman to Iglehart, February 12, July 5, November 4, 1932, and Iglehart to Ehrmann, January 17, 1931, box 4, folder 4, Iglehart Papers.

43. "Proceedings," February 6, 1930 (Thomas Downs, Edward Gough, Col. C. C. and Mrs. Schreeder), June 5, 1930 (Eldora Raleigh, W. D. Robinson), December 4, 1931 (Anna Fellows Johnson), June 9, 1932 (Lucius Embree, George Clifford), June 8, 1933 (Alice Harper Hanby); "Minute Book 2," March 9, 1934 (Thomas de la Hunt, Albion Fellows Bacon), October 26, 1934 (John E. Iglehart, Arthur Fretageot).

44. Iglehart to Johnson, June 5, 1928, box 5, folder 10, Iglehart Papers; Wilson, "Historical Notes on Dubois County," 15 (1933), 588; Ehrmann to Joseph E. Iglehart, February 17, 1937, box 4, folder 5, Iglehart Papers.

45. Ehrmann, *The Missing Chapter,* 148.

46. "Southwestern Indiana Historical Society Annals" (Evansville Public Library, Central Branch, Evansville, IN); I. J. Robinson, *The Lincoln Country of Southwestern Indiana* (Evansville: Southwestern Indiana Civic Association, c. 1935); Kathleen A. Foster, Nanette Esseck Brewer, and Margaret Contompasis, eds., *Thomas Hart Benton and the Indiana Murals* (Bloomington: Indiana University Art Museum in association with Indiana University Press, 2000), 145–46.

47. "Historical Societies," *Indiana History Bulletin,* Vol. 5, no. 12 (September 1928): 250; Michael Kammen, "Carl Becker Redivivus: Or, Is Everyone Really a Historian?," *History and Theory* (2000), 233; David J. Russo, *Keepers of Our Past: Local Historical Writing in the United States, 1820s–1930s* (Westport, CT: Greenwood Press, 1988).

48. Paul M. Angle, *"Here I Have Lived": A History of Lincoln's Springfield, 1821–1865* (Springfield, IL: Abraham Lincoln Association, 1935).

49. Roy Rosenzweig, "Can History Be Open Source? Wikipedia and the Future of the Past," *Journal of American History* 93, no. 1 (June 2006); Anne Kelly Knowles and Amy Hillier, eds., *Placing History: How Maps, Spatial Data, and GIS Are Changing Historical Scholarship* (Redlands, CA: ESRI Press, 2008); Edward L. Ayers, "The Pasts and Futures of Digital History," www.vcdh.virginia.edu/PastsFutures.html; David J. Bodenhamer, John Corrigan, and Trevor M. Harris, *The Spatial Humanities: GIS and the Future of Humanities Scholarship* (Bloomington: Indiana University Press, 2010). Two projects that strive to integrate historical and

geographical information are the Hypercities project at UCLA, www.hypercities .com; and Digital Harlem, www.acl.arts.usyd.edu.au/harlem/.

Conclusion: "A Thousand Minds"

1. J. G. Randall, "Has the Lincoln Theme Been Exhausted?" *American Historical Review* 41, no. 2 (January 1936): 270–94.

2. Mark E. Neely Jr., "The Lincoln Theme since Randall's Call: The Promises and Perils of Professionalism," *Journal of the Abraham Lincoln Association* 1 (1970): 10–70; "Abraham Lincoln at 200: History and Historiography," *Journal of American History* 96, no. 2 (September 2009); Don E. Fehrenbacher, "The Minor Affair: An Adventure in Forgery and Detection," in *Lincoln in Text and Context: Collected Essays* (Stanford, CA: Stanford University Press, 1987), 246–69; Iglehart to Tarbell, March 20, 1929, Ehrmann to Tarbell, June 30, 1932, Tarbell Collection; Benjamin P. Thomas, *Portrait for Posterity: Lincoln and His Biographers* (New Brunswick, NJ: Rutgers University Press, 1947), 265–66.

3. Carl Sandburg and Paul M. Angle, *Mary Lincoln: Wife and Widow* (New York: Harcourt, Brace, 1932); David Donald, *Lincoln's Herndon* (New York: Alfred A. Knopf, 1948); J. G. Randall, "Review of *Abraham Lincoln: The War Years* by Carl Sandburg," *American Historical Review* 45, no. 4 (July 1940): 917–22; J. G. Randall, "Carl," *Journal of the Illinois State Historical Society* (1908–1984) 45, no. 4, *A Tribute to Carl Sandburg* (Winter 1952): 329–33; Harry E. Pratt, "James Garfield Randall, 1881–1953," *Journal of the Illinois State Historical Society* (1908–1984) 46, no. 2 (Summer 1953): 119–31; James Hurt, "Sandburg's 'Lincoln' within History," *Journal of the Abraham Lincoln Association* 20, no. 1 (Winter 1999): 55–65.

4. Abraham Lincoln, "Second Lecture on Discoveries and Inventions" [February 11, 1859], in Roy P. Basler, ed., *Collected Works of Abraham Lincoln,* 8 vols. (New Brunswick, NJ: Rutgers University Press, 1953), 3:362–63.

5. *Indiana, a Guide to the Hoosier State, Compiled by Workers of the Writers' Program of the Work Projects Administration in the State of Indiana: Sponsored by the Department of Public Relations of Indiana State Teachers College* (New York: Oxford University Press, [1941]), vii; George T. Blakey, *Creating a Hoosier Self-Portrait: The Federal Writers' Project in Indiana, 1935–1942* (Bloomington: Indiana University Press, 2005), 117–27; Allan Nevins, *The Gateway to History* (New York: D. Appleton-Century, 1938), iv.

6. James G. Randall, "Sifting the Ann Rutledge Evidence," in *Lincoln the President,* 4 vols. (New York: Dodd, Mead, 1945), 2:321–42; Donald, *Lincoln's Herndon,* 174, 195; Louis A. Warren, "Herndon's Contribution to Lincoln Mythology," *Indiana Magazine of History* 41, no. 3 (September 1945): 221, 223.

7. Ronald J. Grele, *Envelopes of Sound: The Art of Oral History,* 2nd ed. (New York: Praeger, 1999), 126–54.

8. Douglas L. Wilson, "Abraham Lincoln, Ann Rutledge, and the Evidence of Herndon's Informants," *Civil War History* 36 (December 1990): 321. See Charles B. Strozier, *Lincoln's Quest for Union: A Psychological Portrait,* 2d rev. ed. (1982; Philadelphia: Paul Dry Books, 2001); Gabor S. Borritt, ed., *The Historian's Lincoln: Pseudohistory, Psychohistory, and History* (Urbana: University of Illinois Press, 1988).

9. Don E. Fehrenbacher and Virginia Fehrenbacher, eds., *Recollected Words of Abraham Lincoln* (Stanford, CA: Stanford University Press, 1996); Allen C. Guelzo, "Holland's Informants: The Construction of Josiah Holland's 'Life of Abraham Lincoln,'" *Journal of the Abraham Lincoln Association* 23, no. 1 (2002): 1–53; Douglas L. Wilson and Rodney O. Davis,. eds., *Herndon's Informants: Letters, Interviews, and Statements about Abraham Lincoln* (Urbana: University of Illinois Press, 1998); Michael Burlingame, ed., *An Oral History of Abraham Lincoln: John G. Nicolay's Interviews and Essays* (Carbondale: Southern Illinois University Press, 1996). The revival of interest is surveyed in Richard S. Taylor, "Telling Lincoln's Story," *Journal of the Abraham Lincoln Association* 21, no. 2 (Summer 2000): 44–68.

10. John Y. Simon, "Abraham Lincoln and Ann Rutledge," *Journal of the Abraham Lincoln Association* 11 (1990): 13–33.

11. Michael Burlingame, *The Inner World of Abraham Lincoln* (Urbana: University of Illinois Press, 1994), 44, 53–55, 139, 146, 149, 210; Merrill D. Peterson, *Lincoln in American Memory* (New York: Oxford University Press, 1994), 266–70, 410; Michael Burlingame, *Abraham Lincoln: A Life* (Baltimore: Johns Hopkins University Press, 2008), 22, 41–42, 47.

12. Michael A. Capps, "Interpreting Lincoln—A Work in Progress: Lincoln Boyhood National Memorial as a Case Study," *Indiana Magazine of History* 105, no. 4 (December 2009): 327–41.

13. Adin Baber, *Nancy Hanks, the Destined Mother of a President: The Factual Story of a Pioneer Family as Revealed in an Exhaustive Study of Ancestral History* (Glendale, CA: Arthur H. Clark, 1963); David Herbert Donald, *Lincoln* (New York: Simon & Schuster, 1995), 19–20; Burlingame, *Abraham Lincoln: A Life*, 1:12; Wilson and Davis, *Herndon's Informants*, 780.

14. "New Portrait of Abe's Mother," *Chicago News*, February 7, 1964; Elody R. Crimi, Diane Ney, and Ken Cobb, *Jewels of Light: The Stained Glass of Washington National Cathedral* (Washington, DC: Washington National Cathedral, 2004), 72–73.

15. J. G. Randall, "Historianship," *American Historical Review* 58, no. 2 (January 1953), 250–53, 260, 262, 264.

16. John E. Iglehart to Deidré Johnson, September 17, 1926, box 5, folder 8, Iglehart Papers.

Index

KEITH A. EREKSON grew up near Baltimore and earned a PhD in history from Indiana University. He worked on the editorial staff of the *Indiana Magazine of History* and taught courses on U.S. and Indiana history at the Indiana University Kokomo campus. He is currently an assistant professor of history at the University of Texas at El Paso, where he directs the department's history/social studies teacher education program and the university's Center for History Teaching & Learning. An award-winning historian, teacher, and teacher educator, he speaks often to public audiences and media representatives. He lives in El Paso with his wife and four daughters.